CHINA'S SURGING ECONOMY

Adjusting for More Balanced Development

Series on Contemporary China

(ISSN: 1793-0847)

Published

Vol. 1 Legitimacy: Ambiguities of Political Success or Failure in East and Southeast Asia
edited by Lynn White

Vol. 2 China Under Hu Jintao: Opportunities, Dangers, and Dilemmas
edited by Tun-jen Cheng, Jacques deLisle & Deborah Brown

Vol. 3 China's Compliance in Global Affairs: Trade, Arms Control, Environmental Protection, Human Rights
by Gerald Chan

Vol. 4 Political Civilization and Modernization in China: The Political Context of China's Transformation
edited by Yang Zhong and Shiping Hua

Vol. 5 China into the Hu-Wen Era: Policy Initiatives and Challenges
edited by John Wong & Lai Hongyi

Vol. 6 Water and Development in China: The Political Economy of Shanghai Water Policy
by Seungho Lee

Vol. 7 De Facto Federalism in China: Reforms and Dynamics of Central-Local Relations
by Zheng Yongnian

Vol. 8 China's Elite Politics: Political Transition and Power Balancing
by Bo Zhiyue

Vol. 9 Economic Reform and Cross-Strait Relations: Taiwan and China in the WTO
edited by Julian Chang & Steven M Goldstein

Vol. 10 Discontented Miracle: Growth, Conflict, and Institutional Adaptations in China
edited by Dali L Yang

Vol. 11 China's Surging Economy: Adjusting for More Balanced Development
edited by John Wong & Wei Liu

Series on Contemporary China – Vol. 11

CHINA'S SURGING ECONOMY

Adjusting for More Balanced Development

Editors

John WONG
East Asian Institute, Singapore

Wei LIU
Peking University, China

World Scientific

NEW JERSEY · LONDON · SINGAPORE · BEIJING · SHANGHAI · HONG KONG · TAIPEI · CHENNAI

Published by

World Scientific Publishing Co. Pte. Ltd.
5 Toh Tuck Link, Singapore 596224
USA office: 27 Warren Street, Suite 401-402, Hackensack, NJ 07601
UK office: 57 Shelton Street, Covent Garden, London WC2H 9HE

Library of Congress Cataloging-in-Publication Data
China's surging economy : adjusting for more balanced development / edited by John Wong & Wei Liu.
p. cm. -- (Series on contemporary China ; Vol. 11)
Includes bibliographical references and index.
ISBN 978-981-270-627-0 (alk. paper)
1. China--Economic conditions--2000- 2. China--Economic policy--2000-
I. Wong, John, 1939- II. Liu, Wei, 1957-

HC427.95.C4567 2007
330.951--dc22

2007008710

British Library Cataloguing-in-Publication Data
A catalogue record for this book is available from the British Library.

Typeset by Stallion Press
Email: enquiries@stallionpress.com

Printed in Singapore by World Scientific Printers (S) Pte Ltd

Contents

Introduction[1]

I

On account of its successful economic reform and open-door policy, the Chinese economy has achieved spectacular performance since 1979, growing at an average rate of 9.6 percent for over two decades. China's total GDP in 2006 reached US$2.3 trillion to be ranked as the world's fourth largest economy after USA, Japan, and Germany. In PPP (purchasing power parity) terms, China's total GDP has rendered China's economy as the world's second largest after the USA. Thanks to its dynamic export growth (China as the world's third largest exporting country after USA and Germany) and the large influx of foreign capital (China as the world's most attractive destination for foreign direct investment), China's economy has also been rapidly integrated with the global economy. In fact, China has become the world's foremost manufacturing center.

A few years ago, China's economic growth had only impacted its neighboring economies in East Asia. Today, China's economic growth

[1] The authors would like to thank Miss Zheng Yi, Research Officer at EAI, for her assistance in preparing the summary of the book chapters. They also appreciate the efforts of Dr Yang Mu, Senior Visiting Research Fellow at EAI, in organizing the EAI-BEIDA conference and managing the production of this book.

has, beyond doubt, produced significant global implications. By its sheer size, China's high levels of production, consumption, and imports and exports carry world-wide ramifications. Thanks to its persistent twin surpluses (on both current and capital accounts), China has accumulated massive foreign reserves (at US$1 trillion by the end of 2006), which is another telling evidence of China's growing financial clout. Every important financial market in the world has started to watch the movement of the Chinese Renminbi (yuan). In a larger sense, China's economic rise can be a new source of global economic growth as well as a new force of global economic integration. At the same time, it can also aggravate the existing global economic and financial imbalances.

An immediate question can be posed: Is China's dynamic growth sustainable? It is, of course, not possible for any economy to repeat such phenomenally high growth rates year after year without getting overheated or running into constraints. But considering the historical process of East Asian growth and China's own structure of economic growth (from both supply and demand sides), one can be easily optimistic about China's prospects of continuing its high growth in the near future.

However, the Chinese economy today is at a critical crossroads. Long periods of breakneck growth have given rise to a lot of structural strains and stress as well as serious sectoral imbalances that have to be rectified if the growth momentum is to be maintained. China's economic growth has been blatantly urban-biased, and its growth engine is excessively dependent on fixed investment and exports at the expense of domestic consumption. Hence the need to re-balance its economic growth structure. Rapid economic growth has also generated many serious socio-economic problems such as rising income inequality and rural discontent, which, if left unresolved, could well undermine the social foundation of its future economic growth.

Long-term growth is not just about rapid GDP increases. It is also concerned with the crucial issue of "growth sustainability." Viewed from a different angle, this is about the pattern of future growth, which has to be not just politically and socially acceptable, but also physically feasible. The latter means that China's future economic growth needs to take into account the many negative externalities such as environmental degradation and air and water pollution that the growth process has created as unintended consequences. Because of the immense scale of China's industrialization (which is the largest in human history), such physical limits to its economic growth cannot be ignored.

After more than two decades of rapid economic modernization that was unleashed by Deng Xiaoping's economic reform initiatives in late 1978, China's economy today with its per-capita GNP around US$1,800 (soon to breach the US$2,000 level by the combined forces of both economic growth and *Renminbi* appreciation) has reached what the World Bank used to categorize as a lower-middle-income economy. Rapid economic growth has made it possible for China to realize the initial phases of Deng's notion of *Xiaokang* (moderate affluence), satisfying the basic needs of a large number of the Chinese people, particularly those in the coastal provinces. At the same time, it has created many problems that are indeed crying out for attention. It is therefore high time for China to fix those development problems before it embarks on the next lap of high growth.

The current Chinese leadership under Hu Jintao and Wen Jiabao is very much aware of the enormous challenges that China is facing for sustaining its economic growth. At the 5th Party Plenum held in October 2005, the 11th Five-Year Plan was adopted, calling for a redirection of China's past growth-dominated development strategies to one that is more broad-based and more "balanced," and hence more "sustainable" in the long run. Needless to say, structural adjustment for any economy is a long-term undertaking. It is also not easy for any government to effectively deal with so many socio-economic by-products of its past rapid economic growth as these too require long-term solutions.

Rhetoric apart, what is happening now is that the Hu-Wen leadership still counts on maintaining a high level of economic growth as the best means of tackling those challenges, partly because rapid economic growth facilitates faster structural adjustment and partly because growth generates a stronger material base for the government to deal the many socio-economic problems more effectively. At the same time, Hu and Wen also advocate the building of a "harmonious society" to provide an ideological framework for the government as well as the Party to come to grips with those long-term problems.

China is a big country, which readily translates into a colossal economic and social entity in aggregate terms. A big country has many big problems, which define simple and easy solutions. Admittedly, China's future path of economic growth and social development is still riddled with uncertainties.

II

The chapters in this book are selected from the papers presented at the international conference on *China's Surging Economy: Adjusting for More Balanced Development* jointly organized by East Asian Institute, Singapore and the School of Economics, Peking University, China in August 2006. Containing twelve chapters, this volume can be said to represent the product of collaborative efforts of the economists from Beijing, Singapore, and elsewhere in the region by analyzing China's economic growth prospects and their concomitant problems and constraints.

China's dynamic economic growth after its successful economic reform is well known. In Chapter 1, Liu Wei examines the process of China's economic growth and structural changes since 1978. He discusses the changing growth patterns from four perspectives: different growth objectives, different paths to realize the objective, different driving forces, and different constraints. For the whole growth process, he identifies three different modes of economic growth for distinctive phases (1978–1990, 1991–1999, 2000–2006), with each embodying special characteristic features. He argues that institutional innovation, especially the reform of economic system and state-owned enterprises, has been the main driving force of China's past dynamic growth.

In Chapter 2, John Wong analyzes China's economic growth for the past 25 years in the East Asian context. He notes that East Asian economies led by Japan had historically also chalked up dynamic economic growth for a sustained period based on the so-called "Flying Geese" pattern. There is a great deal of similarities between China's present economic growth and what other East Asian economies experienced in the past. It follows that if the past East Asia growth experience could be any guide, then China should continue with its present high growth momentum for many years to come, not to mention that China as a much bigger and more diverse economic entity has much more internal dynamic to sustain its future growth potential. Wong also argues that as a result of its rise, China is fast becoming one of the leading "Geese" in the East Asian growth formation.

Tan Kong Yam, in Chapter 3, provides critical perspectives to examine China's current 11th Five-Year Plan, 2006–2010. China's economic reform has been mostly a gradual step-by-step process. China's high economic growth, particularly in the early years, occurred at the time when China was reforming old institutions and developing new ones. Largely because of its weak institutional support and poor ethical foundation, China's dynamic economic growth has created a lot of social tensions, inequalities, and injustice. The 11th Five-Year Plan, in emphasizing a "pro- people" approach to development along with the advocacy of building a harmonious society, is Beijing's belated attempt to cope with the many socio-economic side effects of past growth to achieve the long-term sustainability of development. In this way, the explosive energy of the Chinese people unleashed by the market reform and liberalization could be more effectively harnessed within a framework based on traditional Chinese ethical and moral foundations.

In Chapter 4, Wu Yanrui characterizes China's growth process as three waves of changes. During the first two waves, capital formation has been the dominant contributor to growth. Not surprisingly, China's growth has been highly resource-intensive and export-oriented. This model of development, however, has serious side effects and may not be sustainable due to a number of internal and external constraints. Wu aruges that China is now at the turning point toward the third wave of transformation under the Hu-Wen leadership. This third wave will have several distinctive features such as emphasizing more domestic consumption, the service sector expansion, greater technological progress, and innovation driven by the development of the western, central, and north-eastern regions, as well as more intensified rural development. China's future development under the new wave is likely to be more "balanced."

In Chapter 5, Yao Yang provides both theoretical analysis and empirical discussion on the relationship between China's trade structure and economic growth. He proposes the concept of "limited catch-up" to describe a country's strategy of exporting products with technological contents higher than what the international division of labor based on comparative advantage would have warranted. The empirical results show that countries adopting the limited catch-up strategy have grown faster than those that have not. China has also successfully adopted the "limited catch-up strategy" to quickly upgrade the technological contents of its exports. And this explains why China has been able to achieve dynamic export growth.

Trade has gained more and more importance in facilitating China's growth. Sarah Tong in Chapter 6 analyzes the emergence of China as one of the leading trading nations and its impact on the world trade structure. She points out that China's rise as a large trading nation in the past fifteen years coincides with the continuing trends of production relocation and outsourcing in manufacturing activities as globalization proceeds. Fragmentation of manufacturing activities, especially within Asia, has led to the formation of global and regional production networks. Thanks to the efforts of the foreign invested enterprises, China is home to many of these production networks, playing a key role in the global development of processing trade. The growth of processing trade has been responsible for China's persistent trade surplus, but it also has adverse effects on Chinese domestic firms.

In Chapter 7, Lin Shuanglin focuses on China's fiscal policy with special reference to the central–local revenue disparity. For various historical and institutional reasons, China's fiscal transfer system is highly centralized and designed to stimulate tax revenue growth.

Despite its higher revenue share, the central government is absent from the provision of social security and welfare, which falls mainly into the responsibility of the local governments. In light of this, Lin proposes that, China's fiscal reform challenges in future should aim at reducing the central–local fiscal disparity, increasing the local government's decision-making power, and increasing social welfare expenditures by the central government.

In line with China's rapid economic growth and trade expansion, China's financial sector reform has made impressive progress and the financial system has also undergone fundamental changes. In the banking sector, the formerly state-owned banks have been overhauled and incorporated into commercial share-holding banks. China's capital markets have also grown rapidly. However, the financial system is still riddled with flaws and problems, and further reform is needed.

In Chapters 8 and 9, He Liping and Lu Ding dig into the processes of China's banking reform and equity market reform, respectively. For banking reform, He highlights a number of important changes such as the reform and transformation of the state-owned banks. However, many problems remain, e.g., the government is still the majority shareholder. Therefore, China's banking sector reform is apt to be a continuing process. Lu, on the other hand, examines the problems of China's equity markets. The main institutional flaws of the equity markets are associated with the "split share structure" and "weak corporate governance." In recent years, the government has taken measures to improve corporate governance and provide greater protection of shareholders' rights. The prospects of China's stock markets have accordingly much improved, leading to their strong recovery in the late 2006.

As noted earlier, China's economic development has been accompanied by increasing income inequalities and regional disparity. The problem is further aggravated by regional disparity in human capital investment. In Chapter 10, Zhao Litao assesses how governmental spending on primary school education varies across provinces, and how this provincial-level inequalities have changed over time. He observes that inequality has been diminishing slowly since the late 1990s due to the faster growth of educational budget in the central region. However, over the last decade, the western region and the minority regions have fallen behind. If such trends should continue, the provincial level inequality would rise again. The central government, therefore, has to play a larger role in balancing regional spending in the compulsory education.

In Chapter 11, Wang Dashu uses the concept of the "demographic dividend" to examine the relationships between demographic transition and economic growth in China. He describes that the demographic dividend has contributed to China's development through three mechanisms: (a) the baby-boomers have left their dependent years to become labor force; (b) lesser number of children and smaller family size have enabled families to emphasize more on better child health and greater educational attainment, thereby boosting human capital accumulation; and (c) lower dependency ratio increases personal savings and contributes to greater investment. Wang also discusses the challenges along with policy remedies that are faced by the world's most populous nation.

In China, as elsewhere, rapid economic growth has brought about dramatic increases in average living standards of many people. However, the rapid growth in health care spending is usually not thought of having benefited the majority of people in China in this way. In Chapter 12, Ake Blomqvist explains how China's health care system has been affected by the process of dismantling the system of central economic management after 1980. He reviews the main elements of the current governmental initiatives for health care reform in urban and rural areas, and argues for a "synthetic approach" under which the proposals in the DRC (Development Research Center) model be integrated with the approaches currently being pursued to strengthen the Basic Urban Insurance system and the Cooperative Medical System in rural areas.

John Wong, East Asian Institute, Singapore
Liu Wei, Peking University, China

Chapter

1

China's Changing Economic Growth Modes in Historical Perspective

Liu Wei and Cai Zhizhou

School of Economics, Peking University, Beijing, PRC

China has kept a long-term rapid economic growth since 1978 when its reform of economic system and opening-up to the outside world began. The GDP annual growth rate is 9.62 percent on average from 1978 to 2005. The GDP in 2005 is 12 times as much as in 1978,[1] and GDP per capita at 1978 constant price is 9 times, and GDP per capita according to US dollar is US$1,700 that is 7 times as much as in 1978. Figure 1.1 shows China's GDPs at 1978 constant price over the past 27 years with a semi-log graph. It can be seen that the GDP curve is approximately a straight line, which means a long-term economic growth with a stable annual growth rate. China's great progress can be depicted with various indices, numerous indicators reflecting economic growth or qualitative indicators reflecting industrial restructure, from the point of view of either economic development or social progress. The proportion of agricultural employment

[1] Total index is 1194.25%.

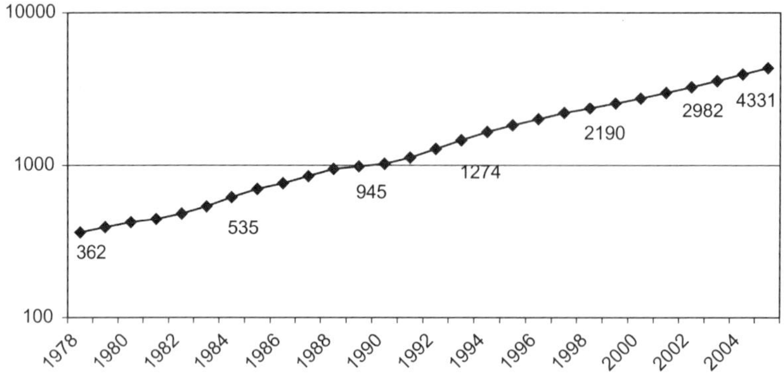

Fig. 1.1: GDP at 1978 constant price of China from 1978 to 2005; billion RMB.

reduced to 47 percent that is lower than the current level in the low-middle income developing countries in the world, from 80 percent in the beginning of the reform, which was higher than the level in the poor countries that time. The Engel coefficient reduced from above 60 percent to lower than 40 percent, which means China has overcome its poverty and entered a higher living standard level. The long-term high-speed economic growth such as of China is rare even if it is observed in a background of world economic development history. Economic growth improved greatly comprehensive national power and people's standards of living as well as international status. The chapter makes a study of China's economic growth mode change, which includes discussion of the understanding of economic growth mode, the characteristics in different growth periods, the progress in the marketing process, effect of technical change, and relationships among economic growth and economic development and social progress.

HOW TO UNDERSTAND THE CHANGE OF CHINA'S ECONOMIC GROWTH MODE

Generally, the resources of economic growth can be attributed to a variety of reasons among which productivity is one of the most important factors. The causes of increase in productivity of China during the past 27 years mainly include to encourage incentives of producers, increase investment of fixed assets, improvement of quality of labor force, to reallocate resources from low to high productivity sectors, technical advances, and so on. The economic growth mode is a kind of combination of factors listed above that should serve the goal to maintain a long-term sustainable growth. Therefore, we regard that the mode not only indicates the relationship between inputs and outputs in the production process but also some more profound contents. At least, it can be discussed from four aspects: (a) objectives of economic growth; (b) paths to realize the objective; (c) drives of economic growth; and (d) constraints of economic growth.

(a) *Objectives of economic growth.* Economic growth serves economic and social development. Therefore, it has economic and social goals. Economic goal is to realize aggregate enlargement to create conditions for enhancing national strength and improving people's standard of living through productive activities; Social goal is to increase people's welfare wholly and promote social progress through income distribution and re-distribution on the basis of economic growth. However, concrete emphases in different periods could be different. In the beginning of the reform, higher attention was paid to aggregate growth, and now, social goal got more concerns.
(b) *Paths to realize the objective.* Economic growth is to realize economic aggregate enlargement in a given period. The promotion of productivity is the main way to achieve growth. There are many ways to increase productivity such as to stimulate incentives of producers through institutional innovation, to increase inputs of capital and other production factors, to develop technical innovation, and so on, among which technical change is the main path to increase productivity and achieve economic growth since the Industrial Revolution. There are differences among paths to promote economic growth during different periods and economic development levels: people always depend on the increase in inputs to increase outputs when the economic development level is low and attach importance to

the improvement of growth quality when a higher development level is reached.

(c) *Drives of economic growth.* The drives are different among different economic backgrounds and historical periods. In the beginning of the 1980s, agricultural development initiated China's economic growth, which was the main drive of China's economy, and then China's main drive transferred from the rural areas to the urban areas. It is an important reason for China's lasting economic growth that the drives to push China's economy are gradually and constantly shifting. Economic growth is stable however its main drives or influencing factors are active.

(d) *Constraints of economic growth.* Economic growth is the basis of economic development and social progress. Especially, for the developing countries, it is impossible to improve its economical and social status greatly without a good economic growth. Otherwise, economic growth cannot deviate from requirements of economic development and social progress. The economic growth objectives can be divided into short-term, mid-term, and long-term according to their duration. The short-term objectives should meet the requirements of consuming and investment goods from the society so that their constraints are a variety of growth conditions to keep the stability of economic growth, which should be coordinated through demand management by governments, especially, the central government. The mid-term objectives are to increase supply capabilities through industrial restructure so that their constraints are industrial equilibriums, which will depend on market mechanism and governmental supply management. Long-term objectives are social progress and sustainable development, which ask for a good combination of resources and economic development and social progress, institutional and legal construction is the base of such a combination. From the viewpoint of development, the higher economic development level of a country is, the more constraints for its economic growth will be asked. This is why currently China's development is becoming more complicated and more objectives should be considered such as energy and resource allocation, employment issue, rural development, income distribution, social security system, etc., whereas the GDP seemed to be the only development objective in the beginning of the 1980s.

INSTITUTIONAL INNOVATION AND THE CHARACTERISTICS IN DIFFERENT GROWTH PERIODS

Institutional innovation is one of the most important factors undoubtedly to change the mode of economic growth in China. Before the reform and opening-up, China had established a high collective planning economy learned from the former Soviet Union. The target of such a system was to allocate social and economic resources through various mandatory plans by the central government, among which investment was paid high attention for an accelerated economic growth and industrialization. However, the intended target was not arrived by the planning system in the practice. First, the planners usually could not understand economic activities clearly and correctly so that they often made mistakes in decision-making to waste resources instead of allocating them reasonably, and various political disturbances worsened these mistakes. The average annual GDP growth rate of China from 1952 to 1978 was 6.15 percent, a rather high growth rate. However, there were no relative improvements of people's living standards and production conditions. Second, the main path to achieve growth was to increase inputs instead of technical change. Natural resources were exploited without limitation to obtain limited return. Third, selfless contributions of labors were encouraged, however, their welfares were always neglected. Laborers had no incentives to work hard so that the productivity increased slowly, sometimes even reduced. It had been proved that traditional planning system cumbered China's economic growth. Therefore, the task to reform the traditional economic system was raised first when China raised its new growth objective that was to make its GDP four times in the beginning of the 1980s. China has to depend on rapid economic growth to get rid of poverty; meanwhile the high-speed growth needed China to change its growth mode. Therefore, the institutional innovation became the starting point of the change.

According to the characteristics and changes of growth mode of China after the reform, China's economic growth can be divided into three periods.

The first is the exploring period from the end of the 1970s to the beginning of the 1990s. The reform to traditional socialism distribution system gave an initial push to China's economy. At that time, China had established a completed system that combined governments and enterprises into an integrated system after the PRC was found. The so-called entire people ownership and collective ownership were the basic formations of various enterprises in the urban areas, and the People's Communes with collective ownership were established widely in the rural areas. The socialism systems for education, medical care, residence, and so on had been set up. The public ownership became the basis of the central planning economy so that the average distribution became the basic distribution method. The system made China stable and stagnating so that it was necessary to break equilibrium to stimulate China active from its bottom. The way to break equilibrium was to adjust income distribution. Mr. Deng Xiaoping said that some people and regions should be allowed to become rich first, then bring others to the same level. Under the guidance of such a thought, a series of changes happened: agricultural production responsibility system was extended in the rural areas; urban enterprises were given more independence and entered markets; foreign direct investments were permitted in some coastal cities, etc. People could have more income if they worked hard after tradition distribution system was reformed so that their demands increased, which pulled economic growth further. Therefore, the industrial structure was changed, output of the consumer goods, such as foods, TV sets, refrigerators, washing machines, grew rapidly so that agriculture and light industry developed faster.

The second is the period of reform of marketing and modern enterprise system in the 1990s, when the institutional innovation played the most important role in promoting economic growth. The reform and economic growth in the 1980s made China understand that the market mechanism is good in pushing economic development. However, whether China should replace the planning system with the marketing one was still a question to be solved as traditional socialism ideology. Therefore, the direction of marketing reform was not clear in the 1980s so that deviations from the intended targets often happened in the try and error process. For example, the reform of price system through the so-called two-way price system failed, in which different prices were given to the same commodity. The price reform had induced inflation and influenced people's life negatively. It had been proved that the commodity price reform could not be processed and should be one part of the integrated marketing reform. The 14th Congress of the Communist Party of China decided the goal of the economic system reform of China was to establish the socialism marketing economy, which meant that China's marketing reform included not only the reform of commodity's prices but also other production factors such as capital, labor, technology, land, natural resource, etc. The core of the reform was to rebuild China's enterprise system that included the reform of state-owned enterprises according to the principle of stock-share system and the establishment of modern enterprise system according to international common standards. During the period, foreign ventures and private enterprises developed rapidly, and the number of state-owned enterprises reduced but the whole quality was improved through the rebuilding. Various markets of production factors were established such as property markets, stock markets, labor markets, and so on. The system of marketing economy had been constructed by the end of the 20th century and become the foundation of China's modernization although its perfection still needed a long process. During the transition from the central planning economy to the marketing one, the potentials in China's economy had been released gradually that pushed economic growth constantly. The tertiary industry developed fast during the period, especially modern tertiary industries such as communication industry, Internet and IT industry, finance industry, and real estate.

The third one is the period of accelerated industrialization and economic globalization from the beginning of the 21st century. The marketing reform was deepened and the stock share reform of the state-owned banks indicated that China's institutional reform entered a higher stage; China's WTO accession marked that the economic connections between China and the rest of the world were enhanced. China's economic growth began to accelerate and enter a new cycle of economic growth with multi-factors promoting this growth during the period: first, development of private enterprises and the reform of state-owned ones improved their management and strengthened their competitive power; second, the economic development level reached a new level and per capita GDP exceeded US$1,000, which meant China had become a low-median income country from a poor developing country; therefore, China's consuming demands had a significant rise, especially, demands for automobiles and houses; third, China's development often depended on economic growth of partial regions in the last two decades, however, economic construction developed all over the country. Each region is eager to develop local economy so that a lot of investment urges were induced to increase huge demands for investment goods; fourth, the demands from the rest of the world increased fast due to the comparative advantage of China's goods. The increases of the supplying capabilities promoted by institutional innovation and of demands from domestic and international markets provided good conditions. The industrial characteristic is the development of manufacture industry, especially, heavy industry.

It can be seen from the discussion above that the institutional innovation, especially the reform of economic system and state-owned enterprises, was the most important drive in the last 27 years. The gradual reform and opening-up not only met the requirements of China's economic development, but also guaranteed stability of the society to avoid recession by the so-called shock therapy. The institutional innovation in the first two periods created conditions for China's accelerated industrial and international development in the new century and induced a new round of economic growth. Figure 1.2 depicts the change of three industries in GDP, it can be seen that the industrial structure has changed obviously as China's economic growth and the proportion of tertiary industry is increasing gradually.

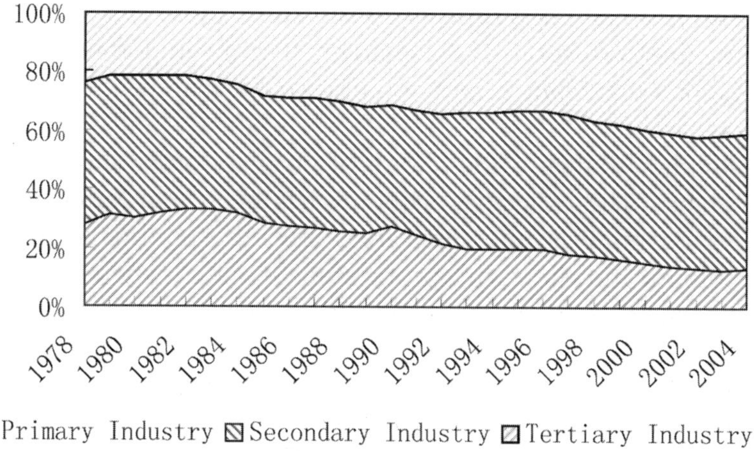

Fig. 1.2: Proportions of primary, secondary, and tertiary industries in GDP.

Three important changes happened as the institutional innovation was taken and deepened from 1978.

One change is the system of marketing economy has been established. From demands and supplies of the national economy, in demanding side the market decides the prices of above 95 percent consuming and capital goods, and in the supplying side most of prices of production factors, such as labor, capital, land, and so on, depend on the market mechanism, whereas over 95 percent prices are decided by the governmental plan before the reform. It is a great progress in China's marketing process. What is important for China now is how to deepen and strengthen the marketing reform of production factors, which is more profound than the marketing reform of commodities. China initiated its marketing reform of commodities in the middle of the 1980s; however, the marketing reform of production factors did not begin until the 1990s. Among various production factors, labor marketing developed faster and wages of most employees were decided by the market; the capital market developed rather slower, in which state-owned banks and other financing companies have a governing status and stock markets only have a small portion of less than 10 percent; the land market developed even slower than capital market, in which property system or trading system, price decision or legal construction, there is a long way to go for the perfection of the market. It is an important objective for China's marketing reform to improve the markets of production factors.

Another change is the reform of property order and traditional ownership. The collective economy has been transferred into the farmer economy in the rural areas after the reform. In the non-agricultural industries the proportion of state-owned enterprises have reduced to about 50 percent from over 90 percent before the reform as private sector developed, and some former state-owned enterprises were transformed or became impoverished.

The third change is the methods of management of national economy. The government adjusted economic activities through mandatory and instructive plans before the reform. The fiscal and monetary policies began to play more and more roles in the economic operation as the reform of economic system was developed. Especially, the monetary policies have been taken as more important measures as the marketing economy was established.

PRODUCTIVITY AND TECHNICAL CHANGE

Institutional innovation liberated labor productivity of China greatly and released the potentials in the economy so that a long-term rapid growth has been achieved since the reform. Table 1.1 lists the GDP, employees, and original value of fixed assets of China after the reform and their comparisons. Three trends can be reflected from the analyses of the time series.

(a) *Labor productivity.* It can be seen from the table that the labor productivity increased quickly after the reform if the indicator is defined as GDP per employee that in 2004 is 5.33 times as much as in 1978. The improvement of labor productivity can be reflected also from the time series of labor elasticity. During the period the trend of the series was diminishing and value in each year is less than 1 significantly, which means labor efficiency in China has been improving.

Table 1.1: GDP, employees, and original value of fixed assets of China, 1978–2004.

Year	GDP		Employees		Original value of fixed assets		Labor productivity (RMB)	Labor elasticity	Capital elasticity
	Billion RMB (at 1978 price)	Growth rate (percent)	Million persons	Growth rate (percent)	Billion RMB (at 1978 price)	Growth rate (percent)			
1978	362	—	402	—	888	—	903	—	—
1979	390	7.62	410	2.17	1001	12.72	951	0.29	1.67
1980	420	7.79	424	3.26	1123	12.18	992	0.42	1.56
1981	442	5.19	437	3.22	1236	10.07	1011	0.62	1.94
1982	483	9.11	453	3.59	1368	10.71	1065	0.39	1.18
1983	535	10.90	464	2.52	1517	10.91	1152	0.23	1.00
1984	616	15.19	482	3.79	1698	11.90	1279	0.25	0.78
1985	700	13.50	499	3.48	1904	12.14	1403	0.26	0.90
1986	761	8.81	513	2.83	2132	11.98	1484	0.32	1.36
1987	850	11.60	528	2.93	2389	12.05	1609	0.25	1.04
1988	946	11.30	543	2.94	2657	11.21	1740	0.26	0.99
1989	984	4.09	553	1.83	2870	8.03	1779	0.45	1.96
1991	1116	9.20	655	1.15	3360	8.43	1578	0.12	0.92
1992	1274	14.20	662	1.01	3677	9.44	1703	0.07	0.67
1993	1452	14.00	668	0.99	4068	10.64	1926	0.07	0.76
1994	1643	13.10	675	0.97	4528	11.31	2174	0.07	0.86

(*Continued*)

Table 1.1: *(Continued)*

Year	GDP		Employees		Original value of fixed assets		Labor productivity (RMB)	Labor elasticity	Capital elasticity
	Billion RMB (at 1978 price)	Growth rate (percent)	Million persons	Growth rate (percent)	Billion RMB (at 1978 price)	Growth rate (percent)			
1995	1822	10.90	681	0.90	5051	11.55	2435	0.08	1.06
1996	2004	10.00	690	1.30	5630	11.45	2676	0.13	1.14
1997	2190	9.30	698	1.26	6243	10.89	2906	0.14	1.17
1998	2361	7.80	706	1.17	6917	10.81	3137	0.15	1.38
1999	2541	7.60	714	1.07	7640	10.45	3343	0.14	1.38
2000	2754	8.40	721	0.97	8431	10.35	3558	0.12	1.23
2001	2983	8.30	730	1.30	9320	10.55	3820	0.16	1.27
2002	3254	9.10	737	0.98	10331	10.84	4084	0.11	1.19
2003	3579	10.00	744	0.94	11541	11.71	4413	0.09	1.17
2004	3941	10.10	752	1.03	12933	12.07	4809	0.10	1.19

Note: The data are estimated through the time series of infrastructure investment, renewal and reconstruction funds, all investments of fixed assets from 1953 and formation of fixed capitals. Calculated at 1978 constant price.

Source: *China Statistical Yearbook*, 2005.

(b) *Investment efficiency.* Obviously, the investment efficiency is much less than labor efficiency during the period. It can be seen from the last column of the table that the capital elasticity is larger than 1 that means in these years the investment efficiency reduced. As a whole, the capital efficiency has been decreasing during the period.

(c) *Technical exchange.* The technical change can be discussed from various points of view. The technical change in narrow sense means the positive impact of technical innovation to production process; and in broad sense it not only includes material production, but also includes social organizations and institutional innovation. With the time series of real GDP (Y), employees (L), and real fixed asset original value (K) from 1978 to 2004 through LS, we fit the Cobb–Douglas aggregate production function (Solow, 1957)

$$Y_t = A_0 e^{\gamma_t} K_t^{\alpha} L_t^{\beta}. \tag{1.1}$$

Under the assumption of neutral technical change, i.e., assuming the output elasticity ratio of capital K and labor L have a relation of $\alpha + \beta = 1$, we have

$$Y = 0.3314 K^{0.9083} L^{0.0917}. \tag{1.2}$$

The fitness coefficient of the regression equation is 0.99 and passed the statistical significant test. The economic explanation of the equation is that the contribution of capital in the economic growth of China from 1978–2004 is much higher than the labor's, assuming the technical change is neutral. Concretely, one unit output would need 91 percent fixed capital investment, whereas only 9 percent labor would be needed. The contribution of capital is 10 times as much as labor's. This is why China's rapid economic growth always goes with high growth rate of fixed capital investment and why the property system reform is so important.

Comparing (1.1) with (1.2), we have

$$A_0 e^{\gamma_t} = 0.3314. \tag{1.3}$$

> Assuming $A_0 = 1$ the coefficient of technical change during the period $\gamma = -1.1044$, which means the technical change did not have any contribution during the period. In other words, that the coefficient of technical change is less than 0 means, to increase one unit output would need more inputs of production factors.

The fact can be derived from China's economic data. The real GDP of China in 2004 is 10.87 times as much as in 1978; the employee number of employee is 1.87 times, and the real fixed asset original value is 14.57 times! It means that labor efficiency had improved significantly; however, the output of one unit investment reduced. The conclusion is that the production capacities induced by the institutional innovation after the reform mainly depended on scale enlargement, especially the increase of investment, instead of technical change.

The analyzing conclusion is close to the reality. The first objective of economic development after the reform was to increase GDP four times in the forthcoming two decades to get rid of poverty in China. Therefore, the growth rate of GDP became the most important objective in the economic development of China for a long period. As a matter of fact, at that time, especially in the 1980s and the early 1990s, it was not important for China how many inputs were utilized to achieve one unit output. Key point was to achieve rapid progress during a given period. It has been proved by the facts after reform that the more investments are introduced the more developments happen in a region so that local governments always concern investment scale instead of investment efficiency. The way to achieve economic growth has both advantages and disadvantages: the main advantage is that a region, even the whole country, can be developed in a short period; and the main disadvantage is that the mode may consume limited natural resources overly.

For its long-term rapid economic growth, China has to resolve a series of development problems and institutional contradictions so that the change of economic growth is important for further growth in the future. From this point of view, the key point to solve development and reform dilemmas is to transfer the current way through increasing inputs into a new way to increase outputs through improvement of efficiency of production factors. The change of growth mode refers to technical innovation, especially promotion of building for indigenous innovation capabilities. It is impossible to improve the efficiency of economic growth without technical change and innovation. However, technical innovation is not only a technical issue but also an institutional one. Promotion of technical innovation capacity depends on reasonable institutions and systems. Therefore, China's institutional innovation faces a new challenge to create development conditions for technical innovation.

From the history of economic development after the reform, there were opinions for a long time to take the improvement of technical efficiency, a main measure to push economic growth, however, which has not been implemented widely in the practice of economic development. The key point is the current economic system did not create an adequate environment for enterprises to compete with each other in the market so that they did not have enough pressures to improve their technologies. This is the reason why the private sector of China improved the efficiency of production factors more than the state-owned enterprises, after the reform. The more the production factors are attributed into the market mechanism, the more improvements in efficiency of technical capacity will be achieved.

ECONOMIC GROWTH AND ECONOMIC DEVELOPMENT AS WELL AS SUSTAINABLE DEVELOPMENT

The economic growth needs improvement of efficiencies, which includes improvement of growth rates, productivities, industrial structure, economic stability, and so on. The institutional innovation of China began from the reform in the distribution field in the beginning of the 1980s. The goal of the reform was to break the equilibrium under the traditional planning system to push economic development to get rid of poverty that was why China had taken the GDP growth objective as almost the only development objective. At that time, the rapid economic growth meant a good development. However, economic growth is different from economic development.

Basically, the growth issue concerns with various aggregates and the development issue concerns with structures and relationships among various economic variables, such as ownership structure, employment, industrial structure, international balance, income distribution, regional differences, and so on. The development issues have become more and more important as China's economic level raised in rapid growth. Therefore, the harmonious society became a new theme of China in the 21st century. From the viewpoint of economic development, what China should do is to rebuild a new equilibrium in a new basis after a long-term economic growth.

To rebuild equilibrium does not mean to give up economic growth. Economic growth is still one of the important objectives in the economic development of China due to a very low starting point in the past and rather low per capita GDP now. The solution of development problems will depend heavily on economic growth. However, what is more complicated is more constraints should be considered in economic growth. Therefore, a rapid growth on development equilibrium will become a new topic in China's future development.

Moreover, the economic development of China should be designed under the background of the sustainable development, which includes three pillars of economy, society, and environment. Balances between partial and whole benefits, current and future benefits, should be considered. At first, the following issues at least should be considered:

- Employment
- Income distribution
- Energy, natural resources, and environmental protection
- Development of export-oriented economy and balance of international payments
- Regional differences
- Reasonable industrial structure
- Technical change and indigenous innovation
- Education, culture, medical care, social security system

Three main important constraints should be considered first in economic growth in the near future.

One issue is the sustainable development. As China entered the accelerated industrializing period, especially in the first decade of the 21st century, the traditional extensive mode brought many problems. Let us take energy consumption as an example. Table 1.2 lists the relationships between the production and consumption of energy and economic growth of China. It can be seen that production and consumption elasticity ratios of energy from 1990 to 2000 are less than 1, which means that the growth rates of energy production and consumption were lower than GDP's, especially, during the period of 1997–2000; the production and consumption of energy reduced because the growth depended on

Table 1.2: Elasticity ratio of energy production and consumption in 1990–2004.

Year	Growth rate of GDP over preceding year (percent)	Growth rate of energy production over preceding year (percent)	Elasticity ratio of energy production	Growth rate of energy consumption over preceding year (percent)	Elasticity ratio of energy production
1990	3.8	2.2	0.58	1.8	0.47
1991	9.2	0.9	0.10	5.1	0.55
1992	14.2	2.3	0.16	5.2	0.37
1993	14.0	3.6	0.26	6.3	0.45
1994	13.1	6.9	0.53	5.8	0.44
1995	10.9	8.7	0.80	6.9	0.63
1996	10.0	2.8	0.28	5.9	0.59
1997	9.3	−0.2	—	−0.8	—
1998	7.8	−6.2	—	−4.1	—
1999	7.6	−12.2	—	−1.6	—
2000	8.4	−2.0	—	0.1	0.02
2001	8.3	13.0	1.57	3.5	0.43
2002	9.1	14.4	1.58	9.9	1.09
2003	10.0	15.6	1.56	15.3	1.53
2004	10.1	15.4	1.52	15.2	1.50

Source: *China Statistical Yearbook*, 2005.

high-tech and new tertiary industries. However, after 2001, the production and consumption of energy grew faster than GDP's and the elasticity ratio of energy production increased to over 1.5 as the growth rate in manufacture industries developed, which indicated that the economic growth of China depend on energy production and consumption.

Another issue is the income distribution. Income inequality is always a sensitive issue in any country. Especially, in a newly industrializing country as China, a "fair" income distribution has direct impacts to economic growth and social stability. However, it is a difficult task to find an optimal solution for the problem because of the contradiction between fair and efficiency. Especially, when growth efficiency and productivity, which asks for higher growth in a given period, are regarded as the primary tasks or objectives of the country, how the income inequity should be controlled within a reasonable scope will become an important social constraint for economic growth. In other words, an equilibrium relationship between fair and efficiency should be established to maintain necessary stability of the society. It is also an important task for China to solve in its development road. The differences between urban and rural areas, among different cities, among different rural areas, and inside the same city or same rural area, have been enlarged as economic reform and growth. Table 1.3 lists the changes of Gini coefficients of China in 1978 and 2003 (Luo, 2005), from which it can be seen that income distributions changed significantly in China after the reform and the national Gini coefficients are much

Table 1.3: The comparisons of household Gini coefficients between rural and urban areas of China in 1978 and 2003.

Year	Urban household Gini coefficient	Rural household Gini coefficient	National household Gini coefficient
1978	0.1806	0.2124	0.298
2003	0.3732	0.3763	0.460

higher than the ones in both rural areas and urban areas that means the income inequity between urban and rural areas is the main factor to induce inequity as the urban areas achieved higher growth rates.

Third issue is the social progress. China had established some good socialism systems before the reform, such as in the fields of education, science, culture, medical care, residence, and so on. However, in the process of marketing reform, some fields that are not suitable with markets have been reformed as industrial sectors, which must influence people's expectancy and standards of living. How to rebuild China's social welfare and security system is an urgent task for China's economic development and social progress.

To realize the development equilibrium on a higher economic level, the following are included as main measures: construction of legal ruling society, administrative and marketing system. Concretely, the development equilibrium is a long-term process for that the development of socialism democratic and legal system, the improvement of government administrative efficiency, completion of marketing system, and development of macro control and regulation through fiscal and monetary policies will provide foundations.

CONCLUSIONS

The paper reviews and analyzes the history of economic growth and changes of its mode from 1978 to date. The following conclusions can be derived from these discussions.

(a) The change of economic growth mode is a complicated topic, which at least can be analyzed from four phases including objectives of economic growth, the paths to realize growth, the main drives to push growth, and the constraints of growth.
(b) From the characteristics in different growth periods, the economic growth of China after the economic system reform and opening-up to the outside world can be divided into three periods.

The first is the exploring period. The reform of income distribution played an important role in pushing economic growth. The industrial characteristic in this period is the development of agriculture and manufacture of consumer goods. The second is the period of marketing reform and modern enterprise system. The industrial characteristic is the development of hi-tech industries and modern tertiary industries such as communication, transportation, finance, real estates, and so on. The third one is the period of accelerated industrialization and economic globalization. Its characteristic is the rapid growth of fixed capital investment and the development of manufacture, especially the development of heavy industry.

(c) The institutional innovation is the main drive of economic growth of China after the reform. China has completed the transformation from the central planning economy into marketing economy in the past 28 years in which China constantly and gradually released its potential and kept a long-term rapid growth. The improvement of marketing mechanism will remain an important factor to push the economic growth in the near future.

(d) The conclusion is derived from an aggregate production function through regression analysis among GDP, labor input, and capital input after the reform that the efficiency of capital input reduced in proportion to economic growth although the efficiency of labor input improved significantly. The negative coefficient of technical change means that the economic growth depended mainly on scale enlargement instead of technical change so that technical innovation should be an important task in the future economic development.

(e) China achieved accelerated economic growth in the initial stages of the reform by breaking the traditional equilibrium of the central planning economy. However, a new development equilibrium should be formatted and maintained in a higher level as a long-term economic growth has been achieved. Economic growth should fit the constraints of economic development and sustainable development.

REFERENCES

China Center for National Accounting and Economic Growth, Peking University (2006), *Economic Growth Report*. Economy Publishing House of China.

Luo, Yuemei (2005), "Gini coefficients and income distribution of households," *Statistical Observation*, Vol. 6.

Solow, R.M. (1957), "Technical change and the aggregate production function," *The Review of Economics and Statistics*, Vol. 39.

Chapter

2

China's Economic Growth in East Asian Context

John Wong

East Asian Institute, Singapore

MANY NEW ECONOMIC MILESTONES IN 25 YEARS

The Chinese economy has experienced spectacular performance on account of its successful economic reform some 25 years ago. Economic growth for the period of 1979–2005 was at an average annual rate of 9.6 percent, with many ups and downs.

As shown in Fig. 2.1, the growth process fluctuated quite a lot in the 1980s caused by the so-called "reform cycles." Since 1990, the growth process has experienced two spurts of high growth: one being sparked off by Deng Xiaoping's *Nanxun* (tour of South China) in early 1992 and the other by China's accession to the WTO in 2001. The *Nanxun* signals China's march into a market economy, while the WTO membership marks the rapid integration of China into the global economy. The second spurt, which coincided with China's 10th Five-Year Plan (2000–2005), was by far more significant, not just because it chalked up an all-time high of 9.9 percent

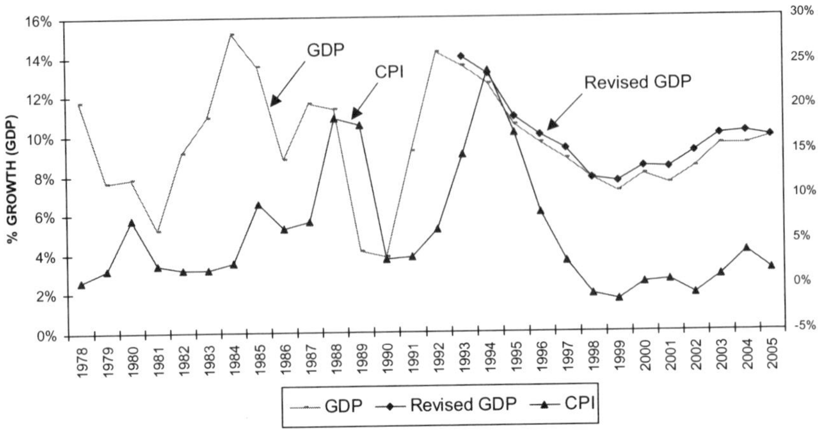

Fig. 2.1: China's economic growth and inflation, 1978–2005.
Source: *China Statistical Abstract 2006*.

growth, but also because it occurred with a much larger base toward the end of the long period.

When Deng introduced economic reform and the open-door policy at the historic Third Party Plenum in December 1978, China's total GDP was only 365 billion yuan. By 2005, the total GDP increased to 18,319 billion yuan or just about 50 times more. In 1978, China nominal GDP per capita was only 381 yuan. In 2005, it increased 37 time to 13,985 yuan.[1] Converted into US dollar at current exchange rate, China's total GDP in 2005 reached US$2.3 trillion to become the world's fourth largest economy after the USA, Japan, and Germany, though China's per-capita GNP, at US$1,700, was still around the 100th in the world. Still, China belongs to what the World Bank called one of the lower middle-income economies. In terms of purchasing power parity (PPP) GDP, i.e., pricing Chinese output at international or US levels, China has been the world's second largest economy after the USA for many years.

China's exports have also been growing very rapidly, averaging at 16 percent a year over the past two and a half decades, rising

[1] *China's Statistical Abstract 2006* (Beijing, 2006).

from US$9.8 billion in 1978 to US$762 billion in 2005, or 78 times more. By 2005, China has become the world's third largest exporting country after the USA and Germany. For foreign direct investment (FDI), since the late 1990s, China has become the world's most favored destination in comparison with all other developing economies. By the end of 2005, China had attracted a total of US$622 billion in FDI, in addition to its external loans of US$147 billion.[2] It may be noted that China has continued to promote FDI, which is not for meeting capital requirements but primarily as a vehicle for technology transfer and the development of the export markets. Not surprisingly, over 80 percent of the world's Fortune 500 largest corporations and its top 100 information technology firms have set up businesses in China.[3]

In recent years, the massive influx of foreign capital into China has indeed continued unabated despite the fact that China has already become a capital-surplus economy on account of its persistent "twin surpluses" on both capital and current accounts. The problem of capital surplus got more serious in 2005 because of China's huge trade surplus of US$102 billion and the rapid accumulation of its foreign reserves to the record level of US$819 million at the end of 2005 (now over US$1,000 billion as the world's largest), despite the revaluation of the *Renminbi* by 2.1 percent on July 21, 2005. Thus, on the one hand, China welcomes FDI in order to catalyze its industrialization and speed up its exports. On the other hand, China is confronted with an enormous problem of how to profitably and smoothly recycle its bulging foreign reserves back to the international financial system.

Turning to the real economy, as a result of intensive and extensive industrialization over the past 25 years, China has become the world's foremost manufacturing production base. Thus, in 2005, China topped the world in the production of 2.2 billion tons of coal, 397 million tons of steel, 1.1 billion tons of cement, 83 million sets of color TV, 68 million units of air-conditioners, 30 million units of

---

[2] Ibid.

[3] "Investors Keep Eyes Peeled on Dragon," *Beijing Review* (June 2, 2005).

refrigerators, and 304 million units of mobile phones. In addition, China produced 5.7 million automobiles (the world's third largest after the USA and Japan) and 81 million personal computers (Asia's number one).[4]

Take steel production, which was used to be regarded as sinew of modern industrialism. When Deng started economic reform in 1978, China's steel output was merely 22 million tons; the level of output in 2005 is 18 times more. In 1978, China churned out only 150,000 units of automobile in all; the output level of 2005 was 38 times more. For many durable consumer products like color TV and refrigerators, China did not even begin their production in 1978. In 1990, China produced only 8,000 units of PCs; but it was 1,000 times more in 2005 (Table 2.1). All this serves to show not just the tremendous progress that China has made in its industrialization efforts during this period, but also the mammoth scale of industrialization that has been going on in China in recent years.

As China is producing millions of units of those commodity items, it will inevitably enjoy enormous economies of scale. The average cost of those products will be very low, while their marginal

Table 2.1: Production of major industrial products, 1978–2005.

	1978	2005	2005 over 1978, %
Coal (million tons)	618	2190.0	354
Steel (million tons)	22	396.9	1804
Cement (million tons)	65	1064.0	1636
Automobiles (million units)	0.15	5.7	3800
Color TV sets (million units)	*	82.8	—
Washing machines (million units)	*	29.5	—
Refrigerators (million units)	*	82.8	—
Air conditioners (million units)	*	67.6	—
Personal computers (million units)	0.08 (1990)	80.8	—

* Ouput just a few hundred.
Source: *China Statistical Abstract 2006* (Beijing, 2006).

[4] *China Statistical Abstract 2006.*

cost will be near to zero. What is less known is that China also reaps the comparative advantage of "external economies" for the production of those manufactured products. Most of China's export-oriented manufacturing activities are concentrated in the Pearl River Delta, the Yangtze River Delta, and Bohai Bay region, which are also blessed with modern infrastructure of ports, airports, and an extensive network of newly built highway. In 1990, China had only 500 km of modern highway; by 2005, China had completed a basic national network of modern highways of 42,000 km, the world's second largest after the USA. When the concentration of various industries complements with an efficient infrastructure, it gives rise to the Marshallian condition of "external economies," which gives China a distinctive edge in competing with other smaller economies.

As China's economy continues to grow and expand rapidly, it will inevitably produce a strong external impact — at first, regionally, but now globally. It may be stressed that the Chinese economic rise is a rare case of speed combining with scale, which tends to expand its disruptive effect on the world economy. Many years ago, China was mostly referred to as a rising regional economic power as its growth had significantly impacted only its neighboring economies, which traded with China or invested in China. By 2005, China's economic growth had, beyond any doubt, produced far-reaching global implications. By its sheer size, China's levels of production, consumption, imports, and exports carry worldwide ramifications. On account of its massive industrialization, China has become the world's top consumer of a wide variety of natural resources and primary commodities from steel and aluminum to oil and gas. China's rising demand in these products in recent years has driven up their world prices. At the same time, China's large-scale fabrication of many industrial products has also brought down their world prices. For boom or for bust, the movement of China's economy has therefore become a significant force in the global economy.

China's external economic impact is best manifested in its unique pattern of trade balances with its major trade partners. Figure 2.2 shows how China in recent years has continued to run substantial trade deficits with its neighboring economies, from Japan, Korea,

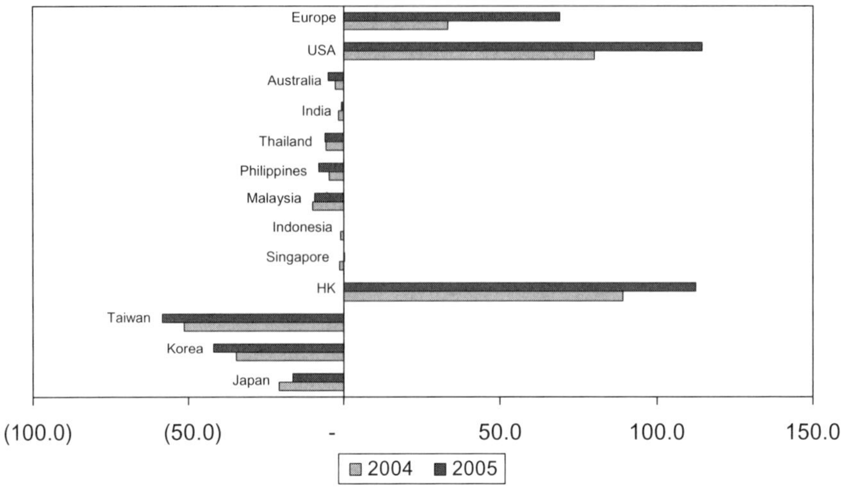

Fig. 2.2: China's trade balance with selected countries (in US billions).
Source: *China Statistical Yearbook 2005*.

Taiwan and the ASEAN-5 to Australia and India; and how China turned around by incurring a large trade surplus with the USA and the EU. In this way, China could still end up with an overall trade surplus. But China's trade deficits with its East Asian neighbors also mean that China has opened up its vast domestic market for their exports (both manufactured products and primary commodities), thereby operating as an engine for their economic growth.

The underlying economic implications of China's overall trade pattern and its trade balances are actually more profound. Because most of China's exports are processed products (55 percent of total exports in 2005) or final products generally with low domestic value-added and low domestic contents (domestic value-added generally around 40 percent, but only 20 percent or lower for many products), China must import in order to export. Since over half of China's exports is handled by its foreign invested enterprises (58 percent on average in 2005, with much higher proportions for some hi-tech products), particularly those from Japan, Korea, Taiwan, and Hong Kong, China's foreign trade is a highly internationalized economic act incorporating foreign trade activities of many other countries. In short,

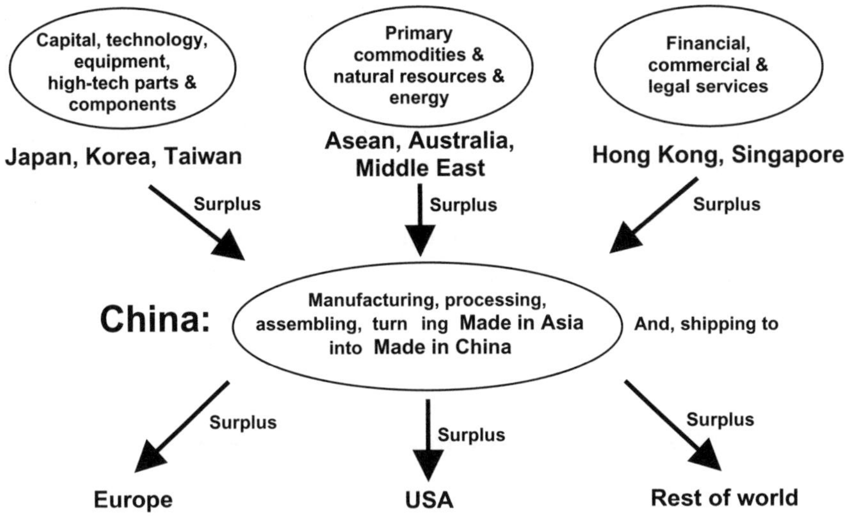

Fig. 2.3: China at the center of global and regional production networks.

China has become a critical link in the East Asian supply chains, spawning numerous regional production networks.

It can further be argued that, as shown in Fig. 2.3, China has in fact become an important "integrator" of global and regional production networks. China's exports embody raw materials, parts and components, technology and equipment, and financial and economic services from different Asian economies, converting "Made-in-Asia" into "Made-in-China" products for the world market. Most international supply chains, be they Asian or global, are centered in China. Therefore, China's exports also generate multiplier effects in other economies, sometimes more than in China itself. In other words, China's own economic growth is also a source of economic growth of other economies. By doing this, China is also a catalyst for regional and global economic integration.

During the past two and a half decades, the Chinese economy has indeed grown by leaps and bounds. It has definitely taken off into self-sustained growth. The economy has been highly industrialized to become the world's manufacturing hub. When Deng started economic reform in 1979, the Chinese economy was insignificant in the global context. China's total GDP is estimated to be just about 0.5 percent of the world's total. By 2004, China's share of the world's GDP increased to 5 percent in nominal terms, or 13 percent in PPP terms.[5] The economy has also been radically transformed from a closed economy based on Mao's tenet of "self reliance" to one that is actively participating in the global economic system in terms of trade and foreign investment. In 2005, China's share of the world's export markets reached 6 percent, compared to the tiny 0.6 percent in 1979. China's economic rise today is no longer a myth, but has become so "real" as to giving rise to the perception of "China Threat."

CHINA AND EAST ASIA'S GROWTH PROCESS

China's highly creditable economic performance after its successful economic reform has inevitably given rise to one critical question. Is China's dynamic economic growth warranted? Is it sustainable?

To begin with, China's past high growth, though very impressive, is actually not exceptional or unprecedented in the historical context of the many high-performance East Asian economies. Hence a good starting point to addressing the future growth potential of China is to put China's growth process in the perspective of East Asia's past development processes.

East Asia's "core growth area" is commonly defined to comprise Japan, China, the four Newly Industrialized Economies (NIEs) of South Korea, Taiwan, Hong Kong, and Singapore, and the four Association of Southeast Asian Nations (ASEAN) of Indonesia, Malaysia, the Philippines, and Thailand — the original ASEAN members. Situated on the western rim of the Pacific, many of these East Asian economies have displayed dynamic growth for a sustained period until 1997 when they were hit, in varying degrees, by the regional financial crisis. The World Bank in its well-known study referred to their high growth phenomenon as the "East Asian Miracle."[6]

---

[5] World Bank, *World Development Report 2006.*

[6] *The East Asian Miracle* (New York: Oxford University Press, 1994).

Historically speaking, the East Asian growth process, as shown in Table 2.2, is marked by three waves. Japan was the first non-Western country to become industrialized. Its high growth dated back to the 1950s beginning with its rapid postwar recovery, and carried the growth momentum over to the 1960s and much of the 1970s. Japan's economic growth engine was initially based on the export of labor-intensive manufactured products; but it was soon forced by rising wages and increasing costs to shed its comparative advantage for labor-intensive manufacturing in favor of the four NIEs, which started their industrial take-off in the 1960s. These four NIEs, once dubbed "Asia's Four Little Dragons," were arguably the most dynamic economies in the world at that time, as they had sustained near double-digit rates of growth for three decades, from the early 1960s to the 1980s. The rise of the NIEs constituted the second wave of the region's growth and integration.

By the early 1980s, high costs and high wages had similarly caught up with these four NIEs, which had to restructure their economies toward more capital-intensive and higher value-added activities by passing their comparative advantage in labor-intensive products to the late-comers of China and the four ASEAN economies and thereby spreading economic growth to the latter. In this way, China and some ASEAN economies were able to register high growth through the 1980s and the 1990s. Many Japanese scholars used to depict this pattern of development in Asia as the "Flying Geese" pattern.[7] The "Flying Geese Model" for all its simplicity still provides an instructive and in fact highly intuitive explanation of East Asia's past successful economic growth until the recent rise of the Chinese economy.

Figure 2.4 clearly brings out the "flight formation" of these four East Asian economies over several decades. In the decades of the 1950s and the 1960s, Japan took the lead while Taiwan and Korea just started to industrialize; and China was the laggard. In the 1970s, Taiwan and Korea, having achieved their industrial take-off, were in

---

[7] The "flying geese" concept of development was originally coined by a Japanese economist, Kaname Akamatzu. ["A Historical Pattern of Economic Growth in Developing Countries," *Developing Economies* 1 (March/August 1962)].

Table 2.2: East Asian economic performance indicators.

	Population (million)	GNP per-capita (US$)	PPP estimates of GNP per-capita (US$)	Growth of GDP (%)							
	2004	2004	2004	Total GDP (US$ billion), 2004	1960–1970	1970–1980	1980–1990	1990–2000	2000–2004	2004	2005
China	1,297	1,290	5,530	1,930	5.2	5.5	10.3	9.7	9.2	10	9.9
Japan	128	37,180	30,040	4,623	10.9	4.3	4.1	1.3	1.3	2.7	2.7
NIEs											
South Korea	48	13,980	20,400	680	8.6	10.1	8.9	5.7	4.7	4.6	4
Taiwan	23	14,033	n.a.	321	9.2	9.7	7.9	5.7	3.3	6.1	4.1
Hong Kong	7	26,810	31,510	163	10	9.3	6.9	3.8	3.2	8.6	7.3
Singapore	4	24,220	26,590	107	8.8	8.3	6.7	7.4	2.8	8.7	6.4
ASEAN-4											
Indonesia	218	1,140	3,460	258	3.9	7.2	6.1	3.8	4.6	5.1	5.6
Malaysia	25	4,650	9,630	118	6.5	7.9	5.3	6.5	4.3	7.1	5.3
Philippines	83	1,170	4,890	86	5.1	6	1	3.3	4.2	6	5.1
Thailand	62	2,540	8,020	163	8.4	7.1	7.6	3.8	5.3	6.2	4.5
India	1,080	620	3,100	692	—	—	5.8	5.5	5.9	8.5	8.5

Sources: *World Development Report 1995*, *2000/2001*, *2002*, *2003*, *2004*, *2006*; *EIU* Countrydata, *EIU Dataservice*; Asian Development Bank; *World Investment Report 2004*, UNCTAD.

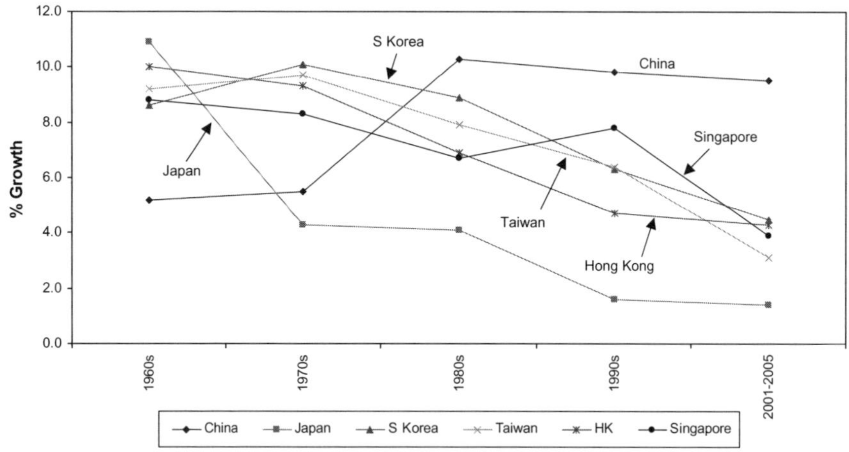

Fig. 2.4: East Asia's economic growth — the flying geese pattern.
Sources: *Hong Kong Statistics*; www.stat.gov.tw; www.singstat.gov.sg; Bank of Korea; *Japan Statistical Yearbook*; *China Statistical Yearbook*.

the lead while Japan as a mature economy was slowing down in growth. In the 1980s, China's economic growth was taking off on the back of successful economic reform and has since been in the lead while Japan succumbed to a decade of low growth and recession. Indeed, the rapid economic rise of China coupled with the long economic recession of Japan has considerably weakened the "Flying Geese" theory, which was originally put forward to explain how Japan was leading East Asian growth, though much in a "static" way.

The "Flying Geese" pattern is also reflected in the distribution of per-capita GDP in East Asia (which is commonly used to denote the level of economic development of an economy). As shown in Fig. 2.5, individual per-capita levels of the East Asian economies tend to bunch much closer in their initial phase of development. However, their income gaps tend to get widened after decades of rapid development, even though they have all enjoyed high rates of economic growth. China's per-capita GDP always tends to be low because of China's vast population size, while Japan is, without doubt, the most developed of all in the pack. But still, Japan's per-capita GDP level should not be so much higher than that of the four NIEs,

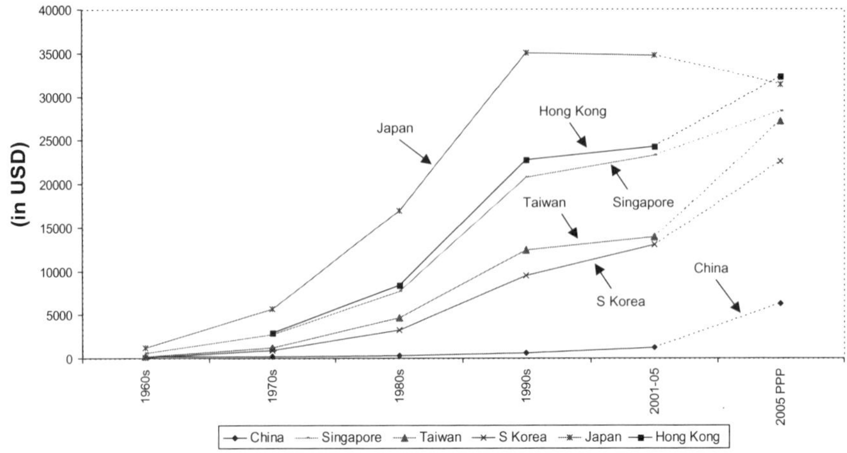

Fig. 2.5: Per-capita GDP of East Asian economies: The flying geese pattern. Sources: *IMF World Economic Outlook*; *China Statistical Yearbook*; *Hong Kong Statistics*; *Korea Statistical Yearbook*; www.statgov.tw; www.singstat.gov.sg; *Japan Statistical Yearbook*.

which have also become developed economies. The main explanation lies in Japan's high domestic price levels, especially for the non-tradable service sector. Hence, using PPP level of per-capita GNP for 2004 has considerably narrowed their income gaps: the lower the nominal GDP, the higher will be the adjustment for the PPP level of GDP. Hence, in PPP terms, China's per-capita GDP is sharply raised while that of Japan is brought down.

Figure 2.6 shows the process of structural change of these economies. In the 1960s, the Japanese economy was dominated by the manufacturing sector, while the agricultural sector remained large for China, Korea, and Taiwan. In the 1980s, the manufacturing sector was predominant for China, Korea, and Taiwan, while it started to decline for Japan. In 2004, manufacturing was the leading sector for China, while Japan, Taiwan and Korea are moving toward the so-called post-industrial phase as marked by the rapid expansion of the service sector along with the further dwindling of the agricultural sector.

How does China's economy stand in the context of the other East Asian economies today (2005)? Figure 2.7 brings out a sharp

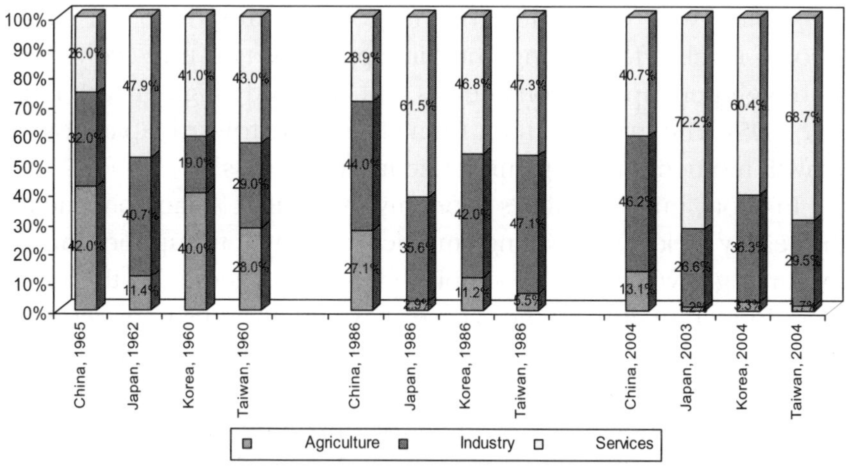

Fig. 2.6: Structure of output — China, Japan Korea, and Taiwan.
Sources: ADB; World Bank; *Japan Yearbook 2006*.

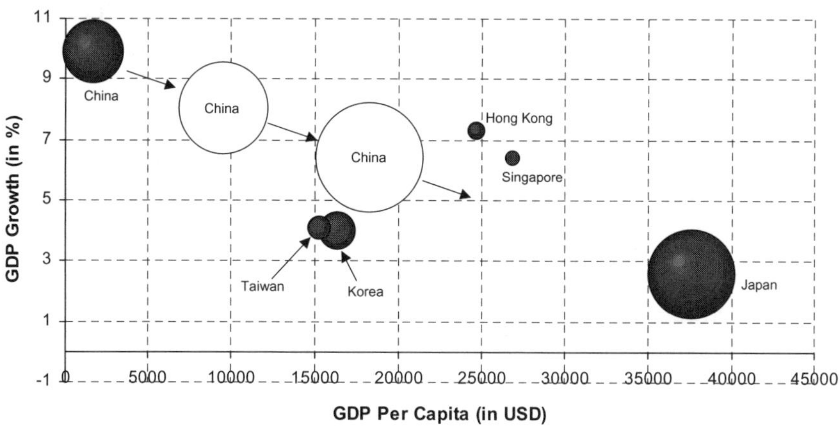

Fig. 2.7: East Asia growth performance, 2005 (growth rate, economic size, and per-capita GDP level).
Sources: World Bank; *IMF World Economic Outlook*.

contrast between East Asia's two largest economies: Japan and China. Japan is a high-income but slow-growing economy, while China stands at the other end as a fast-growing but low-income economy. Korea and Taiwan stand in between the two as mid-sized economies with moderate growth rates and fairly high per-capita income levels. Hong Kong and Singapore are two tiny economies with high per-capita income levels and also fairly high growth rates (for 2005). The future path for China is moving toward Japan, losing growth momentum but gaining size in the process.

In short, putting China's economy in the East Asian context can thus easily yield a compelling empirical argument to support China's dynamic growth. China is simply one of the "geese" in the rapid flight formation, and all the "geese" have taken turns to experience their dynamic economic growth, one after another. In simple language, it should run like this: If the Japanese have achieved successful industrialization, why can't the Koreans? Why can't the Chinese?

Furthermore, if Japan historically had over 25 years of high economic growth while the four NIEs had over 30 years, why not China? China's present run of high growth covers only about 25 years, and it could easily continue for another decade more. In fact, China's economy is much larger and more diverse, and it should therefore have much more internal dynamic to sustain higher growth for a longer period.

By considering the historical pattern of East Asian economic growth, we can easily be optimistic about China's future growth potential. In fact, one can also add that China has been, historically speaking, one of the high growth economies in East Asia. Even before Deng's economic reform in 1979, the Chinese economy still grew at a relatively fast rate of 5–6 percent (during 1952–1978) as compared to the long-term growth rates of 3–4 percent of India and other economies in South Asia, despite all the inherent economic inefficiencies of central planning and all the disruptions caused by Mao's political campaigns. The reform after 1978 has merely set free the latent dynamic economic and social forces for China to realize its "natural" potential of high growth that is much characteristic of the other East Asian economies.

EXPLAINING CHINA'S DYNAMIC GROWTH

How then do we explain East Asia's dynamic growth and its successful development? What are the underlying causes? Economic development is a highly complex multidimensional process involving not just the interactions of such primary economic factors as capital, labor, and technology, but also changes in the value and belief systems, social structure, and institutional mechanism.[8]

We may start with the observation that the East Asian region as a whole has developed many favorable social and institutional preconditions for rapid modern economic growth (or modern industrialism). By and large, the region is land scarce and resource poor. To overcome their physical constraints, many East Asian economies have to intensify their human resource development by emphasizing education and training. As shown in Table 2.3, East Asian economies do possess many growth-inducing social indicators such as high levels of human capital formation. Without stepping into the controversial zone of cultural determinism, one may even argue that East Asia has the necessary socio-cultural milieu that fosters capitalism and encourages risk taking and entrepreneurship. In East Asia at least, anti-materialism has not come, and the private accumulation of capital and wealth is not socially frowned upon.

One can further argue that since East Asian societies all share the mainstream cultural traditions of Confucianism, the aspect of Confucian ethic as manifested in its emphasis on thrift and hard work, respect for education, and social harmony based on communitarian action, is just the kind of social driving force that is most conducive to modern industrialization. In fact, Confucian argument has been advanced by many scholars as the major social explanation of the economic success of East Asia.[9]

The institutional explanation for East Asia's success is more compelling. "Good policy and good development strategy" are actually

---

[8] Bert F. Hoselitz, "Economic Growth and Development: Non-Economic Factors in Development," *American Economic Review* (May 1957).

[9] See, e.g., Peter Berger and Michael Hsiao Hsin-Huan, *In Search of An East Asian Development Model* (Transactions Books, 1988); Michio Morishima, *Why Has Japan Succeeded? Western Technology and Japanese Ethos* (Cambridge University Press, 1982); and Harry Oshima, *Economic Growth in Monsoon Asia: A Comparative Survey* (Tokyo University Press, 1987).

Table 2.3: East Asia Social Indicators.

	GDP per-capita (US$)	Total fertility rate (births per woman)	Life expectancy at birth	Life expectancy at birth	Infant mortality rate (per 1000 live births)	Literacy rate15 years and older (%)		Gross school enrolment ratio (%)							Human development index	
								Primary		Secondary		Teritary		Year	HDI 2002	Ranking 2002
	2005	2003	Male 2003	Female 2003	2003	Female 2000–2004	Male 2000–2004	Female	Male	Female	Male	Female	Male			
China	1,700	1 80	69	73	30	87	95	115	115	69	71	14	17	2002	0.745	94
Japan	37,566	1 29	78	85	3	99	99	100	100	102	102	—	—	2000–04	—	—
NIEs																
South Korea	16,294	1.40	71	78	5	97	99	105	106	91	90	64	105	2003	0.888	28
Taiwan	15,271	1.20			5	87	95	101	100	100	98	93	88	2003	—	—
Hong Kong	24,626	1.00	78	83	2	90	97	106	107	81	79	31	31	2002	0.903	23
Singapore	26,833	1.30	76	80	3	89	97	95	96	73	75	40	47	2001	0.902	25
ASEAN-4																
Indonesia	1,267	2.30	65	69	31	83	93	111	113	60	61	15	18	2002	0.692	111
Malaysia	4,930	2.90	71	76	7	85	92	93	93	74	67	33	26	2002	0.793	59
Philippines	1,077	3.10	68	72	27	93	93	112	113	88	80	34	26	2002	0.753	83
Thailand	2,665	1.90	67	72	23	91	95	95	99	77	77	42	36	2002	0.768	76
India	678	3.00	63	64	63	48	73	104	111	47	58	10	14	2002	0.595	127

Human Development Index combines life expectancy, educational attainment, and income indicators to give a composite measure of human development.

Sources: *World Development Report 2006*; Asian Development Bank.

very important for successful economic development.[10] It is well known that East Asian economies have all shared the salient common feature of operating effective export-oriented development strategies for their export-oriented industrialization, as reflected in their generally high export-GDP ratios and their relative high shares of the world export markets. Export orientation has propelled them to high growth through reaping the gains from international trade and specialization.[11]

In particular, the political leadership of East Asia was highly committed to economic development, which was regarded as vital for national economic survival — for postwar Japan, postwar Korea, the KMT-governed Taiwan, the post-independence Singapore and Hong Kong under UN Embargo. The political systems or regimes of East Asia at the time of industrial take-off were not democratic in the Western sense; but the governments in East Asia proved to be highly pro-business and pro-development. They succeeded in developing an effective, "market-friendly" institutional environment to foster competition and more efficient resource allocation.

China today, by comparison, is equally pro-development, if not more so than the other East Asian economies in the past. In fact, the Chinese society today, in the name of following Deng Xiaoping's calling of "get rich first," is blatantly materialistic. The Chinese leadership is also dedicated to the single-minded pursuit of GDP growth, either as means of boosting its political legitimacy or just as an end in itself (e.g., for China to achieve the "*Xiaokang* society"). Stripped of all its socialistic trappings, the Chinese government is basically pro-growth and pro-capitalism. Growth is relentlessly pursued not just by the central government, but also by all local leaders, whose personal career and the social stability of their individual

[10] For a detailed discussion, see Ian M.D. Little, *Economic Development: Theory, Policy, and International Relations* [A Twenty Century Fund Book] (New York: Basic Books, 1982).

[11] For further discussion of this topic, see John Wong, "The East Asian Phenomenon and the Implications for Economic Development," in Basant K. Kapur *et al.* (eds.) *Development, Trade and the Asia-Pacific*, Essays in honour of Professor Lim Chong Yah (Singapore: Prentice Hall, 1996).

regions have come to depend critically on continuing high economic growth and rising prosperity. It is hard to find any other country today which is politically and socially so "growth-obsessed!"

By comparison, economic theory offers a much more "direct" and cogent explanation of East Asia past and China's present dynamic growth. Economic growth as increases in GDP can be easily explained, on the supply side, by increasing labor force and increasing productivity. For a developing economy at its early phase of development, growth occurs when surplus labor is transferred from the low-productivity agriculture to the high-production manufacturing, i.e., industrialization. China's vast rural labor force is undoubtedly a huge reservoir of unexploited labor supplies for the future. It may, however, be stressed that in accounting for growth, it is usually quite hard for economists to measure the exact level of productivity growth, especially since "productivity" in the real world is the outcome of both skilled labor (hence human capital formation) and technological progress (capital investment in new machines).

On the demand side, economic growth occurs when aggregate demand, which is made up of domestic demand (comprising household consumption, domestic investment, and government spending) and external demand (exports net of imports). For most economies, with a few exceptions like Singapore and Hong Kong, domestic demand constitutes the mainstay of their economic growth.

As can be seen in Fig. 2.8, East Asian economies have generally committed a high proportion of their GDP (at around 30 percent) to domestic investment during their critical periods of industrial take-off. Furthermore, their high levels of gross domestic investment were largely matched by their equally high levels of domestic savings (Fig. 2.9). In short, high investment and high savings constitute the single most important and yet simple neo-classical economic explanation of East Asia's dynamic growth. They operate much like a "virtuous circle": High rates of investment induce high export growth, and then high GDP growth, leading to high savings and finally high investment again.

China's case is even more compelling. China's high growth over the past two decades essentially stems from its exceedingly high levels

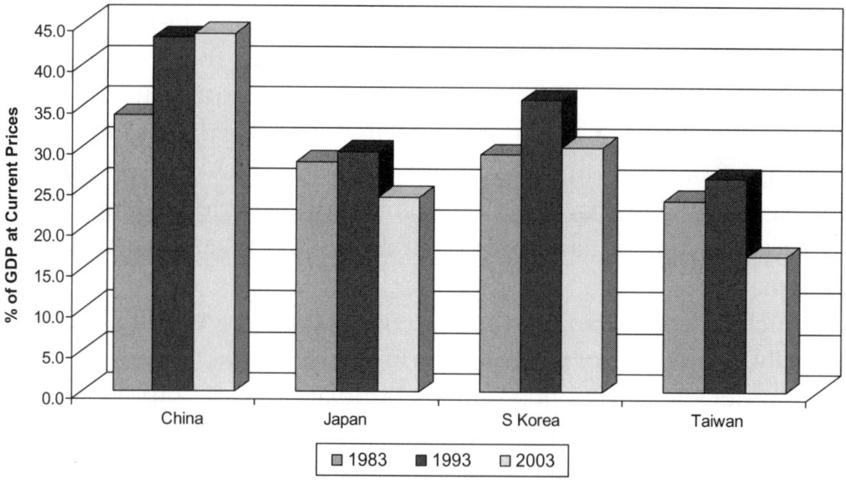

Fig. 2.8: Gross domestic investment in East Asia.
Sources: ADB; *IMF World Economic Outlook*; *Japan Statistical Yearbook 2006*.

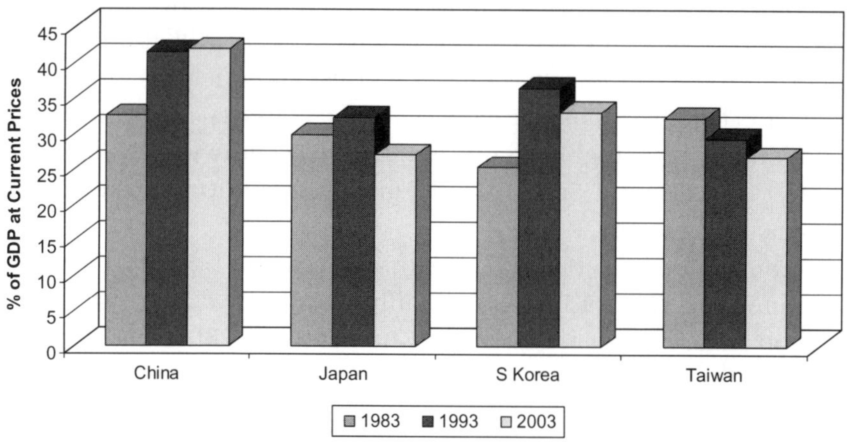

Fig. 2.9: Gross domestic savings in East Asia.
Sources: ADB; *IMF World Economic Outlook*; *Japan Statistical Yearbook 2006*.

of domestic investment at over 40 percent of GDP and equally high levels of domestic savings, also at over 40 percent. In fact, China's economic growth since Deng Xiaoping's *Nanxun* has been basically investment driven. Recently, China's economy has become "overheated," and that has largely been the result of over-investment.[12] At the same time, this also serves to indicate that China's past growth, primarily fuelled by the sheer input of more capital, is not an efficient form of economic growth, i.e., growth without much coming from productivity (TFP or total factor productivity) increases. Several East Asian economies had experienced little or no TFP growth in their early periods of development, as pointed out by Krugman.[13]

Such a demand analysis also suggests that, given China's exceptionally high levels of domestic savings (which can come down one or two decades later once China's population starts rapidly aging), China's economy should continue to carry on with its high growth momentum as long as its domestic demand continues to grow.

For domestic investment, China will continue to have enormous need for infrastructural investment in transportation, communications, ports, airports, and power plants. Very soon, China will also need to invest more heavily in environmental protection like cleaning up the rivers and water supply sources. There will also be rising demand for social infrastructure like housing, education, and medical-care facilities. This explains why fixed assets investment will continue to be a highly significant source of growth for China for many years to come. Subsequently, growth needs to be sustained by productivity growth.

China's future economic growth can also be boosted by rising consumption. With a moderately affluent middle class of over 100 million, mainly in large cities and numerous small towns, China's appetite for consumption goods is enormous. When the urban elites have satisfied their material consumption needs, they will go for consumption in services like travels and entertainment, which are

---

[12] For further discussion of China's recent economic growth and its problems, see John Wong, "China's Economy in 2005: At a New Turning Point and Need to Fix Its Development Problems," *China & World Economy* 14, 2 (March 14, 2006).

[13] Paul Krugman, "The Myth of Asia's Miracle," *Foreign Affairs* (Nov–Dec., 1994). See also, Kim Jong-Il and Lawrence Lau, "The Sources of Growth of the East Asian Newly Industrialized Countries," *Journal of the Japanese and International Economies* (September 1994).

still in their early phases of development in China. Recent government efforts in stepping rural development will also add a new source of domestic consumption from the millions of peasants. In short, for a large and diverse economy like China, domestic demand rather than external demand will be more viable for its long-term growth.[14] Currently, one of China's priorities as contained in the 11th Five-Year Plan is to expand domestic demand in order to achieve a more balanced growth in future.

All in all, one can be justifiably optimistic about China's continuing growth potential over one to two decades. The historical dimension of East Asia's past growth process clearly suggests that China's dynamic growth potential will not be exhausted in the short to medium term. An analysis of China's economic and social structures also unfolds many growth-inducing features as well as new sources of growth, which are not about to be dried up any time soon. China's high growth is therefore sustainable for many years to come.

LESSON OF EXPERIENCE FOR CHINA

With over 25 years of unbridled growth, China's economic growth process has inevitably created a lot of structural stress and socio-economic side-effects, which are crying out for attention. How will East Asia's past development experience be instructive for China?

It may be emphasized that the East Asian development model is not just about rapid economic growth, but it is also a success story of social development and political transformation. East Asia's past economic growth has been accompanied by a high level of equity. At the peak of its industrialization, income distribution in Japan, Korea, and Taiwan had been among the most equal with the Gini ratio just over 0.3, though the Gini ratio for Hong Kong and Singapore have always been above 0.4. This is a far-cry for China

[14] For a more detailed discussion of this subject, see John Wong and Sarah Chan, "Why China's Economy Can Sustain High Performance: An Analysis of Its Sources of Growth," *East Asian Institute Background Brief no.* 138 (November 14, 2002).

today, whose rapid economic growth has brought about widening income disparities not just between rural and urban populations but also across various social classes. In other words, Chinese economic development has not been accompanied by an effective "trickle-down" process as happened in Japan, Korea, and Taiwan. China seems to have carried Deng's adage of "let some people get rich first" a bit too far!

In Japan, Korea, and Taiwan, the economic process has also been accompanied by an orderly transfer of agricultural surplus (redundant rural labor and food) for industrial development in the urban areas. The agricultural sector carried the main burden of development in the early phases; but the rural population were not "over-squeezed." In contrast, China's present development has been blatantly and excessively "urban-biased," and the development benefits have not been extensively diffused to the rural sector, which is often made to suffer the negative consequences of urban economic growth from pollution to water shortages. Even the central government in Beijing had openly admitted the many rural excesses now prevailing in China, which include land seizures without adequate compensation.

Rapid economic development also means rapid industrialization and urbanization, which is apt to give rise to many negative social externalities such as rising crime, as quite common in China today. But this phenomenon did not happen in Japan because of its well-known high level of social discipline. Nor was it serious in Korea and Taiwan at the time of their industrial take-off, partly because their industrialization took place under the martial law. One may also argue that the scale of China's industrialization is by far larger than that of Korea and Taiwan, and that China's economic development of the past 25 years has also been a simultaneous process of reform and system transformation, all happening at the same time. And this exaggerates China's problems.

Overall, the Chinese leadership has come to realize that China's past development patterns are physically unsustainable (in terms of mounting pressures on the environment and natural resources, including water) and socially unacceptable (in terms of rising income inequalities). They have also broadly embraced the need to re-balance and re-orient China's development policies. The new development paradigm is contained in the recently approved 11th Five-Year Programme. China has the capacity and resources to deal with the negative consequences of its economic growth if the leadership also has the required political will.

Chapter

3

China's 11th Five-Year Plan: A Critical Perspective

Tan Kong Yam

Nanyang Technological University, Singapore

INTRODUCTION

On October 11, 2005, the fifth plenum of the 16th Communist Party Central Committee passed the party's proposals for the 11th five-year plan, covering the period 2006–2010. The full plan was then ratified as a government document the following spring at the National People's Congress on March 2006. The document marked the formal adoption of the economic strategy and program of the new leaderships of Hu Jintao and Wen Jiabao.

The plan recognized the reality that future economic growth and development in China will be shaped by "rapid growth, industrialization, urbanization, marketization and an accelerating pace of internationalization." Recognizing the increasing dominance of market forces, the document is actually called a program (guihua) rather than a plan (jihua). In addition, the document no longer listed any priority areas and key quantitative targets to develop. The document set only two quantifiable targets: GDP per capita should double between 2000 and 2010 and energy consumption per unit of GDP in 2010 should decline by 20 percent compared to that in 2005.

KEY THEMES

The program fundamentally focused on two key themes. Firstly, what should the government do to ensure that long-term growth is sustainable? Secondly, what should the government do to ensure that the fruits of growth and development are spread more broadly to the people and the various regions. The objective is to ensure a harmonious society as the earlier headlong growth has been viewed as not unsustainable. It has led to poverty in the rural area, greater rural–urban and regional inequality, social tensions and rising polarization of society as well as environmental degradation. It is perceived that for some segment of the population, economic growth has not led to better human welfare, a higher quality of life and greater social stability. To ensure sustainability and better distribution in the fruits of growth, the program advocated the adoption of a scientific view of the development process, the strategy of putting people first and emphasized a comprehensive, coordinated and sustainable view of development.

Under this rubric of new philosophy in development, the major task and key policies include:

(i) establishing a new socialist countryside and balancing rural and urban development;
(ii) strengthening the independent capability for innovation and the upgrading of industrial structure;
(iii) pushing forward a coordinated and balanced regional development strategy;
(iv) improving the efficiency in resource and energy utilization and focus on environmental and ecological protection;
(v) further deepening of reform and opening to the outside world as well as continued institutional reform consistent with the scientific view of development;

(vi) emphasizing on the development of education, science and technology and the priority in talent development;
(vii) creating greater employment opportunities, perfecting the social security system and focus on the establishment of a harmonious society.

CRITICAL PERSPECTIVES ON THE PROGRAM

Putting People First and the Creation of a Harmonious Society

As indicated in Fig. 3.1, household consumption as a share of GDP has fallen from 52 percent in 1985 to 46 percent in 1995 and further to 39 percent by 2005. The household sector has been squeezed substantially over the past decade. As indicated in Fig. 3.2, urban disposable income per capita declined from 85 percent of GDP per capita in 1995 to 76 percent of GDP per capita in 2005. Rural cash income per capita fell from 31 percent to 23 percent of GDP per capita during the same period. Overall, empirical evidence on growth over the past two decades appeared to indicate that the household sector has been squeezed and is getting a smaller and

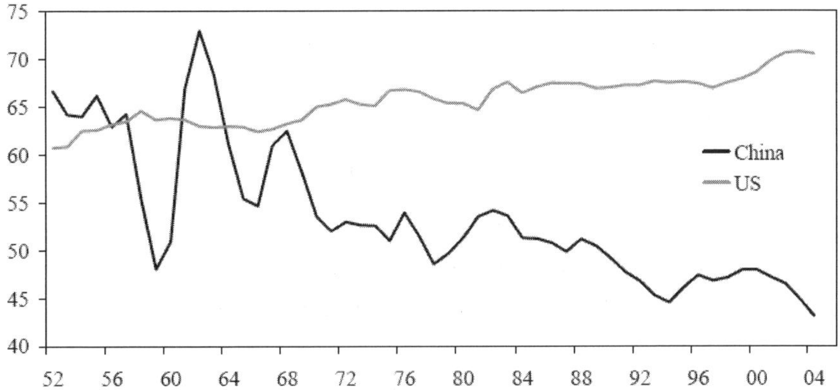

Fig. 3.1: Personal consumption as a percent of GDP.
Source: *China National Bureau of Statistics, Bureau of Economic Analysis, Morgan Stanley Research.*

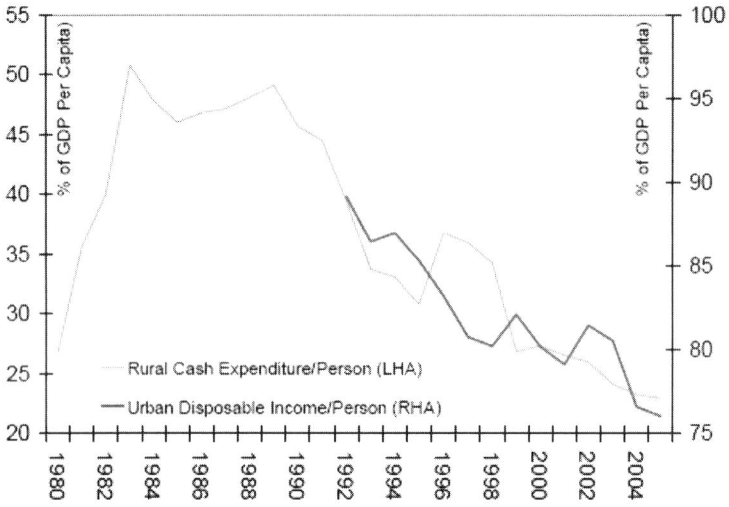

Fig. 3.2: China: People's share in economy declines.
Source: *CEIC and Morgan Stanley*.

smaller share of the value added created. Central government, local governments and state-owned enterprises, have garnered an increasing share of the value added created in the growth process.

China's saving and investment rates are very high. The bulk of investment is financed by domestic savings with FDI playing a minor financing role. According to World Bank studies (Kuijs, 2005, 2006), much of China's high saving, especially in recent years, is due to high savings of enterprises and government (see Fig. 3.3). Empirical analysis by the World Bank indicates that much of the high savings in China is the result of peculiar policies in China. The effect of particular policies is estimated to have contributed to an additional 15–20 percentage points of GDP to the saving rate.

Empirical evidence indicates that profitability has risen substantially over the past decade. Profit as a share of value added for the industrial sector has increased from 10.6 percent in 1995 to

	1996	2000	2004	2005
Households				
S	20	15	16	16
S-I	14	10	10	10
Enterprises				
S	13	15	19	20
S-I	-16	-11	-13	-11
Government				
S	5	6	6	6
S-I	3	3	3	2
China				
GNS (above the line)	37	35	41	44
Gross capital formation	38	34	41	40
Current account (bop data) :	1	2	4	7

Fig. 3.3: China: Saving and investment by sectors.
Source: *NBS, and author's estimates.*

17.3 percent in 2000 and further to 21.6 percent in 2005. This was partly due to the fact that retrenchment and restructuring in SOEs have moved most of the social responsibility to local governments and back to the household sector. Hence, almost three-quarter of enterprise investment have been financed by retained earnings.

The government and state-owned enterprises dominated industries with super-normal profits as they have significant barriers to entry. As indicated in Fig. 3.4, the profit rate of mining is very high compared to highly competitive industries dominated by the private sector like textile and other light manufactured products (see Figs. 3.5 and 3.6). For the machinery and equipment industry which has both state-owned and private enterprises, the profit rate is somewhere in between (see Fig. 3.7).

Government savings have been high. About 5 percent of GDP of these savings have been transferred to enterprises to finance capital investments.

Central and local governments' command over resources has been underestimated by the official fiscal data as a large part of the fiscal revenue and spending consist of extra-budget revenue and expenditure. These have been estimated at 19–27 percent of GDP (Bird and Wong, 2005). This extra-budgetary revenue includes

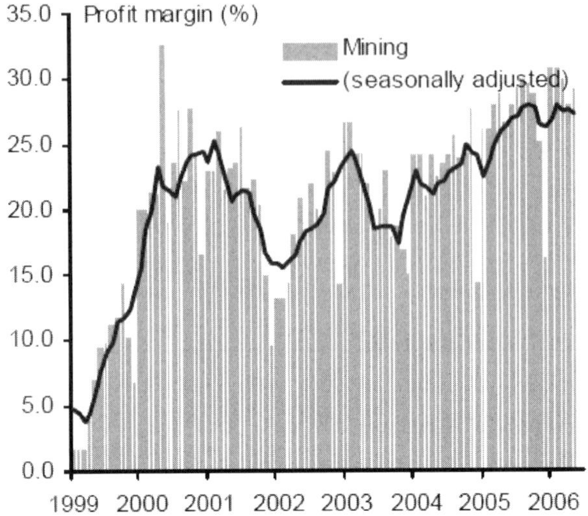

Fig. 3.4: Mining.
Source: *CEIC, UBS estimates.*

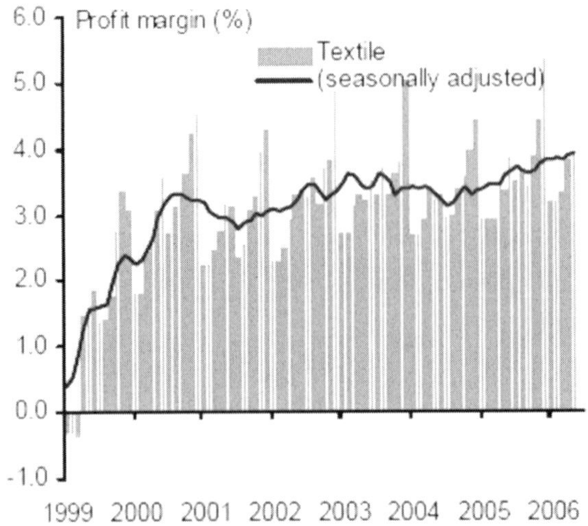

Fig. 3.5: Textile.
Source: *CEIC, UBS estimates.*

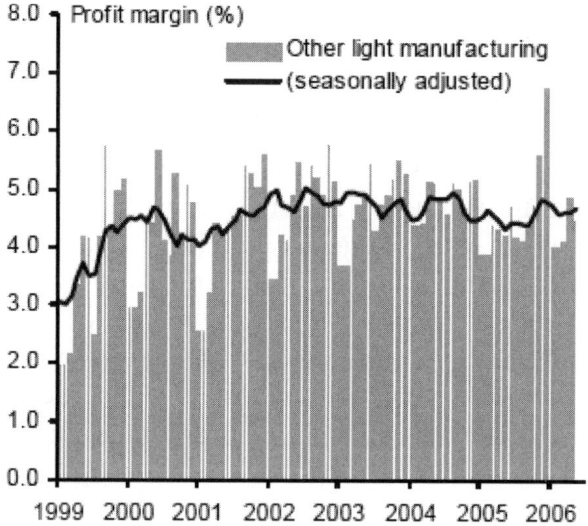

Fig. 3.6: Other light manufacturing.
Source: *CEIC, UBC estimates*.

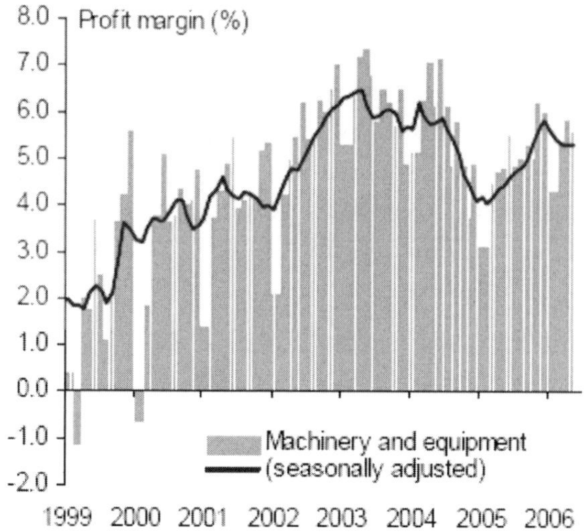

Fig. 3.7: Machinery and equipment.
Source: *CEIC, UBS estimates*.

extra-budgetary revenue collected by branches of government in the performance of services, quasi-fiscal fund of the government, enterprises, and public service units.

A nationwide audit report by the Ministry of Finance, State Planning Commission, State Council Audit Office, and Peoples Bank of China, and the Ministry of Supervision in 1996 found more than 384 billion yuan in extra-budgetary fund (EBF) or about 6 percent of GDP. In 1998, estimates of the EBF rose substantially, with the Ministry of Finance estimating it at 8–10 percent of GDP. However, the office of the State Administration of Taxation often used an estimate of 15 percent of GDP. Hence it is likely that the complex and opaque fiscal system has also played a not insignificant role in the squeeze of the household sector.

The state sector has shifted the financial burden of education, health care, retirement income as well as housing to the household sector. The resulting increase in local government surplus, state-owned enterprises profits have led to substantial increase in government and enterprises' savings which have been channeled largely into fixed assets investments. On the other hand, household spending in health care, education, housing, and savings for retirement have greatly increased the burden of households, leading to falling consumption expenditure and lower household saving rate (see Figs. 3.1 and 3.8). Not surprisingly, a recent survey by the *China Youth Daily* showed that 85.3 percent of the population felt a greater financial burden compared to ten years ago.

Household survey data suggest that household saving rate in the urban and rural area is being roughly equal at 26 percent in the rural and 24 percent in the urban area from 2004. High household savings is partly due to the withdrawal of the government from the financing of health care, education and housing, and retirement. Most survey data confirmed that household savings are largely motivated by precautionary motives.

Shifting the composition of government spending away from capital investment transfer to enterprises to boosting spending on health, education, and social services would reduce the burden of households and reduce precautionary savings and increase private

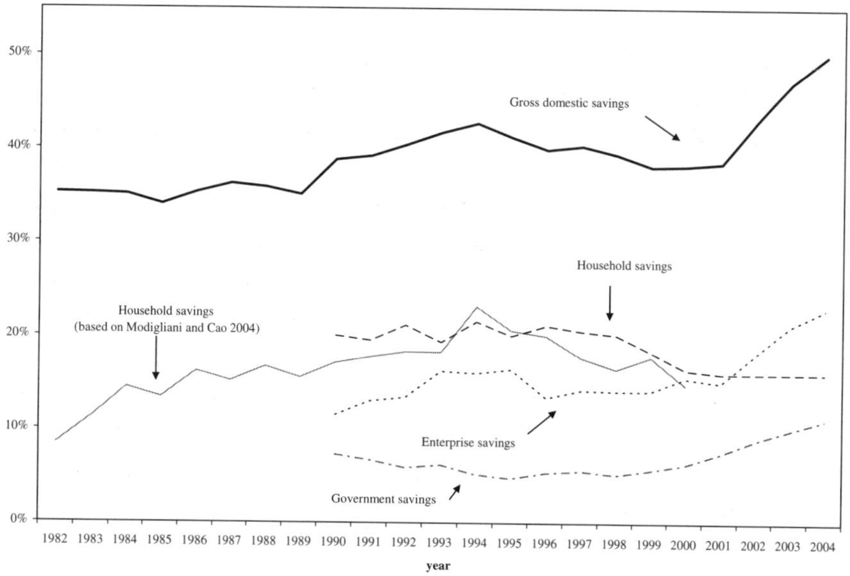

Fig. 3.8: Savings as a percentage of GDP.

consumption expenditure. This would require the performance evaluation criteria for local governments to be tilted from GDP, fixed assets investment, and visible hardware development indicators toward greater weightage on soft infrastructure like social expenditure and services that improve the welfare of the people. In addition, the production-based value added tax structure has also led to local government policies favoring the industrial sector.

Instead of state-owned enterprises channeling their increasing profit into fixed assets investments, they could be asked to channel them partly into dividends to the central government and then used to reduce the burden of households. Based on existing level of profit, the World Bank estimated that a paid out rate of only 50 percent could raise existing government health and education spending by 100 percent. This would drastically reduce the existing heavy burden of the household sector in shouldering these spending. It would also significantly shift the GDP spending pattern away from fixed assets investment toward private consumption.

Existing policies that discriminate in favor of the development of industries against services include the under-pricing of resources and energy inputs to industry, as well as a financial sector that favor lending to the large state-owned enterprises and the industrial sector at the expense of small medium enterprises which predominate in the services sector. This has pushed the economy toward a capital intensive path of development. A more service-oriented, labor-intensive path development would result in a greater share of value added distributed to labor rather than capital, and a higher propensity to consume.

Affordable housing is an important contributing factor to household welfare. However, effective solutions are likely to run counter to the vested interest and profit opportunities of local governments and property developers. It is heartening that given the weak power of households, the central government has taken up this issue and recently promulgated various policies to protect the interest of the average household sector.

State monopolistic power over education, a service of enormous demand due to the cultural focus on education, has led to undue bargaining power for the state suppliers. Their flexibility in fees charges have led to a big squeeze on the household sector. Similarly, state monopolistic power over health-care supply has also given the health-care industry undue bargaining power in levying charges, adding to the burden of households. This is aggravating the existing household income inequality (see Fig. 3.9). In line with "putting people's welfare first" development strategy, the government should introduce public-funded basic education and basic health care to achieve equity while promoting private sector competition in both education and health care beyond the basic level to achieve greater efficiency.

Resource Prices and Energy Security

As indicated in Fig. 3.10, the rapid expansion of the Chinese economy has resulted in China being ranked first or second in the global

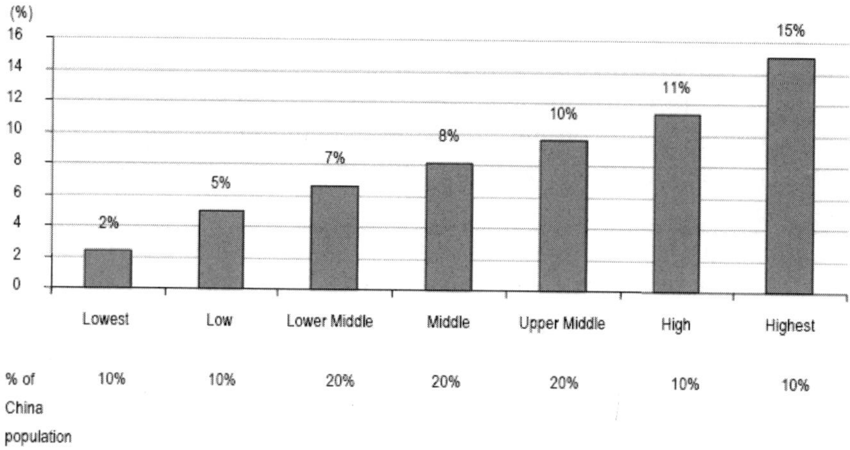

Fig. 3.9: Growth in different income groups in the PRC.
Source: *China Statistical Yearbook 1999–2005 inclusive*.

	World Rank 2004	% World 2004	% World Growth 2004
Oil	2	7	31
Aluminium	2	20	49
Iron ore	1	32	107
Nickel	2	11	100
Copper	1	22	52
Steel	1	28	37
Thermal coal [1]	1	31	157
Alumina	1	19	33

Fig. 3.10: China's consumption rankings.
[1] Note: Coal data for 2003.
Source: *International Lead and Zinc Survey, International Aluminium Institute, World Metal Statistics, China Non-ferrous Metals Yearbook, China Metals, BP*.

demand for oil, aluminum, iron ore, nickel, copper steel, thermal coal, and alumina. More significantly, the share of world demand has reached 7–32 percent and the contributions to incremental growth are even higher, surpassing 100 percent for iron ore and thermal coal. The substantial expansion in demand from China has been an important contributing factor to the major rise in commodities and oil prices in recent years (See Fig. 3.11). Consequently, China's dependence on import in these commodities and resources has also reached 40–50 percent within a very short period of time (see Fig. 3.12).

A contributing factor to the enormous expansion in the demand for resources and energy is the underpricing of these resources. Based on international comparative analysis, water is underpriced by about 50–60 percent, refined oil by 15–20 percent, contract coal by 10–15 percent, and power by 45–50 percent (see Fig. 3.13).

Given China's relative poor endowment of resources per capita and the substantial disparity between endowment and consumption per capita relative to the global average (see Fig. 3.14), China cannot afford to maintain the underpricing policies that lead to substantial wastage and inefficiency.

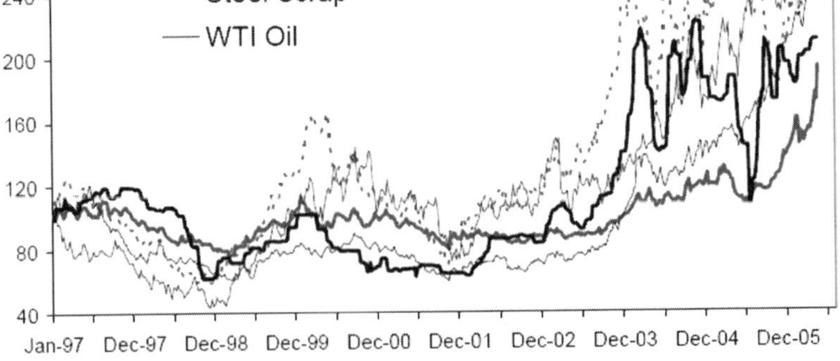

Fig. 3.11: Commodities have "gone parabolic," led by the metals.
Source: *Datastream, Morgan Stanley Research*.

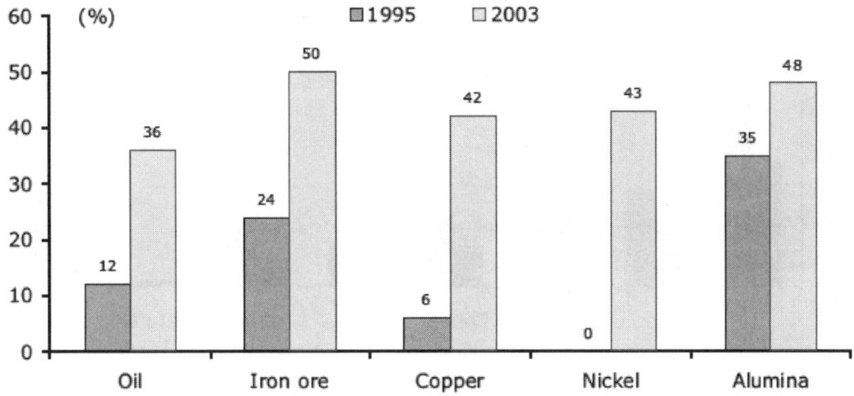

Fig. 3.12: China's rising import dependency (share of net imports in consumption).
Source: *CLSA*.

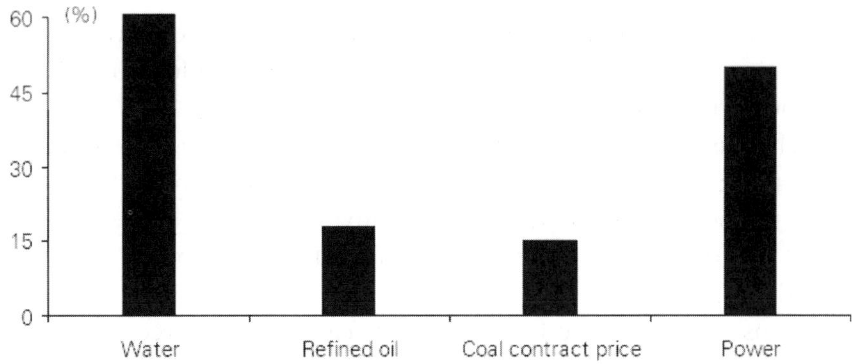

Fig. 3.13: Estimated under-pricing of natural resources in China.
Source: *Deutsche Bank estimates*.

The underpricing of energy and resources has resulted in the higher profit margin and the overdevelopment of the energy and resource-intensive industrial sectors like steel, cement, aluminum, and chemicals. It has led to excessive consumption of resources and energy and severe environmental degradation. In addition, it has aggravated regional inequality as the resource rich but poorer central and western provinces have subsidized the resource poor but

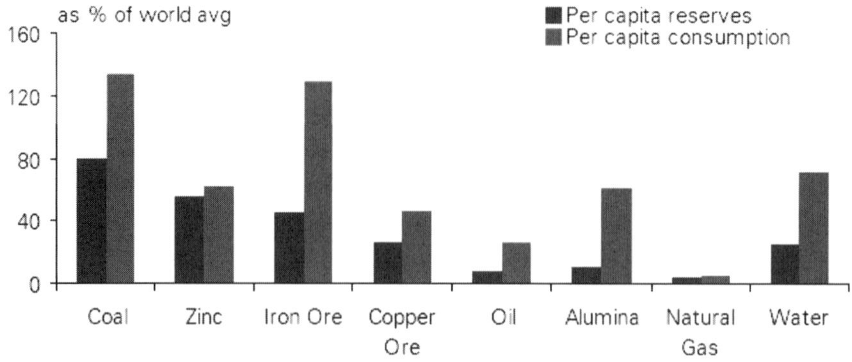

Fig. 3.14: China's per capita reserves and per capita consumption of natural resources.
Source: *State Council (2005), Deutsche Bank estimates.*

richer industrial coastal provinces. Insufficiently strict environmental regulations and enforcement are also a form of hidden subsidy to the industrial sector development.

The distortion effect on the economic structure can be seen from the fact that industry and construction as a share of GDP has risen to about 54 percent, fixed asset investment as a share of GDP to 50 percent. These ratios are the highest among countries in the world (Fig. 3.15).

Consequently, there is a need to re-calibrate resource prices for oil, gas, water, coal, electricity, and land. The ultimate objective is to gradually increase these resource prices eventually to their equilibrium levels.

The need for energy conservation and security is urgent. In November 2004, the NDRC published a very detailed policy document with precise policy targets called the "Medium to Long Term Plan in Energy Conservation." In July 2005, two other documents on the acceleration of a "renewable economy" and the "development of a society geared towards conservation" were issued by the Sate Council. In addition, in October 2005, the central committee gave greater political weight to these government policies.

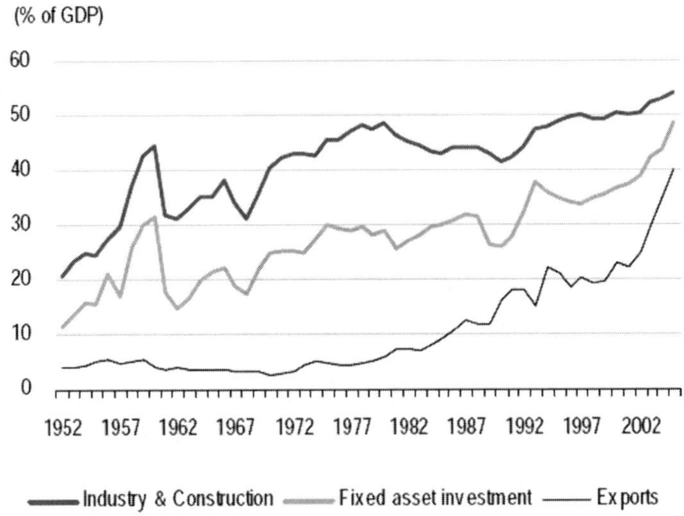

Fig. 3.15: Share of industrial, export, and investment activities.
Source: *CEIC*.

During the reform period, energy demand per unit of GDP has declined steadily by over half from 1981 to 2000 (see Fig. 3.16). This reflected the substantial improvement in energy efficiency as market forces were allowed to operate on the previously central planned industrial structure. In particular, inefficient coal utilizing industries have declined. It has risen somewhat since then (see Fig. 3.16). However, the level of energy intensity (oil) per unit of GDP is still very high in China. Compared to the OECD, they are 2–4 times high (Fig. 3.17). While part of this disparity is due to the different structure composition of the GDP, energy efficiency at the industrial level has also been a factor. For example, energy consumed to produce a unit of steel in China is 50 percent larger than Japan, and 45 percent higher than Korea (Fig. 3.18).

On the other hand, after successive raising of residential IPP tariff, utilities rate appear to be more reasonable in Chinese cities like Shanghai and Shenzhen relatively to other international rates (Fig. 3.19).

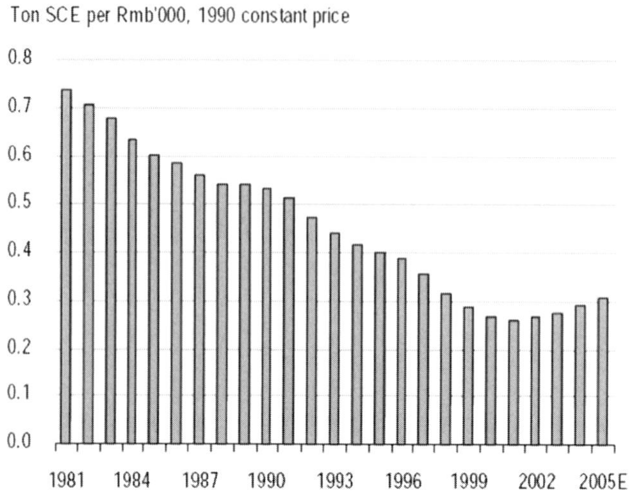

Fig. 3.16: Energy demand per unit of GDP.
Source: *CEIC*.

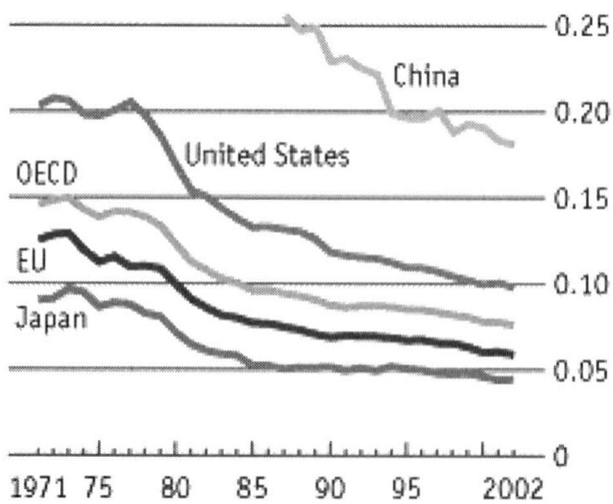

Fig. 3.17: Ratio of oil use to GDP* (tonnes of oil equivalent, per $'000, 1995 prices).
Source: *IFA*.

Oil product price has been lower in China compared to even other developing countries. (Fig. 3.20). A major reason is due to the low rate of fuel tax in China (Figs. 3.20 and 3.21). The raising of final product price as well as the introduction of higher fuel tax

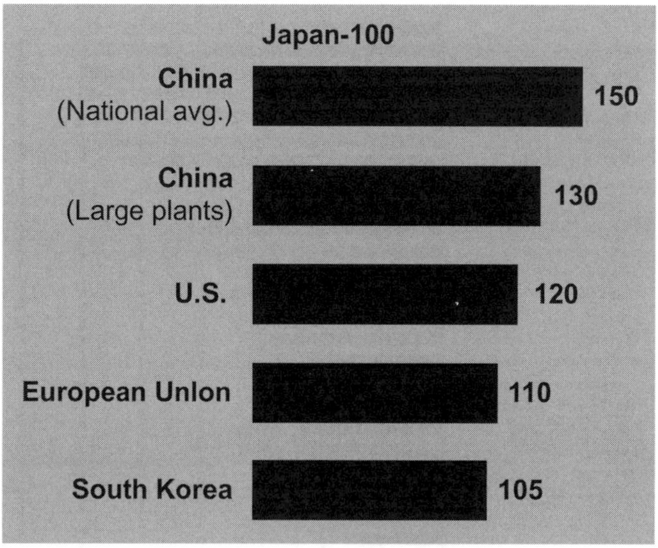

Fig. 3.18: Amount of energy used to produce a ton of steel, with Japan's consumption used as a baseline of 100 units.
Source: *Japan Iron & Steel Federation*.

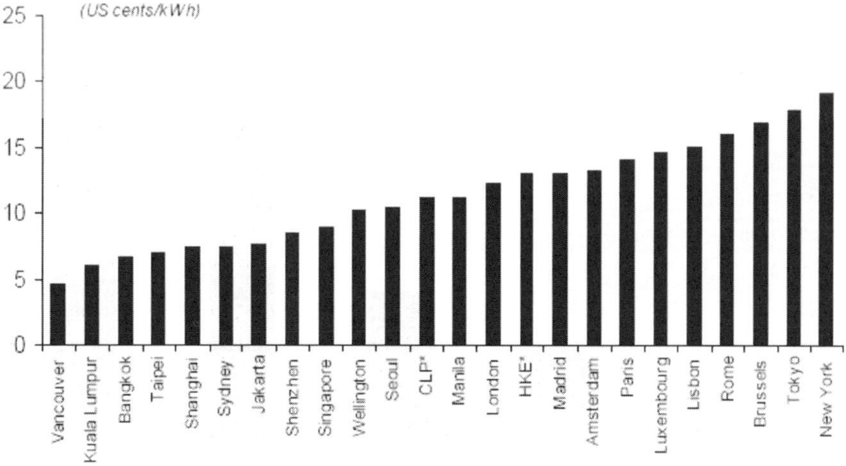

Fig. 3.19: Residential IPP tariffs — China (Shenzhen) and International.
Source: *Deutsche Bank AG*: *Company data*.

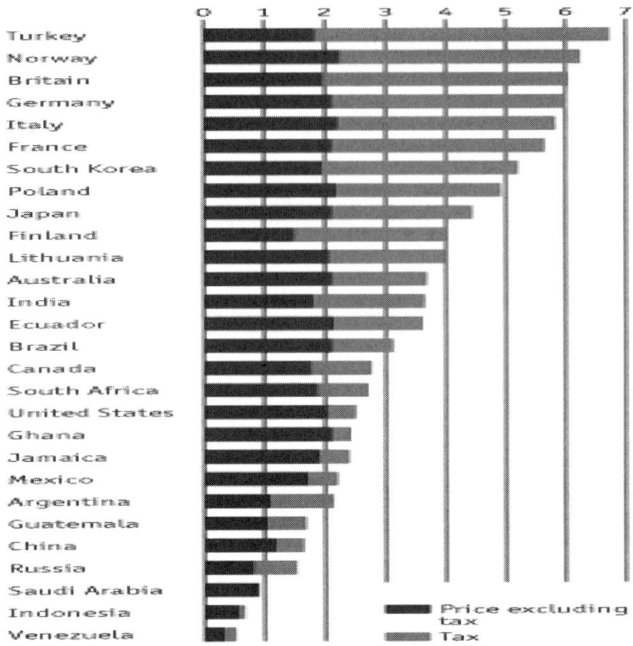

Fig. 3.20: Petrol prices (latest 2005 observations, $ per US gallon).
Source: *IMF*.

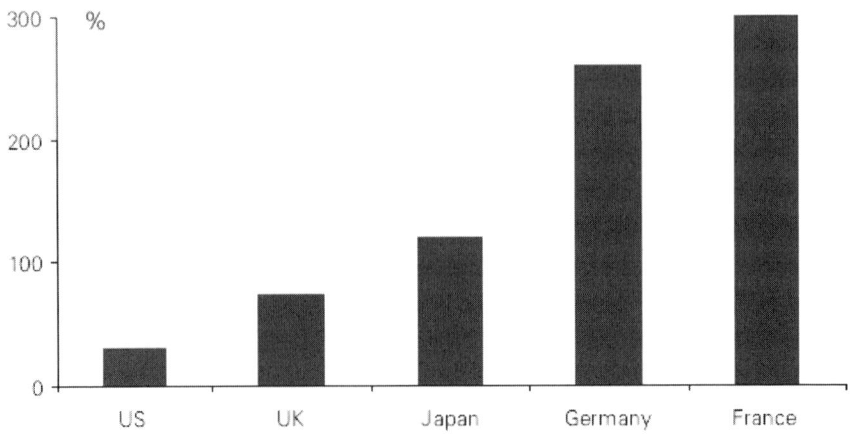

Fig. 3.21: Fuel (Gasoline) tax rates in selected countries.
Source: *Deutsche Bank*.

would help to reduce overconsumption and excessive import dependence and reduce energy insecurity. At the up-steam level for the oil sector, there could be the substantial raising of the resource tax for crude oil production which is at a low Rmb 8–30 per ton. In addition, there is a need to consider the introduction of the windfall tax to capture the windfall gains due to high oil prices, as well as the introduction of open bidding for the exploration of rights of oil fields.

Oil is a significant resource that is critical for China's future industrial development. As indicated in Fig. 3.22, China has become a net oil importer since 1993. Given existing and past discovery, production in China is expected to peak around 2008 and decline steadily over the next 50 years, precisely the time when China's rapid industrial development will continue to need substantial oil and energy (Fig. 3.23). This implies that China's dependence on the volatile Middle East and Caspian region for oil will rise as the bulk of global reserves are in these regions (Fig. 3.24).

For water, rates have been rather low compared to other international countries (Fig. 3.25). This has resulted in poor efficiency usage of water. In Fig. 3.26, World Development Indicators of the

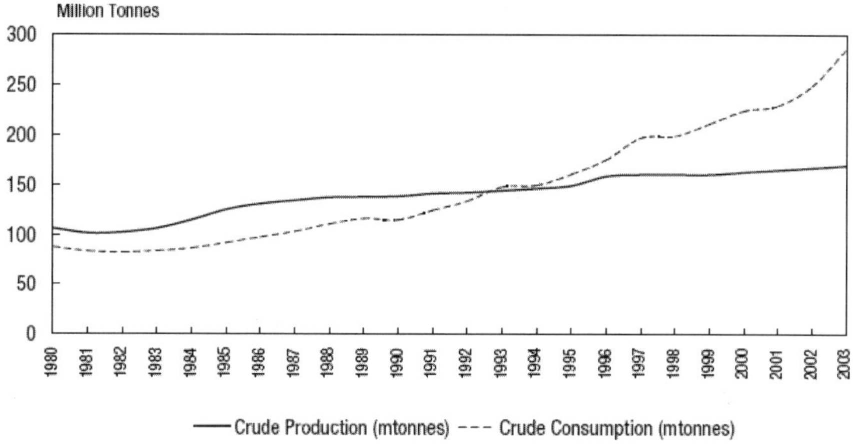

Fig. 3.22: China's total oil consumption and domestic oil production, 1978–2002 (millions of tonnes).
Source: *CEIC, BP, Citigroup estimates.*

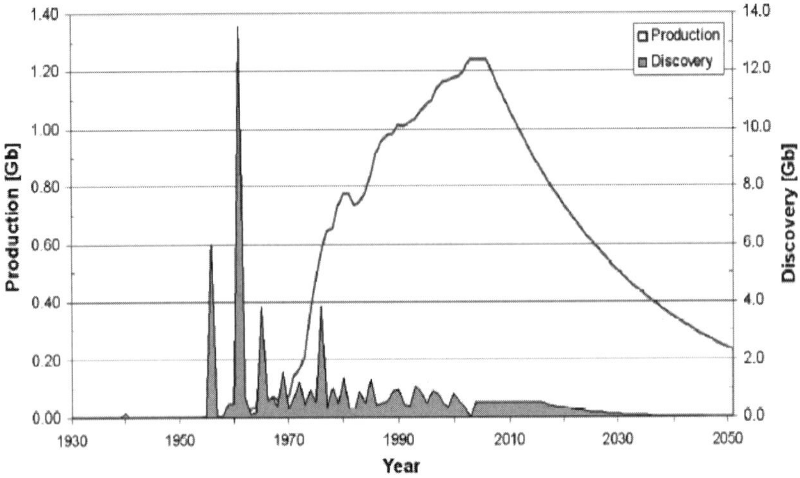

Fig. 3.23: Oil discovery and production of China.

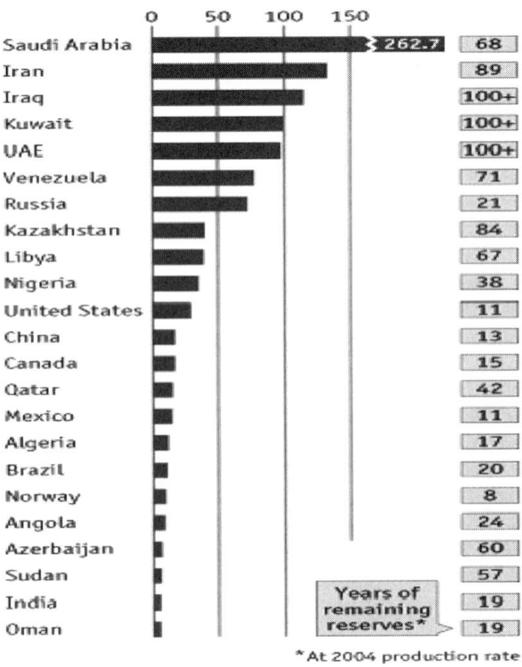

Fig. 3.24: Oil reserves (end 2004, barrels bn).
Source: *BP*.

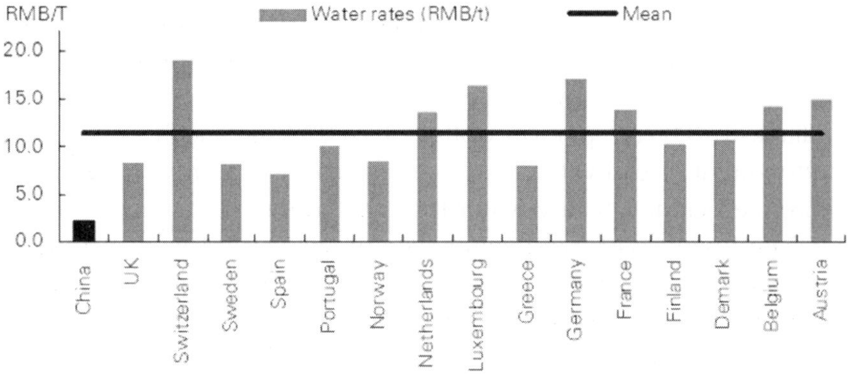

Fig. 3.25: China's water rates.
Source: *Deutsche Bank AG*.

	Total	Agricul ture	Non Agriculture	Freshwater Resource per capita (m^3)
China	**0.38**	**1.95**	**0.10**	**2,210**
Brazil	**0.12**	**1.22**	**0.05**	**41,941**
Indonesia	**0.36**	**1.96**	**0.03**	**13,405**
India	**0.85**	**3.39**	**0.09**	**1,819**
Malaysia	**0.13**	**1.08**	**0.03**	**23,863**
Mexico	**0.13**	**2.46**	**0.03**	**4,543**
Thailand	**0.23**	**2.36**	**0.02**	**6,653**
Argentina	**0.23**	**1.59**	**0.07**	**24,644**
Korea	**0.04**	**0.83**	**0.02**	**1,465**

Fig. 3.26: Efficiency in water usage (m^3 per US dollar GDP): 2003.
Source: *Author's Estimates, World Bank*.

World Bank for 2003 is used to assess China's efficiency in water usage. More importantly, it compares China's efficiency in water usage with other large developing countries with significant agriculture sector. In addition, separate water efficiency indicators are compiled for the agriculture and non-agriculture sector.

For the economy as a whole, efficiency of water usage in China is very low, at 0.38 m^3 for each US dollar of GDP produced. The only country that is more inefficient than China in using water is India with 0.85 m^3 per US dollar of GDP. China with poor water endowment (freshwater resource per capita at only 2210 m^3) is more inefficient in using water than the countries that are far more well endowed with freshwater like Brazil (41,941 m^3), Indonesia (13,405 m^3), Malaysia (23,863 m^3), Mexico (4,543 m^3), Thailand (6,653 m^3), and Argentina (24,644 m^3).

Separating out water usage for the agriculture and non-agriculture sector, the results become very revealing. The non-agriculture sector in China (manufacturing, services, and urban sector) is the least efficient in water usage, consuming 0.10 m^3 for each US dollar of GDP produced. This is even more inefficient than India (0.09 m^3), let alone Argentina (0.07 m^3), Brazil (0.05 m^3), Indonesia (0.03 m^3), Malaysia (0.03 m^3), Mexico (0.03 m^3), Thailand (0.02 m^3), and Korea (0.02 m^3). It is very significant that water efficiency in the non-agriculture sector in China is half that of Brazil, and less than one-third that of Indonesia, Mexico, Malaysia and only one-fifth that of Thailand and Korea.

Examining the water efficiency in the agriculture sector, while China (1.95 m^3) is more efficient than India (3.39 m^3), Indonesia (1.96 m^3), Mexico (2.46 m^3), Thailand (2.36 m^3); these are countries (except India) with far larger water resource endowment per capita than China and hence can afford to waste water. It is astonishing that water efficiency in the agriculture sector in China is actually similar to that of Indonesia (1.96 m^3) and worse than Malaysia (1.08 m^3) though these two countries are far better endowed with water resources. The only country that is poorly endowed with water and uses it inefficiently, especially in the agriculture sector, is India.

The non-agriculture sector in China is least efficient in water usage among the large developing countries. This indicates the wastage and inefficiency resulting from price distortion as well as industrial structure. China's agriculture sector is also very inefficient in using water, especially considering its poor water endowment per capita.

Consequently, there is a need for increase in water charges to urban consumers, better management of uses and charges in the rural area, raising of waste water treatment charges in cities and developing the market for the transfer of water supply rights.

For coal, charges for the transportation of coal by railway are still tightly controlled. There is a need to raise the transport charges to reflect railway transport tariff. This would lead to higher market prices for coal in the coal consuming region. It would also reduce the over-expansion of electricity-intensive industries as cheap coal for power generation is a major subsidy toward electricity for industries.

The key aspect of land price reform is to increase the proportion of land for industrial, commercial, and residential development being sold in open bidding rather than through private transfer or negotiation.

The New Socialist Countryside

Over the past two and a half decades of dynamic economic growth, a clear concern is the rise of inequality. Figure 3.27 shows that the Gini coefficient has risen significantly over the reform period and

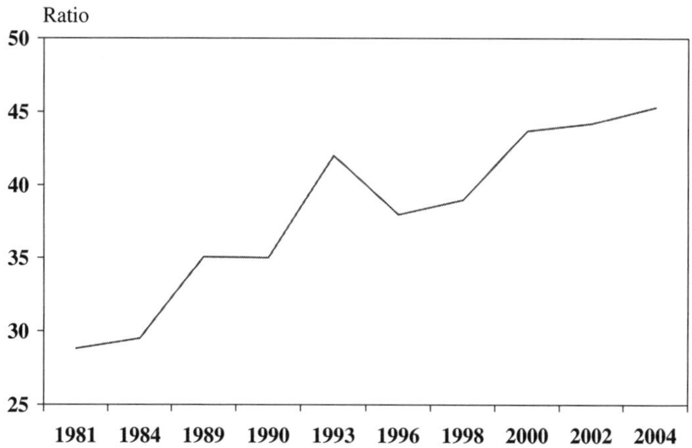

Fig. 3.27: Gini index.
Source: *World Bank*.

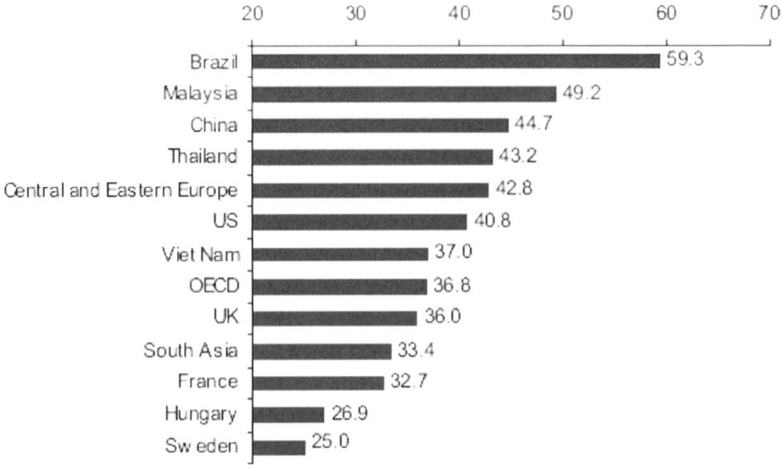

Fig. 3.28: Gini Coefficients of selected countries and regions.
Source: *Human Development Report 2005, United Nations Development Programme.*

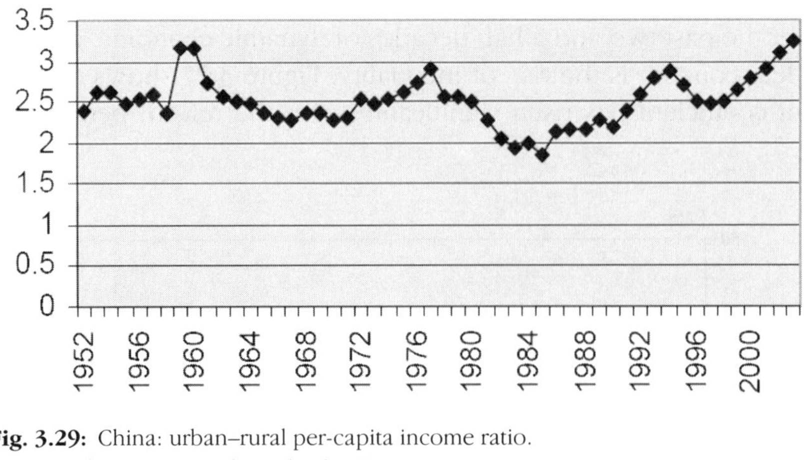

Fig. 3.29: China: urban–rural per-capita income ratio.
Source: *China Statistical Yearbooks*, SSB.

has reached 0.45 by 2005. This is very high by international standard (Fig. 3.28). Rural–urban per capita income ratio has risen to 3.2 by 2005 (Fig. 3.29), compared to 1.6 in India (Fig. 3.30). It is clear that unlike the poor Indian farmers, Chinese farmers have lacked an effective voice in the system. In particular, during the period

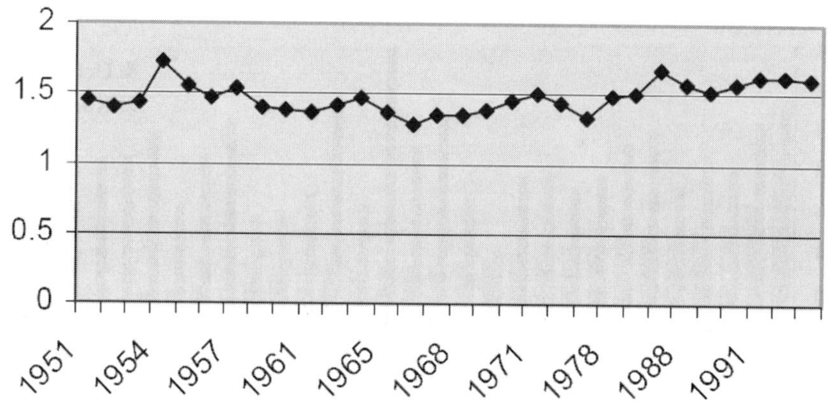

Fig. 3.30: India; urban–rural per-capita income ratio.
Source: *Datt* (1998).

1998–2002, rural per capita income increased at a much slower rate than that of the urban per capita income across all the provinces; in provinces like Jilin, Guangxi, Liaoning and Heilongjiang, rural per capita income actually fell while the urban per capita income rose by 8–10 percent (Fig. 3.31).

Presently, bigger cities in the administrative hierarchy are favored by government policies in the allocation of public sector investment for infrastructure, tax subsidy policies on foreign direct investment, and allocation of funds for industrial enterprises. These distorted policies have slowed the natural process of the upgrading of bigger cities, especially those in the coastal region, into higher value added services sector and the skilled manufacturing activities. This has retarded the process of migration of lower and medium skilled manufacturing activities from coastal to the central and western region, as well as to smaller and medium cities in the coastal region, aggravating regional inequality.

Anti-rural policies have also contributed to substantial resource flows from the agriculture and rural sectors to the non-agriculture and urban sectors. Figure 3.32 indicates that through the fiscal and financial system as well as the implicit tax in grain marketing, the annual resource transfer from the agriculture and rural sectors has

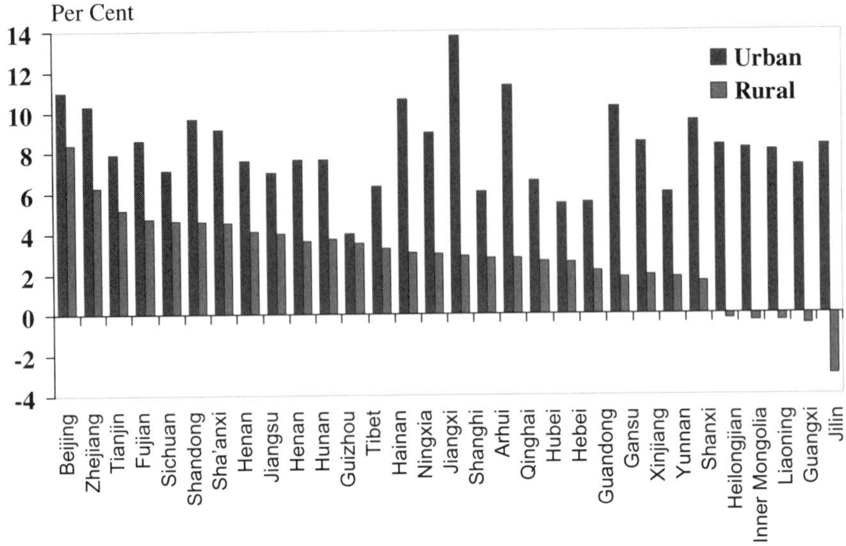

Fig. 3.31: Annual average per-capita income growth by province, 1998–2002. Source: *World Bank*.

been very substantial. Huang *et al*. (2004) estimated that from 1980 to 2000, China has extracted a total value of about 1,289 billion (in 2000 prices) of capital from the agriculture sector to finance industrialization (Fig. 3.32). The capital outflow from rural to urban sector was 2,297 billion (in 2000 prices) for the same period.

The most important theme of the NPC meeting on the 11th Five-Year Plan was the building of the "new socialist countryside." The key policy measures include the abolishment of the agricultural tax by 2006 (the first time in 2500 years of Chinese history!), an increase in agriculture subsidy to farmers, and a major increase in government fiscal allocation to rural infrastructure, education, and health expenditure. The slogan is to "give more and take less." For example, tuition for the nine-year compulsory education in the western rural region will be made free this year and expanded to all the rural areas next year. A rural cooperative health-care system will be built by 2008. In particular, the government has allocated 340 billion Rmb (1.7 percent of GDP) for rural support. This was an increase of

	Fiscal system		Financial system		Grain Marketing (implicit tax)	Cash flow from	
	Agri to Industry	Rural to urban	Agri to Industry	Rural to Urban		Agri to Industry	Rural to Urban
1980	-33.6	-25.8	15.9	7.2	39.3	21.6	20.7
1985	-14.9	13.2	29.5	9.2	11.3	25.9	33.7
1990	-29.6	14.5	62.5	28.8	33.3	66.2	76.6
1995	-18.4	115.8	131.7	89.1	33.5	146.8	238.4
2000	-46.5	153.2	206.9	247.8	-0.1	160.3	400.9
Total: 1980-2000	-533.2	1069.7	613.4	1734.7	613.9	1289.3	2297.0

Fig. 3.32: Capital flows (billion yuan in 2000 price) from agriculture to industry and form rural to urban through fiscal, financial, and grain procurement systems, 1980–2000.
Source: Huang *et al.* (2004).

14 percent over last year. Rural road and irrigation work will receive 1.2 trillion Rmb over the Five-Year Plan period (2006–2010). Specifically, the Minister of Transport has outlined an ambitious plan to reach 95 percent of the counties and 80 percent of the villages with paved road by 2010. Overall, additional annual investment in rural infrastructure would amount to 1.3 percent of GDP.

The policies on "new socialist countryside" will have significant multiplier effect throughout the economy and various industries. Rural consumption will be significantly boosted. For example, the abolishment of the agricultural tax and the free nine-year education will inject 150 billion Rmb into the pocket of the farmers. With an estimated propensity to consume of about 74 percent, farmers consumption spending would increase by 111 billion Rmb or 5 percent of existing total rural consumption. The two key items in rural consumption are food (40 percent) and housing (17 percent). The significant improvement in rural income would boost the food and beverages, supermarket and retail sector. An increase in housing construction would benefit the construction material industry and consumer durables, and even low-end computers. The huge increase in rural infrastructural spending would lead to strong demand for basic materials and also benefit construction contractors in the inland region. The upgrading in the rural transport network between small towns, counties, and villages and rising rural income would generate strong demand for passenger and cargo transportation like minibus, vans, light trucks, and motorcycles. Other industries that are likely to benefit include agriculture machinery, garment, and footwear.

Since the new leadership of Hu Jintao and Wen Jiabao assumed power in 2002, the focus on the rural sector and other relative losers in economic reform have become a prominent theme. This is the third consecutive year China's first government document has focused on the rural sector. Unlike the previous leadership of Jiang Zemin, Zhu Rongji, and Li Peng, Hu and Wen have spent extensive period of their early career in poor and remote provinces like Gansu, Guizhou, and Tibet. They are generally more aware and sympathetic to the plight of the farmers and migrant workers. There is greater concern to ensure that the fruits of economic reform in China are not confined to the urban sector as well as some connected interest groups but also increasingly trickle down extensively to the vast majority in the rural sector.

By 2006, there have already been some visible results of benefits trickling to the rural sector. Figures 3.33 and 3.34 indicate that while the urban sector continued to show good increase in income and expenditure over the past three years, it is the rural sector that has improved substantially in terms of income and expenditure increases due to the policies of the Hu–Wen new leadership.

In addition, the rise in relative inequality, with the urban–rural income ratio reaching 3.2 by 2005 (compared to 2.1 in 1985 and 1.6 for India in 2004) has also led to greater social conflicts in the rural sector. The anger against rural government officials in the acquisition of land and poor compensation, the increase in arbitrary fees and levies, the poor conditions in health and education facilities have also led to greater tension. A recent survey indicates that rural

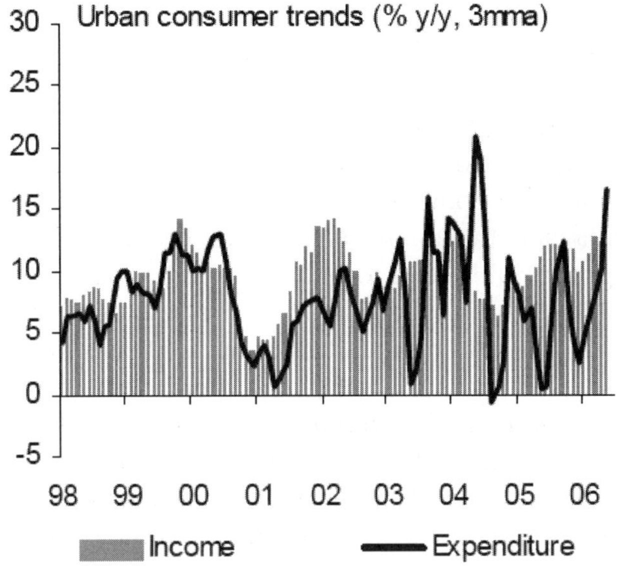

Fig. 3.33: Growth in urban income and expenditure.
Source: *CEIC, UBS*.

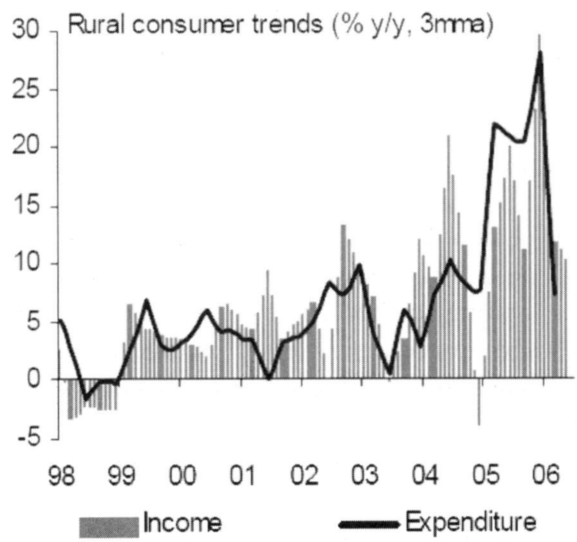

Fig. 3.34: Growth in rural income and expenditure.
Source: *CEIC, UBS*.

population paid 87 percent of health-care expenditure out of their own pocket, compared to 44 percent in the urban sector. Consequently, the new leadership needs to increasingly turn their attention to address the grievances of the rural sector.

From a stage of development perspective, it is also a natural sequence of development. The other East Asian countries like Japan, Korea, and Taiwan, have also gone from the earlier stage of "exploiting" the rural sector to finance the urban sector to the stage of "subsidizing" the rural sector from the resources of the urban sector. A major development in China that facilitates this support of the rural sector now is the substantial improvement in the fiscal condition of the central government over the past few years. As Chen Xiwen, the key official in charge of rural policy under the Central Financial Work Leading Group in the CCP highlighted, these programs are now fiscally affordable as the government revenue has reached 3.2 trillion Rmb in 2005, more than double that in 2000.

An important objective of this policy is to increase consumption expenditure and domestic demand. This would lead to less dependence on investment and export as sources of growth. Given the rising trade surplus and tension (Ministry of Commerce data indicate that over 21 anti-dumping investigations were initiated by 11 trading partners in 2005), as well as overinvestment and excess capacity, this policy would also serve to re-balance the overall economy.

The improvement in income pertaining to social services in the rural sector could increase the "reservation wages" of the rural workers in migrating to the urban factories as this sets the basic benchmark wage. Consequently rural income improvement could lead to an increase in the wage necessary to entice rural workers to move to urban factories. These rising wages could exert pressure on firms producing labor-intensive products, especially those without specific technological advantage or brand attraction. The increasing wages in the coastal factories could also accelerate the existing trend of firms relocating inland or to other Asian countries like Vietnam.

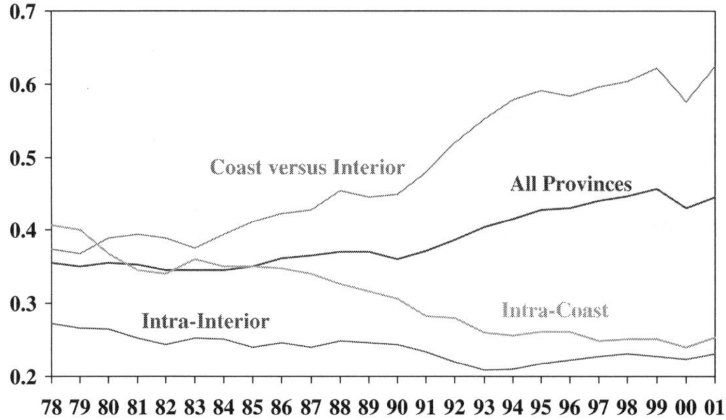

Fig. 3.35: Regional income disparities, 1978–2001.
Source: *World Bank*.

Fragmentation of the Factor Market and Balanced Regional Development

Coupled with the rural–urban inequality, unbalanced regional growth has also aggravated over the reform period. Figure 3.35 shows that while regional inequality has risen, intra-coastal and intra-interior inequalities have both declined. Consequently, the key factor leading to greater regional inequality is the rapidly rising disparity between the coastal and interiors provinces. There is increasing danger that while the coastal provinces have been moving rapidly like the Japanese bullet trains, the lower interior provinces have been plodding along like a Bangladesh bullock cart (Fig. 3.36). There is a danger of centrifugal forces been generated leading to greater regional tensions. An important contributing factor is the overwhelming concentration of foreign direct investments at the eastern coastal provinces (Fig. 3.37).

Fragmentation of the Labor Market

Using detailed provincial data, we examine the fragmentation of the labor and capital market across the regions and sectors in the

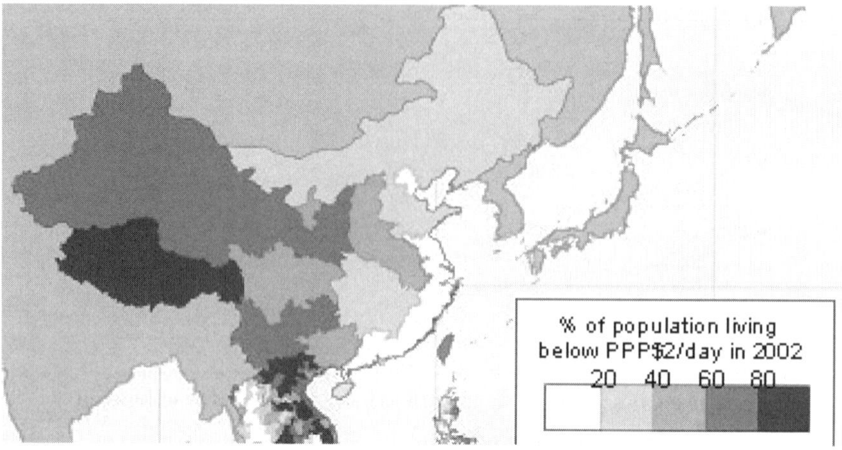

Fig. 3.36: Regional disparities: coastal to central to inland provinces.
Source: *World Bank*.

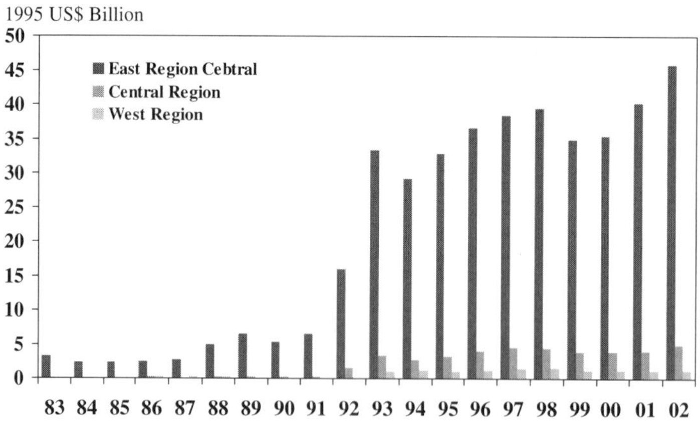

Fig. 3.37: FDI inflows into China by region, 1983–2002.
Source: *World Bank*.

economy for the period 1978–2001 (see Annex. 1 for details). Regional and sectoral differences in labor productivity are large and increasing. Tables 3.1 and 3.2 present labor and capital productivities by region and sector for the period 1978–2001. They highlight the dramatic change in factor markets and economic structure over the

Table 3.1: Labor and capital productivity by region.

Year	Labor productivity					Capital productivity				
	China	East	Central	Western	Northeast	China	East	Central	Western	Northeast
1978	868.1	1073.3	707.2	618.6	1672.1	36.5	41.5	37.8	25.4	44.7
1979	921.3	1147.9	761.8	656.5	1681.5	37.1	42.2	38.9	26.1	43.7
1980	974.0	1249.5	792.4	683.5	1714.2	38.0	43.3	39.1	27.1	45.0
1981	989.0	1302.6	810.9	667.7	1681.7	37.8	43.1	39.4	26.4	43.7
1982	1045.5	1374.6	864.9	713.6	1717.5	38.5	43.0	40.4	27.9	43.3
1983	1122.7	1468.9	930.0	766.1	1861.2	39.6	43.5	41.4	29.3	45.0
1984	1259.9	1655.2	1045.9	853.0	2072.0	41.6	45.4	43.1	31.6	47.1
1985	1403.9	1859.7	1169.5	950.6	2214.1	42.6	45.5	44.4	33.6	46.9
1986	1472.3	1966.3	1221.4	989.3	2315.6	41.7	43.9	43.4	33.9	45.6
1987	1599.6	2157.5	1302.9	1061.9	2597.6	42.2	43.9	43.7	34.9	46.9
1988	1751.2	2410.6	1402.5	1150.9	2822.0	43.3	45.0	44.3	36.6	47.4
1989	1794.0	2475.7	1442.5	1166.9	2919.2	42.2	42.9	43.6	36.3	46.4
1990	1840.6	2578.2	1470.5	1200.6	2912.0	41.1	41.9	42.5	36.3	43.2
1991	1966.0	2821.7	1543.4	1267.7	3032.4	42.0	43.6	42.8	37.4	42.9
1992	2261.6	3358.9	1761.5	1406.5	3331.4	45.4	47.7	46.5	39.8	44.5

(*Continued*)

Table 3.1: *(Continued)*

Year	Labor productivity					Capital productivity				
	China	East	Central	Western	Northeast	China	East	Central	Western	Northeast
1993	2640.8	4045.2	2023.2	1605.0	3723.4	49.3	52.2	50.4	42.8	46.7
1994	2993.2	4657.7	2291.7	1769.4	4115.9	51.8	54.8	53.4	44.6	48.4
1995	3356.2	5429.0	2566.9	1841.7	4409.2	52.8	55.9	55.0	43.3	51.0
1996	3709.0	5979.6	2837.1	2099.1	4718.9	54.0	56.1	55.9	46.3	53.5
1997	4052.3	6526.9	3135.3	2281.8	5058.3	53.8	54.6	56.5	47.0	54.9
1998	4562.9	7337.3	3358.9	2852.6	5663.0	54.3	54.0	54.7	54.0	54.7
1999	4915.3	7880.8	3622.0	3047.4	6167.5	53.5	52.7	54.4	53.5	55.3
2000	5190.4	8538.6	3882.1	2848.2	6768.2	51.9	51.8	53.9	46.8	56.7
2001	5616.8	9035.5	4255.7	3087.4	7293.9	52.2	52.2	53.9	46.9	57.5
Growth rates (percent)	8.5	9.8	8.1	7.3	6.9	1.9	1.3	1.8	3.1	1.1

Note: The unit of labor productivity is 1978 constant yuan and the unit of capital productivity is 1978 constant yuan per 100 yuan of capital stock.

Table 3.2: Labor and capital productivity by sector.

Year	Labor productivity					Capital productivity				
	China	Agri	Urban industry	Urban service	Rural nonfarm	China	Agri	Urban industry	Urban service	Rural nonfarm
1978	868.1	346.5	3245.4	1949.0	622.8	36.5	52.3	45.7	19.2	22.4
1979	921.3	367.1	3256.4	1943.5	807.0	37.1	54.8	45.5	19.9	23.1
1980	974.0	368.9	3386.5	2026.8	902.0	38.0	55.0	46.5	21.5	23.3
1981	989.0	385.1	3240.2	2104.3	972.4	37.8	58.3	44.1	22.6	23.5
1982	1045.5	423.5	3267.8	2303.0	908.9	38.5	64.0	42.9	23.6	24.3
1983	1122.7	452.8	3494.7	2502.7	906.6	39.6	68.4	43.4	24.6	26.1
1984	1259.9	509.0	3783.3	2882.8	856.5	41.6	73.6	45.0	26.0	30.2
1985	1403.9	532.8	4601.3	3221.4	777.9	42.6	73.5	46.2	27.2	37.8
1986	1472.3	546.0	4803.1	3420.4	873.5	41.7	74.2	43.1	27.9	42.9
1987	1599.6	565.9	5086.3	3790.3	1020.8	42.2	75.6	42.9	29.0	47.2
1988	1751.2	562.9	5549.0	4238.4	1248.7	43.3	74.4	43.4	30.6	54.0
1989	1794.0	559.0	5649.3	4432.3	1397.1	42.2	74.8	41.0	30.4	56.1
1990	1840.6	584.9	5712.9	4615.2	1509.7	41.1	78.3	38.4	29.7	58.6
1991	1966.0	580.3	6102.4	5015.9	1690.9	42.0	77.7	39.1	31.2	62.3
1992	2261.6	611.7	6944.3	5528.4	2182.8	45.4	78.9	42.1	33.4	74.1

(*Continued*)

Table 3.2: *(Continued)*

Year	Labor productivity					Capital productivity				
	China	Agri	Urban industry	Urban service	Rural nonfarm	China	Agri	Urban industry	Urban service	Rural nonfarm
1993	2640.8	660.5	7582.1	6189.6	3012.5	49.3	79.5	44.3	34.3	94.4
1994	2993.2	708.8	8254.0	6050.6	3862.8	51.8	78.0	45.9	33.8	108.7
1995	3356.2	761.0	8636.0	6312.7	4867.3	52.8	74.0	45.4	32.9	119.8
1996	3709.0	826.9	9245.6	6062.1	5769.6	54.0	70.9	46.9	30.5	136.5
1997	4052.3	856.1	10754.6	6329.3	6072.3	53.8	66.8	49.2	29.7	140.5
1998	4562.9	917.1	13239.3	7003.5	6728.7	54.3	64.9	51.0	29.0	152.3
1999	4915.3	942.5	15089.2	6920.4	7666.2	53.5	62.0	49.4	27.4	170.5
2000	5190.4	945.2	17060.3	7362.1	7488.2	51.9	58.0	50.4	25.7	173.9
2001	5616.8	988.0	18613.3	7797.9	7944.2	52.2	57.0	51.6	25.2	187.1
Growth rates (percent)	8.5	4.7	8.1	6.3	12.4	1.0	0.4	0.5	1.5	10.5

Note: The unit of labor productivity is 1978 constant yuan and the unit of capital productivity is 1978 constant yuan per 100 yuan of capital stock.

reform period. Labor and capital productivities are measured as the ratios of GDP to labor and capital. The unit of labor productivity is 1978 constant Yuan and the unit of capital productivity is 1978 constant Yuan per 100 Yuan of capital stock. As shown in Table 3.1, there exists a large regional variation in labor productivity. Initially, the northeast region had the highest labor productivity, but it fell behind the eastern region by 2001. Overall, labor productivity in the eastern region has grown the fastest (averaging 9.8 percent per year), followed by the central (8.1 percent), western (7.3 percent) and the northeast (6.9 percent). Consequently, the regional gap between the coastal and inland region has worsened over the period.

Tables 3.3(a)–3.3(d) indicate that, over the period 1978–2001, the fragmentation between the urban industry and the agriculture sector has increased considerably. The ratio in labor productivity has risen from 9.4 in 1978 to 18.8 by 2001. (While we were unable to adjust the labor data for quality, the rising disparity in labor productivity could be indicative of greater distortion, especially when this huge disparity is not likely to be credibly accounted for by the increasing difference in the quality of labor.) This rising disparity between the urban industry and agriculture sector is most serious in the western region, with the ratio standing at an astonishing 23.7 by 2001. The situation in the northeast appears to show smaller increase in the degree of fragmentation. It should be highlighted that in view of the well-known limitations of data on employment and GDP, especially at the provincial level, as well as the weak data series for rural industry, the analysis and computed marginal returns to labor and capital by sectors and regions should be viewed as indicative of magnitude and trends rather than definitive.

This urban industry versus agriculture fragmentation is the most serious, overwhelming the regional fragmentation. In fact, even the labor productivity in the urban industry in the poor western region improved faster than that of the agriculture sector in the booming eastern region over the reform period.

Overall, the data indicates that the rural non-farm sector has the fastest growth in both labor and capital productivities while the

Table 3.3(a): Labor and capital productivity by sector and region.

Region	Year	Labor productivity				Capital productivity			
		Agriculture	Urban industry	Urban service	Rural nonfarm	Agriculture	Urban industry	Urban service	Rural nonfarm
East	1978	345.4	3800.2	2350.3	677.8	48.1	73.1	18.4	25.7
	1979	379.0	3853.9	2359.8	866.4	51.5	70.8	18.9	26.4
	1980	389.1	4156.4	2558.3	885.7	51.5	71.4	20.4	26.3
	1981	413.6	4077.3	2721.0	945.3	53.7	68.1	21.3	26.5
	1982	480.7	3940.6	3017.5	819.2	60.5	64.3	21.8	27.4
	1983	506.2	4121.7	3419.1	841.9	63.2	64.6	22.2	29.0
	1984	598.6	4396.3	4132.6	824.5	70.6	66.3	22.9	31.3
	1985	627.3	6238.7	4728.6	747.9	70.0	65.3	23.1	39.8
	1986	653.6	6490.3	4817.7	874.2	71.7	59.4	23.4	44.2
	1987	690.8	6943.5	5216.5	1043.5	74.1	58.0	23.7	47.2
	1988	706.7	7596.6	5813.5	1351.7	75.3	57.5	25.0	54.2
	1989	698.1	7727.9	6144.3	1481.9	76.1	53.2	24.4	53.2
	1990	713.3	7818.6	6476.0	1667.6	77.4	50.2	24.1	56.0
	1991	741.8	8213.7	7079.7	1924.9	79.6	51.6	25.8	58.7
	1992	786.5	9534.2	7984.7	2635.5	81.1	56.5	27.9	67.3

(Continued)

Table 3.3(a): *(Continued)*

Region	Year	Labor productivity				Capital productivity			
		Agriculture	Urban industry	Urban service	Rural nonfarm	Agriculture	Urban industry	Urban service	Rural nonfarm
	1993	852.5	10426.5	9187.9	3830.5	82.6	59.3	29.6	82.3
	1994	934.5	11807.5	8470.8	4769.1	82.4	64.4	29.6	86.2
	1995	1040.8	12694.5	9504.0	6129.6	81.0	64.4	29.7	92.6
	1996	1117.3	13795.5	9478.0	6975.5	73.3	65.2	28.3	102.1
	1997	1120.5	15541.2	9890.1	7635.6	66.9	63.3	26.9	109.4
	1998	1199.3	17793.5	10954.2	8789.3	64.5	60.6	26.3	122.5
	1999	1260.7	19969.9	9832.2	10212.9	61.8	56.5	24.6	139.9
	2000	1281.0	22197.0	10500.4	10705.7	56.6	56.4	23.6	147.9
	2001	1310.5	22554.6	10530.0	11779.0	55.3	55.2	23.0	166.9

Table 3.3(b): Labor and capital productivity by sector and region.

Region	Year	Labor productivity				Capital productivity			
		Agriculture	Urban industry	Urban service	Rural nonfarm	Agriculture	Urban industry	Urban service	Rural nonfarm
Central	1978	347.1	2615.8	1855.4	658.7	69.2	36.9	23.4	18.2
	1979	372.2	2672.4	1920.5	824.0	73.8	37.2	24.6	18.8
	1980	356.2	2807.7	1974.4	957.9	70.9	38.4	26.6	19.2
	1981	392.0	2657.5	2003.5	987.3	81.8	35.6	27.1	19.4
	1982	421.0	2732.2	2214.2	1053.2	88.7	34.8	29.2	20.2
	1983	446.0	2966.8	2357.4	1027.5	95.1	34.6	30.8	21.9
	1984	500.5	3147.9	2733.6	921.3	102.5	35.2	32.5	27.1
	1985	543.3	3550.0	2953.6	826.9	107.5	35.7	34.9	33.1
	1986	542.3	3827.7	3189.7	886.1	106.2	33.5	35.8	39.1
	1987	564.4	3882.0	3281.8	1020.8	108.1	32.5	37.3	44.4
	1988	550.4	4263.9	3624.8	1162.6	102.9	33.4	39.1	50.7
	1989	559.3	4203.8	3934.8	1327.4	105.1	31.1	39.3	55.8
	1990	577.1	4307.4	4129.6	1370.7	109.3	29.1	38.3	58.0
	1991	536.9	4775.4	4505.9	1538.8	102.9	29.5	40.3	63.9
	1992	571.6	5425.6	4871.6	1888.5	104.2	31.3	44.0	82.3

(*Continued*)

Table 3.3(b): (*Continued*)

Region	Year	Labor productivity				Capital productivity			
		Agriculture	Urban industry	Urban service	Rural nonfarm	Agriculture	Urban industry	Urban service	Rural nonfarm
	1993	625.4	5702.6	5385.2	2489.4	99.0	32.6	45.0	114.0
	1994	670.4	5903.2	5428.9	3300.9	91.1	32.4	44.4	148.6
	1995	718.4	5767.1	5375.7	4397.2	81.7	30.3	41.1	183.3
	1996	781.9	5910.8	4894.5	5363.3	77.2	30.5	35.3	206.0
	1997	826.4	7526.9	5304.9	5343.4	71.4	36.1	35.0	194.5
	1998	849.6	9467.2	5082.6	5608.1	64.2	38.4	31.5	193.6
	1999	852.6	10332.0	5424.9	6490.6	59.7	37.0	30.7	213.4
	2000	881.7	12998.9	6141.1	6069.2	56.7	41.8	29.8	208.3
	2001	929.3	15563.6	6895.0	6071.3	54.5	46.1	28.9	209.7

Table 3.3(c): Labor and capital productivity by sector and region.

Region	Year	Labor productivity				Capital productivity			
		Agriculture	Urban industry	Urban service	Rural nonfarm	Agriculture	Urban industry	Urban service	Rural nonfarm
West	1978	290.2	2743.4	1749.5	420.4	36.9	25.2	15.7	25.6
	1979	298.7	2811.3	1678.6	610.3	37.8	26.1	16.6	26.4
	1980	312.1	2821.8	1776.6	761.9	40.5	25.9	18.0	27.1
	1981	298.8	2629.3	1796.3	899.2	39.7	24.2	19.2	27.3
	1982	326.2	2825.4	1915.6	766.8	43.7	24.8	20.4	27.8
	1983	336.4	3230.2	2090.5	703.6	45.0	26.6	21.6	30.2
	1984	368.1	3592.9	2362.5	632.6	48.3	28.7	23.8	35.0
	1985	391.1	3914.0	2646.2	595.0	48.8	31.4	25.7	41.9
	1986	401.1	4119.1	2762.7	627.0	49.5	31.0	26.5	44.6
	1987	407.1	4426.4	3310.7	686.1	50.0	31.7	28.5	47.2
	1988	404.1	4936.6	3653.8	800.9	49.5	33.9	30.5	51.8
	1989	409.8	5112.6	3538.7	901.5	50.5	32.5	30.5	56.0
	1990	422.9	5244.1	3776.1	940.6	52.2	31.6	30.8	59.4
	1991	439.5	5516.4	4012.3	983.4	54.0	32.3	31.8	64.4
	1992	456.0	6130.2	4439.3	1215.0	54.4	34.4	33.7	81.4

(*Continued*)

Table 3.3(c): *(Continued)*

Region	Year	Labor productivity				Capital productivity			
		Agriculture	Urban industry	Urban service	Rural nonfarm	Agriculture	Urban industry	Urban service	Rural nonfarm
	1993	480.9	6911.2	4850.3	1676.6	56.1	37.2	33.3	111.1
	1994	504.8	7285.2	4708.3	2228.1	57.1	37.4	32.3	141.1
	1995	531.0	7610.1	4507.8	2348.2	57.3	36.1	30.2	139.5
	1996	570.5	8639.5	4316.9	2954.1	58.7	40.3	28.6	166.5
	1997	601.2	10180.2	4637.6	2874.8	59.6	43.8	28.1	161.8
	1998	701.4	12852.8	6041.7	3355.9	66.8	54.0	31.1	189.7
	1999	725.5	16332.3	5789.6	3553.7	66.4	55.3	29.5	201.5
	2000	689.8	15761.1	5354.0	3040.4	61.3	49.9	24.3	190.0
	2001	717.8	17011.4	5654.3	3387.5	61.8	50.3	23.6	212.3

Table 3.3(d): Labor and capital productivity by sector and region.

Region	Year	Labor productivity				Capital productivity			
		Agriculture	Urban industry	Urban service	Rural nonfarm	Agriculture	Urban industry	Urban service	Rural nonfarm
Northeast	1978	674.9	3706.8	1529.2	734.1	85.2	52.8	21.0	25.0
	1979	670.8	3472.6	1502.9	885.8	80.7	51.4	21.5	25.9
	1980	701.6	3367.9	1438.7	1052.0	83.0	52.8	23.0	25.2
	1981	710.1	3103.1	1551.8	1225.4	83.8	49.1	25.2	25.0
	1982	726.2	3128.2	1704.6	1296.4	87.9	47.4	26.5	24.8
	1983	923.2	3230.4	1778.0	1441.7	108.5	46.7	27.1	26.5
	1984	970.8	3656.0	1933.5	1528.3	103.8	48.8	29.9	32.2
	1985	836.1	4126.7	2232.8	1378.6	86.7	50.4	30.9	42.7
	1986	921.4	4073.4	2512.6	1693.2	91.3	46.0	32.5	50.8
	1987	951.6	4439.7	3049.2	2040.7	90.3	46.8	34.8	60.1
	1988	949.5	4702.5	3559.3	2456.3	88.6	45.8	37.5	71.6
	1989	817.3	4962.0	3795.0	2925.3	76.9	44.8	37.8	81.4
	1990	1038.9	4756.8	3610.4	3157.4	94.9	39.4	34.1	82.0
	1991	1010.2	4920.9	3865.9	3331.2	93.0	39.0	34.8	85.3
	1992	1066.0	5367.1	4133.5	3992.6	96.4	40.5	35.2	100.2

(*Continued*)

Table 3.3(d): *(Continued)*

Region	Year	Labor productivity				Capital productivity			
		Agriculture	Urban industry	Urban service	Rural nonfarm	Agriculture	Urban industry	Urban service	Rural nonfarm
	1993	1158.3	5920.5	4478.3	4997.4	100.1	41.8	35.0	126.7
	1994	1251.8	6260.2	4432.4	7569.9	97.9	41.0	34.2	180.2
	1995	1266.9	6557.8	4584.0	9330.1	80.5	42.3	36.4	203.6
	1996	1461.2	6529.6	4276.7	12645.6	78.0	42.4	34.8	238.0
	1997	1477.3	7247.3	4008.3	16970.3	69.9	43.3	35.1	256.4
	1998	1404.3	9932.8	4718.9	17412.4	64.1	43.5	33.8	263.4
	1999	1456.7	10980.7	5181.0	16959.9	60.6	44.2	32.0	282.6
	2000	1423.2	13340.5	5575.2	16857.5	60.2	48.3	30.8	291.5
	2001	1532.0	15652.0	6076.3	15932.4	62.4	52.8	31.7	271.6

traditional agricultural sector has the lowest labor productivity and the slowest growth. Consequently, transforming rural labor force from farm to non-farm and urban activities will undoubtedly enhance the overall economic growth.

The wedge between agricultural and industrial labor productivity is particularly large in China. Table 3.4 compares the ratio of labor productivity of the industry and services sector to that of the agricultural sector between China and several other countries. The differences are very stark. By 2001, labor productivity ratio of urban

Table 3.4: Ratio of labor productivity of industry and services sector to that of the agriculture sector.

Year	UI/AG	US/AG	RI/AG	Year	IB/AG	SE/AG
China				Indonesia		
1978	9.4	5.6	1.8			
1988	9.9	7.5	2.2	1993	7.2	3.6
1995	11.3	8.3	6.4	1998	7.0	2.8
2001	18.8	7.9	8.0	2002	6.5	3.0
Philippines				Malaysia		
Year		IN/AG	SE/AG			
1989		4.4	2.1	1987	2.7	1.5
1995		4.5	2.1	1995	2.1	1.8
2002		4.2	1.8	2001	2.5	1.9
Korea				Taiwan		
				1981	2.4	3.9
1987		2.5	2.6	1988	2.6	3.9
1995		2.4	1.9	1995	2.9	4.7
2002		3.1	1.7	2002	3.0	4.5
Japan				US		
1990		3.2	3.0	1987	1.5	1.6
1995		3.1	3.4	1995	1.8	1.7
2001		3.3	3.4	2001	1.4	1.3

Note: AG: agriculture; IN: industry; SE: services; UI: urban industry; US: urban services; RI: rural industry.

industry, urban services, and rural nonfarm to that of agriculture in China is an astonishing 4–10 times that of the other countries. More significantly, while the ratios of the other countries have generally been stable or falling, that of China has risen substantially over the past 20 years. On the one hand, these extremely high ratios as well as their rising trends are symptomatic of the major distortions in the factor markets, especially in its bias against the agricultural sector. On the other hand, the figures highlight the tremendous potentials for efficiency gains and economic growth as well as sectoral and regional equity through reallocating resources between the agricultural sector and the other three sectors.

The above partial productivity analysis is the evidence of resource allocation distortions among sectors and regions over the reform period. To examine the patterns of resource allocation and figure out the sources of disequilibria in factor markets, we analyze the marginal product of factor inputs. Theoretically, resource allocation is optimal when the marginal products of factor inputs (suitably adjusted) equalize across sectors and regions. While the absolute levels of marginal products of factor inputs differ across regions and sectors due to a host of reasons like risks, infrastructure, transportation network, tax regime, etc., the relative change across sectors and regions is indicative of the degree and trend of fragmentation. By calculating the inter-sectoral and inter-regional marginal returns of factor as well as their variations over time, the opportunities for achieving efficiency gains by reallocating factors across sectors or regions can be uncovered. Having known labor and capital productivities, we further estimate labor and capital elasticities by calculating marginal returns to labor and capital using the formula below:

$$\frac{\partial Y}{\partial L} = \alpha \frac{Y}{L}; \quad \frac{\partial Y}{\partial K} = \beta \frac{Y}{K},$$

where α and β are labor and capital elasticity, respectively; Y/L and Y/K are labor and capital productivity, respectively.

The decomposition into sectoral and regional polarization indicates that the bulk of the fragmentation in the labor market is due to sectoral effects, especially between urban industry and rural agriculture, rather than regional effect. On the other hand, the empirical evidence indicates that the fragmentation in the financial market has increased in the 1990s compared to the 1980s. The fragmentation in the financial market is overwhelmingly due to sectoral rather than regional, particularly between urban industry and rural agriculture and rural industry.

Marginal Returns to Labor across Sectors and Regions

As indicated in Tables 3.5(a)–(j), the marginal return of labor in the agriculture sector has been rising steadily since the early 1990s. However, it remained by far the lowest at 365, compared to 11,884 in urban industry, 4,672 in rural nonfarm and 2,009 in urban services. While the analysis is unable to adjust for the quality of labor due to data constraint, these huge disparities are clearly indicative of the barriers toward free labor mobility, especially from the agriculture sector to urban industry and rural nonfarm. These large disparities in marginal returns to labor are observed across all the four regions, especially in the west, east, and central regions.

Most significantly, the ratio of the marginal return of labor in urban services against that in the agriculture sector rose from 4.6 in 1978 to reach 20.6 in 1993. Since then, it has fallen dramatically to reach 5.5 in 2001 (see Table 3.5(b)). This indicates the increasing mobility of agriculture labor to the urban services sector since 1993, especially the unskilled segment. Clearly, the rapid absorption of migrant agriculture workers had led to the rapid decline in the marginal return of workers in the urban services sector which fell from 4,228 in 1993 to reach 2,009 in 2001. This indicates the steady convergence between these two sectors. This absorption of agriculture workers in the urban services sector can be observed across all the four regions (see Tables 3.5(g)–(j)). In particular, the ratio of marginal returns has fallen to 2.8 in the northeast region by 2001, compared to 5.6 in the other three regions. This indicates that the urban services sector in the northeast region, unlike its urban industry sector, has been most effective in absorbing the surplus worker from its

Table 3.5(a): Marginal returns to labor and capital by sector and region.

Year	MR (L)				MR (K)			
	Agriculture	Urban industry	Urban service	Rural nonfarm	Agriculture	Urban industry	Urban service	Rural nonfarm
1978	247.4	2885.7	1126.6	255.9	0.8	11.0	3.5	6.6
1979	244.6	2892.6	1208.3	359.6	1.2	11.0	3.6	6.9
1980	229.4	3002.2	1338.0	430.9	1.4	11.4	3.8	7.1
1981	223.5	2863.8	1458.9	493.4	1.9	10.9	4.0	7.3
1982	229.4	2876.5	1661.0	485.9	2.4	10.7	4.2	7.7
1983	229.4	3060.4	1861.9	507.2	3.1	11.0	4.5	8.5
1984	240.8	3292.7	2195.0	498.3	3.8	11.5	4.9	10.0
1985	236.2	3975.4	2492.3	468.1	4.4	12.0	5.3	12.8
1986	227.4	4114.9	2670.2	540.9	5.0	11.4	5.7	15.0
1987	222.2	4316.0	2965.7	647.4	5.7	11.6	6.3	16.0
1988	209.2	4658.3	3301.7	807.7	6.3	12.0	7.1	20.0
1989	197.7	4686.1	3414.1	917.8	7.0	11.6	7.6	21.4
1990	198.1	4676.6	3490.7	1003.5	8.1	11.1	8.0	23.0
1991	189.6	4923.3	3697.6	1132.8	8.8	11.6	9.0	25.2
1992	194.3	5514.2	2940.6	1468.5	9.8	12.8	10.4	31.0

(*Continued*)

Table 3.5(a): *(Continued)*

Year	MR (L)				MR (K)			
	Agriculture	Urban industry	Urban service	Rural nonfarm	Agriculture	Urban industry	Urban service	Rural nonfarm
1993	205.7	5917.3	4228.4	2027.8	10.8	13.8	11.6	40.8
1994	218.5	6321.6	3922.4	2592.1	11.4	14.7	12.4	48.6
1995	234.5	6480.6	3839.2	3244.2	11.7	15.0	13.0	55.4
1996	257.0	6786.7	3411.9	3805.4	12.1	15.9	13.0	65.3
1997	271.0	7708.5	3242.2	3947.9	12.3	17.2	13.6	69.5
1998	298.3	9248.4	3196.7	4295.0	12.8	18.4	14.4	77.9
1999	317.5	10252.2	2736.2	4783.8	13.1	18.4	14.6	90.3
2000	332.2	11249.9	2422.9	4547.4	13.2	19.3	14.8	95.4
2001	364.6	11884.2	2008.6	4672.0	13.7	20.4	15.5	106.2

Table 3.5(b): Marginal returns of labor and capital by sector.

Year	MR(L)			MR(K)		
	Urban industry/ Agri.	Urban service/ Agri.	Rural nonfarm/ Agri.	Urban industry/ Agri.	Urban service/ Agri.	Rural nonfarm/ Agri.
1978	11.7	4.6	1.0	13.0	4.1	7.8
1979	11.8	4.9	1.5	9.6	3.1	6.0
1980	13.1	5.8	1.9	7.9	2.6	4.9
1981	12.8	6.5	2.2	5.8	2.1	3.9
1982	12.5	7.2	2.1	4.4	1.7	3.1
1983	13.4	8.1	2.2	3.6	1.5	2.8
1984	13.7	9.1	2.1	3.0	1.3	2.6
1985	16.8	10.6	2.0	2.8	1.2	2.9
1986	18.1	11.7	2.4	2.3	1.2	3.0
1987	19.4	13.3	2.9	2.0	1.1	3.0
1988	22.3	15.8	3.9	1.9	1.1	3.2
1989	23.7	17.3	4.6	1.6	1.1	3.0
1990	23.6	17.6	5.1	1.4	1.0	2.8
1991	26.0	19.5	6.0	1.3	1.0	2.9
1992	28.4	20.3	7.6	1.3	1.1	3.2
1993	28.8	20.6	9.9	1.3	1.1	3.8
1994	28.9	18.0	11.9	1.3	1.1	4.2
1995	27.6	16.4	13.8	1.3	1.1	4.7
1996	26.4	13.3	14.8	1.3	1.1	5.4
1997	28.4	12.0	14.6	1.4	1.1	5.7
1998	31.0	10.7	14.4	1.4	1.1	6.1
1999	32.3	8.6	15.1	1.4	1.1	6.9
2000	33.9	7.3	13.7	1.5	1.1	7.3
2001	32.6	5.5	12.8	1.5	1.1	7.8

agriculture hinterland. Overall, there is clear evidence that the urban services sector, especially restaurant, construction, catering, personal services, recreational services, etc., have become significantly more open to agricultural labor as well as acting as a sponge to absorb retrenched urban industry workers over the past decade.

The greatest distortion in the labor market is in the barrier of mobility between agriculture and urban industry. The ratio of the

Table 3.5(c): Marginal returns of labor and capital by region and sector.

Region	Year	MR (L)				MR (K)			
		Agriculture	Urban industry	Urban service	Rural nonfarm	Agriculture	Urban industry	Urban service	Rural nonfarm
East	1978	246.6	3378.9	1358.6	278.6	0.8	17.7	3.4	7.5
	1979	252.6	3423.4	1467.1	386.0	1.1	17.2	3.4	7.9
	1980	241.9	3684.7	1688.8	423.1	1.4	17.4	3.6	8.0
	1981	239.9	3603.7	1886.5	479.6	1.7	16.8	3.7	8.2
	1982	260.3	3468.6	2176.3	438.0	2.3	16.0	3.9	8.7
	1983	256.0	3609.5	2543.6	471.0	2.8	16.3	4.0	9.4
	1984	283.2	3826.1	3146.7	479.7	3.7	17.0	4.3	10.4
	1985	278.0	5390.0	3658.4	450.0	4.2	17.0	4.5	13.5
	1986	272.2	5560.4	3761.1	541.3	4.8	15.7	4.8	15.4
	1987	271.2	5892.0	4081.6	661.8	5.6	15.7	5.2	16.9
	1988	262.6	6377.3	4528.7	874.3	6.4	15.9	5.8	20.0
	1989	246.9	6410.3	4732.9	973.6	7.1	15.0	6.1	20.3
	1990	241.6	6400.3	4898.1	1108.4	8.0	14.5	6.5	22.0
	1991	242.3	6626.7	5219.1	1289.6	9.0	15.3	7.5	23.8
	1992	249.8	7570.8	5691.4	1773.1	10.1	17.2	8.7	28.2

(*Continued*)

Table 3.5(c): (*Continued*)

Region	Year	MR (L)				MR (K)			
		Agriculture	Urban industry	Urban service	Rural nonfarm	Agriculture	Urban industry	Urban service	Rural nonfarm
	1993	265.5	8137.2	6276.7	2578.4	11.2	18.5	10.0	35.6
	1994	288.1	9043.1	5491.4	3200.3	12.1	20.6	10.8	38.5
	1995	320.7	9526.2	5780.0	4085.6	12.8	21.2	11.7	42.8
	1996	347.3	10126.5	5334.4	4600.8	12.5	22.1	12.1	48.8
	1997	354.7	11139.3	5066.2	4964.4	12.3	22.1	12.4	54.1
	1998	390.1	12429.7	4999.9	5610.3	12.7	21.8	13.1	62.7
	1999	424.7	13568.4	3887.5	6373.0	13.0	21.0	13.1	74.1
	2000	450.2	14637.1	3455.7	6501.3	12.7	21.6	13.5	81.1
	2001	483.6	14400.7	2712.4	6927.2	13.3	21.8	14.2	94.7

Table 3.5(d): Marginal returns of labor and capital by region and sector.

Region	Year	MR (L)				MR (K)			
		Agriculture	Urban industry	Urban service	Rural nonfarm	Agriculture	Urban industry	Urban service	Rural nonfarm
Central	1978	247.8	2325.8	1072.5	270.7	1.1	8.9	4.3	5.3
	1979	248.1	2373.9	1194.0	367.2	1.6	9.0	4.4	5.6
	1980	221.5	2489.0	1303.3	457.6	1.9	9.4	4.7	5.8
	1981	227.4	2348.8	1389.0	501.0	2.6	8.8	4.8	6.0
	1982	228.0	2405.0	1597.0	563.1	3.4	8.7	5.2	6.4
	1983	225.6	2598.1	1753.8	574.8	4.3	8.7	5.6	7.1
	1984	236.8	2739.6	2081.5	536.0	5.3	9.0	6.1	9.0
	1985	240.8	3067.1	2285.1	497.6	6.4	9.3	6.8	11.3
	1986	225.8	3279.3	2490.2	548.7	7.1	8.9	7.4	13.6
	1987	221.6	3294.1	2567.9	647.4	8.2	8.8	8.2	15.9
	1988	204.6	3579.5	2823.6	752.0	8.7	9.2	9.1	18.7
	1989	197.8	3487.1	3030.9	872.1	9.8	8.8	9.8	21.3
	1990	195.5	3526.1	3123.5	911.1	11.3	8.4	10.3	22.8
	1991	175.4	3852.8	3321.7	1030.9	11.7	8.7	11.7	25.9
	1992	181.5	4308.3	3472.4	1270.5	12.9	9.5	13.8	34.5

(Continued)

Table 3.5(d): *(Continued)*

Region	Year	MR (L)				MR (K)			
		Agriculture	Urban industry	Urban service	Rural nonfarm	Agriculture	Urban industry	Urban service	Rural nonfarm
	1993	194.8	4450.4	3678.9	1675.6	13.4	10.2	15.2	49.3
	1994	206.7	4521.1	3519.4	2215.0	13.4	10.4	16.2	66.4
	1995	221.3	4327.7	3269.3	2930.9	13.0	10.0	16.2	84.7
	1996	243.1	4338.8	2754.8	3537.4	13.2	10.4	15.1	98.5
	1997	261.6	5395.0	2717.4	3474.1	13.1	12.6	16.1	96.2
	1998	276.3	6613.4	2319.9	3579.7	12.7	13.8	15.6	99.1
	1999	287.2	7020.0	2145.0	4050.2	12.6	13.8	16.4	113.0
	2000	309.9	8571.7	2021.1	3685.7	12.8	16.0	17.1	114.2
	2001	342.9	9937.0	1776.1	3570.5	13.1	18.2	17.8	119.0

Table 3.5(e): Marginal returns of labor and capital by region and sector.

Region	Year	MR (L)				MR (K)			
		Agriculture	Urban industry	Urban service	Rural nonfarm	Agriculture	Urban industry	Urban service	Rural nonfarm
West	1978	207.2	2439.3	1011.3	172.8	0.6	6.1	2.9	7.5
	1979	199.0	2497.3	1043.6	271.9	0.8	6.3	3.0	7.9
	1980	194.0	2501.6	1172.8	364.0	1.1	6.3	3.2	8.2
	1981	173.3	2323.9	1245.4	456.2	1.3	6.0	3.4	8.5
	1982	176.6	2487.1	1381.6	410.0	1.7	6.2	3.6	8.8
	1983	170.1	2828.8	1555.3	393.6	2.0	6.7	3.9	9.8
	1984	174.1	3126.9	1798.9	368.1	2.5	7.4	4.5	11.6
	1985	173.4	3381.6	2047.3	358.1	2.9	8.2	5.0	14.2
	1986	167.0	3528.9	2156.8	388.3	3.3	8.2	5.5	15.6
	1987	159.8	3756.1	2590.5	435.1	3.8	8.6	6.2	17.0
	1988	150.2	4144.2	2846.2	518.0	4.2	9.3	7.1	19.1
	1989	144.9	4240.9	2725.8	592.3	4.7	9.2	7.6	21.3
	1990	143.2	4292.8	2856.1	625.2	5.4	9.1	8.3	23.3
	1991	143.6	4450.6	2957.8	658.8	6.1	9.6	9.2	26.1
	1992	144.8	4867.8	3164.3	817.4	6.8	10.4	10.5	34.1

(*Continued*)

Table 3.5(e): *(Continued)*

Region	Year	MR (L)				MR (K)			
		Agriculture	Urban industry	Urban service	Rural nonfarm	Agriculture	Urban industry	Urban service	Rural nonfarm
	1993	149.8	5393.7	3313.5	1128.6	7.6	11.6	11.3	48.1
	1994	155.6	5579.6	3052.3	1495.2	8.4	12.0	11.8	63.1
	1995	163.6	5710.7	2741.5	1565.1	9.1	11.9	11.9	64.5
	1996	177.3	6341.7	2429.7	1948.4	10.0	13.7	12.2	79.6
	1997	190.3	7296.7	2375.6	1869.1	10.9	15.3	12.9	80.0
	1998	228.1	8978.4	2757.6	2142.1	13.2	19.5	15.4	97.1
	1999	244.4	11096.9	2289.1	2217.6	14.0	20.6	15.8	106.7
	2000	242.4	10393.2	1762.0	1846.4	13.8	19.1	13.9	104.2
	2001	264.9	10861.4	1456.5	1992.2	14.8	19.9	14.6	120.5

Table 3.5(f): Marginal returns of labor and capital by region and sector.

Region	Year	MR (L)				MR (K)			
		Agriculture	Urban industry	Urban service	Rural nonfarm	Agriculture	Urban industry	Urban service	Rural nonfarm
Northeast	1978	481.8	3295.9	884.0	301.7	1.4	12.7	3.8	7.4
	1979	447.0	3084.6	934.3	394.7	1.7	12.5	3.8	7.7
	1980	436.2	2985.7	949.7	502.5	2.2	12.9	4.0	7.7
	1981	412.0	2742.6	1075.8	621.7	2.7	12.1	4.4	7.7
	1982	393.3	2753.5	1229.4	693.1	3.4	11.8	4.7	7.8
	1983	467.0	2829.0	1322.7	806.6	4.9	11.8	4.9	8.6
	1984	459.2	3181.8	1472.2	889.2	5.4	12.5	5.6	10.7
	1985	370.6	3565.4	1727.5	829.6	5.1	13.1	6.1	14.5
	1986	383.7	3489.7	1961.5	1048.5	6.1	12.2	6.7	17.8
	1987	373.6	3767.4	2385.8	1294.3	6.8	12.6	7.6	21.6
	1988	352.9	3947.7	2772.7	1588.8	7.5	12.6	8.7	26.5
	1989	289.1	4116.0	2923.3	1921.9	7.2	12.6	9.4	31.0
	1990	351.9	3893.9	2730.7	2098.7	9.8	11.4	9.2	32.2
	1991	330.0	3970.1	2849.9	2231.7	10.6	11.6	10.1	34.6
	1992	338.6	4261.9	2946.3	2686.0	12.0	12.3	11.0	41.9

(Continued)

Table 3.5(f): (*Continued*)

Region	Year	MR (L)				MR (K)			
		Agriculture	Urban industry	Urban service	Rural nonfarm	Agriculture	Urban industry	Urban service	Rural nonfarm
	1993	360.8	4620.6	3059.3	3363.8	13.5	13.0	11.8	54.8
	1994	385.9	4794.5	2873.4	5079.8	14.4	13.1	12.5	80.6
	1995	390.3	4921.1	2787.8	6218.8	12.8	13.9	14.4	94.1
	1996	454.2	4793.0	2407.0	8340.5	13.3	14.4	14.9	113.8
	1997	467.7	5194.6	2053.2	11033.4	12.9	15.1	16.2	126.8
	1998	456.7	6938.6	2153.9	11114.5	12.6	15.7	16.8	134.8
	1999	490.7	7460.8	2048.5	10583.2	12.8	16.4	17.1	149.7
	2000	500.2	8797.0	1834.8	10237.1	13.5	18.5	17.7	159.8
	2001	565.3	9993.5	1565.2	9369.8	15.0	20.9	19.5	154.1

Table 3.5(g): Marginal returns of labor and capital by region and sector.

Region	Year	MR (L)				MR (K)			
		Agriculture	Urban industry	Urban service	Rural nonfarm	Agriculture	Urban industry	Urban service	Rural nonfarm
Northeast	1978	481.8	3295.9	884.0	301.7	1.4	12.7	3.8	7.4
	1979	447.0	3084.6	934.3	394.7	1.7	12.5	3.8	7.7
	1980	436.2	2985.7	949.7	502.5	2.2	12.9	4.0	7.7
	1981	412.0	2742.6	1075.8	621.7	2.7	12.1	4.4	7.7
	1982	393.3	2753.5	1229.4	693.1	3.4	11.8	4.7	7.8
	1983	467.0	2829.0	1322.7	806.6	4.9	11.8	4.9	8.6
	1984	459.2	3181.8	1472.2	889.2	5.4	12.5	5.6	10.7
	1985	370.6	3565.4	1727.5	829.6	5.1	13.1	6.1	14.5
	1986	383.7	3489.7	1961.5	1048.5	6.1	12.2	6.7	17.8
	1987	373.6	3767.4	2385.8	1294.3	6.8	12.6	7.6	21.6
	1988	352.9	3947.7	2772.7	1588.8	7.5	12.6	8.7	26.5
	1989	289.1	4116.0	2923.3	1921.9	7.2	12.6	9.4	31.0
	1990	351.9	3893.9	2730.7	2098.7	9.8	11.4	9.2	32.2
	1991	330.0	3970.1	2849.9	2231.7	10.6	11.6	10.1	34.6
	1992	338.6	4261.9	2946.3	2686.0	12.0	12.3	11.0	41.9

(*Continued*)

Table 3.5(g): *(Continued)*

Region	Year	MR (L)				MR (K)			
		Agriculture	Urban industry	Urban service	Rural nonfarm	Agriculture	Urban industry	Urban service	Rural nonfarm
	1993	360.8	4620.6	3059.3	3363.8	13.5	13.0	11.8	54.8
	1994	385.9	4794.5	2873.4	5079.8	14.4	13.1	12.5	80.6
	1995	390.3	4921.1	2787.8	6218.8	12.8	13.9	14.4	94.1
	1996	454.2	4793.0	2407.0	8340.5	13.3	14.4	14.9	113.8
	1997	467.7	5194.6	2053.2	11033.4	12.9	15.1	16.2	126.8
	1998	456.7	6938.6	2153.9	11114.5	12.6	15.7	16.8	134.8
	1999	490.7	7460.8	2048.5	10583.2	12.8	16.4	17.1	149.7
	2000	500.2	8797.0	1834.8	10237.1	13.5	18.5	17.7	159.8
	2001	565.3	9993.5	1565.2	9369.8	15.0	20.9	19.5	154.1

Table 3.5(h): Marginal returns of labor and capital by region and sector.

Region	Year	MR (L)			MR (K)		
		Urban ind./ Agri.	Urban ser./ Agri.	Rural nonfarm/ Agri	Urban ind./ Agri.	Urban ser./ Agri.	Rural nonfarm/ Agri.
Central	1978	9.4	4.3	1.1	8.0	3.8	4.8
	1979	9.6	4.8	1.5	5.8	2.8	3.6
	1980	11.2	5.9	2.1	5.0	2.5	3.1
	1981	10.3	6.1	2.2	3.4	1.8	2.3
	1982	10.5	7.0	2.5	2.6	1.5	1.9
	1983	11.5	7.8	2.5	2.1	1.3	1.7
	1984	11.6	8.8	2.3	1.7	1.1	1.7
	1985	12.7	9.5	2.1	1.5	1.1	1.8
	1986	14.5	11.0	2.4	1.2	1.0	1.9
	1987	14.9	11.6	2.9	1.1	1.0	2.0
	1988	17.5	13.8	3.7	1.1	1.0	2.2
	1989	17.6	15.3	4.4	0.9	1.0	2.2
	1990	18.0	16.0	4.7	0.7	0.9	2.0
	1991	22.0	18.9	5.9	0.7	1.0	2.2
	1992	23.7	19.1	7.0	0.7	1.1	2.7
	1993	22.8	18.9	8.6	0.8	1.1	3.7
	1994	21.9	17.0	10.7	0.8	1.2	5.0
	1995	19.6	14.8	13.2	0.8	1.3	6.5
	1996	17.9	11.3	14.6	0.8	1.1	7.5
	1997	20.6	10.4	13.3	1.0	1.2	7.3
	1998	23.9	8.4	13.0	1.1	1.2	7.8
	1999	24.4	7.5	14.1	1.1	1.3	9.0
	2000	27.7	6.5	11.9	1.3	1.3	8.9
	2001	29.0	5.2	10.4	1.4	1.4	9.1

marginal return of labor between urban industry and agriculture has risen steadily from 11.7 in 1978 to 23.6 in 1990 and further to 33.9 by 2000. There is a tentative decline to 32.6 by 2001 (see Table 3.5(b)). This clearly shows that there has been sustained divergence in the marginal return in urban industry against that for the agriculture sector, indicating that the urban industrial sector probably has become increasingly relatively more capital intensive, as well as having very

Table 3.5(i): Marginal returns of labor and capital by region and sector.

Region	Year	MR (L)			MR (K)		
		Urban ind./ Agri.	Urban ser./ Agri.	Rural nonfarm/ Agri	Urban ind./ Agri.	Urban ser./ Agri.	Rural nonfarm/ Agri.
Central	1978	9.4	4.3	1.1	8.0	3.8	4.8
	1979	9.6	4.8	1.5	5.8	2.8	3.6
	1980	11.2	5.9	2.1	5.0	2.5	3.1
	1981	10.3	6.1	2.2	3.4	1.8	2.3
	1982	10.5	7.0	2.5	2.6	1.5	1.9
	1983	11.5	7.8	2.5	2.1	1.3	1.7
	1984	11.6	8.8	2.3	1.7	1.1	1.7
	1985	12.7	9.5	2.1	1.5	1.1	1.8
	1986	14.5	11.0	2.4	1.2	1.0	1.9
	1987	14.9	11.6	2.9	1.1	1.0	2.0
	1988	17.5	13.8	3.7	1.1	1.0	2.2
	1989	17.6	15.3	4.4	0.9	1.0	2.2
	1990	18.0	16.0	4.7	0.7	0.9	2.0
	1991	22.0	18.9	5.9	0.7	1.0	2.2
	1992	23.7	19.1	7.0	0.7	1.1	2.7
	1993	22.8	18.9	8.6	0.8	1.1	3.7
	1994	21.9	17.0	10.7	0.8	1.2	5.0
	1995	19.6	14.8	13.2	0.8	1.3	6.5
	1996	17.9	11.3	14.6	0.8	1.1	7.5
	1997	20.6	10.4	13.3	1.0	1.2	7.3
	1998	23.9	8.4	13.0	1.1	1.2	7.8
	1999	24.4	7.5	14.1	1.1	1.3	9.0
	2000	27.7	6.5	11.9	1.3	1.3	8.9
	2001	29.0	5.2	10.4	1.4	1.4	9.1

significant and persistent barrier to entry to agriculture labor, especially when compared to the urban services sector. Apparently, the absorption of rural migrant workers from the inland provinces in the labor-intensive industries in the coastal region have been confined to the young and constituting a relatively small share of the total urban industrial labor force. They have not made any significant impact on the divergence between the marginal returns of the two

Table 3.5(j): Marginal returns of labor and capital by region and sector.

Region	Year	MR (L)			MR (K)		
		Urban ind./ Agri.	Urban ser./ Agri.	Rural nonfarm/ Agri	Urban ind./ Agri.	Urban ser./ Agri.	Rural nonfarm/ Agri.
Northeast	1978	6.8	1.8	0.6	9.3	2.8	5.3
	1979	6.9	2.1	0.9	7.4	2.3	4.5
	1980	6.8	2.2	1.2	5.9	1.9	3.5
	1981	6.7	2.6	1.5	4.5	1.6	2.9
	1982	7.0	3.1	1.8	3.5	1.4	2.3
	1983	6.1	2.8	1.7	2.4	1.0	1.8
	1984	6.9	3.2	1.9	2.3	1.0	2.0
	1985	9.6	4.7	2.2	2.6	1.2	2.8
	1986	9.1	5.1	2.7	2.0	1.1	2.9
	1987	10.1	6.4	3.5	1.9	1.1	3.2
	1988	11.2	7.9	4.5	1.7	1.2	3.5
	1989	14.2	10.1	6.6	1.8	1.3	4.3
	1990	11.1	7.8	6.0	1.2	0.9	3.3
	1991	12.0	8.6	6.8	1.1	1.0	3.3
	1992	12.6	8.7	7.9	1.0	0.9	3.5
	1993	12.8	8.5	9.3	1.0	0.9	4.0
	1994	12.4	7.4	13.2	0.9	0.9	5.6
	1995	12.6	7.1	15.9	1.1	1.1	7.4
	1996	10.6	5.3	18.4	1.1	1.1	8.5
	1997	11.1	4.4	23.6	1.2	1.3	9.9
	1998	15.2	4.7	24.3	1.2	1.3	10.7
	1999	15.2	4.2	21.6	1.3	1.3	11.7
	2000	17.6	3.7	20.5	1.4	1.3	11.8
	2001	17.7	2.8	16.6	1.4	1.3	10.3

sectors. (It is possible that there has been convergence in the marginal return of labor between the private and foreign urban industry sector with the agriculture sector but the overall divergence could have been driven by the state-owned urban industry sector. In addition, the contributory effect of human capital could become more significant, especially since the mid-1990s (Zhang and Tan, 2004).) More significantly, the ratio has been rising most rapidly in the western region, reaching an astonishingly high ratio of 41.0 by 2001 (Table 3.5(i)). This could indicate that the SOE dominated urban industrial sector in the western region has been most resistant to absorbing agriculture labor in its hinterland. This is clearly one of the biggest distortion and greatest inefficiency in the system. In fact, the marginal return of labor in the urban industry sector in the western region is actually higher than that of the northeast and central region and only 25 percent lower than the booming eastern region, indicating the heavy industry and SOE effect. The tentative decline in this ratio from 45.4 in 1999 to 41.0 in 2001 in the western region could be indicative of the beginning of a trend, resulting from the restructuring and privatization process of the urban industrial sector, leading to steady gradual converging trend in the future. The same beginning in the decline or stabilization in the ratio can be observed in the eastern, central, and northeast regions.

Comparing the ratio of the marginal returns to labor of the rural nonfarm to agriculture sector, the trend has also been rising steadily from 1.0 in 1978 to reach 15.1 in 1999 before declining to 12.8 in 2001 (see Table 3.5(b)). This is very significant as it indicated that the rural nonfarm sector has actually greater barrier to agriculture labor mobility than the urban services sector. This phenomenon is observed across all the four regions, especially in the northeast and eastern region (Tables 3.5(g)–(j)). By 2001, marginal return of labor in the rural nonfarm sector has risen to 4,672, more than double the 2,009 in the urban services sector! This disparity is even larger in the eastern and northeastern region. Partly reflecting the effect of skill level differential, this huge disparity and diverging trend is also clearly indicative of the barrier in the mobility of agriculture labor to the rural nonfarm sector. Local governments in the TVE sector have clearly erected substantial barriers to labor mobility, resulting in substantial distortion in the labor market. The earlier survey results clearly confirm these empirical findings.

In particular, the ratio has been higher in the northeast and eastern region, compared to the central and western region (Tables 3.5(g)–(j)). It is noteworthy that the ratio has been lower and falling since 1996 in the western region, possibly indicating that the rural nonfarm sector in the western region has been more open in the absorption of its own agriculture labor. The same phenomenon can be observed in the central region to a lesser extent. With the rapid pace of privatization of the TVE sector on recent years, the decline in the ratio since 1999 could be sustained, leading to gradual convergence and reversing the diverging trend from 1978 to 1999.

Other research findings confirm this observation. Empirical evidence indicates that rural industrial labor market is not competitive, industrial wages are not responsive to experience and education, but strongly biased against women and significantly influenced by government intervention (Yao, 1999). Labor market segmentation is even worse in highly developed villages with a strong collective economy and attracting many outside workers. In these villages, local people were assigned to occupy almost all the management jobs in the village factories though their educational levels and managerial skills were below that of many of the outsiders (Chen, 2002). In their study on the improvement of city competitiveness through the investment climate in 23 cities (Dollar *et al.* 2004), labor market flexibility was found to be important for firm performance. In particular, their results showed that firms with a higher share of non-permanent workers (including contract and temporary workers) had higher level of productivity and labor growth rates.

Examining the marginal returns of labor in the agriculture sector across all the four regions, it is clear that the ratio (using western level as the base) has been relatively stable at 1.2–2.5 over the past 20 years. This clearly indicates that there were no significant increases in fragmentation of labor market in the agriculture sector across the four regions. For the marginal product of labor in the urban industry sector across the four regions, the ratio (again using western level as the base) has also been relatively stable at 0.7–1.7 over the past 20 years. This is again indicative of the fact that there are no significant increases in fragmentation of labor market in the urban industry sector across the four regions. In fact, there is some indication of steady convergence across the four regions. Examining the marginal product of labor in the urban services sector across the four regions, the ratio (using western level as the base) again shows stability at around 0.8–2.2 over the past 20 years. This again indicates that there are no significant increases in fragmentation of the labor market in the urban services sector across the four regions. For the marginal returns of labor in the rural nonfarm sector across the four regions, the ratios (using the western level as the base) have been rising steadily, particularly for that between the east and northeast versus the western region. This is indicative of the fact that there exist considerable fragmentations in the labor market in the rural nonfarm sector across the four regions, particularly between east–west and northeast–western region. The degree of fragmentation has actually been increasing especially over the past decade. Local governments managing TVEs in the northeast and eastern region have clearly been erecting barriers against workers from the western region. The barriers against western workers appear to be somewhat less in the central region.

Consequently, it is clear that the key barrier to national integration in the labor market is fragmentation of the labor market across sectors, particularly between agriculture and urban industry and not across the four regions. The main labor market fragmentation at the regional level is actually in the rural nonfarm sector. This fragmentation could be due to the protectionist measures of local governments in the TVEs as well as the rural services sector.

Ongoing rapid and extensive privatization processes in both the TVEs and local SOE sectors could speed up the integration of the labor market across sectors and regions. Some of the initial indication of convergence over the past 2–3 years could be the tentative signs of the initial effect resulting from the privatization processes in these two sectors in the recent years.

To assess the economic costs of the existing distortions in the labor market, we use the estimated production functions to conduct policy simulations. Table 3.6 below reports the growth impact of different policy interventions. Considering the low labor productivity in the agricultural sector, the first experiment is to move labor out of the agricultural sector. Using 2001 as a baseline, the report examines three scenarios: moving 1 percent, 5 percent, and 10 percent of labor

Table 3.6: Policy simulations.

Moving labor out of agriculture (percent)	1	5	10
Change in GDP (percent)	0.7	3.3	6.4
Reallocating investment from cities to rural areas (percent)	1	5	10
Change in GDP (percent)	0.7	3.2	5.9
Adding investment in rural areas (billion yuan)	10	50	100
Change in GDP (percent)	0.2	0.8	1.7
Change in GDP (billion yuan)	21.4	85.4	181.5

Note: Using 2001 as baseline.

force out of the agriculture sector and distributing them equally into the other three sectors. With a mere 1 percent labor reallocation, the economy will gain 0.7 percent. If the share of labor outflow reaches 5 percent and 10 percent, the economy will grow by 3.3 percent and 6.4 percent, respectively. This represent the one time static gain, not taking into account the more significant dynamic gains as rural migrants acquire new skills, exposure as well as experience in the urban sector.

In view of the disparity in marginal productivity of labor across sectors and regions, Table 3.7(a) shows the policy simulations and its impact across different regions. In moving 1 percent, 5 percent, 10 percent of labor out of the rural areas (i.e., from agriculture and rural nonfarm sector) to the urban areas (i.e., into urban industry and urban services), the overall economy would gain by 0.5 percent, 2.5 percent, 5.0 percent of GDP, respectively. More significantly, the gains are much higher in the western and central region compared to the east and northeastern region. With 10 percent of labor movement, the western and central region would gain by 8.2 percent and 5.7 percent, compared to 3.5 percent and 3.1 percent for the northeast and eastern region, respectively.

The policy simulations highlight the economic gains from reallocating resources from low productivity sector to high productivity sector. Removing barriers to labor movement will enhance the overall economic growth. In addition to economic efficiency, these policies

Table 3.7(a): Policy simulations and regional impact.

Changes in GDP (percent) resulting from moving labor out of the rural into the urban areas

Region	1 percent	5 percent	10 percent
East	0.32	1.57	3.12
Central	0.59	2.92	5.74
West	0.85	4.19	8.19
Northeast	0.36	1.76	3.49
China	0.51	2.52	4.96

will also bring about distributional effect by reducing regional and sectoral inequality. Hence, these policies are both efficiency improving and equity enhancing. Since large inequality is a potential source for social conflict and political instability, the far-reaching social impact of these policies is equally important.

Fragmentation of the Capital Market

As indicated in Table 3.5(a), the marginal return of capital is highest at 106.2 for the rural nonfarm sector in 2001, compared to 20.4, 15.5, and 13.7 for the urban industry, urban services, and the agriculture sector, respectively. (The unit of labor productivity is 1978 constant yuan and the unit of capital productivity is 1978 constant yuan per 100 yuan of capital stock.) This indicates that there is substantial underinvestment, especially for the rural industry sector. It clearly shows that small and medium enterprises, particularly those in the rural areas, face serious credit constraint. It is also noteworthy that the marginal returns of capital of the urban industry and urban services sector have been increasing at the lowest rate, compared to that of the agriculture and rural nonfarm sectors. There are indications that capital has been getting a better rate of returns in the rural compared to the urban areas. This indicates that while there has been substantial expansion in fixed assets investment and capital stock in the urban industry sector, capital productivity has increased at a very low rate of only 0.5 percent over the past two decades, compared to 10.5 percent for rural nonfarm sector and 1.5 percent for the urban services sector. Only the agriculture sector grew at the comparable rate of 0.4 percent during the period (see Table 3.2). This phenomenon of weak increase in capital productivity in the urban industry sector is observed across all the four regions.

Examining the level of capital productivity by region, it is clear that there is much less disparity across the four regions. As indicated in Table 3.1, capital productivity is at a comparable rate of 52, 54, 47, 57 across the east, central, west, and northeast region. Between 1978–2001, capital productivity has grown the slowest at 1.1 percent in the northeast, compared to 1.3 percent in the east, 1.8 percent in the central region, and the fastest at 3.1 percent in the western region. This could indicate the underinvestment in the western region, relative to the northeast and eastern region. Again, it should be highlighted that in view of the well-known limitations of data on employment and GDP, especially at the provincial level, as well as the weak data series for rural industry, the analysis and computed marginal returns to labor and capital by sectors and regions should be viewed as indicative of magnitude and trends rather than definitive.

Comparing the disparity in the marginal return of capital across all the four sectors in each region, it is clear that the biggest disparity is between the rural nonfarm sectors against the other three sectors (see Tables 3.5(a)–(j)). This indicates that there has been substantial underinvestment in the rural nonfarm sector, particularly in the northeast, west, and central region. Analyzing the marginal product of capital of agriculture across the four regions, it appears that there are no substantial differences among the four regions. The same can be said for the urban industry sector and urban services sector across all the four regions. However, for the rural nonfarm sector, there is a much larger difference among the four regions, with the northeast, western, and central regions having higher marginal return for capital, compared to the eastern region. This could indicate the substantial underinvestment in the rural industry sector, especially outside of the coastal region. This could be partly due to poor property ownership rights as well as credit constraint. Overall, the fragmentation in the capital market is mostly along sectoral rather than regional line. The impediment of capital into the rural nonfarm sector is particularly serious.

In summary, the empirical evidence indicates that the greatest disparity is in the rural–urban division and not in the coastal–western inequality. In the agriculture sector, marginal product of labor and capital do not diverge by more than 2.1 times across all the four regions. Similarly, they also do not diverge by more than 1.4 times in urban industry or more than 1.9 times in urban services. The disparity is somewhat larger by 3.5–4.7 times for the rural nonfarm sector across all the four regions.

On the other hand, the disparity in the marginal return of labor and capital is much more substantial across sectors. At the overall national level, marginal product of labor in the urban industry sector (11,884.2) is 32.6 times that of the agriculture sector, 5.9 times that of the urban services, and 2.5 times that of the rural nonfarm sector. At the national level, the marginal product of capital in the rural nonfarm sector (106.2) is 7.8 times that of the agriculture sector, 6.9 times that of the urban services, 5.2 times that of the urban industry sector. These disparities are significantly larger than the disparities across the four regions.

These disparities across sectors, especially between the agriculture and urban industry sectors, are observed across all the four regions. In fact, for the disparity in marginal return of labor between the urban industry and agriculture sectors, the worst is in the western region at 41. This indicates that the misallocation of capital and labor between the agriculture and urban industry sectors, is particularly in the western region.

Consequently, the largest gain in efficiency as well as equity could be obtained by shifting agriculture labor into urban industry as well as into the rural nonfarm sector. This applies to all the four regions of the country. In addition, substantial gain could be obtained by expanding investment in the rural industry sector, especially in the northeast, western, and central regions. These are the two areas where policy measures could have the most impact in reducing the existing fragmentation in the factor markets, improving efficiency as well as enhancing equity.

The empirical evidence suggests that there is substantial room to improve efficiency by reallocating resources, in particular capital, among sectors than among regions. Reversing the long-hold urban-biased investment policy will improve not only economic efficiency but also equity as most of the poor live and work in the rural areas.

To estimate the economic gains from greater financial market integration, the report conducts a simulation by changing the long-existing urban bias policy through the movement of investment from cities to rural areas while keeping the total amount investment constant. The magnitude of impact of reallocating capital is similar to that of labor reallocation. The analysis indicate that if we move 1 percent, 5 percent, and 10 percent of urban investment to the rural areas, the whole economy will gain an additional 0.7 percent, 3.2 percent, and 5.9 percent in GDP, respectively (see Table 3.6). In the second simulation, the report assumes that the government makes additional investment in the rural areas, dividing equally between the agricultural sector and the rural nonfarm sector. An additional 10 billion investments in rural areas contribute to an increase of GDP by 0.2 percent, which equals to 21 billion yuan. In view of the fact that in the rural areas, most productions are labor-intensive, a large share of the gain will go to labor compensation and benefit to farmers. When the size of investment increases to 50 and 100 billion, the overall GDP will increase by 0.8 percent and 1.7 percent, or 85 and 182 billion yuan, respectively (see Table 3.6).

In the policy simulations of moving 1 percent, 5 percent, and 10 percent of capital investment out of the urban into the rural area, the efficiency gains are much higher for the northeast and western region. While the overall economy would gain by 0.7 percent, 2.9 percent, and 5.0 percent respectively, the gains for the northeast region is much larger at 0.9 percent, 4.1 percent, and 7.0 percent respectively. The gains in the western and central region are also larger than those in the eastern region (see Table 3.7(b)).

These policy simulations highlight the economic gains from reallocating resources from low productivity sector to high productivity sector. Reversing the urban bias investment policy will enhance overall economic growth. In addition to economic efficiency, these

Table 3.7(b): Policy simulations and regional impact.

Changes in GDP (percent) resulting from moving capital investment from the urban to the rural areas

Region	1 percent	5 percent	10 percent
East	0.57	2.52	4.33
Central	0.69	3.09	5.39
West	0.88	3.84	6.53
Northeast	0.93	4.09	7.01
China	0.65	2.89	4.99

policies will also bring about distributional effect by reducing regional and sectoral inequality. Hence, these policies are both efficiency improving and equity enhancing.

CONCLUSIONS

The collapse of Maoist ideology resulted in an ideological vacuum. The disruption of the Cultural Revolution has weakened the hold of traditional culture and ethical values on the population. Into this ideological and moral vacuum, the open-door policy of the Deng era ushered in the early stage of capitalism, with its greed, materialism, ruthless competition, not moderated by human compassion. This cocktail has undoubtedly created an explosion of growth and expansion. With no moral compass and ethical foundation, as well as weak legal institutions and regulation framework, it has also led to rising social tension, gross inequality, great injustice, and rampant greed. The rise of the Hu–Wen leadership ushered in the beginning of the corrective adjustment to this development path as the costs have mounted. It is an attempt to continue to harness the explosive energy unleashed by the market economy and liberalization, but to put the path of development within a framework of traditional Chinese ethical and moral foundation, to blunt its ruthless sharp edges. The emphasis on putting people first, human welfare, harmonious society, harmony with nature, sustainability of development with respect to resources and the environment, would lead to a development model similar to the mixed economy of the West, with traditional Chinese culture and values serving the role of moderating the greed impulse of harsh and cold-blooded capitalism. It will prevent the development path from veering to extremes and instability. In the international arena, with China's rise being viewed as a potential threat, this development model moderated by the softness of traditional Chinese culture would also be viewed as less threatening. It would help to provide a more conducive and friendly international environment for China to peacefully emerge.

Like an angry rural young man ashamed of his poverty and backwardness, China has rejected his traditional values and culture and stormed off to the city to embrace a new radical ideology and developmental framework. The collapse of the ideology and the rejection of traditional values led to a moral vacuum. With the embrace of market economy leading to explosive growth, the young man has become richer and more confident. Returning to the village, he discovered that his total rejection of the traditional values might have been an over-reaction of a hot-headed youth. The recovery of some of the age-old wisdom and values could provide the ethical foundation for a more fulfilling life and a more balanced society.

ANNEX 1

Data on Provincial GDP, Labor, and Capital by Sectors and Regions for the Period 1978–2001

GDP

(1) Both nominal GDP and real GDP growth indices for various sectors from 1978 to 1995 are available from SSB's "The Gross Domestic Product of China" (SSB, 1997a). The data sources and construction of national GDP estimates was published by the State Statistical Bureau (SSB, 1997b). This publication indicates that the SSB has used the U.N. standard SNA (system of national accounts) definitions to estimate GDP for 29 provinces by three economic sectors (primary, secondary, and tertiary) in Mainland China for the period

1952–1995. Since 1995, the *China Statistical Yearbook* has published GDP data every year for each province by the same three sectors. Both nominal and real growth rates are available from SSB official publications.

(2) We use four sectors in our analysis: agriculture, urban industry, urban services, and rural enterprises. The agriculture sector is equivalent to the primary sector used by SSB. The following procedures were used to construct GDP for the other three sectors. Until 1996, China published annual gross production value for rural industry and services. Since 1996, they began to publish value added figures in *China Township* and *Village Enterprise Statistical Yearbook* (SSB). The definition of value added is GDP originating in the sector, the data we need. The Ministry of Agriculture published data on both gross production value and value added for rural industry (including construction) and services in *China's Agricultural Yearbook*, 1996. The data on nominal value added for rural industry and services prior to 1995 were estimated using the growth rate of gross production value and 1995 value-added figures, assuming no change in the ratio of value added to gross production value.

(3) GDP for rural industry was subtracted from GDP for industry as a whole (or the secondary sector as classified by SSB) to obtain GDP for urban industry. Similarly, GDP for rural services was subtracted from aggregate service sector GDP (or the tertiary sector as classified by SSB) to obtain GDP for the urban service sector. GDP for rural enterprises is the sum of GDP for rural industry and rural services.

(4) The implicit GDP deflators by province for the three sectors are estimated by dividing nominal GDP by real GDP. These deflators are then used to deflate nominal GDP for rural industry and services to obtain their GDP in real terms.

Labor

(5) Labor input data for the primary, secondary, and tertiary sectors at the provincial level after 1989 can be found in SSB's statistical

yearbooks (various issues), while provincial labor data prior to 1989 are available in SSB (1990). Labor is measured in stock terms as the number of persons at the end of each year. For rural industry and services, prior to 1984, labor input data at the township and village level, but not at the individual household level, are available in SSB's rural statistical yearbooks. The omission of individual-household, nonfarm employment data will not cause serious problems, as the share of this category in rural employment was minimal prior to 1984. Urban industry labor is estimated by subtracting rural industry labor from total industry labor, and urban service labor is similarly estimated as total service labor net of rural service labor.

Capital Stock

(6) Capital stocks for the four sectors are calculated from data on gross capital formation and annual fixed asset investment. For the three sectors classified by SSB, the data on gross capital formation by province after 1978 was published by SSB (1997). Gross capital formation is defined as the value of fixed assets and inventory acquired minus the value of fixed assets and inventory disposed. To construct a capital stock series from data on capital formation, we used the following procedure. Define the capital stock in time t as the stock in time $t-1$ plus investment minus depreciation:

$$K_t = I_t + (1 - \delta)K_{t-1}, \tag{1}$$

where K_t is the capital stock in year t. I_t is gross capital formation in year t, and δ is the depreciation rate. *China Statistical Yearbook* (SSB, 1995) reports the depreciation rate of fixed assets of state-owned enterprises for industry, railway, communications, commerce, and grain for the years 1952 to 1992. We use the rates for grain and commerce for agriculture and services, respectively. Since 1992, SSB has ceased to report official depreciation rates. For the years after 1992, we used the 1992 depreciation rates.

(7) To obtain initial values for the capital stock, we used a procedure similar to Kohli (1982). That is, we assumed that prior to 1978,

real investment has grown at a steady rate (r), which is assumed to be the same as the rate of growth of real GDP from 1952 to 1977. Thus,

$$K_{1978} = \frac{I_{1978}}{(\delta + r)}. \quad (2)$$

(8) This approach ensures that the 1978 value of the capital stock is independent of the 1978–1995 data used in our analysis. Moreover, given the relatively small capital stock in 1978 and the high levels of investment, the estimates for later years are not sensitive to the 1978 benchmark value of the capital stock.

(9) Estimates of capital stocks for rural industry and services are constructed using the annual fixed asset investment by province from 1978 to 1995, which are available in the annual *China Statistical Yearbooks* and the *China Fixed Asset Investment Statistical Materials*, 1950–1995. Initial values are calculated using Eq. (2), but the growth rate of real investment prior to 1978 is assumed to be 4 percent. Again, the initial capital stock is low, so that the estimated series is not sensitive to the benchmark starting value. The capital stocks data from 1996 to 2001 are obtained directly from SSB.

(10) Capital stock for rural industry was subtracted from that of total industry (or secondary industry as classified by SSB) to obtain capital stock for the urban industry sector. Similarly, capital stock for rural services was subtracted from the aggregate service sector (or tertiary sector as classified by SSB) to obtain the capital stock for the urban service sector. Finally, capital stock for rural enterprises is the sum of capital stocks for both rural industry and services.

(11) Prior to constructing capital stocks for each sector, annual data on capital formation and fixed asset investment was deflated by a capital investment deflator. The SSB began to publish provincial price indices for fixed asset investment in 1987. Prior to 1987, we use the national price index of construction materials to proxy the capital investment deflator.

REFERENCES

Bird, Richard M. and Christine P.W. Wong (2005), "China's Fiscal System: A Work in Progress," Available at SSRN: http://ssrn.com/abstract=875416.

Chen, Donqi 陈东琪 (2002),《打破地方市场分割》中国计划出版社。

Dollar, David, Anqing Shi, Shuilin Wang, and Lixin Colin Xu (2004), "City Competitiveness and the Investment Climate: Ranking 23 Chinese Cities," World Bank.

Huang, Jikun, Keijiro Otsuka and Scott Rozelle (2004), "China's Rural Economy and the Path to a Modern Industrial State" In *Proceeding for International Symposium on China's Rural Economy: Problems and Strategies*, pp. 16–50.

Kohli, Ulrich (1982), "A Gross National Product Function and the Derived Demand for Imports and Supply of Exports," *Canadian Journal of Economics* 18, 369–386.

Kuijs, Louis (2005), "Investment and Saving in China," World Bank policy research paper series no. 3633.

Kuijs, Louis (2006), "How Will China's Saving-Investment Balance Evolve?" World Bank policy research paper series no. 3958.

State Statistical Bureau (1978–2001), *China Statistical Yearbook*.

Yao, Y. (1999), "Rural Industry and Labor Market Integration in Eastern China," *Journal of Development Economics* 59, 463–496.

Zhang, X. and K. Y. Tan (2004), "Blunt to Sharpened Razor: Incremental Reform and Distortions in the Product and Capital Markets in China," IFPRI Discussion Paper No. 13.

Chapter

4

China in Search of New Sources of Growth

Wu Yanrui

School of Economics and Commerce, University of Western Australia, Australia

Since the end of the notorious Cultural Revolution in 1976 and subsequent initiative of economic reform in 1978, China has maintained impressive economic growth for almost three decades (1976–2005). This growth has raised the standard of living of Chinese citizens and lifted China's status internationally. Subsequently, the Chinese economy has attracted a lot of attention among economists and policymakers who are interested in understanding the sources of China's robust growth in recent decades.[1] This paper adds to the literature by reviewing the existing studies of the sources of China's growth and identifying potential new sources of growth in the coming years. It is concluded that the Chinese economy is now heading toward the third wave of changes after continuous high growth since 1978. This third wave of changes would be characterized by

[1] Examples include Bramall (2000), Chow (2002), Young (2003), Wu (2004), and Garnaut *et al.* (2005).

domestic consumption growth, expansion of the service sector, further productivity improvement, and balanced development. The rest of the chapter first presents a brief review of the existing literature examining economic growth in China. It then discusses the key features of the third wave of economic growth. This is followed by some concluding remarks in the final section.

ACCOUNTING FOR CHINA'S GROWTH: THE EXISTING LITERATURE

Since the foundation of the People's Republic of China in 1949, the Chinese economy has undergone through two waves of changes. The first wave of changes was dominated by collectivization and centralization during the heydays of communism movement from 1949 to 1977. Although there were some successes initially, the first wave of changes ended with major disasters and inefficiency in the Chinese economy.[2] The complete collapse of that system in Eastern Europe is testament to its problems which are well documented (e.g. Kornai 1980, Lin *et al.*, 1996). To overcome these problems, Deng Xiaoping, the former leader of China, engineered economic reforms in 1978 and hence triggered the second wave of changes for nearly three decades. The consequence of these changes is sustained high economic growth since 1978, with an average annual rate of growth of 9.6 percent.[3] Such impressive performance is unprecedented in the Chinese history and has attracted the world news headlines. As a result, a huge literature accounting for China's growth in the past three decades has emerged. The popular approach used in the literature is the traditional growth accounting framework which decomposes the rate of economic growth into three components associated with labor, capital, and productivity changes, respectively. Table 4.1 presents a summary of the main findings in several

[2] For reviews, see Wang (1982), Wu and Zhao (1987), Reynolds (1987), Feuchtwang *et al.* (1988), Perkins (1988), World Bank (1990), and Lin *et al.* (1996).

[3] This is the average annual rate of growth during the period 1978–2005 (National Bureau of Statistics, 2006).

Table 4.1: Sources of China's growth.

Authors	Period	*K*	*L*	TFP
Hu and Khan (1997)	1979–1994	46	13	41
World Bank (1997)	1978–1995	37	17	46
Maddison (1998)	1978–1995	49	21	30
Chow and Li (2002)	1978–1998	55	13	32
Swamy (2003)	1980–1997	39	16	45
Bosworth and Collins (2003)	1980–1990	23	31	46
Bosworth and Collins (2003)	1990–2000	32	18	50
Wu (2006)	1980–2004	50	11	39
Average		41	18	41

Notes and Sources: Statistics in this table are author's own compilation from the studies cited. Modifications where applicable were made so that the statistics are compatible.

studies. These studies support the conclusion that capital formation has been the main driver of China's economic growth over the past decades. The literature also provides evidence that productivity has played a positive role in China's economic growth. This is in sharp contrast to claims about the role of technological progress in East Asian growth by some authors.[4] A positive contribution from productivity change implies that growth may be sustainable in the long run.

While the traditional growth accounting framework has focused on the role of labor, capital, and productivity (i.e. the conventional factors), the framework has also been extended to assess the impact of other factors on economic growth. These factors include efficiency improvement due to sectoral reallocation and spillover effects of foreign trade and economic openness. Sector reallocation captures the flow of resources from low to high productivity sectors such as labor movement from farming to manufacturing and from the state to the non-state sectors. For example, the World Bank

[4] These authors include Krugman (1994), Young (1994), and Kim and Lau (1994) who argued that technological progress hardly made any contribution to East Asian growth in particular economic growth in Singapore, Hong Kong, Korea, and Taiwan.

(1997) found that sectoral reallocation amounted to about 1.5 percentage points of China's growth (out of 9.4 percentage points) during 1978–1995. This finding is supported by Borensztein and Ostry (1996) and Woo (1998). Furthermore, Lin and Li (2003) demonstrated that an increase of 10 percent in exports could lead to one percentage point growth in China's GDP. In addition, another strand of literature has examined the relationship between economic growth and certain factors though no quantitative assessment is presented. For instance, Zhang (1999) argued that foreign direct investment (FDI) contributed to China's growth through spillover effects in various forms, Wong (2006) found that information and communication technology (ICT) made a positive contribution to recent growth, Wu (2004) showed that infrastructure development was positively related to economic growth in the 1980s and 1990s, Wang and Yao (2003) examined the role of human capital which accounted for 11 percent of China's economic growth during 1978–1999, and Lin and Liu (2000) illustrated that fiscal decentralization made a positive contribution to China's growth during 1970–1993.

However, after rapid growth for almost 30 years, several problems have emerged in the Chinese economy. To state broadly, these problems include unbalanced development, high resource-intensity, and over reliance upon external markets. Geographically, unbalanced development appears in the form of rural–urban disparity and coastal–noncoastal gap. Figure 4.1 shows the widening gap in disposable income between rural and urban households. In addition, according to the National Bureau of Statistics (2005), the mean urban household disposable income per capita among 12 western regions was equal to 92 percent of national average in 1990, and this figure fell to 85 percent in 2004.[5] There is also evidence of enlarging inequality among the households within the urban and rural areas, respectively (Knight *et al.*, 2004).

[5] The 12 western regions include five autonomous regions (Tibet, Inner Mongolia, Guangxi, Ningxia, and Xinjian), six provinces (Sichuan, Guizhou, Yunnan, Shaanxi, Gansu, and Qinghai) and one municipality (Chongqing). They are covered by the Western Development Program initiated in 1999.

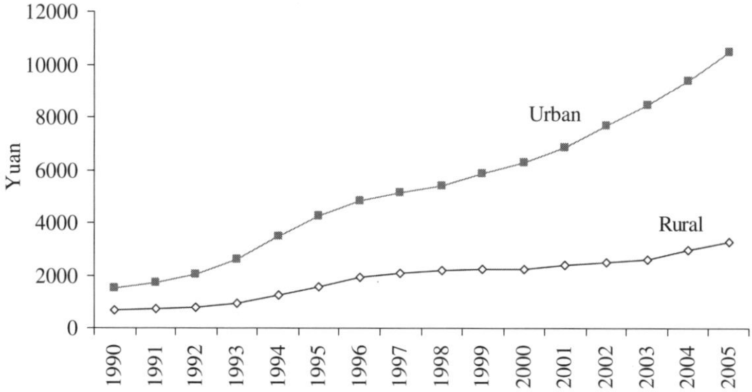

Fig. 4.1: Household disposable income per capita 1990–2005.
Source: *National Bureau of Statistics (2006)*.

China's growth in the past decades has also adopted a resource-intensive strategy. For instance, China's intensity of energy use in 2002 was 0.82 kgoe/US$ (kilogram oil equivalent per US dollar of GDP) which is far higher than 0.24 kgoe/US$ in Mexico and 0.22 kgoe/US$ in the US, not to mention 0.13 kgoe/US$ in Japan in the same year.[6] Furthermore, in 2004, the intensity of steel use was 140 t/US$m (tons per 1 million US dollars) in China, 10 t/US$m in the USA, 69 t/US$m in South Korea, and 17 t/US$m in Japan.[7] Finally, in 2005, China's consumption share of world total was 8.3 percent of oil, 34.4 percent of coal, 21 percent of aluminum, 30 percent of steel, and 51.4 percent of cement (Garnaut and Song, 2006). Seemingly unsaturated demand for raw materials has made China an easy target of blame for being the cause of high world commodity prices in recent years. The high resource-intensity in China's growth has also put great pressure on the environment and raw material supply. Environmental damage is

[6] Data are author's own estimates using statistics from the National Bureau of Statistics (2005), World Economic Outlook database 2005 (IMF, 2005), and World Development Indicator 2005 database (World Bank, 2005).

[7] These statistics are defined as tons of steel used over GDP (millions of U.S. dollars) and calculated using the World Development Indictor 2006 database (World Bank, 2006) and World Steel in Figures 2006 (International Iron and Steel Institute, 2006).

evident everywhere in China, though more efforts have been put for environmental protection in recent years (World Bank, 1997).

Finally, China's total value of trade as a proportion of GDP rose from 9.4 percent in 1978 to 33.9 percent in 1992 and to 64.1 percent in 2005.[8] This figure is now far higher than 21 percent in Japan and 24 percent in the US, for instance.[9] It implies that China's domestic market is relatively small. As a result, China has been accused of relying on others' markets for economic growth and hence causing global imbalance and job losses in other countries (The Economists, 2005). Subsequently, the country has become the world's number one target for antidumping activities (UNCTAD, 2005).

In summary, recent studies have focused on the explanation of China's economic growth since 1978. The consensus view is that capital formation has been the dominant contributor to China's growth. Other contributing factors include productivity gains associated with relocation of resources, economic openness, and technological progress. Thus, growth since 1978 has been resource-intensive and export-oriented. This model of development has serious consequences and may not be sustainable due to both internal and external constraints. It calls for an alternative development strategy which is the focus of the following section.

NEW SOURCES OF GROWTH: THE THIRD WAVE

As discussed in the preceding section, having gone through the second wave of growth, the Chinese economy is now confronted with emerging issues such as rising inequality, environmental deterioration, and external trade frictions. These problems could potentially detour the course of China's development if they are not managed properly. Thus, China is now at the crossroads. For this reason, the economy is being steered toward a third wave of changes. While the second wave of growth was reflected in propaganda slogans such as

[8] These statistics are derived from the National Bureau of Statistics (2006).

[9] These figures are 2002 statistics calculated using data from the World Development Indicator 2005 database (World Bank, 2005).

"getting rich is glorious" and "letting some get rich first," the third wave of change is also policy driven and campaigned by China's current leadership under the concept of developing a "pro-people, harmonious society" which is well documented in the 11th Five-Year Plan (FYP). This wave of changes is hence expected to have several features emphasizing the importance of domestic consumption, the service sector, innovation and technological progress, and balanced development. These are discussed in detail in the following sections.

Domestic Consumption

Following any standard economics textbook, national income can be defined as the sum of investment, net exports, and consumption. It is well known that China has achieved substantially in both investment and net exports. However, in international perspective, domestic consumption accounts for a relatively small share of China's GDP, in particular over the past two decades. This is confirmed in Fig. 4.2 which shows that, among the selected countries,

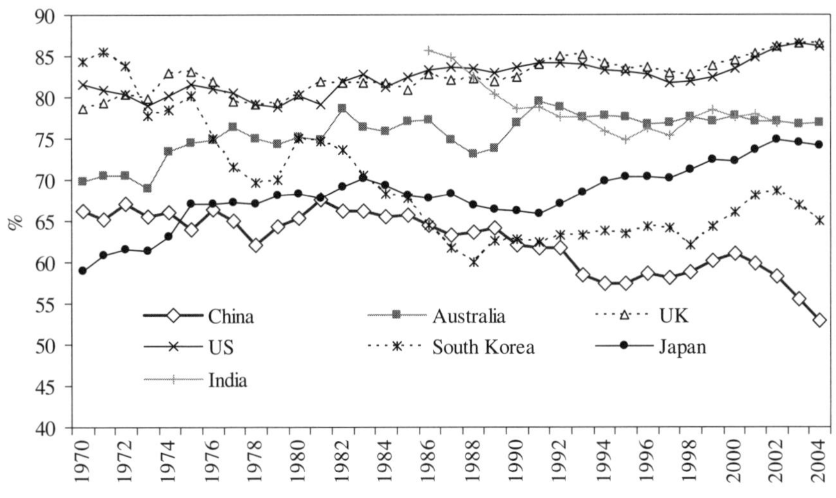

Fig. 4.2: Domestic consumption over GDP 1970–2004.
Sources: *OECD national accounts database (www.oecd.org), and the National Bureau of Statistics (various issues, 2006).*

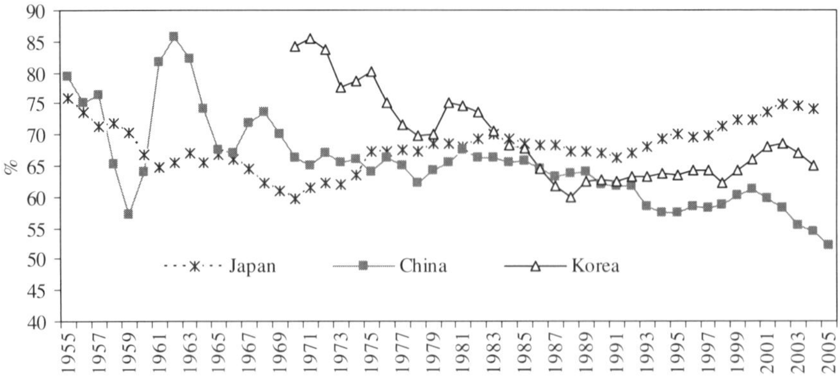

Fig. 4.3: Domestic consumption over GDP in China, Japan, and South Korea. Sources: *OECD national accounts database (www.oecd.org), Japan online database (xx), and the National Bureau of Statistics (various issues, 2006).*

China is at the bottom of the chart. China's consumption share over GDP has shown the tendency of decline as the country's economy takes off. This pattern is however not unusual in comparison with Japan and South Korea at the similar stages of development. Figure 4.3 shows that domestic consumption as a proportion of GDP in both Japan and South Korea has followed a V-shaped pattern over time, with the trough point being reached around 1970 in Japan and around 1988 in South Korea. China is currently at the bottom of the V curve. It can be anticipated that domestic consumption is to pick up and act as one of the main contributors to China's growth. Especially, there is great potential for expansion in rural consumption which has lagged far behind the economic growth and urban consumption over the past decade (Fig. 4.4). These changes will be driven by several factors.

First, China is in the process of developing a nationwide social security system which will boost government spending on pension payment, unemployment benefits, health care, and education. This is already happening. For example, social welfare expenditure (pension, special assistance, and unemployment benefits) as a proportion of government spending is raised from 11 percent in 2000 to

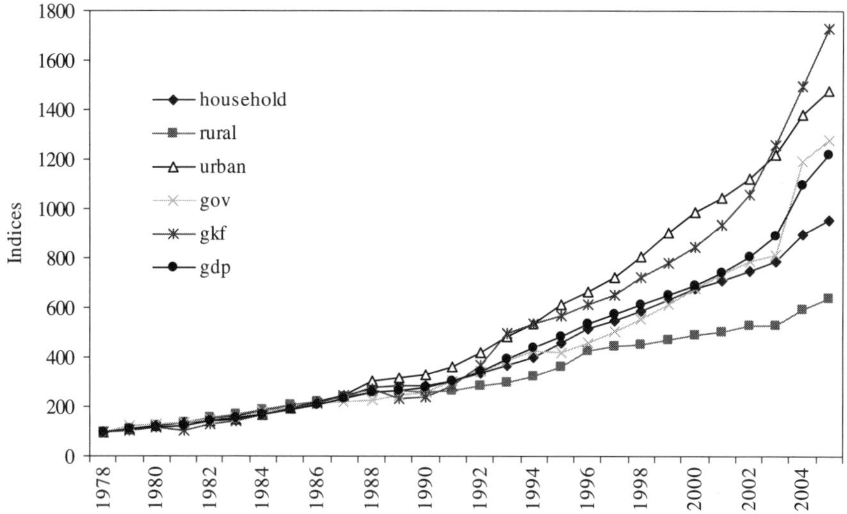

Fig. 4.4: Real indices of China's GDP and its components 1978–2005.
Source: *Author's own estimates.*

13 percent in 2005.[10] This figure amounting to about 2.5 percent of China's GDP in 2005 is however still very low in comparison with 5.0 percent in Mexico and 5.6 percent in South Korea in 2000, not to mention the OECD average of 20.5 percent in the same year.[11]

Second, recent policy shift to deal with *San Nong* issues (i.e., agriculture, countryside, and peasants) will trigger a new round of rural growth and hence lift the level of income in the rural areas. During the period of 1999–2003, the rate of growth in the agricultural sector hovered around 2.5–2.9 percent while the rest of the economy enjoyed a two-digit rate of growth per annum. This situation has changed under recent policy shift. As a result, the agricultural sector recorded rates of growth of 6.3 percent and 5.2 percent in 2004 and 2005, respectively (National Bureau of Statistics, 2006).

[10] The sources of the data are the National Bureau of Statistics (2001, 2006).

[11] The Chinese statistic is author's own estimate using data from the National Bureau of Statistics (2006). Others are drawn from the OECD online database (www.sourceoecd.org/factbook).

Table 4.2: Ownership of selected consumer goods in 2005.

Goods	Urban (per 100 households)	Rural
Air conditioner	80.7	6.4
Color TV	134.8	84.0
Fixed-line telephone	94.4	58.3
Home computer	41.5	2.1
Mobile phone	137.0	50.2
Refrigerator	90.7	20.1
Washing machine	95.5	40.2

Source: *National Bureau of Statistics (2006).*

As more tax incentives are offered to farmers, further growth in the agricultural sector is expected in the coming years. This growth will boost rural households' affordability and hence give rise to potential demand for consumer goods and other products, many of which are facing saturated markets in urban areas. Table 4.2 illustrates the huge difference in terms of rural and urban ownership of consumer goods. As income rises, rural consumers will certainly catch up with their urban counterparts. Thus, China's vast rural market is yet to be exploited by both domestic and international producers.

Third, some key markets such as the Chinese real estate and automotive markets are becoming more and more mature, and expanding rapidly. According to the National Bureau of Statistics (2006), the value of housing sales increased from 394 billion yuan in 2,000 to 1,808 billion yuan in 2005, and the number of private motor vehicles rose from 6 million to 19 million during the same period. These developments will continue and hence contribute to the growth in China's domestic consumption in the coming decade.

Services

Service is another area with huge growth potential. The latest statistics show that services amounted to just over 40 percent of China's GDP in 2005 (National Bureau of Statistics, 2006). This figure makes China

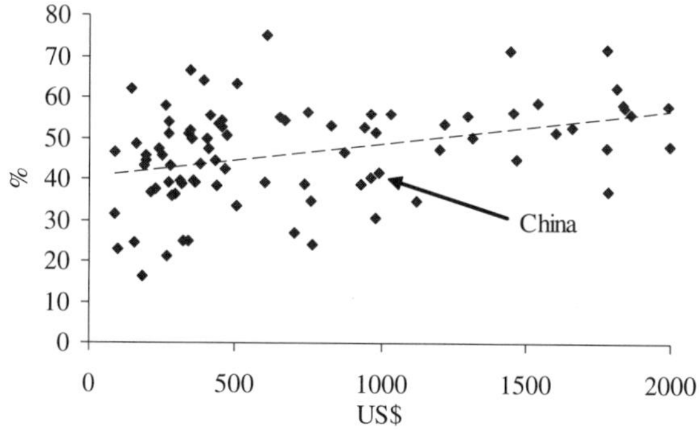

Fig. 4.5: Services as proportion of GDP in low income countries, 2003.
Source: *World Development Indicator 2005 online database (www.worldbank.org)*.

an outlier in comparison with countries at the similar stage of development, not to mention advanced economies in the world (Fig. 4.5). The latter normally have a service sector which generates more than 70 percent of a country's GDP. Accordingly, services also account for about 70 percent of total employment in OECD economies.

For example, in 2004, services amounted to 77 percent of GDP and 72 percent of total employment in the US, 68 percent of GDP and 66 percent of total employment in Japan, and 70 percent of GDP and 69 percent of total employment in Germany.[12] In China, the service sector had an employment share of 31 percent in 2005 (NBS, 2006). There is hence a gap between income (40 percent) and employment shares too. While China's manufacturing sector has attracted the world's headlines and been nicknamed as the world factory, the service sector still created twice (40 million) as many jobs as the manufacturing sector (19 million) during 2001–2005. Most new jobs in China will be created in the service sector.

Chinese policy makers are aware of the above-stated problems and have put in place specific policies promoting growth in services

[12] These numbers are either drawn or estimated using data from the OECD online database (www.sourceoecd.org/factbook) and the World Development Indicator 2006 database (World Bank, 2006).

Table 4.3: Selected statistics of services.

Categories	2000	2005	Average rate of growth (percent)
Number of tourists			
Domestic (million)	744	1212	10.3
International outbound (million)	10	31	25.4
International inbound (million)	83	120	7.7
Tourism revenue			
Domestic (billion yuan)	318	529	10.7
International (U.S.$ billion)	16	29	12.6
Banking revenue (billion yuan)	27,707	62,698	17.7
Security investment funds (billion yuan)	56	471	53.1
Insurance workforce (000)	167	367	17.1
Insurance premium (billion yuan)	160	493	25.2
Assets	61	128	16.0
Life	99	365	29.8
No. of students (million)			
Tertiary	56	156	22.7
High schools	737	858	3.1
Vocational	50	63	4.7
Government expenditure (billion yuan)	1,589	3,371	16.2

Source: *National Bureau of Statistics (2006)*.

and hence stimulating structural transformation in the economy. For example, the introduction of week-long holidays for the Chinese New Year, May Day, and National Day has greatly stimulated domestic tourism and hence tourism-related services. Table 4.3 shows that the growth in the number of domestic tourists has kept pace with economic growth over the past five years, though the fastest growing area is the number of international outbound tourists. The growth in revenues from both domestic and international tourists has exceeded the rate of economic growth according to Table 4.3.

Other areas with potential growth include government services, banking, and finance. In particular, banking and financial services are the new areas with considerable growth potential. This is confirmed by the statistics presented in Table 4.3 which shows rapid

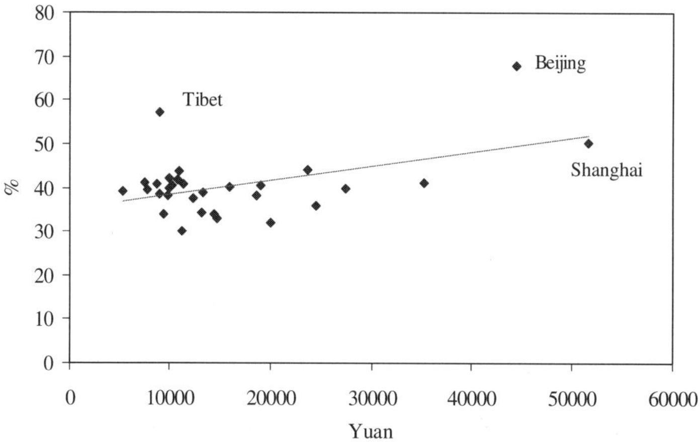

Fig. 4.6: Service sector shares and per capita GDP among Chinese regions, 2005. Source: *National Bureau of Statistics (2006)*.

expansion in banking, insurance, and investment funds. In terms of education services, tertiary education has no doubt been the fastest growth sector over the past five years according to Table 4.3.

Growth in services is not only policy driven but also determined by the process of economic development. Most developed economies have gone through the path of industrialization with manufacturing development taking off first then followed by service growth. China is no exception. As income grows, the service sector as a share of China's GDP has increased from 24 percent in 1978 to 40 percent in 2005 (National Bureau of Statistics, 2006). This positive relationship between income and service development is also observed at the regional level in China (Fig. 4.6).

Innovation and Technological Progress

While empirical studies show that productivity has made a positive contribution to economic growth in China, there is still scope for further growth in productivity through innovation and efficiency improvement. The latter will come from further relocation of rural surplus labor to the urban sector, spillover effects from foreign

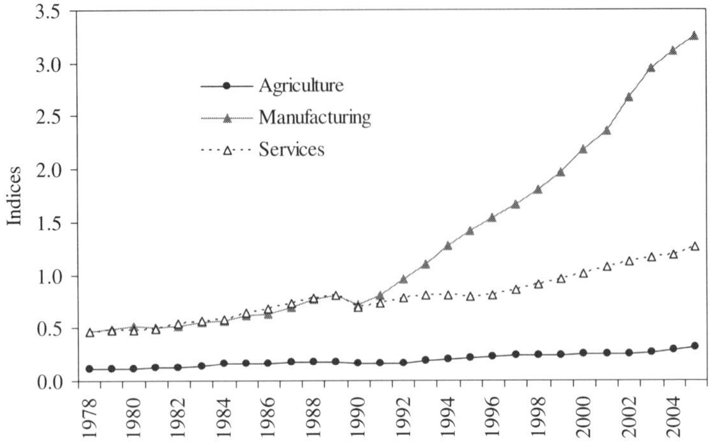

Fig. 4.7: Labor productivity indices, 1978–2005.
Source: *Derived using data from the National Bureau of Statistics (2006).*

investment, and export sectors and privatization of the still sizable state-owned enterprise sector.

First, while several hundreds of million of rural workers have migrated to the cities, there are still over 300 million rural workers who accounted for 45 percent of China's workforce in 2005 (National Bureau of Statistics, 2006). Empirical evidence shows that productivity gap between farming and non-farming is widening as shown in Fig. 4.7. Thus, rural employment share is expected to decline further as the Chinese economy advances. Even if this share falls by only a half, it implies that there are at least 150 million to be relocated. There will be efficiency gains from further relocation of workers from farming to manufacturing and services due to variation in productivity across the sectors.

Second, empirical evidence demonstrates that the spillover effect of foreign direct investment is generally positive in China (Ho, 2007). As China complies with WTO rules and the Chinese economy becomes more open, more foreign investment will flow to China and be invested in various sectors. In addition, due to improved protection of intellectual property rights over time, the quality of foreign investment should also improve. At present, foreign investment is more active in the labor-intensive manufacturing sector. Over time, more capital will likely flow to capital- and skill-intensive sectors. A good example is the increasing interest by foreign banks in investing in the Chinese banking sector since 2005. These developments will bring about more positive spillover effects into the Chinese economy.

Third, relocation of resources would also likely occur due to the expansion of the private sector. In general, private enterprises with lower operating cost per unit of profit are more labor-intensive than the state-owned enterprises (SOEs) according to Table 4.4. The private sector in China has expanded substantially, but its growth is limited because of poor resource access such as lack of access to bank credits. Under the recent policy shift, the private sector will have more access to bank loans including foreign exchange reserves. There will be efficiency gains due to resource flow from the state sector to the private sector. In addition, efficiency gains will also be possible due to resource-saving. During the second wave of growth in the last 27 years, China basically followed a resource-intensive model. It is common knowledge that China has abundant

Table 4.4: Selected performance indicators in 2004.

Categories	*K/L*	Cost/profit	Export/output
State-owned enterprises	27.8	23.17	3.7
Collectively owned enterprises	12.8	16.33	6.9
State joint-ventures	32.6	16.63	8.3
Collective joint-ventures	11.3	14.11	3.3
State-collective joint-ventures	16.9	44.20	8.8
Other joint-ventures	15.5	17.10	8.2
Private enterprises	12.1	17.18	10.0
Private solely owned enterprises	8.2	10.87	5.7
HMT-funded enterprises	16.1	17.83	43.6
Chinese-foreign joint-ventures	24.7	12.87	29.5
Foreign-funded	18.1	19.95	62.3

Notes: *K/L*, cost/profit and export/output represent the ratios of the value of assets over labor compensation, operating cost over profit, and export value over gross output value. HMT is the abbreviation of Hong Kong, Macau, and Taiwan.
Source: *China Economic Census Yearbook 2004* (*Economic Census Office, 2006*).

relatively cheap labor and hence enjoys comparative advantage in labor-intensive production. In the meantime, China's consumption of main commodities per unit of GDP is relatively high as discussed in the preceding section. A high intensity of use not only implies waste and inefficiency in the economy but also leads to pressure on resource supply both domestically and internationally. For example, by 2030, China's primary energy use is projected to be 6.4 btoe (billion tons oil-equivalent), i.e., about 30 percent of global energy use, which will generate about 5.8 billion tones of carbon (Sheehan and Sun, 2006). Such outcomes, if they come to be true, will have major impacts on the world energy markets and the global climate.

Finally, productivity growth will also stem from innovation which helps lift China's production frontier and which is vital for sustained growth in the long run. While efficiency improvement can be short-lived and limited in scope, innovation is long lasting and unlimited. The sources of innovation will in turn be due to increased R&D activities and competition associated with globalization. For example, during the decade of 1996–2005, China's government spending on R&D activities and education and health sciences maintained an average annual rate of growth of 9.3 percent and 12.7 percent, respectively.

Balanced Development

Since 1978, when economic reform was initiated, China basically adopted an unbalanced development model following the doctrine of Deng Xiaoping's "letting some get riches first." Under this strategy, coastal regions and urban areas have forged ahead of the rest of the country. This unbalanced development strategy has serious consequences, i.e., the enlarging inequality in the Chinese society. The preceding section presented evidence of widening gap between rural and urban households (Fig. 4.1). Inequality within the urban and rural areas, in particular within urban households, has also deteriorated in recent years, though the gap between the rich and the poor is larger in rural areas than in urban areas according to Table 4.5. The consensus among policy makers as well as the general public is

Table 4.5: Household income by groups, 2000 and 2005.

Year	Income groups					
	Low	Lower-middle	Middle	Upper-middle	High	Ratio of high over low
Rural households						
2000	802	1,440	2,004	2,767	5,190	6.47
2005	1,067	2,018	2,851	4,003	7,747	7.26
Urban households						
2000	3,132	4,624	5,898	7,487	11,299	3.61
2005	4,017	6,711	9,190	12,603	22,902	5.70

Notes: The numbers refer to disposable income per capita in urban households and net income per capita in rural households. The unit is yuan.
Source: *National Bureau of Statistics (2006)*.

that economic development should be more even. The responses have been the development of the western regions commenced in 1999, the revitalization program of the northeast regions (China's old industrial areas), and the campaigns of *San Nong* issues and for the rise of the central regions (the six inland provinces).[13]

As a result, investment shares of the noncoastal regions increased in recent years. There was also a substantial increase in government spending in the western regions after the launch of the western development program in 1999 according to Table 4.6. In addition, development of the noncoastal regions can benefit from the experience of coastal development in the past decades. For example, the western regions have exploited their advantages by promoting tourism, while more strict environmental protection measures are maintained. Thus, from the very beginning, developers and policy makers in the noncoastal regions are more conscious of environmental issues and sustainable development. This shift in development

[13] "Western regions" are defined in footnote 5. "Northeast China" refers to Liaoning, Jilin, and Heilongjiang. "San Nong" means agriculture, rural areas, and peasants. The middle six provinces include Anhui, Henan, Hubei, Hunan, Jiangxi, and Shanxi.

Table 4.6: Regional shares (percent), 1999 and 2005.

Regions	Total investment		Government spending		Population		GDP	
	1999	2005	1999	2005	1999	2005	1999	2005
Middle 6	17.1	18.7	18.8	18.7	28.6	27.4	20.7	18.8
Western 12	18.7	20.3	25.3	24.9	28.9	28.0	17.5	17.0
Northeast 3	8.2	8.9	11.3	10.4	8.6	8.4	10.0	8.7
Rest of China	56.0	52.1	44.6	46.0	34.0	36.1	51.8	55.5

Notes: The numbers are derived using data from NBS (2000, 2006). The regions refer to six middle regions, 12 western regions, and three northeast regions as defined in footnote 13. The "rest of China" mainly includes the coastal regions.

strategy will not only boost economic growth in these regions but also contributes to the sustainability of economy-wide growth. In addition, China is in the process of developing a nation-wide social security system to look after the disadvantaged groups in the society. This will help in reducing inequality.

CONCLUDING REMARKS

Since the communist government took office in 1949, the Chinese economy has gone through three waves of changes. The first two cover the pre-1978 and post-1978 periods. China is now at the turning point toward the third wave of changes under the new leadership of Hu Jintao and Wen Jiabao. This round of economic growth is characterized with some distinct features representing the new sources of growth including domestic consumption, the service sector, innovation, and balanced development.

China's development pattern is similar to that followed by South Korea and Japan. The latter replied on capital accumulation and exports to boost economic growth at the early stage of development. Over time, domestic consumption has replaced capital accumulation and exports to become the leading contributor to economic growth in both South Korea and Japan. After continuous high growth of almost 30 years, China's domestic market is growing rapidly and will gradually overtake exports and investment to become the main driver of economic growth in the coming decades. This trend of change is also assisted by government policies encouraging ownership of private housing and cars and deregulating the education and health care systems. Associated with this consumption expansion will be accelerated urbanization and growth in the service sector.

The role of innovation is also expected to expand due to increased investment in R&D, education, and information technology, and because of the spillover effects from foreign direct investment and trade after China's WTO accession in 2001. During the third wave of growth, China's development will be more balanced. This will be driven by the development of the western, central, and northeast regions as well as the latest round of reforms in rural China. The eventual development of a nation-wide social security system will also help reduce imbalances in the Chinese society.

REFERENCES

Borensztein, Eduardo and Jonathan D. Ostry (1996), "Accounting for China's Growth Performance," *American Economic Review (Papers and Proceedings)* 86, 225–228.

Bosworth, Barry and Susan M. Collins (2003), "The Empirics of Growth: An Update," unpublished, Brookings Institution, Washington, DC.

Bramall, C. (2000), *Sources of Chinese Economic Growth, 1978–1996*, Oxford and New York: Oxford University Press.

Chow, G.C. (2002), *China's Economic Transformation*, Malden, MA: Blackwell Publishers.

Economic Census Office (2006), *China Economic Census Yearbook 2004*, Beijing: China Statistics Press.

Feuchtwang, S., A. Hussain and T. Pairault (eds.) (1988), *Transforming China's Economy in the Eighties*, Vols. 1 and 2, Boulder, CO: Westview Press.

Fouquin, M. and F. Lemoine (eds.) (1998), *The Chinese Economy*, Paris: Economica Ltd.

Garnaut, R., Ligang Song, Stoyan Tenev and Yang Yao (2005), *China's Ownership Transformation: Process, Outcomes and Prospects,* International Finance Corporation, World Bank.

Garnaut, Ross and Ligang Song (2006), "Rapid Industrialization and Market for Energy and Minerals: China in East Asian Context," Paper presented at the

ACESA2006 Conference on Emerging China: International Challenges and Global Implications, Victoria University, Melbourne.

Ho, Owen (2007), Foreign Direct Investment and Its Impacts in China, PhD dissertation, University of Western Australia.

Hu, Z.F. and Mohsin S. Khan (1997), "Why Is China Growing So Fast?," *IMF Staff Papers* 44, 103–131.

IMF (2005), "World Economic Outlook April 2005 Database," International Monetary Fund (http://www.imf.org/external/pubs/ft/weo/2005/01/index.htm).

International Iron and Steel Institute (2006), "World Steel in Figures 2006," online document (http://www.worldsteel.org).

Kim, J.I. and L. Lau (1994), "The Sources of Economic Growth in the East Asian Newly Industrialised Countries," *Journal of the Japanese and International Economies* 8, 235–271.

Knight, John, Shi Li and Renwei Zhao (2004), "Divergent Means and Convergent Inequality of Incomes among the Provinces and Cities of Urban China," *Research Paper No. 2004/52*, WIDER (World Institute for Development Economics Research), United Nations University.

Kornai, Janos (1980), *Economics of Shortage*, Amsterdam and New York: North-Holland Pub. Co.

Krugman, P. (1994), "The Myth of Asia's Miracle," *Foreign Affairs* 73(6), 62–78.

Lin, J. Yifu and Yongjun Li (2003), "Export and China's Economic Growth: A Demand-Oriented Analysis," *China Economic Quarterly* 4(2), 779–794.

Lin, J.Y. and Z. Liu (2000), "Fiscal Decentralization and Economic Growth in China," *Economic Development and Cultural Change* 49(1), 1–21.

Lin, J.Y., F. Cai and Z. Li (1996), *The China Miracle: Development Strategy and Economic Reform*, Hong Kong: The Chinese University Press.

Maddison, A. (1998), *Chinese Economic Performance in the Long Run*, Paris: OECD Development Centre.

National Bureau of Statistics (2005), *China Statistical Yearbook 2005*, Beijing: China Statistics Press.

National Bureau of Statistics (2006), *China Statistical Abstract 2006*, Beijing: China Statistics Press.

National Bureau of Statistics (various issues), *China Statistical Yearbook*, Beijing: China Statistics Press.

Perkins, D. (1988), "Reforming China's Economic System," *Journal of Economic Literature* 26(2), 601–645.

Reynolds, Bruce L. (ed.) (1987), *Reform in China: Challenges and Choices*, New York: M.E. Sharpe.

Sheehan, Peter and Fiona Sun (2006), "Energy Use and CO_2 Emissions in China: Retrospect and Prospect," Paper presented at the *ACESA2006 Conference on Emerging China: International Challenges and Global Implications*, Victoria University, Melbourne.

Swamy, S. (2003), *Economic Reforms and Performance: China and India in Comparative Perspective*, New Delhi: Konark Publishers Pvt Ltd.

The Economist (2005), "Leaders: Meeting the Superpower; China and the West," *Economist* 377(8453), 12.

UNCTAD (2005), "China in a Globalizing World," *United Nations Conference on Trade and Development*, United Nations, New York and Geneva.

Wang, George C. (ed.) (1982), *Economic Reform in the PRC*, Boulder, CO: Westview Press.

Wang, Y. and Y.D. Yao (2003), "Sources of China's Economic Growth 1952-1999: Incorporating Human Capital Accumulation," *China Economic Review* 14(1), 32–52.

Wong, Chee Kong (2006), ICT, Productivity and Economic Growth in China, PhD dissertation, University of Western Australia.

Woo, W.T. (1998), "Chinese Economic Growth: Sources and Prospects," in *The Chinese Economy*, eds. M. Fouquin and F. Lemoine, Paris: Economica Ltd.

World Bank (1990), *China: Plan and Market*, a World Bank country study, Washington, DC: World Bank.

World Bank (1997), *China 2020: Development Challenges in the New Century*, Washington, DC: World Bank.

World Bank (2005), "World Development Indicator 2005 Database," World Bank, Washington, DC (www.worldbank.org).

World Bank (2006), "World Development Indicator 2006 Database," World Bank, Washington, DC (www.worldbank.org).

Wu, Jinglian and Renwei Zhao (1987), "The Dual Pricing System in China's Industry," *Journal of Comparative Economics* 11, 309–318.

Wu, Yanrui (2004), *China's Economic Growth: A Miracle with Chinese Characteristics*, London: Routledge Curzon.

Wu, Yanrui (2006), "Why Does the Dragon Fly While the Elephant Walks? Comparing Economic Growth in China and India," EAI Background Brief No. 276, National University of Singapore.

Young, A. (1994), "Lessons from the East Asian NICs: A Contrarian View," *European Economic Review* 110, 641–680.

Young, A. (2003), "Gold into Base Metals: Productivity Growth in the Peoples Republic of China during the Reform Period," *Journal of Political Economy* 111(6), 1220–1261.

Zhang, Xiaoguang (1999), "Foreign Investment Policy, Contribution and Performance," in *Foreign Direct Investment and Economic Growth in China*, eds. Yanrui Wu, Cheltenham, England, and, Northampton, USA: Edward Elgar Publishing.

Chapter

5

Limited Catch-up and China's Economic Growth[1]

Yang Rudai and Yang Yao

China Center for Economic Research, Peking University, Beijing, PRC

INTRODUCTION

With a bourgeoning foreign reserve that is soon to reach a trillion US dollars, it becomes a hotly debated issue whether China is exporting too much. It is widely believed that China heavily relies on labor-intensive exports and this strategy is not sustainable. However, most studies fail to assess China's export strategy from an international perspective. The world trade pattern has generally followed the rule of comparative advantage with poorer countries exporting labor-intensive products and richer countries exporting capital-intensive products. Does China fit into this international division of labor, or has it overtaken it? The purpose of this chapter is to

[1] We thank Robert Feenstra for providing us with part of the data. Huiwen Li, Kai Guo, and participants of the East Asian Institute–School of Economics, Peking University Conference on Chinese Economy provided useful comments. Shi'e Zhu provided excellent support in data analysis.

provide an answer to this question and link a country's trade strategy with its record of economic growth.

We propose the concept of "limited catch-up" to describe the trade strategy by which a country exports products that have higher technological contents than what the comparative advantage-based international division of labor allows it to. The limited catch-up strategy, or the LC strategy subsequently, is different from the catch-up strategy defined by Lin *et al.* (1994) in that it advocates a catch-up relative to a country's position in international division of labor, not an absolute catch-up that aims at catching up with the most advanced technology in the world. When it is compared with the world technological leaders, a country with the LC strategy is still located at a lower position in the world technological ladder. However, the LC strategy is also different from the comparative advantage strategy (subsequently, the CA strategy) defined by Lin *et al.* (1994) in that it indeed advocates a catch-up relative to a country's position in international division of labor.

We define an index to measure limited catch-up and call it the limited catch-up index (LCI). The definition is based on a method developed by Hausmann *et al.* (2005) to measure the technological contents of a country's exports. The key element of Hausmann *et al.* (2005)'s method is what we call the technological sophistication index (TSI) for each exported product. It is the average per-capita GDP of countries that export the product, weighted by each country's relative weight of the product in world trade. Then, the technological content index (TCI) of a country's exports is defined as the weighted average of the TSIs of the country's exported products. Using the COMTRADE data, we have calculated the TCIs for 112 countries in the period of 1965–2005. Then, for each year, we estimate a linear function between the logarithm of TCI and the logarithm of per-capita GDP. This linear function defines a match between each value of per-capita GDP and a value of TCI. Naturally, a country with a lower per-capita GDP tends to have a lower TCI, so the function defines what we call the comparative advantage-based international division of labor. Then, the LCI is defined as the gap between a country's actual TCI and the value projected by the linear function based on its per-capita GDP. A positive LCI implies that a country's exports have higher technological contents than that is allowed by the international division of labor, so this country has limited catch-up. On the other hand, a negative LCI implies that a country falls behind the international division of labor.

Theoretically, the LC strategy can bring faster economic growth than the pure CA strategy. By the CA strategy, a country should improve the productivity of the products that it has comparative advantage on. However, this strategy will not expand the scope of a country's exports. In the case of a developing country, such a strategy will reinforce its position at the lower end of the technological ladder. On the contrary, the LC strategy requires that a country improve its productivity beyond the products that it currently has comparative advantage. As a result, its competitiveness edge moves outward toward the higher end of the technological ladder so that it can export more products with higher technological contents.

Our descriptive and econometric studies have confirmed the theoretical prediction. We divide the period 1965–2005 into eight five-year sub-periods and four ten-year sub-periods and use the LCI of the beginning year of each sub-period to predict the average growth rate of per-capita GDP in that sub-period. Our econometric analysis shows that following the LC strategy significantly increases a country's average growth of the next five and ten years by a significant margin. In addition, this positive effect exhibits an inverse U curve, which means that there exists an optimal level of catch-up. We have also found that China has not followed its comparative advantage defined by the international division of labor, but instead has followed the LC strategy. Our detailed analysis further shows that China has fast upgraded its exports in the last 20 years.

The rest of the chapter is arranged as follows. The second section uses a simple theoretical model to link the LC strategy with economic growth. Third section defines the LCI. The fourth section provides econometric results. Fifth section presents data on China's technological upgrading in its exports in the last 20 years. Sixth section concludes the chapter.

A SIMPLE MODEL OF LIMITED CATCH-UP

Our simple theoretical model is adapted from Krugman (1990). The key idea of the model is as follows. Countries compete with each other in exporting the same set of products. The competition is based on the real wage that a country has to pay in producing a specific product, which is defined as the wage rate weighted by the labor productivity. If a country has the lowest relative cost, then this country produces and exports the product, and all the other countries do not produce it. Low-income countries have the advantage to have lower labor cost, but high-income countries have the advantage to have higher labor productivity. It is usually the case that higher labor productivity is corresponding to higher technological contents. Therefore, there will emerge an international division of labor by which low-income countries produce and export products with low technological contents and high-income countries produce and export products with high technological contents. In the following analysis, we restrict our attention to the case of two countries.

We start with assuming that the only factor needed to produce a product is labor and the technology exhibits constant return to scale. This second assumption ensures that there is only one producer for each product. There is a continuum of products ordered by their technological contents from the lowest to the highest. Let z be the index of the products as well as their technological contents. A larger z represents a product with a higher level of technological contents. There are two countries competing to produce the products. One of them is the technological leader, and the other is the technological follower. Let $a_L(z)$ represent the leader's labor productivity in producing the product z, and $a_F(z)$ represent that of the follower. We follow Krugman (1990) to assume that both a_L and a_F increase in z, but a_L is higher than a_F for any z, that is, the follower has lower labor productivity than the leader in producing every product. Figure 5.1 shows this assumption. The figure also present the wage rates of the leader and the follower, w_L and w_F. It is natural to assume that w_L is higher than w_F.

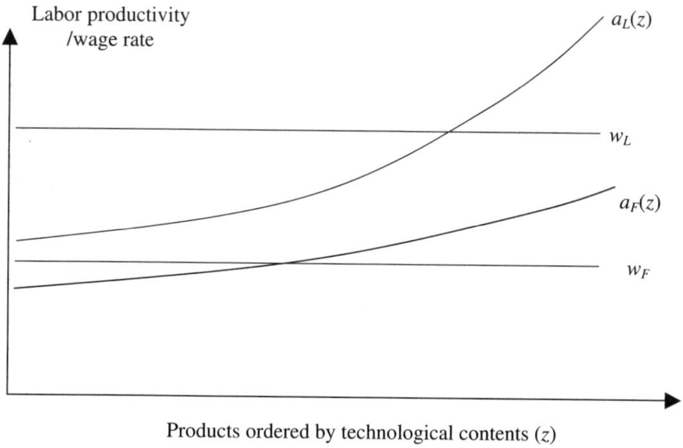

Fig. 5.1: Labor productivity and wage rates in the two countries.

The competition between the two countries is centered at the two countries' real wage rates, which are defined as $w_L^*(z) = w_L/a_L(z)$ and $w_F^*(z) = w_F/a_F(z)$, respectively. If a country can produce a product with lower real wage than the other country, then it can drive out the other country out of the market by lowering the price of the product. Because of our assumption about the labor productivity and wage rates, the real wage rates in both countries decline as z increases, but the leader's decline faster than the follower's. This leads to a single cross, z^*, between the two wage rate schedules, as shown in Fig. 5.2. Thus, for products with $z < z^*$, $w_F^*(z) < w_L^*(z)$, so the follower has an advantage to produce them; for products with $z > z^*$, $w_F^*(z) > w_L^*(z)$, so the leader has an advantage to produce them.

Now suppose that the follower wants to improve its labor productivity. Should it make improvements on the products that it has comparative advantage over and is currently producing, i.e., the products with an index less than z^*, or do that on the products beyond z^*? If improvements are made to products below z^*, the competitiveness and profitability of these products are enhanced. However, since the competitiveness of the products beyond z^* has not been improved, the country cannot expand its range of exports.

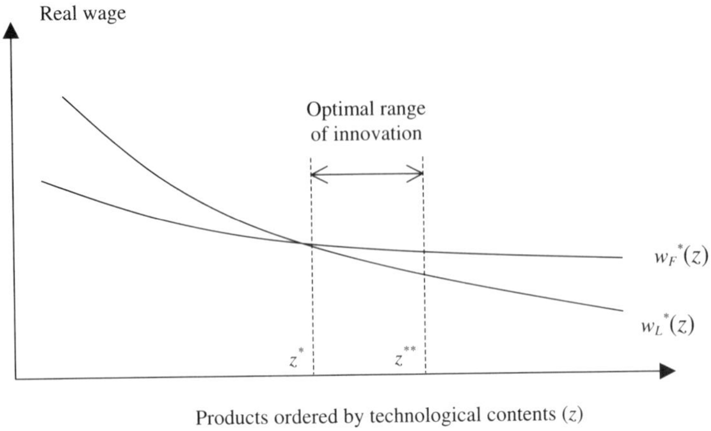

Fig. 5.2: Real wage rates and the division of labor.

Moreover, if the leader keeps innovating new products, sticking to its comparative advantage will enlarge the follower's technological gap with the leader. In the long run, economic growth depends on the expansion of the range of products. Therefore, improving the productivity of products above z^* will help more with a country's growth than improving the productivity of products below z^*.

However, the cost of innovation was not considered in the above analysis. It is conceivable that the cost of innovation increases with the sophistication of products. Therefore, a country faces the trade-off between producing a wider range of products and higher marginal costs of innovation when it improves the labor productivity of products beyond z^*. This trade-off leads to an optimal cutoff point for innovation, denoted by z^{**} in Fig. 5.2, at which the marginal revenue of producing a new product is equal to the marginal cost of it. The interval $(z^*, z^{**}]$ thus is the optimal range of innovation. It is natural to predict that a country grows the fastest in the long run when it produces and exports products up to z^{**}. When its range of production is below or above z^{**}, the country grows slower.

Therefore, limited catch-up means that a country expands its production, and thus exports, beyond z^* and up to z^{**}. It is a catch-up because it defies the international division of labor defined by comparative advantage (which allows a country to produce and export up to z^*); it is "limited" because the catch-up has a limit, i.e., it is not profitable for the country to produce and export beyond z^{**} given its comparative advantage defined by z^*. This implies that there is an inverse-U relationship between limited catch-up and economic growth: between z^* and z^{**}, expanding the scope of exports leads to higher growth rates; beyond z^{**}, expanding the scope of exports leads to lower growth rates.

THE LIMITED CATCH-UP INDEX

First, in this section, we will implement an empirical test of the LC strategy. The key to the implementation is to empirically identify the international division of labor and to measure limited catch-up. This section will take up these two tasks. Our strategy to identify the international division of labor is similar to that of the revealed comparative advantage. Unlike what we have assumed in the simple theoretical model, in reality each country exports a wide range of products instead of those below a certain level of technological contents (i.e., z^* in the model). Therefore it is a question how we assess whether a country is following its comparative advantage. We deal with this issue by adopting the method developed by Hausmann *et al.* (2005) to obtain a compounded index, i.e., the TCI, of the technological contents of a country's exports. Then we regress TCI on per-capita income to obtain the world average export pattern, which defines the international division of labor. Having a higher TCI than what is predicted on the regression line implies that a country adopts the LC strategy. Below, we first introduce the data that we are going to use.

Data

We obtain trade data for 112 countries/regions in the period 1965–2005 from two sources. One is the World Trade Flow (WTF) compiled by Robert Feenstra that provides us data for the period 1965–2000. The other is the COMTRADEE maintained by the United Nations that provides us data for the period 2001–2005. Appendix 1 lists the names of these countries/regions. WTF uses SITC four-digit product classification system and has about 1200 products. It gives primacy to the trade flows reported by the importing country, assuming that these are more accurate than reports by the exporters (Feenstra *et al.* 2005). If the importer report is not available for a country-pair, then the corresponding exporter report is used. From 1984 to 2000, WTF excludes trade flows at four-digit SITC classification when they are less than US $1000.

COMTRADEE uses the HS six-digit system and has more than 5000 products. It relies on the reports by the exporting countries. In our sample countries, there were countries that failed to report their trade data in certain years. Some countries had a lag of several years in reporting their data. Therefore, data missing is more severe in more recent years. But the total trade volume in the resulted sample accounts for about 80 percent of the actual world total in each year. We do not convert the two systems into one because our main purpose is to get the compounded TCI at the country level; using the two systems for different years will not affect our results in significant ways.

GDP figures are in PPP US dollars complied by PWT 6.1. We have obtained data from three sources. For 1965–2000, we get data from PWT 6.1. Detailed description of the data can be found in Heston *et al.* (2002). For 2001–2005, we get data for most countries from the data source compiled by the Groningen Growth and Development Centre (GGDC). We use the GGDC figures primarily because GGDC uses PPP converters similar to those used by PWT 6.1. In the cases where GGDC does not provide data, we use the figures published in the UNDP *Human Development Report*.[2]

[2] GDP figures of the following countries/regions in 2001–2003 come from the HDR: Barbados, Benin, Bolivia, Burkina Faso, Burundi, Cameroon, Central African Republic, Costa Rica, Dominica, El Salvador, Fiji, Gabon, Gambia, Guinea, Guyana, Honduras, Jamaica, Madagascar, Malawi, Mali, Mauritius, Mozambique, Nepal, Nicaragua, Niger, Panama, Papua New Guinea, Paraguay, Rwanda, Senegal, Seychelles, Togo, Trinidad and Tobago, Tunisia, Uganda, Tanzania, Uruguay, Zambia, and Zimbabwe. The HDR has not published data after 2004. We extrapolate the GDP figures of the above countries for 2004 and 2005 by assuming that they grew by their respective average growth rates of 2001–2003.

Construction of the LCI

We start with constructing the TSI for each four-digit product. Our method is directly adopted from Hausmann *et al.* (2005). To start, we use subscript j to index countries and l to index products, and superscript t to denote years. Then, let Y_j^t stand for the per-capita GDP of country j in year t, and x_{jl}^t stand for the export value of product l in country j in year t. The total export value of country j in year t is $X_j^t = \sum_l x_{jl}^t$. Then, the TSI of product l in year t is defined as

$$\mathrm{TSI}_l^t = \sum_j \frac{x_{jl}^t / X_j^t}{\sum_j x_{jl}^t / X_j^t} Y_j^t. \tag{1}$$

The reason that the share, rather than the absolute value, of a particular product is used as the weight is to avoid the dominance of large countries. Higher income countries tend to have higher labor productivity, so by our theoretical model they tend to produce products with more technological contents. The construction of the TSI uses an approach similar to that used by the revealed comparative advantage: a product has a higher TSI if it is exported more by high-income countries.

The TCI of country j's exports is then defined as the weighted average of the TCIs of its exported products:

$$\mathrm{TCI}_l^t = \sum_l \frac{x_{jl}^t}{X_j^t} \mathrm{TSI}_l^t. \tag{2}$$

This definition facilitates our treatment of the relationship between TCI and per-capita GDP as a way to represent the international division of labor. TCI of a country is a weighted average of the per-capita GDP of all the countries in the world. Indeed, for any year, we have $\sum_j \mathrm{TCI}_j^t = \sum_j Y_j^t$, that is, the TCI and per-capita GDP have the same mean. It is well understood that only a weak form of comparative advantage exists when the number of products exceeds two (Dixit and Norman 1980). It is thus a question as to how we represent comparative advantage in international trade. In the framework of our theoretical model, high-income countries tend to produce and export products with more technological contents. A corollary is that the international division of labor should require that a country's TCI depend positively on its per-capita GDP. One scenario is that the TCI is equal to per-capita GDP for each country in each year. In reality, though, a positive correlation between the two variables suffices to show comparative advantage at working.

We still adopt the "revealed" approach to use the existing trade pattern of a particular year to represent the working of comparative advantage. For that, we run a linear regression of the logarithm of TCI on the logarithm of per-capita GDP for each year and treat the fitted line as the representation of the international division of labor defined by comparative advantage in each year. Figure 5.3 shows the data and the regression lines for 1980 and 2003. The goodness of fit is almost perfect for both years (and actually for all the years).

Let $(\ln \mathrm{TCI}_{jt})^f$ be the fitted value of $\ln \mathrm{TCI}_{jt}$ on the regression line. Then we define the LCI of country j in year t as

$$\mathrm{LCI}_{jt} = \ln \mathrm{TCI}_{jt} - (\ln \mathrm{TCI}_{jt})f. \tag{3}$$

When the index is positive, a country is exporting goods that have higher technological contents than what are implied by its per-capita GDP in line with comparative advantage; when the index is negative, the reverse is true. Since it is defined in logarithm terms, the TCI provides an intuitive interpretation to a deviation from the comparative advantage. If the TCI is 0.1 for a country in a specific year, then we can say that this country is catching up by a pace of 10 percent over its comparative advantage. Our theoretical prediction is that a country's growth rate depends on its LCI in an inverse-U relationship. This makes our approach to catch-up different from Hausmann *et al.* (2005)'s approach. Hausmann *et al.* use the absolute value of TCI to predict a country's growth rate, so the catch-up in their study is the absolute catch-up in our framework. However, as our theoretical model has shown, catch-up beyond a

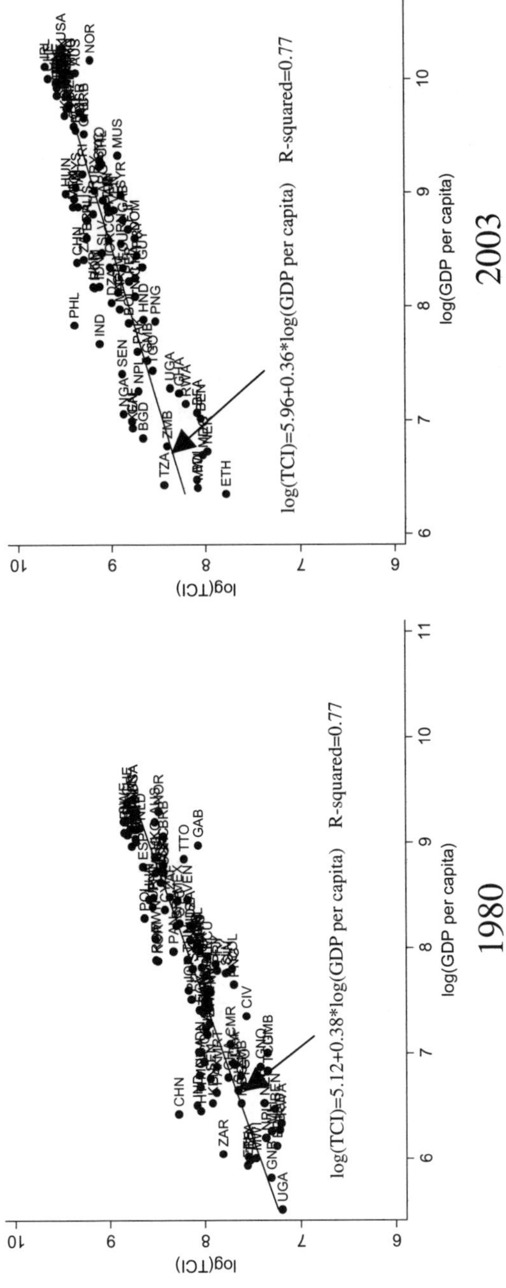

Fig. 5.3: International division of labor: 1980 and 2003.

certain level is detrimental rather than helpful to growth. So our approach is more sensible than theirs.[3]

Some descriptive evidence

Our aim is to study the relationship between the LC strategy and economic growth. To establish a positive relationship between the two, we ought to show that countries with higher TCIs grow faster than countries with lower TCIs. Here we compare several countries/regions in terms of TCIs. Figure 5.4 shows the trends of TCIs in several economies in the period 1965–2005. The figure on the left is for South Korea and Taiwan, and the figure on the right is for the US, UK, and France. It is evident that the world technological leader should have a TCI of zero because by definition it does not need to catch up with anyone, nor does it fall behind anyone. Another interpretation is that the technological leader strictly follows its comparative advantage. Interpreting in this way, we find that there was a clear trend of convergence in the case of South Korea and Taiwan. Both economies started with very high LCIs but have followed a declining trend in the last 40 years. By 2005, South Korea approached zero, which means that it was close to its position of comparative advantage. USA started in 1960 with a TCI equaling to zero, but has since followed a downward trend. This shows that the US is falling behind in technological innovations relative to its income. The UK and France started with small positive TCIs but gradually fell down, and began to have negative TCIs in the recent years.

Figure 5.5 further compares the TCIs of three countries, China, India, and Argentina in the period 1985–2005. Argentina maintained

[3] In their regression analysis, Hausmman *et al.* (2005) add per-capita income as a control variable, so our approach is the same as theirs if we only run a linear regression. However, our theoretical model predicts that the relationship between GDP growth rate and our LCI follows an inverse-U curve. This means that we need to consider nonlinearity in our regression. Then our approach differs from that of Hausmman *et al.* (2005).

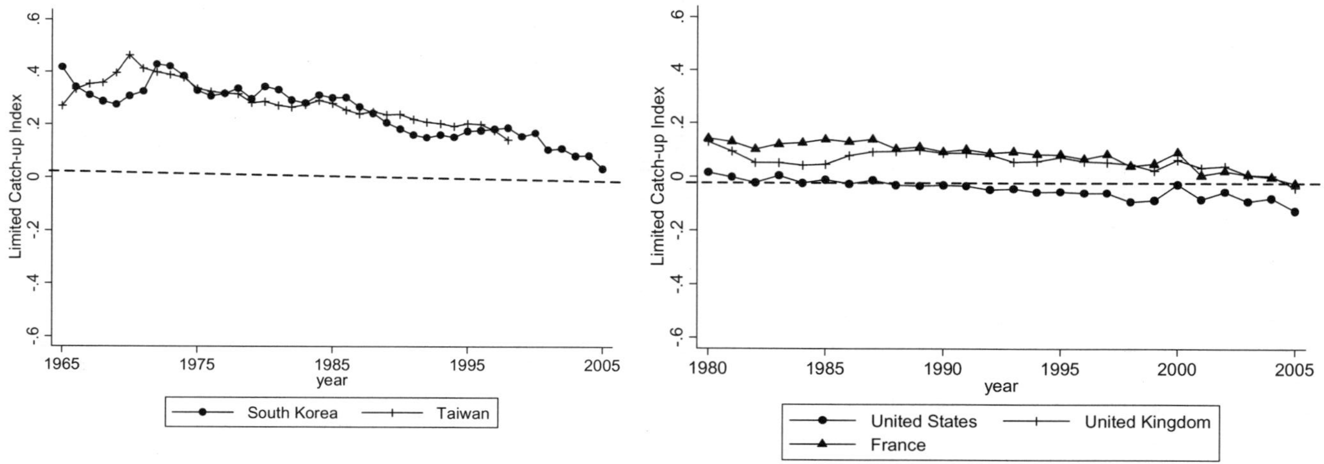

Fig. 5.4: TCIs of several advanced economies.

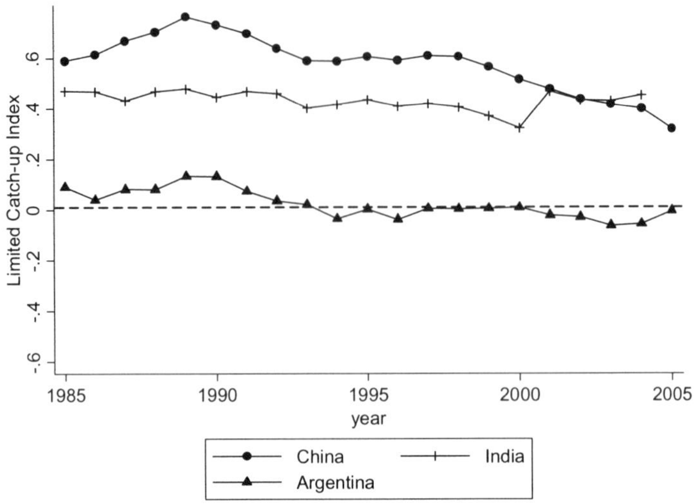

Fig. 5.5: TCIs of China, India, and Argentina.

positive but small TCIs before 1992, but has since fallen below zero. China has maintained very high TCIs. It was 0.5 in 1985, and increased in the late 1980s. However, China's TCI has been decreasing since 1990 although it was still higher than 0.3 in 2005. Before 2001, India had had smaller TCIs than China, but began to overtake China in 2004. While Argentina had converged to its comparative advantage in the early 1990s, China still has a long way to do that despite that its speed of convergence is high. Comparing Figs. 5.4 and 5.5, we find that China's TCI in 2005 was the same as that of South Korea and Taiwan around 1985. Therefore, China will have 20 some years before it converges to its comparative advantage. To the extent that catch-up leads to higher economic growth rates, we expect that China's high growth will last for another 20 years.

Porter (1990) distinguishes three stages for a country's development in terms of its competitiveness. The first stage is the investment stage. In this stage, a country does not need to engage in innovations, but can simply adopt technologies innovated by advanced countries. The second stage is the innovation stage. Countries in this stage need to innovate in order to maintain their competitiveness.

The third stage is the consumption stage. When countries achieve this stage, innovations slow down and people can enjoy the benefits of innovations accumulated in the second stage. Putting Porter's theory into our framework, we find that the investment stage corresponds to the period when a country has both negative TCIs and low income; the innovation stage corresponds to the period when a country maintains positive TCIs; and the consumption stage corresponds to the period when a country has high income and zero or negative TCIs. In this regard, the US, UK, and France have entered the consumption stage, but Argentina is a pre-mature consumption society because it began to have negative TCIs with relatively low income. Taiwan and South Korea are nearing the end of their innovation stage and are about to enter the consumption stage. China and India are still in the innovation stage. If the recent trend is to last, India will stay longer in the innovation stage than China in the future. This is because China started its take-off earlier than India did.

CROSS-COUNTRY ANALYSIS

To provide a flavor to our analysis, we take 1985, 1990, 1995, and 2000 as the starting years, respectively, and plot in Fig. 5.6 the average per-capita GDP growth rates of the next five years against the TCIs in each starting year.[4] It is evident that higher TCIs lead to higher average economic growth in the next five years. The coefficient of LCI in the simple linear regression is 6.9, 4.8, 3.6, and 4.7 for the four periods, respectively. This means that when a country increases its degree of catch-up by 10 percentage points, its income growth rate will increase by 0.69, 0.48, 0.36, and 0.47 percentage points. Because of the impacts of the Asian Financial Crisis, the coefficient for the period of 1996–2000 is relatively low.

Using the above calculated figures, we can gauge the contribution of limited catch-up to economic growth in China. In the period of 1990–2005, China's per-capita GDP grew by an average of 8.7 percent per annum and its average TCI was 0.58. Using the average of the

[4] We only plot data of larger economies and exclude a few cases with military coups.

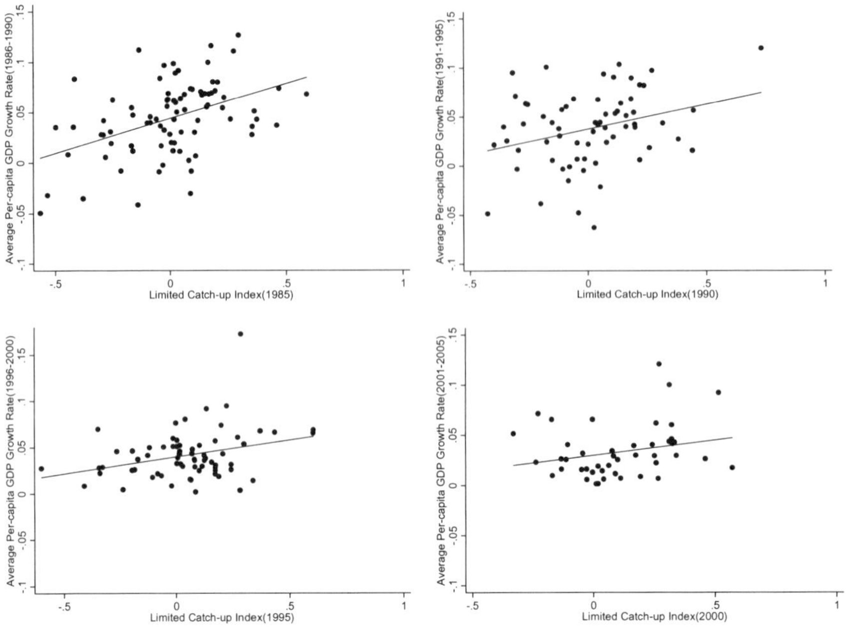

Fig. 5.6: LCI and per-capita GDP growth: 1985–2005.

three coefficients of TCI in the period, which is 4.37, as the marginal contribution of limited catch-up, we get the contribution of limited catch-up to be 2.53, which is 29 percent of China's average growth rate in this period. This is a very large effect.

Our econometric analysis adopts the two-way fixed-effect panel model as control for time and country-specific effects. According to our theoretical model, the impact of LCI on economic growth should exhibit an inverse-U relationship. Therefore, the LCI and its square in the starting year are the major concerns for us.

We will also include in our regressions the following control variables, all measured in the starting year, the logarithm of per-capita GDP (PPP USD), share of investment in GDP (percent), share of trade in GDP (percent), share of government expenditure in GDP (percent), a political liberty index, an exchange rate regime index, and the illiteracy rate (percent). Data for the shares of investment, government expenditure, and trade are from PWT 6.1. The political liberty index is provided by Polity IV (Marshall and Jaggers, 2004), which is a widely accepted dataset to measure world democratization. Polity IV includes annual composite indicators measuring both "institutionalized autocracy" and "institutionalized democracy." The polity score is defined as the difference between the democracy indicator and the authoritarian indicator. Since each indicator is an additive eleven-point scale (0–10), the index is scaled between −10 and 10 consequently. The higher the number, the higher is the level of political liberty of a country. The exchange rate regime index is from Reinhart and Rogoff (2002) who study the exchange rate regimes across more than one hundred countries after World War II. They develop a novel system of re-classifying historical exchange rate regimes. One important difference between their study and previous classification efforts is that they employ an extensive data base on market-determined parallel exchange rates. They arrive at 14 classes of exchange rate regime and give each class a number between 1 and 14; the larger the number, the more liberal is the exchange regime. Finally, the illiteracy rates are from Barro and Lee (2000).

We run two sets of regressions. One set is based on data of five-year averages, and the other is based on data of ten-year averages. The results are presented in Tables 5.1 and 5.2, respectively. For each dataset, we first run four regressions that use different control variables. The first only includes the share of investment in GDP and the share of trade in GDP; the second adds log per-capita GDP to control the Solow-type convergence; the third adds the share of government expenditure in GDP, the political liberty index, and the exchange regime index; and the last adds the illiteracy rate. Changes of the illiteracy rate in most countries are small, so its results in panel estimation are not reliable. We also run one regression with all the control variables but with the square of LCI being dropped.

By the results of regression (5) in Table 5.1, increasing the LCI by 10 percentage points will result in an increase in the average GDP growth rate in the next five years by 0.48 percentage points. This result is significant at the 1 percent significance level. Regression (5) in Table 5.2 shows that the effect is smaller for the next ten years, which is only 0.34, but still statistically significant.

Table 5.1: Effects of the LC strategy on economic growth: Five-year averages (1965–2005).

	(1)	(2)	(3)	(4)	(5)
LCI	4.92***	3.96***	7.09***	4.95***	4.79***
	(1.37)	(1.30)	(1.72)	(1.17)	(1.10)
LCI^2	−3.59	−4.31	−4.07	1.83	
	(4.05)	(4.02)	(4.23)	(3.04)	
Share of investment in GDP (percent)	0.14*	0.12*	0.12*	0.01	0.01
	(0.08)	(0.07)	(0.69)	(0.03)	(0.03)
Share of trade in GDP (percent)	0.00	0.01	0.01	−0.00	−0.01
	(0.01)	(0.01)	(0.01)	(0.01)	(0.01)
Log (per-capita GDP)		−0.21E−3***	−0.08E−3**	−0.16E−3***	−0.16E−3***
		(0.04E−3)	(0.04E−3)	(0.05E−3)	(0.05E−3)
Share of government expenditure in GDP (percent)			0.04	0.02	0.02
			(0.04)	(0.03)	(0.03)
Political liberty index (−10–10)			0.02	0.01	0.02
			(0.03)	(0.03)	(0.03)
Exchange rate regime (1–14)			0.35***	0.28***	0.28***
			(0.08)	(0.05)	(0.05)
Illiteracy rate (percent)				0.07***	0.07***
				(0.02)	(0.03)
Number of observations	849	849	773	662	662
Number of countries	112	112	95	84	84
Adjusted R^2	0.35	0.36	0.41	0.49	0.49

Notes: Standard errors are reported in the parentheses; *, **, and *** indicate, respectively, the 10 percent significance level, 5 percent significance level, and 1 percent significance level.

The inverse-U curve is not found in any of the regressions using the dataset of five-year averages, but is found in three out of the four regressions using the dataset of ten-year averages. The insignificant result of regression (4) has something to do with the illiteracy rate whose lack of variations could have caused a multi-collinearity problem. Using the results of regression (3), it is found that the peak of the inverse-U curve is at LCI = 0.27. That is, a catch-up of 27 percent is the best for GDP growth.

Table 5.2: Effects of the LC strategy on economic growth: 10-year averages (1965–2005).

	(1)	(2)	(3)	(4)	(5)
LCI	4.91***	3.72**	6.00***	3.28***	3.35***
	(1.87)	(1.72)	(2.01)	(1.20)	(1.10)
LCI^2	−10.26*	−11.47*	−11.09*	−0.92	
	(5.93)	(5.98)	(5.96)	(2.90)	
Share of investment in GDP (percent)	0.15	0.12	0.11	−0.03	−0.03
	(0.10)	(0.09)	(0.07)	(0.03)	(0.03)
Share of trade in GDP (percent)	−0.00	0.01	0.00	−0.011*	−0.011*
	(0.01)	(0.01)	(0.01)	(0.006)	(0.006)
Log (per-capita GDP)		−0.27E−3***	−0.12E−3***	−0.22E−3***	−0.22E−3***
		(0.06E−3)	(0.05E−3)	(0.06E−3)	(0.05E−3)
Share of government expenditure in GDP (percent)			0.11**	0.01	0.01
			(0.05)	(0.03)	(0.03)
Political liberty index (−10–10)			0.04	0.02	0.02
			(0.04)	(0.04)	(0.03)
Exchange rate regime (1–14)			0.36***	0.19***	0.19***
			(0.10)	(0.06)	(0.06)
Illiteracy rate (percent)				0.07***	0.07***
				(0.02)	(0.02)
Number of observations	435	435	394	334	334
Number of countries	112	112	95	84	84
Adjusted R^2	0.31	0.33	0.41	0.56	0.56

Notes: Standard errors are reported in the parentheses. *, **, and *** indicate, respectively, the 10 percent significance level, 5 percent significance level, and 1 percent significance level.

Judging by this result, China is now catching up too much. One explanation is that more than 60 percent of Chinese exports are processing trade so the technological contents of its own manufacturing are not as high as its TCI shows. Ping *et al.* (2006) finds that about 20 percent of China's exports can be explained by vertical integration. Taking 20 percent as the share of contribution made by imported inputs to China's TCI, then China's pace of catch-up was about at the optimal level in 2005 (Fig. 5.5).

Among the control variables, initial level of GDP and the exchange rate regime have the most robust results. Initial per-capita GDP unambiguously reduces the average growth rate in both the next five and ten years. The speed of convergence is about 0.2 percentage points of reduction in GDP growth rate for 1 percent increase of per-capita GDP. A more flexible exchange rate regime strongly supports GDP growth. Moving up by one category from a less flexible regime to a more flexible regime increases GDP growth rate by 0.28 percentage points in the next five years and by 0.19 in the next ten years. Investment share in GDP has a positive effect only in the next five years, but not in the next ten years.

TECHNOLOGICAL UPGRADING IN CHINESE EXPORTS

Up to this point, we have shown that China has adopted the LC strategy and shown that this strategy leads to higher economic growth in the world. In this section, we move a step further to provide more detailed information on how China has upgraded the technological contents in its exports.

Technological upgrading and competitiveness of Chinese exports

In the last 20 years, the sophistication of Chinese exports has improved fast. Figure 5.7 compares the situations in 1980 and 2000. The horizontal axis is the TSI of SITC four-digit products. We divide the products into ten equal groups on the TSI scale. The vertical axis is the share of export of each group of products. It is clear that in the 20 years between 1980 and 2000, Chinese exports have uniformly moved from low TSI to high TSI products. In 1980, Chinese exports were highly concentrated in the first and second groups; in 2000, the concentration was fairly spread from the second to the fifth groups.

Table 5.3 lists the top five exports in China in 1985, 1990, 1995, 2000, and 2005. The information provided by this table reinforces the information that we wanted to convey in Fig. 5.7. Although

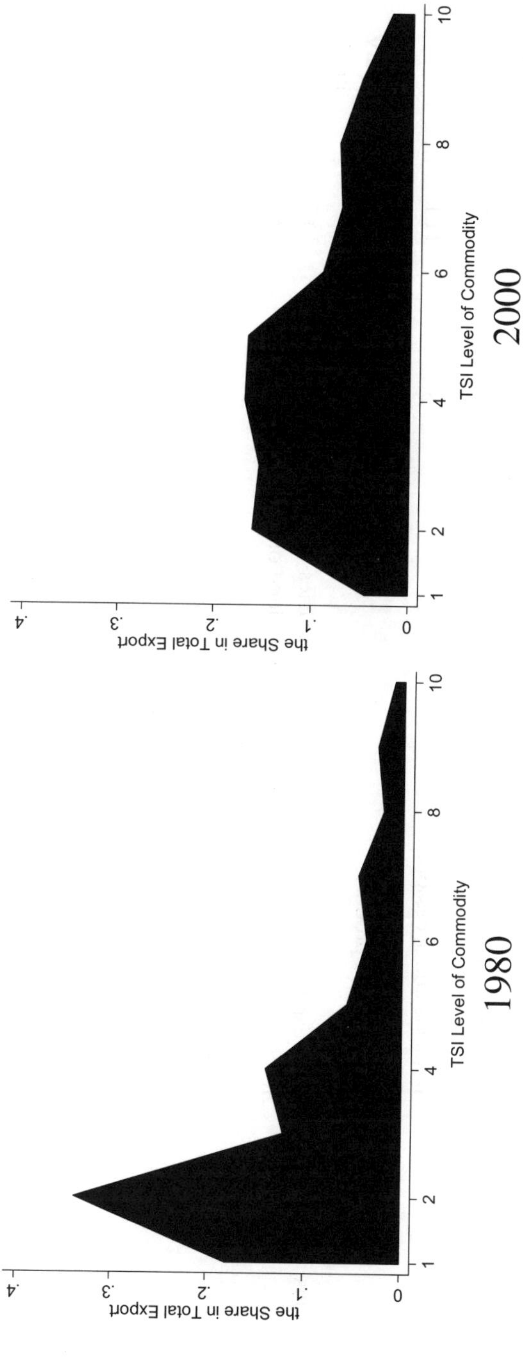

Fig. 5.7: Technological upgrading in Chinese exports: 1980–2000.

Table 5.3: Five most exported products in China.

Year	Product code	Product name	Value (billion USD)	The share in total export (percent)	Notes
1985	05	Vegetables and fruits	1.3	3.8	Primary products
	26	Cotton and other fibers	2.1	6.2	Primary products
	84	Garments and accessories	3.7	11.1	
	65	Textile fibers and related products	4.3	12.8	
	33	Crude oil and products	6.9	20.8	Primary products
1995	64	Footwear, gaiters and the like; parts of such articles	6.7	4.5	
	61	Articles of apparel and clothing accessories, knitted or crocheted	6.9	4.7	
	84	Nuclear reactors, boilers, machinery and mechanical appliances; parts thereof	8.7	5.8	
	62	Articles of apparel and clothing accessories, not knitted or crocheted	14.3	9.6	
	85	Electrical machinery and equipment and parts thereof; sound recorders and reproducers, television image and sound recorders and reproducers, and parts and accessories of such articles	19.0	12.8	
2000	64	Footwear, gaiters and the like; parts of such articles	9.9	4.0	
	61	Articles of apparel and clothing accessories, knitted or crocheted	13.4	5.4	

(Continued)

Table 5.3: (*Continued*)

Year	Product code	Product name	Value (billion USD)	The share in total export (percent)	Notes
	62	Articles of apparel and clothing accessories, not knitted or crocheted	18.9	7.6	
	84	Nuclear reactors, boilers, machinery and mechanical appliances; parts thereof	26.8	10.8	
	85	Electrical machinery and equipment and parts thereof; sound recorders and reproducers, television image and sound recorders and reproducers, and parts and accessories of such articles	46.1	18.5	
2005	90	Optical, photographic, cinematographic, measuring, checking, precision, medical or surgical instruments and apparatus; parts and accessories thereof	25.5	3.3	
	61	Articles of apparel and clothing accessories, knitted or crocheted	30.9	4.1	
	62	Articles of apparel and clothing accessories, not knitted or crocheted	35.0	4.6	
	84	Nuclear reactors, boilers, machinery and mechanical appliances; parts thereof	149.7	19.6	
	85	Electrical machinery and equipment and parts thereof; sound recorders and reproducers, television image and sound recorders and reproducers, and parts and accessories of such articles	172.3	22.6	

Notes: The classification of commodities for 1985 is SITC–Four digits. Data are from Feenstra *et al*. (2005). The classification of commodities for 1995, 2000, and 2005 is HS — Six digits. Data are from the Bureau of Customs of China.

Table 5.4: The RCA index of key Chinese exports in selected years.[5]

Year	Product code									
	01	05	33	65	69	75	76	77	84	85
1985	186	206	175	453	84	5	30	17	398	176
1990	80	123	85	289	114	21	187	70	506	438
1995	51	108	33	225	127	78	211	80	483	804
2000	45	91	18	191	151	137	181	99	420	726

Source: Feenstra *et al.* (2005).

exports of garments and shoes have always been strong, Chinese exports have decisively moved away from resource-based products, and the presence of electronic and other manufacturing goods has been greatly enhanced.

We can also use Ballasa (1965)s RCA index to show the upgrading of Chinese exports. Table 5.4 presents the RCA indices for several key products in selected years. It is clear that China's revealed comparative advantage has been decreasing in resource-intensive products including meats and meat products (01), vegetables and fruits (05), crude oil and related products (33), and textile fibers (65). On the other hand, China has become much more competitive in capital and technology-intensive products, including metal products (75), office automation and data processing equipment (76), and electric equipment (77). Finally, China has maintained a strong position in garments (84) and shoes (85).

The problem of value-added

It is often argued that the contribution of domestic firms to China's technological upgrading has been weak because 60 percent of

[5] The product codes in the table are SITC two-digit codes. Code 01 is meat and meat products; 05 is vegetables and fruits; 33 is crude oil and products; 65 is textile fibers; 69 is metal products; 75 is office and automation and data processing equipment; 76 is telecom and recording equipment; 77 is electric equipment; 84 is garment and accessories; and 85 is shoes.

China's exports are processing trade. By this view, China is the world factory, but it is only an assembling factory. We do not deny that processing trade plays an important role in China's exports, but at the same time we believe that processing trade alone cannot fully account for China's technological upgrading. Table 5.5 presents Ping *et al.* (2006)'s calculation of the ratio of processing trade in the value-added of China's exports from 1992 to 2003. This ratio had indeed increased but the highest was only 22 percent. Therefore, processing trade cannot fully explain China's export upgrading.

To further explore the issue, we compare the import and export values of products in SITC 7 in the period of 1985–2000. SITC 7 includes capital-intensive products. Figure 5.8 presents the comparison.

Table 5.5: Ratio of processing trade in value-added: 1992–2003.

Year	1992	1993	1994	1995	1996	1997	1998	1999	2000	2001	2002	2003
Ratio of specialization	0.14	0.14	0.15	0.15	0.15	0.15	0.16	0.15	0.20	0.20	0.21	0.22

Source: Ping *et al.* (2006).

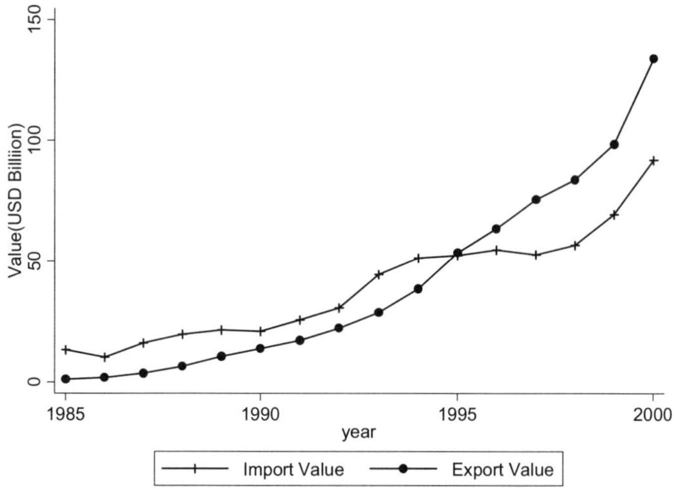

Fig. 5.8: Export and import values of SITC 7: 1985–2000.

Before 1995, the export value of SITC 7 was smaller than its import value; after 1995, the trend has reversed. This transition from a net importer to a net exporter shows that China has gained competitiveness in capital-intensive products. At the minimum, the fact that China can now compete in the world market itself is a sign for China's technological progress because now it can produce products that it could not in the past.

CONCLUSIONS

In this paper we have studied China's trade strategy and linked it to its economic growth. Our central idea is the concept of limited catch-up. We have shown that China has adopted the limited catch-up strategy instead of the comparative advantage strategy in its exports. Our theory shows that the limited catch-up strategy could lead to higher economic growth, and our empirical analysis has proved this assessment. By our calculation, about 29 percent of China's annual per-capita GDP growth rate in the period 1990–2005 was contributed by its adoption of the limited catch-up strategy. We have also provided detailed data on the technological upgrading of Chinese exports in the last 20 years.

One important implication of our analysis is that a developing country has to overtake its comparative advantage in order to catch up with advanced countries. In the long run, however, each country will converge to its comparative advantage. To reach a higher income level, however, the task for a country is to postpone this convergence. To use Porter (1990)'s jargon, a country should stay longer in the innovation stage. Our theory and empirical analysis provide a hint to reconcile comparative advantage and catch-up: in the short run, catch-up is necessary for a country to close its gap with advanced countries; in the long run, every country follows its comparative advantage.

Our empirical analysis shows that China is still in the catch-up stage. Using Korea and Taiwan as the reference, we have shown that China has about 20 years more for fast economic growth. This will ensure that China's per-capita GDP converges to nearly

US $8,000 before it falls to its comparative advantage. It is a decent income and would enable China to comfortably compete in the international market by then.

APPENDIX: COUNTRIES IN THE DATASET

Algeria, Angola, Argentina, Australia, Austria, Bangladesh, Barbados, Belgium, Benin, Bolivia, Brazil, Burkina Faso, Burundi, Cameroon, Canada, Cent. Afr. Rep, Chad, Chile, China, China HK SAR, Colombia, Congo, Costa Rica, Cote Divoire, Cyprus, Dem. Rp. Congo, Denmark, Dominican Rp, Ecuador, Egypt, El Salvador, Eq. Guinea, Ethiopia, Fiji, Finland, France, Monac, Gabon, Gambia, Germany, Ghana, Greece, Guatemala, Guinea, Guinea Bissau, Guyana, Haiti, Honduras, Hungary, Iceland, India, Indonesia, Iran, Ireland, Israel, Italy, Jamaica, Japan, Jordan, Kenya, Korea Rep., Madagascar, Malawi, Malaysia, Mali, Mauritania, Mauritius, Mexico, Morocco, Mozambique, Nepal, Netherlands, New Zealand, Nicaragua, Niger, Nigeria, Norway, Pakistan, Panama, Papua N. Guin, Paraguay, Peru, Philippines, Poland, Portugal, Romania, Russian Fed, Rwanda, Senegal, Seychelles, Sierra Leone, Singapore, South Africa, Spain, Sri Lanka, Sweden, Switz. Liecht, Syria, Taiwan, Tanzania, Thailand, Togo, Trinidad Tbg, Tunisia, Turkey, UK, USA, Uganda, Ukraine, Uruguay, Venezuela, Zambia, Zimbabwe.

REFERENCES

Balassa, B (1965), "Trade liberalization and revealed comparative advantage," *Manchester School* 33, 99–123.

Barro, Robert and Jong-Wha Lee (2000), "International data on educational attainment: updates and implications," *CID Working Paper*, No. 42, April.

Dixit, Avinash and Victor Norman (1980), *Theory of International Trade : A Dual, General Equilibrium Approach*, Cambridge: Cambridge University Press.

Feenstra, Robert, Robert Lipsey, Haiyan Deng, Alyson Ma and Hengyong Mo (2005), "World trade flows, 1962–2000," *NBER Working Paper*, 11040.

Groningen Growth and Development Centre (2006), "Total Economy Database," http://www.ggdc.net, May.

Heston, Alan, Robert Summers and Bettina Aten (2002), "Penn world table version 6.1," *Center for International Comparisons at the University of Pennsylvania (CICUP)*, October.

Hausmann, Ricardo, Jason Hwang and Dani Rodrik (2005), "What you export matters," *NBER Working Paper*, 11905.

Krugman, Paul (1990), *Rethinking International Trade*, Cambridge, MA: MIT Press.

Lin, Justin, Fang Cai and Zhou Li (1994), *The China Miracle: Development Strategy and Economic Reform*, Shanghai: Shanghai Sanlian Bookstore.

Marshall, Monty and Keith Jaggers (2004), "Polity IV project," dataset available at http://www.cidcm.umd.edu.

Ping, Xinqiao *et al.* (2006), "Vertical specialization in China's export and Sino-U.S. Trade," *The Journal of World Economy*, 333, 3–11.

Porter, Michael (1990), *The Competitive Advantage of Nations*, New York: Free Press.

Reinhart, Carmen and Kenneth Rogoff (2002), "The modern history of exchange rate arrangements: a reinterpretation," *NBER Working Paper*, 8963.

Chapter

6

Manufacturing Fragmentation and the Emergence of China as a Trading Nation

Sarah Y. Tong

East Asian Institute, Singapore

GLOBAL TRADE EXPANSION AND THE EMERGENCE OF CHINA

Global trade has expanded significantly faster relative to production in recent decades, especially since 1990s. Between 1990 and 2004, according to the World Trade Organization (WTO)[1], world export grew by 5.8 percent a year on average, while production increased by only 2.5 percent a year on average. During the same period, the growth gap for manufacturing goods is even larger, with 6.3 percent a year for export and 2.6 percent for production.

As a late comer, China has emerged rapidly as a trading nation since the 1990s. From a very much closed economy 25 years ago, China has become one of the leading exporters and importers in the world. In 1993, China's trade accounted for about 2.5 percent

[1] *International Trade Statistics 2005*, World Trade Organization.

of the world total export and 2.8 percent of the world total import. In 2004, China overtook Japan to become the world's third largest exporter in merchandise trade, following Germany and the US. A year earlier, in 2005, China was already the world's third largest importer in merchandise trade, after the US and Germany. China's trade to GDP ratio has increased quickly from 30 percent in 1990 to 64 percent in 2005 (Fig. 6.1). In 2005, China's export and import made up 6.5 percent and 5.9 percent of the total export and import of the world, respectively. Even in the trade of commercial services, China is among the top 10 largest nations, ranking #9 for export and #8 in import in 2004.

China's rapid emergence as a trading nation is one outcome of China's economic reform and transition started more than a quarter century ago in the late 1970s. Since then, China has attained economic growth of nearly 10 percent a year on average. In 2005, China's GDP amounted to RMB 18.23 trillion (US$2.23 trillion based on official exchange rate, slightly less than a quarter of US GDP). To a large extent, China's fast economic growth has been sustained by an even more rapid expansion in trade, about 17 percent a year on average.

Due to the large size and great diversity, China's rapid economic growth and associated trade expansion have generated significant

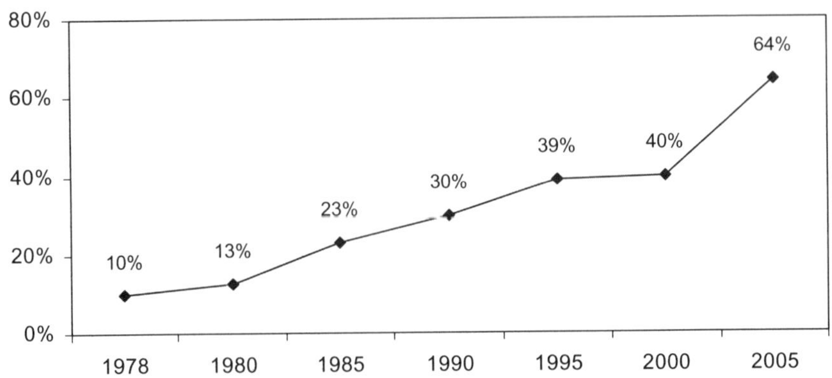

Fig. 6.1: Trade to GDP ratio, 1979–2005.
Source: *China Statistical Abstract 2006*, National Bureau of Statistics of China.

impact for the world as well as for economies in the region. This is particularly true in recent years as China has sustained substantial and growing trade surpluses. In 2005, China's total trade surplus reached US$102 billion, a threefold increase from the previous year. On the one hand, China has accumulated large foreign reserves, and has overtaken Japan to have the world largest foreign reserves. By June this year, China has piled up US$940 billion in foreign reserves.

More importantly, China's growing trade surplus has been reflected most notably by its huge trade imbalances with two of the world's most important economies, the US and the European Union. According to China's Customs Statistics, China's trade surpluses with the two economies in 2005 reached US$114 billion and US$70 billion, respectively.[2] They represent sharp increases from those in 2004 with US$80 billion and US$37 billion surpluses with the two.

On the other hand, China has also become one of the most important export markets for its Asian Neighbors in recent years. Between 2000 and 2004, the share of export to China in total Asian exports increased from 7 percent to 12 percent. For Japan, the share of export to China increased from 9 percent to 17 percent; while those for the four East Asian traders, including Hong Kong, Singapore, Taiwan, and South Korea, rose from 13 percent to 22 percent over the same four year period (Fig. 6.2).

China's rise as a significant economic power and a large trading national has lead to both applause and some degree of unease. There has been continuing and increasing pressure, mainly from the US, for China to revalue its currency and to relax its exchange rate. There were also heated disputes over China's export of textile and clothing (T&C) to the US and the European Union last year, which resulted in re-imposition of curbing measures to restrict bilateral trade in T&C. Within East and Southeast Asia, on the other hand, there have been growing efforts to facilitate further economic integration, in terms of negotiating regional and bilateral trade arrangements.

---

[2] The US reported a trade deficit of US$201 billion with China for 2005. The European Union reported a trade deficit of EURO 106 billion (about US$133 billion) in 2005.

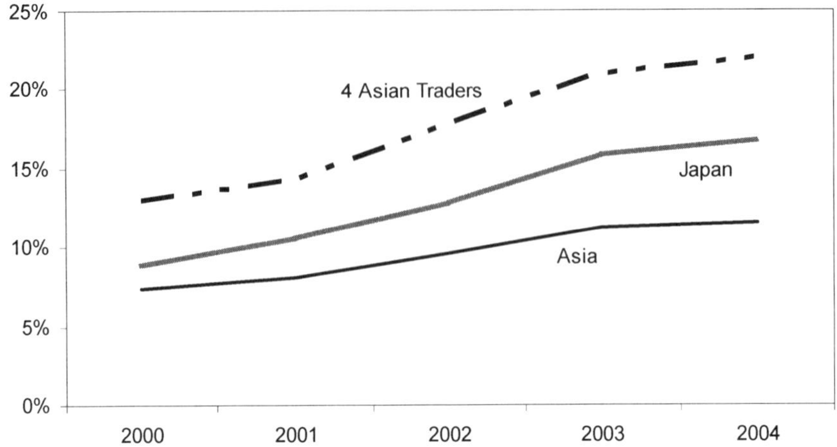

Fig. 6.2: Share of export to China in total by source, 2000–2004.

To understand these diverse approaches to China's changing role in trade and in world economy, it is essential to evaluate China's development from a broader regional perspective.

GLOBAL TRADE AND THE MANUFACTURING FRAGMENTATION

Since the end of World War II (WWII), global trade expanded more rapidly, with an average annual rate of about 6 percent, relative to production that had grown at an annual rate of 4 percent between 1950 and 2004. Furthermore, global trade expansion has been associated with significant changes in regional composition. Europe, as an increasingly integrated region, has become the most import in world trade. While intra-regional trade within Europe accounted for about three quarters of its total trade in recent years, Europe remained the world largest exporting and importing region, accounting for about 45 percent of the world total (Table 6.1).

The account for North America is quite different. Its share in total world imports decreased most consistently, from 28 percent post-WWII to less than 15 percent in 2004. For import, the share of North America has been relatively stable at a slightly above 20 percent

Table 6.1: Composition of world trade by regions, 1948–2004.

	1948	1953	1963	1973	1983	1993	2003	2004
Share in world merchandise export								
North America	28.3	24.9	19.9	17.3	16.8	18.0	15.8	14.9
Europe	31.5	34.9	41.4	45.4	43.5	45.4	46.1	45.3
Asia	13.6	13.1	12.4	14.9	19.1	26.1	26.1	26.8
China	0.9	1.2	1.3	1.0	1.2	2.5	6.0	6.7
Share in world merchandise import								
North America	20.6	20.7	16.2	17.3	18.5	21.5	22.7	21.8
Europe	40.4	39.4	45.4	47.4	44.2	44.8	45.4	44.8
Asia	14.2	15.1	14.2	15.1	18.5	23.3	23.0	24.0
China	1.1	1.7	0.9	0.9	1.1	2.8	5.4	6.1

level for most of the period, except during the 1960s to 1980s. The development of Asia's trade is in apparent contrast to that of North America, and the changes came most dramatically during the 1970s and 1980s. For export, Asia's share rose from about 15 percent of the world total in early 1970s to 26 percent in early 1993 and has remained stable since then. The pattern is similar for import, though Asia's share in the world import had increased slowly and thus remained lower than that in the world export.

The result has been that North America has sustained a large and growing trade deficit since 1970s. On the other hand, Asia began to carry trade surplus with the rest of the world. Large and growing trade imbalance emerged between the two regions and sometimes had led to trade disputes, for example those between the US and Japan in the 1980s.

The post-WWII trade expansion has been largely a tale of manufacturing expansion. Between 1950 and 2004, manufacturing export grew by 7.8 percent a year on average, while manufacturing production grew by 4.6 percent a year. There are two possible explanations. First, unlike primary goods, such as oil and copper, manufacturing goods are more differentiated. As a result, a large portion of manufacturing trade is intra-industry trade, which means a country will export and import large quantity of goods within the same category such as cars. This is more likely the case for trade between countries with similar development levels.

The second explanation is the growing importance of manufacturing fragmentation across countries. It has become increasingly feasible to separate manufacturing activities into different stages to be carried out in different locations within and across countries. This explanation is important to understand the rising importance of Asian newly industrialized economies (NIEs) in world trade during the 1970s and 1980s, as well as that of China since 1990s.

Indeed, China's rise as a large trading nation in the past 15 years coincide with the continuing trend of production relocation and outsourcing in manufacturing activities. Fragmentation of manufacturing activities, especially that within Asia, has led to the formation of global as well as regional production networks in which China is set to be an important link. Due to its large size and great diversity, China has become a main export platform for large multinational as well as for small and medium sized companies from neighboring economies.

As is shown in Table 6.1, while China's share in global trade expanded considerably, the share of Asia as a whole only increased modestly over the past decade. Between 1993 and 2004, China's share in the world merchandise export went up significantly, from 2.5 percent to 6.7 percent. Over the same period, Asia's share increased slightly from 26.1 percent to 26.8 percent. This is also true for manufacturing trade. Between 1999 and 2004, while China expanded rapidly in world trade, Asia's shares in the world manufacturing export and import remained largely stable, at around 30 percent and 20 percent, respectively (Fig. 6.3).

Behind the relative stable regional composition in world trade, in the broader sense, and China's rising importance, it has been the growing intra-regional trade associated with manufacturing fragmentation in recent years where China is increasingly integrated to become a key export platform for other economies in the region. Between 2000 and 2004, for example, the share of intra-regional trade in Asia's total export went up from 48.8 percent to 50.3 percent. More

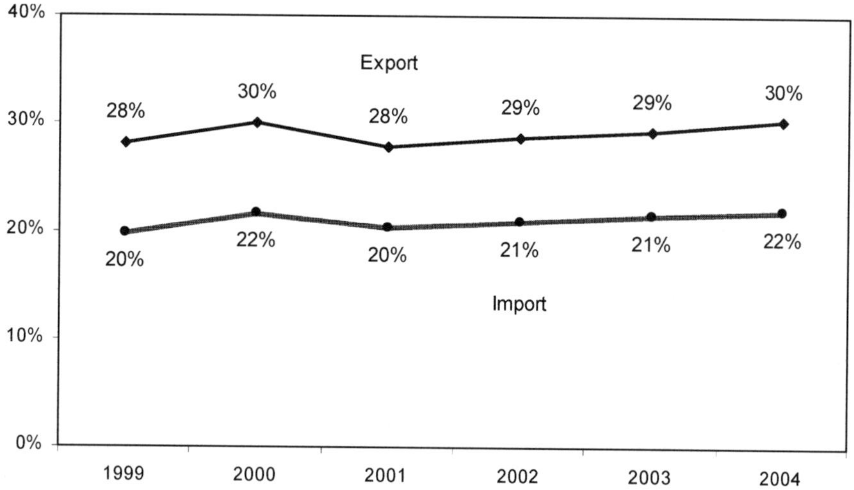

Fig. 6.3: Asia's share in world manufacturing trade, 1999–2004.

significantly, the share of Asian's export to China increased from 6.2 percent to 9.6 percent.

As China is increasingly integrated with economies in the region and serves as an important export platform, it, on the one hand, sustains large and growing trade surplus with the US and the European Union, and, on the other hand, has maintained increasing trade deficits with its Asian neighbors.[3] In 2005, for example, while China had trade surpluses of US$114 billion and US$70 billion with the US and the European Union (Fig. 6.4), respectively, it had trade deficits amounting to US$20 billion with ASEAN, US$16 billion with Japan, US$42 billion with South Korea, and US$57 billion with Chinese Taipei (Fig. 6.5).

The increasing importance of manufacturing fragmentation can also be seen from growing trade in parts and components in recent years. This is especially important regarding Asian economies. According to Gaulier *et al.* (2006), the shares of Asia's intra-regional

[3] Mainland China has maintained large trade surpluses with Hong Kong, SAR. Trade with Hong Kong includes a substantial portion of re-export from and to third markets. This may result in inaccurate estimation of China's import and export figures with its trading partners, but most likely under-estimate China's net export.

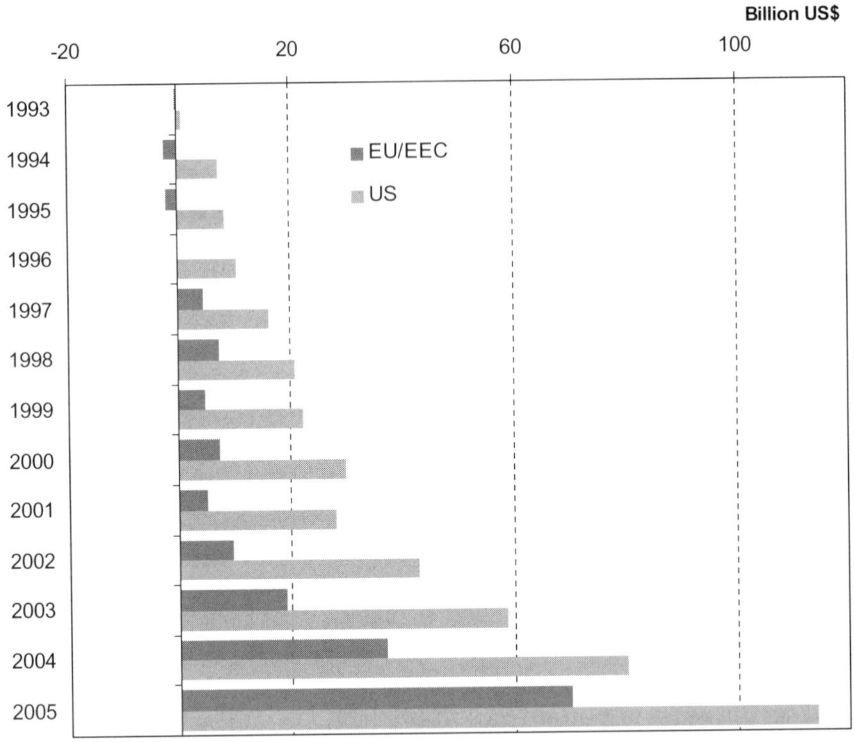

Fig. 6.4: China's trade balance with EU/EEC and USA, 1993–2005.

exports and imports in parts and components[4] increased significantly in the last decade. In 1993, intra-regional exports and imports accounted for 46.2 percent and 61.2 percent of Asian economies' total export and import of parts and components. The figures went up to 58.7 percent and 69.1 percent in 2003, respectively.

International trade data suggest that China has become an increasingly visible trading nation through its participation in regional as well as global production networks, especially of manufacturing. To gain a comprehensible insight into the process by which China

[4] In the study by Gaulier *et al.* (2006), parts and components include 42 parts and components of capital goods, except transport equipment, and 53 parts and accessories of transport equipment under the BEC classification (Broad Economic Categories of the United Nations of production stages).

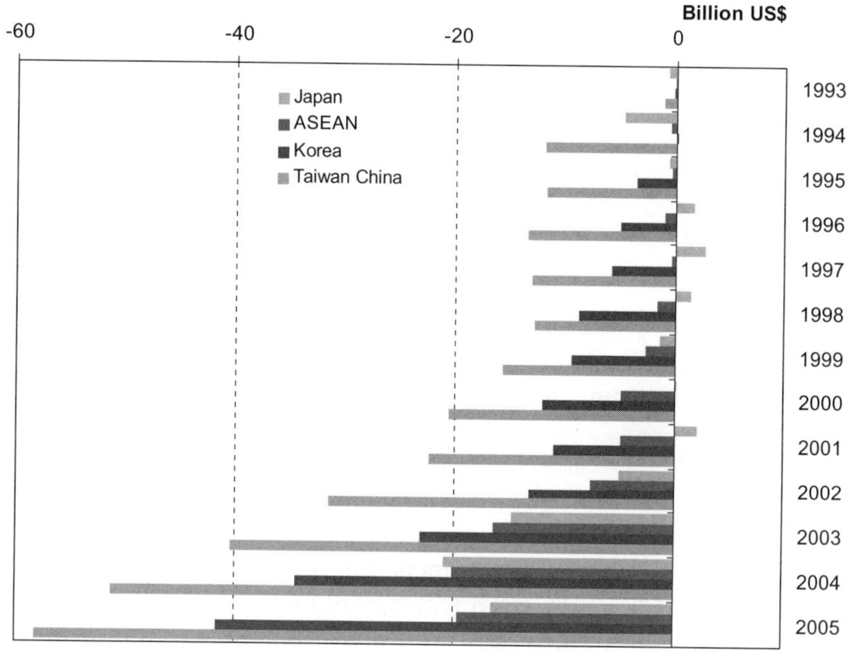

Fig. 6.5: China's trade balance with Asian economies, 1993–2005.

attained its objective of trade development, it is essential to review the important role of foreign invested enterprises and that of processed trade in China.

FOREIGN INVESTMENT AND PROCESSED TRADE

Attracting foreign investment and promoting trade have been a major component of China's reform efforts. Investment in high technology industries and export oriented industries are particularly encouraged. Processed trade that utilizes imported materials by foreign invested enterprises (FIEs) has been mostly favored as it is considered the least disruption to domestic market. As a result, China's trade expansion and its emergence as a trading nation rely crucially on the active participation by foreign affiliates in global and regional production networks through processed trade.

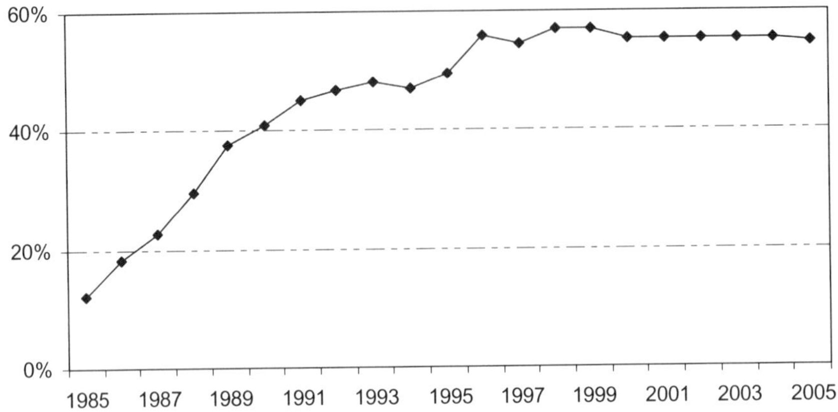

Fig. 6.6: Share of process export in total export, 1985–2005.

According to Chinese government statistics,[5] the share of processed export in China's total export rose rapidly from 12 percent in 1985 to 50 percent in 1995. Since then it has become stable at about 55 percent of the total export during the past 10 years (Fig. 6.6). While the total share of the processed trade in the total export has remained stable in recent years, it is important to note that the shares of the total trade and the processed trade by FIEs have risen significantly. From 1995 to 2005, FIEs' share in China's total export rose from 32 percent to 58 percent. At the same time, processed exports by foreign affiliates increased from 28 percent to 45 percent of China's total exports (Fig. 6.7).

A direct outcome of FIEs' growing participation in trade, especially in processed trade, is the dramatic changes in China's trade composition. The share of manufactures in export has increased consistently and significantly since the mid-1980s. For import, on the other hand, the share of manufactures rose in the early 1980s; since then it has been on a slow downward trend. Over the past quarter century, the share of manufactures in China's total export rose by 44 percentage points, from 50 percent in 1980 to 94 percent in 2005

[5] *China Statistical Abstract 2006*, National Bureau of Statistics of China.

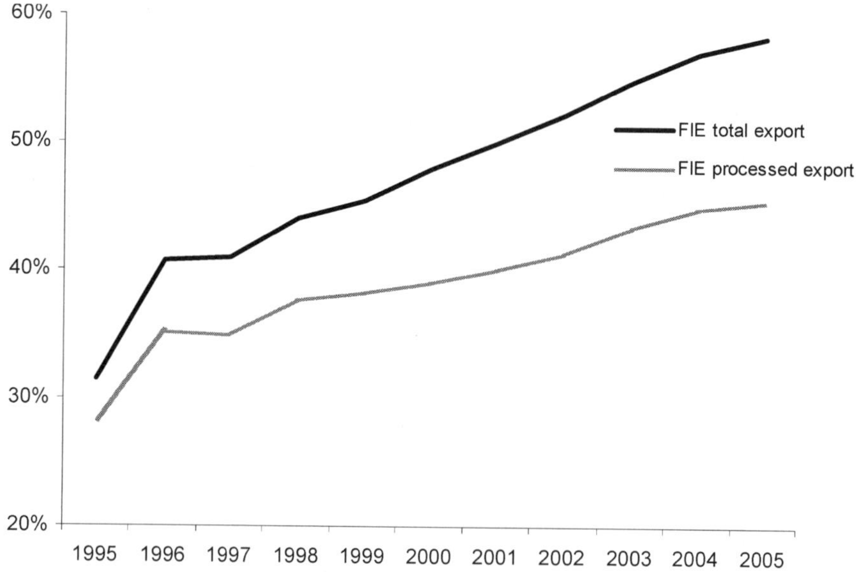

Fig. 6.7: Share of FIEs in total exports, 1995–2005.

(Fig. 6.8). The share of manufactures in the total import reached its peak of 87 percent in 1985 and then dropped to less than 80 percent in recent years.

Even more significantly, the rising share of manufacturers in the total export is significantly driven by the emerging and rapidly expanding exports of machinery and transport equipment. In the 1980s, exports of machinery and transport equipment made up less than 10 percent of the total export. In 2005, they accounted for nearly half of China's total export (Fig. 6.9a). In contrast, the relative importance of light and textile industrial products, rubber products, minerals, and metallurgical products has remained relatively stable over the decades between 15 percent and 23 percent of total exports (Fig. 6.9b).

It is noted that, while the share of machinery and transport equipment in the total export increased significantly, its share in the total import fluctuated during the earlier years and overall changed only modestly, from less than 30 percent in 1980 to around 45 percent in recent years. There are possibly two explanations. First, it

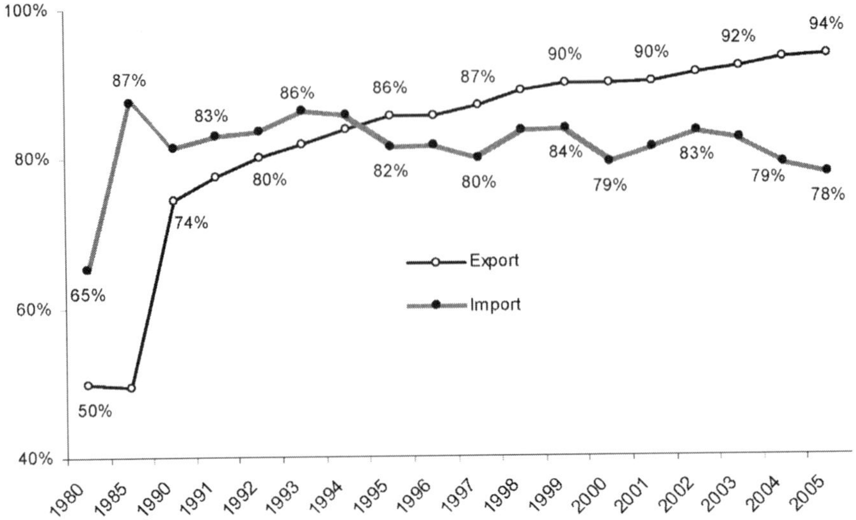

Fig. 6.8: Shares of manufacture in China's trade, 1980–2005.

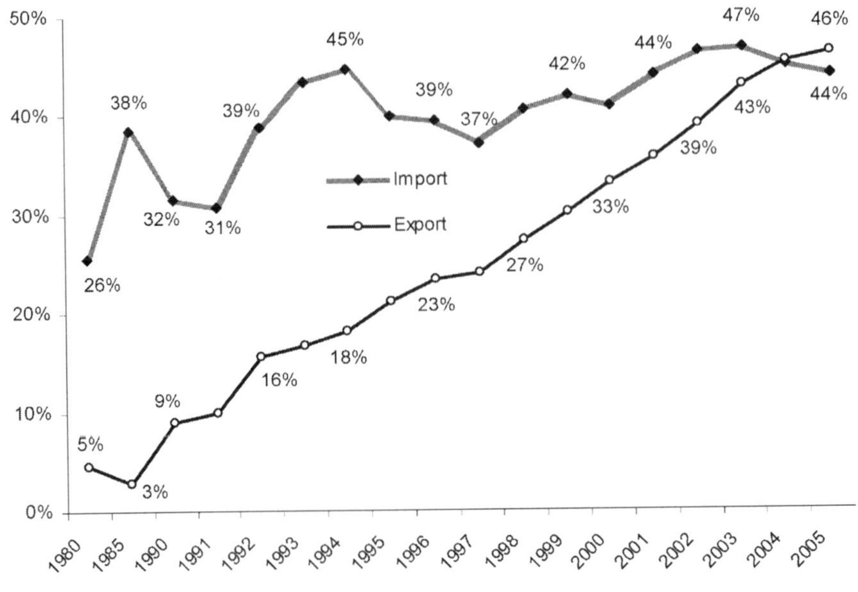

Fig. 6.9a: Shares of machinery and transport equipment in trade, 1980–2005.

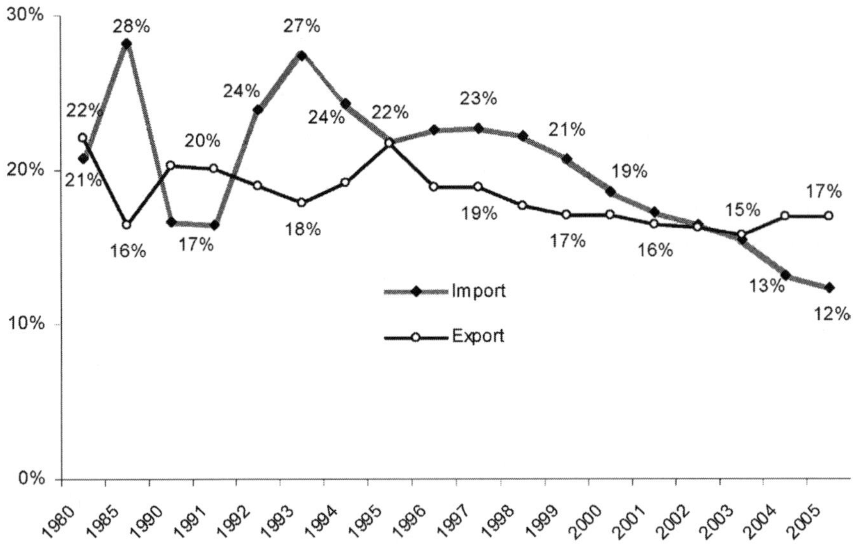

Fig. 6.9b: Shares of light and textile industrial products, rubber products, minerals and metallurgical products, 1980–2005.

may be that export of machinery and transport equipment products has become less dependent on imported materials, parts, and components, and thus relatively less processed export. This is consistent with the recent leveling off in the share of the processed export. Second, it is also possible that exporters in China, domestic and foreign, have increased their value-added contribution to their exports.

However, the relative magnitude of the processed trade remains high for trade in high-tech manufactures. This may be shown by export composition of the Guangdong province. Located in Southeastern China, Guangdong is the first to open to foreign investment and to trade in China. It is therefore the pioneer and the main player in the processed trade. In 1997, nearly three quarters of Guangdong's exports are processed exports. The shares of the processed trade in exports, however, vary greatly across industries. Those who have the highest shares of the processed export include cultural and office machinery (98 percent), computers (97 percent), other electronic and telecommunication equipment (96 percent), consumer electronics (96 percent), electrical equipment (95 percent), and printing and record medium reproduction (95 percent).[6]

At present, the processed trade is crucial in China's trade in high-tech products in which foreign affiliates remain the main players. It is reported that, while processed exports accounted for more than 90 percent of total exports of computer and telecommunication equipment in the first half of 2006, exports by foreign invested enterprises made up nearly 90 percent of the overall export (73 percent by wholly foreign owned enterprises and another 16 percent by foreign equity joint ventures).[7]

After more than a quarter century of reform and opening up, China's economy has become dramatically different, especially in trade, thanks to the increasing participation of foreign firms. Since 1990s, as manufacturing activities have been increasingly fragmented, China has been more deeply incorporated trade and production networks, including those of high-tech goods. As is shown in Table 6.2, within only five years, i.e., from 1998 to 2005, the items included in the top 10 exporting industries changed considerably. Specifically, industries producing products with higher technology contents increased their presence significantly. For example, computer peripherals and computer industries combined accounted for more than 15 percent of total exports by state and above-scale non-state enterprises in 2003, up from only 4 percent in 1998. Mobile communication terminal equipment, electronic components, and consumer video and audio equipment accounted for another 11 percent. On the other hand, the total shares of three traditional exporting industries, apparel, lather shoes, and toys, went down from 14 percent in 1998 to 10 percent in 2005.

Given the increasingly important role of foreign invested firms and of the processed trade, we aim to explore two questions in the

---

[6] These are author's own calculation based on data provided by Development Research Center in Beijing.

[7] Source: Website for the Ministry of Commerce of P. R. China.

Table 6.2: Top exporting industries, 1998 and 2003.

1998		Rank	2003	
% in total	Industry		Industry	% in total
8.8	Apparel	1	Computer peripherals	8.0
3.6	Electronic components	2	Computers	7.1
3.3	Computer peripherals	3	Apparel	6.5
3.1	Leather shoes	4	Electronic components	3.7
2.2	Toys	5	Mobile communication termal equipment	2.8
2.1	Cotton spinning	6	TV sets and other video equipment	2.7
2.0	Cotton printing and dyeing	7	Spinning and weaving of cotton and other fiber	2.2
1.9	Radio receivers and sound recording equipment	8	Leather shoes	2.1
1.6	Crude petroleum extraction	9	Consumer audio equipment	2.1
1.4	Cotton weaving	10	Printing and dyeing of cotton and other fiber	1.5
29.8		Above 10		38.6
	RMB 1084 billion	All industries	RMB 2551 billion	

Note: Include state firms and above scale non-state firms.

following section with respect to China's increasing integration in global production networks through the increasing foreign participation in the Chinese economy. First, what is the implication on China's trade imbalance with its key partners? Second, what is the effect on Chinese domestic firms?

FIEs, TRADE IMBALANCE, AND DOMESTIC CHINESE INDUSTRIES

As demonstrated earlier, foreign affiliates and the process trade are central to understand China's recent emergence as a large trading nation. It is then not difficult to predict that FIEs are most responsible in China's increasing trade imbalance with its major trading partners in recent years. This is indeed the case.

As shown in Figs. 6.10a and 6.10b, trade surpluses realized by FIEs have accounted for large and increasing portions of China's overall net export to the US and the European Union in recent years. For the Sino-US bilateral trade imbalance, the contribution

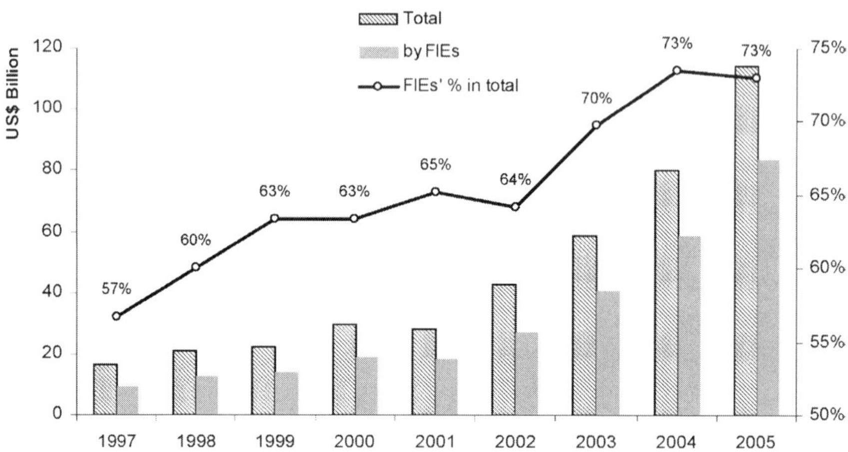

Fig. 6.10a: China's net export to USA: total and by FIEs, 1997–2005.

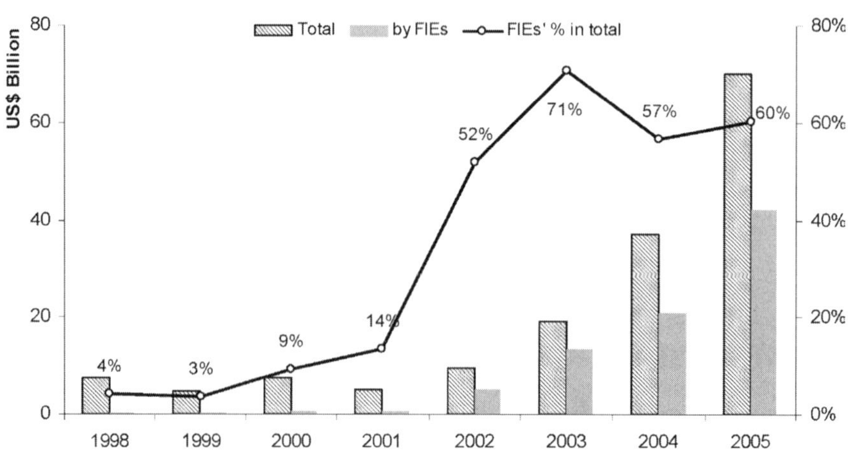

Fig. 6.10b: China's net export to EU: total and by FIEs, 1998–2005.

made by foreign firms has increased from 57 percent in 1997 to 73 percent in 2005. Similarly for the Sino-EU trade imbalance, FIE's contribution rose from only 4 percent in 1998 to 60 percent in 2005. The story for China's trade imbalance with its Asian neighbors is quite similar, though the direction is that China is maintaining growing deficits.

Roughly speaking, FIEs in China, from neighboring economies as well as from other regions, form a crucial link in regional production networks of manufactures, producing final goods in the form of processing using parts and components imported from economies in the region, most importantly Taiwan, Korea, Japan, and ASEAN members, which are then exported to the US and European Union markets.

This may be demonstrated more clearly in China's trade in high-tech products (Figs. 6.11a and 6.11b). On the supply side, China imported heavily from its neighbors, including ASEAN, Japan, Chinese Taipei, and South Korea. These four jointly made up 64 percent of China's total import of hi-tech products in 2004. On the other hand,

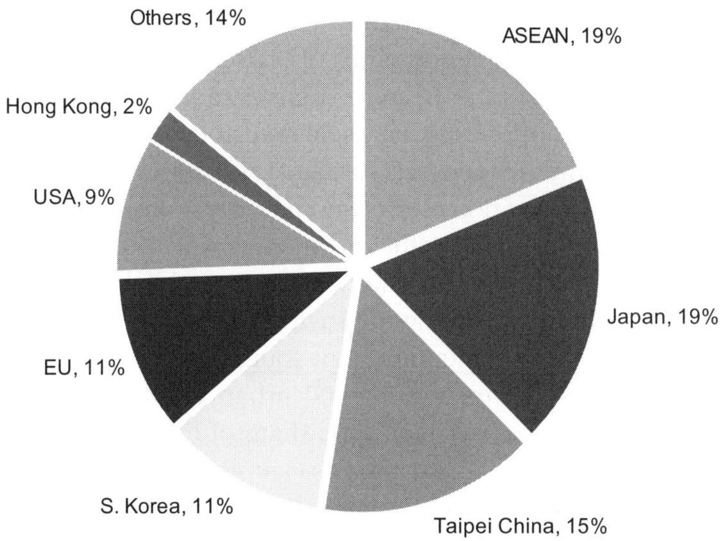

Fig. 6.11a: Percentage in China's imports of high-tech products by source, 2004.

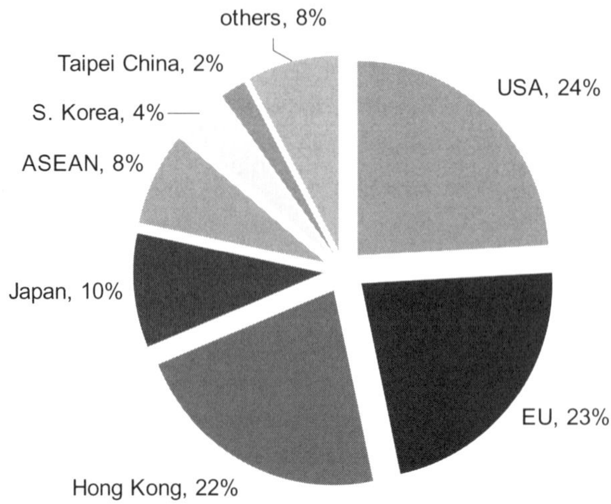

Fig. 6.11b: Percentage in China's export of high-tech products by destinations, 2004.

China sent most of its high-tech products to the industrial world outside the region, 45 percent directly to the US and the European Union and probably indirectly through its export to Hong Kong. Therefore, to single out China as the sole responsible party for deteriorating trade imbalance in the US is certainly an over-statement.

We demonstrated the importance of FIEs and the process trade in China's trade expansion to become a large trading nation. It is also important not to under-estimate their contribution are the China's domestic economy. In general, foreign investment and associated foreign trade may affect domestic economies in various ways, and there have always been disputes in the direction as well as the magnitudes of such effects. As a demonstration, we will highlight a number of figures here without attempting to provide a comprehensive account.

First, FIEs have become important sources of increased employment. While their percentage in total urban employment remains relatively low, at about 5 percent, the share of FIEs in overall industrial employment by state and above-scale non-state firms has gone up from 11 percent 1998 to 27 percent in 2005. Moreover, FIEs' contribution to the industrial value-added has also increased significantly, from 21 percent in 1998 to 29 percent in 2005.

Table 6.3: Ratio of domestic firms labor productivity to FIEs.

	1998	2003	% of FIEs in 2003
All industries	48%	53%	9
TV sets and other video equipment	42%	40%	22
Computers and computer peripherals	42%	102%	30
Electronic components	41%	56%	26
Apparel	83%	85%	18

More importantly, increasing participation of FIEs has likely helped technological advancement and productivity improvement of domestic firms, through technology spillover and more intensified competition. It is shown that, measured by value-added per employee, domestic firms have narrowed their gap with foreign invested firms. As is shown in Table 6.3, average domestic productivity amounted to 48 percent to that of foreign invested firms[8] in 1998. The ratio increased to 53 percent in 2003. To see if this is caused by the changing composition of Chinese industries, we also examine the industries where there has been a heavy presence of foreign firms. For firms producing computers and computer peripherals, labor productivity ratio of domestic to foreign firms increased from 42 percent to 102 percent. For electronic components, the ratio increased from 41 percent to 56 percent. Even for apparels, there is slight increase over the five year period. Only for TV and other video equipment, among the top exporting industries, labor productivity ratio of domestic to foreign firms decreased, though only slightly.

[8] Foreign invested firms here exclude those with investment from Hong Kong, Macao, and Taiwan.

Chapter

7

China's Central–Local Fiscal Disparity

Lin Shuanglin

Department of Public Finance, Peking University, Beijing, PRC

INTRODUCTION

The 1994 tax reforms in China has greatly increased the revenue share of the central government in total revenue and reduced the revenue share of local governments. Since the tax reform, every province has run fiscal deficits every year, while the central government has run surplus every year. Both the central government's surplus and the local governments' deficit have grown rapidly. As a result, local governments have become heavily dependent on the central government for revenue transfers. The imbalanced fiscal power between China's central and local governments has become one of the central concerns among academics and policy-makers in China. This chapter will analyze the central and local fiscal disparity and provide some policy suggestions.

Government became a major economic player in both developed and developing countries. In the industrial countries, market failures, income inequality, environmental damages, workplace safety, social security, and periodical economic recessions called for government intervention. In the non-industrialized countries, the demand for government to stimulate economic development increased. Thus, the size of government in many countries has increased dramatically.[1]

Recent decades have seen calls for fiscal decentralization, i.e., the devolution of fiscal powers and responsibilities from central to local governments. The advantages of fiscal decentralization include the following. First, local governments have better access to the local needs for public goods and services and can serve the local public better than the central government Hyek, 1945. Second, local government can collect the appropriate taxes according to the local characteristics. Third, competition among local governments can improve resource allocation since high-tax and high-regulation local governments will lose investors and residents (Tiebout, 1956; Brennan and Buchanan, 1980). Taxes are the price of public goods and services, and competition will yield the right price. Fourth, decentralization also permits those decision-makers to be held directly accountable to the local public through voters.

The revenues collected by different levels of government may not match their expenditures, and thus, intergovernmental transfers become necessary. Intergovernmental transfers are grants from one level of government to another, most often from a higher level of government to a lower level of government. The rationales of grants from a higher level of government to a lower level of government are as follows (Fisher, 2007): (1) Grants may be used to correct the inefficiency caused by inter-jurisdictional externalities or spillovers. If nonresidents of another region benefit from a public good provided by a given region, then social marginal benefits will be underestimated and too little of the public good is provided. A central government grant can bc uscd to inducc the regional government to provide more public goods and improve efficiency. Because the grant funds are from taxes, those nonresidents end up paying for part of the service through their taxes to the central government.

[1] According to Adolph Wagner (1835–1917), government size will increase as the development of industrial economy.

(2) A tax generated by the national government may cost less than that collected by local governments, while the tax revenue may be spent more efficiently by the local governments. Thus, the central government can collect more and spend less to improve efficiency. (3) Intergovernmental grants can be used as a method of explicit income redistribution for equity reasons. Transfers can serve as an inter-regional redistribution of income, and make the provision of public goods more equitable.

China's economic reforms started with decentralization in which the central government designated some decision-making powers to state-owned enterprises and local governments. As the local government spending increased, the local government budgetary revenue became insufficient, and the central government gave local government rights to collect extra-budgetary revenues. However, decentralization led to a large decline in the central government revenue share in the total revenue, and the expansion on the extra-budgetary revenue was accompanied by a decline in the total budgetary revenue in GDP.[2] In 1994, a tax sharing system was established, thus beginning the process of fiscal recentralization. The fiscal landscape has dramatically changed. The size of the budgetary revenue and the fiscal power of the central government have increased significantly. Nevertheless, provincial government's fiscal responsibilities have actually increased. Every province relies heavily on the central government for transfers, and many governments below the provincial level have severe debt problems.

China's central and local government finance has been a fascinating subject of research. Many prior studies are concerned with the decline in the government budgetary revenue (Bahl and Wallich, 1992, p. 20; Stiglitz, 1998; Brean, 1998; Wong *et al.*, 1995, p. 6; Lin, 2000) and the excessive fee collections by local governments and central government agencies and the large extra-budgetary revenue (Wu, 1997; Fan, 1998; Jia, 2000; Lin, 2004). Recent years have

[2] The share of the central government revenue in the total government revenue was only 22 percent in 1993, and the share of the total government revenue in GDP declined from 31.2 percent to 12.6 percent in 1993.

seen studies on the effects of fiscal decentralization on regional economic development (see for example, Knight and Li, 1999; Lin and Liu, 2000; and Jin *et al.*, 2004), and the effect of local election on local public goods provisions (Zhang *et al.*, 2004). However, analyses of China's current central–local fiscal disparity are still limited.

Balancing the fiscal power and responsibilities between the central and local governments can help China in solving the problems such as growing local government debt and unbalanced regional development. This study will discuss China's central–local fiscal disparity, identify the missing role of China's central government, and provide urgently needed policy suggestions. The organization of the paper is as follows: the second section discusses China's tax system and central–local fiscal disparity, and addresses the issue of fiscal centralization; the third section analyzes the structures of central and local governments' revenues and expenditures, and identifies the missing role of the central government; and the last section provides concluding remarks.

CHINA'S TAX SYSTEM AND THE CENTRAL–LOCAL FISCAL DISPARITY

Tax System

In China, tax laws are made by the National People's Congress and its Standing Committee. Provincial governments have the right to pass limited tax laws. But they have seldom used the right. Prefecture, county, and township governments have no right to enact their own tax laws. All of the local governments (provincial, prefecture, county, and township) have no right to independently issue bonds. Since the 1980s, the central government has delegated some authority to the lower levels in collecting revenues and disposing the revenue in order to solve the local revenue shortage problem.

The budgetary process for provincial is usually as follows: every year, provincial governments submit the budget to the central government, the central government provides feedbacks, the provincial government revises the budgets and submits the revised budget to the central government, and the central government approves provincial budgets. The process is called "Two-ups and Two-downs" (Niu, 2005).

In 1994, a tax sharing system was established. Taxes were reduced from 37 to 23 and were divided into three categories: national taxes which were paid to the central government, joint taxes which were shared by the central and local governments, and local taxes which were paid to local governments. Central tax bureaus (*guo shui ju*) and local tax bureaus (*di shui ju*) were set up, and the central to local tax rebate (*shuishou fanhuan*) system was established.

Central government taxes include (1) tariff, (2) consumption tax (similar to excise tax in the US), (3) corporate income tax from central government-owned enterprises, (4) income tax from local banks and foreign banks and other financial institutions, (5) income tax from rail road, headquarters banks, headquarters insurance companies (including business tax, income tax, profit and urban construction and maintenance tax), and (6) profits from central government-owned enterprises.

Local government taxes include (1) business tax (excluding business tax from rail road, headquarters banks, and headquarters insurance companies),[3] (2) income tax from local enterprises (excluding income tax from local banks and foreign banks and other financial institutions), (3) profits from local enterprises, personal income tax, urban land tax, and fixed investment direction adjustment tax, (4) urban construction and maintenance tax (excluding the tax from rail road, headquarters banks, and headquarters insurance companies), (5) housing tax, (6) vehicle license tax, (7) urban real estate tax, (8) vehicle tax, (9) stamp tax, (10) land appreciation tax, (11) slaughtering tax, (12) agricultural (animal husbandry) tax, (13) cultivated land occupation tax, and (14) contract tax.

Taxes shared by the central and local governments include (1) value-added tax (the share of the central government is 75 percent),

[3] Business tax is levied on the transfer of intangible assets or sale of immovable properties, primarily "service enterprises" including transportation, communications, financial services, real estate sales, and entertainment. Education institutions and hospitals are exempted from this tax.

(2) natural resource tax (only ocean oil resource tax belongs to the central government), and (3) stamp tax from stock exchange (the share of the central government is 50 percent).[4]

The most important shared tax is the value-added tax. Currently, there are two rates: for products related to agricultural production (such as fertilizer, feeds, and machines) and basic consumption goods (such as foods, cooking oil, water, and natural gas) the tax rate is 13 percent; for most other goods the rate is 17 percent. Of the value-added tax revenues, 75 percent are remitted to the central government, and 25 percent remains in the province.

As the size of personal income taxes increases, the central government has decided to share the personal income tax with local governments. In 2002, the central government share of personal income tax was 50 percent; in 2003, the central government share increased to 60 percent. Meanwhile, the Chinese government completely eliminated the agricultural tax in 2006.

Central-Local Fiscal Disparity

The new tax system has greatly strengthened the central government's fiscal power and weakened the local governments' fiscal power. Table 7.1 shows budgetary revenues and expenditures of central and local governments from 1978 to 2005. From 1978 to 1984, local governments as a whole ran huge surpluses every year, although the surpluses were decreasing year by year. From 1985 to 1993, the local governments' budget was basically balanced every year. As a result of the tax reform, the central government share in the total revenue increased from 22 percent in 1993 to 54.9 percent in 2004! The central government revenue share was down to 52.3 percent in 2005. Meanwhile, the central government expenditure share actually declined from 28.3 percent in 1993 to 26.0 percent in 2005. After the tax reform in 1994, every provincial government has run budget deficits every year.

[4] Since 2001, personal income tax has also become the shared tax between the central government and local governments.

Table 7.1: Budgetary revenues and expenditures of central and local governments.

Year	Central and local budgetary revenue				Central and local budgetary expenditure				Local government self-sufficiency rate (%)
	Absolute amount (100 million yuan)			Proportion (%)	Absolute amount (100 million yuan)			Proportion (%)	
	National	Central	Local	Central	National	Central	Local	Central	
1978	1,132.26	175.77	956.49	15.5	1,122.09	532.12	589.97	47.4	162.1
1979	1,146.38	231.34	915.04	20.2	1,281.79	655.08	626.71	51.1	146.0
1980	1,159.93	284.45	875.48	24.5	1,228.83	666.81	562.02	54.3	155.8
1981	1,175.79	311.07	864.72	26.5	1,138.41	625.65	512.76	55.0	168.6
1982	1,212.33	346.84	865.49	28.6	1,229.98	651.81	578.17	53.0	149.7
1983	1,366.95	490.01	876.94	35.8	1,409.52	759.6	649.92	53.9	134.9
1984	1,642.86	665.47	977.39	40.5	1,701.02	893.33	807.69	52.5	121.0
1985	2,004.82	769.63	1,235.19	38.4	2,004.25	795.25	1,209.00	39.7	102.2
1986	2,122.01	778.42	1,343.59	36.7	2,204.91	836.36	1,368.55	37.9	98.2
1987	2,199.35	736.29	1,463.06	33.5	2,262.18	845.63	1,416.55	37.4	103.3
1988	2,357.24	774.76	1,582.48	32.9	2,491.21	845.04	1,646.17	33.9	96.1
1989	2,664.90	822.52	1,842.38	30.9	2,823.78	888.77	1,935.01	31.5	95.2
1990	2,937.10	992.42	1,944.68	33.8	3,083.59	1,004.47	2,079.12	32.6	93.5
1991	3,149.48	938.25	2,211.23	29.8	3,386.62	1,090.81	2,295.81	32.2	96.3
1992	3,483.37	979.51	2,503.86	28.1	3,742.20	1,170.44	2,571.76	31.3	97.4
1993	4,348.95	957.51	3,391.44	22.0	4,642.30	1,312.06	3,330.24	28.3	101.8
1994	5,218.10	2,906.50	2,311.60	55.7	5,792.62	1,754.43	4,038.19	30.3	57.2
1995	6,242.20	3,256.62	2,985.58	52.2	6,823.72	1,995.39	4,828.33	29.2	61.8

(*Continued*)

Table 7.1: *(Continued)*

Year	Central and local budgetary revenue				Central and local budgetary expenditure				Local government self-sufficiency rate (%)
	Absolute amount (100 million yuan)			Proportion (%)	Absolute amount (100 million yuan)			Proportion (%)	
	National	Central	Local	Central	National	Central	Local	Central	
1996	7,407.99	3,661.07	3,746.92	49.4	7,937.55	2,151.27	5,786.28	27.1	64.8
1997	8,651.14	4,226.92	4,424.22	48.9	9,233.56	2,532.50	6,701.06	27.4	66.0
1998	9,875.95	4,892.00	4,983.95	49.5	10,798.18	3,125.60	7,672.58	28.9	65.0
1999	11,444.08	5,849.21	5,594.87	51.1	13,187.67	4,152.33	9,035.34	31.5	61.9
2000	13,395.23	6,989.17	6,406.06	52.2	15,886.50	5,519.85	10,366.65	34.7	61.8
2001	16,386.04	8,582.74	7,803.30	52.4	18,902.58	5,768.02	13,134.56	30.5	59.4
2002	18,903.64	10,388.64	8,515.00	55.0	22,053.15	6,771.70	15,281.45	30.7	55.7
2003	21,715.25	11,865.27	9,849.98	54.6	24,649.95	7,420.10	17,229.85	30.1	57.2
2004	26,396.47	14,503.10	11,893.37	54.9	28,486.89	7,894.08	20,592.81	27.7	57.8
2005	31,627.89	16,535.94	15,092.04	52.3	33,708.12	8,775.73	24,932.39	26.0	60.5

Notes: (a) The central and local revenues in this table represent the income from the central and local level government themselves.

(b) The figure here excludes debt revenue.

Sources: Ministry of Finance (1997); China Statistical Bureau (2005, 2006).

*The figures in this table do not include the revenues from issuing internal and external debts, and do not include interest payment on internal and external debts and basic construction expenditures financed by foreign debts.

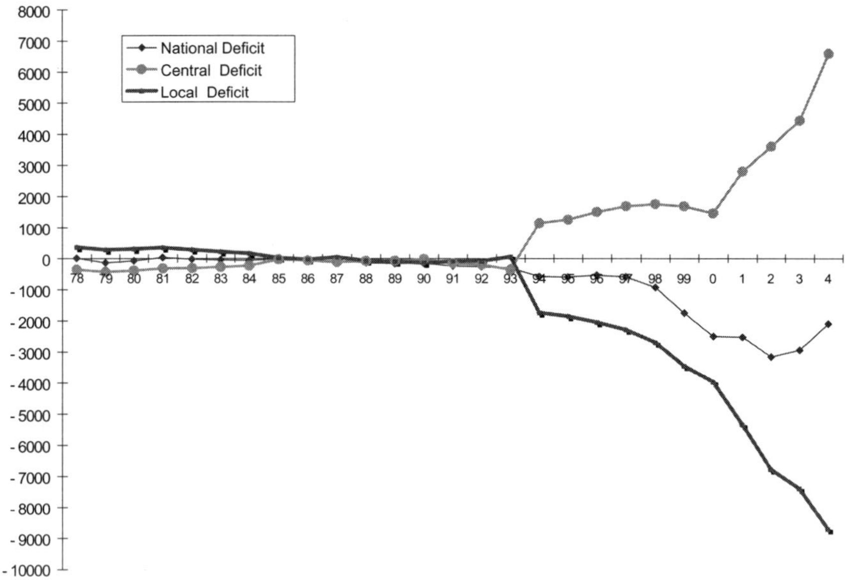

Fig. 7.1: China's central and local government budget deficits.
Data sources: Ministry of Finance, *Finance Yearbook China*, 2005.

Figure 7.1 shows budget deficits for various levels of governments. It can be seen that the central government surplus has been increasing, while the local government budget deficit has been increasing.

Table 7.1 also shows the self-sufficiency rate for the local government (the ratio of local government revenues to local government expenditures). This rate reached 56 percent in 2002, and was 60.5 percent in 2005. That is to say, about 40 percent of local government expenditures were financed by central government transfers.

The central government approves the budgets of provincial governments and covers every provincial government's fiscal deficits through its transfers. So, from accounting books, after the central government transfers, provincial governments have no deficits.

Besides budgetary revenues and expenditures, there exist extra-budgetary revenues and expenditures for both central and local governments. Extra-budgetary revenues are collected and disposed of by local governments, government agencies and institutions, and state enterprises. Extra-budget revenues include user-charges for the service provided by government agencies and institutions, administrative fees (license fee, etc.), and revenues from businesses run by administrative units. Extra-budgetary revenues are used for investment in fixed assets, city maintenance, welfare, bonuses and awards, administrative and business activities, etc. Extra-budgetary revenues have increased dramatically during the reform period, and local governments heavily rely on extra-budgetary revenues.

Table 7.2 shows the extra-budgetary revenues and expenditures of central and local governments. The ratio of the extra-budgetary revenue to the budgetary revenue was 66.2 percent in 1982, reached 110.7 percent in 1992, and declined to 21 percent in 2003. The central government share of the extra-budgetary revenue was 33.7 percent in 1982, reached 44.3 percent in 1992, and declined to 8.3 percent in 2003. It can be seen that the extra-budgetary revenue is now mainly collected and utilized by local governments. As fee reforms have proceeded in recent years, the extra-budgetary revenue has declined significantly.[5]

Local governments often initiate their own projects and finance these projects with their own funds. Thus, there exist off-budget revenues and expenditures, which are out of the central government's monitor and supervision. Off-budgetary revenues (called "third source of finance") are the revenues not included in either budgetary or extra-budgetary revenues. Most of the off-budgetary revenues are not legal, and thus this budget is sometimes called "the Little Golden Box (*xiao jin ku*)." Many local governments are in severe fiscal difficulties. For example, in the Guangxi province, 65 out of 81 counties (including cities and districts) owned wages and salaries of government employees. By the end of 2000, the accumulated debt of various levels of governments reached 22.84 billion yuan, of which internal debt was 8.94 billion yuan and external (foreign) debt was 13.92 billion yuan.[6]

[5] See Lin (2004) for a discussion of fee reforms in China.

[6] Lu (2003).

Table 7.2: Extra-budgetary revenues and expenditures (100 million yuan) of central and local governments.

Year	National total		Central government		Local government		Central government's share (%)	
	Revenue	Expenditure	Revenue	Expenditure	Revenue	Expenditure	Revenue	Expenditure
1982	802.74	734.53	270.70	227.05	532.04	507.48	33.7	30.9
1983	967.68	875.81	359.90	300.38	607.78	575.43	37.2	34.3
1984	1,188.48	1,114.74	470.54	420.24	717.94	694.50	39.6	37.7
1985	1,530.03	1,375.03	636.10	562.05	893.93	812.98	41.6	40.9
1986	1,737.31	1,578.37	716.63	640.94	1,020.68	937.43	41.2	40.6
1987	2,028.80	1,840.75	828.03	741.61	1,200.77	1,099.14	40.8	40.3
1988	2,360.77	2,145.27	907.15	842.86	1,453.62	1,302.41	38.4	39.3
1989	2,658.83	2,503.10	1,072.28	975.87	1,586.55	1,527.23	40.3	39.0
1990	2,708.64	2,707.06	1,073.28	1,037.69	1,635.36	1,669.37	39.6	38.3
1991	3,243.30	3,092.26	1,381.10	1,263.27	1,862.20	1,828.99	42.6	40.9
1992	3,854.92	3,649.90	1,707.73	1,592.81	2,147.19	2,057.09	44.3	43.6
1993	1,432.54	1,314.30	245.90	198.87	1,186.64	1,115.43	17.2	15.1
1994	1,862.53	1,710.39	283.32	225.02	1,579.21	1,485.37	15.2	13.2
1995	2,406.50	2,331.26	317.57	351.38	2,088.93	1,979.88	13.2	15.1
1996	3,893.34	3,838.32	947.66	1,034.92	2,945.68	2,803.40	24.3	27.0

(*Continued*)

Table 7.2: (*Continued*)

Year	National total		Central government		Local government		Central government's share (%)	
	Revenue	Expenditure	Revenue	Expenditure	Revenue	Expenditure	Revenue	Expenditure
1997	2,826.00	2,685.54	145.08	143.91	2,680.92	2,541.63	5.1	5.4
1998	3,082.29	2,918.31	164.15	139.74	2,918.14	2,778.57	5.3	4.8
1999	3,385.17	3,139.14	230.45	164.82	3,154.72	2,974.32	6.8	5.3
2000	3,826.43	3,529.01	247.63	210.74	3,578.79	3,318.28	6.5	6.0
2001	4,300.00	3,850.00	347.00	258.13	3,953.00	3,591.87	8.1	6.7
2002	4,479.00	3,831.00	440.00	259.00	4,039.00	3,572.00	9.8	6.8
2003	4,566.80	4,156.36	379.37	329.32	4,187.43	3,827.04	8.3	7.9

Notes: The scope of extra-budgetary revenues and expenditures was adjusted between 1993 and 1995 and 1996, not comparable with previous years; since 1997, the extra-budgetary revenue and expenditure has not included those funds (fees) which have been brought into budgetary management, not consistent with previous year. Each year's growth rate was calculated by constant figures.

Sources: Ministry of Finance (2000, 2005).

Fiscal Centralization

We have mentioned that China's local government spending accounted for 74 percent of the total government spending in 2005. Is the Chinese fiscal system decentralized? To answer this question, we need to discuss the definition of decentralization. A general definition of decentralization is given by Rondinelli (1981). That is, the transfer of responsibility for planning, management, and resource-raising, and allocation from the central government to (a) field units of central government ministries or agencies; (b) subordinate units or levels of government; (c) semi-autonomous public authorities or corporations; (d) area-wide regional or functional authorities; or (e) Non-Governmental Organizations (NGOs). Bennet (1990) emphasized the distinction between two general decentralizing thrusts: *intergovernmental decentralization,* which involves transfers of authority, responsibility, power, and resources downward to lower levels of government, and *market-based decentralization,* where these are transferred from governments to the firms and NGOs.

In many economic analyses, the share of the sub-national government expenditure or revenue in the consolidated general government expenditure or revenue is used as a proxy for the degree of decentralization of a fiscal system.[7] These measures can be misleading in the Chinese case.

Table 7.3 shows the share of central government revenues in total government revenues and the share of central government expenditures in total government expenditures. If a high ratio of central government revenues in the total revenue or a higher ratio of central government expenditures in the total expenditure implies a high level of centralization, then the degree of centralization is not high in China, compared to the other countries. In 2004, the share of the central government revenue in the total revenue was 54.9 percent and the share of the central government expenditure in the total expenditure was only 27.7 percent for China, while these ratios are, respectively, 61.9 percent and 67.9 percent for Argentina, 89.7 percent

[7] See Oates (1972) for a discussion.

Table 7.3: Shares of central government revenue and expenditure for some selected countries in 2004 (percent).

Country	Share of central government revenue in total revenue	Share of central government expenditure in total expenditure	Share of central government revenue in total revenue excluding social contributions	Ratio of central government expenditure to its revenue	Ratio of central government transfers to its total revenue
Argentina	61.9	58.9	57.5	87.2	13.4
Australia	73.8	55.4	73.8	71.2	25.4
China	57.2	27.7	57.2	52.2	68.9
Chile	89.7	83.4	89.1	76.5	4.0
Czech	85.3	76.6	76.0	91.8	16.5
Denmark	64.6	36.5	63.6	55.4	39.9
France	87.1	80.8	79.8	97.9	9.9
Germany	66.9	61.0	45.2	99.5	8.6
Hungary	85.8	75.6	80.2	93.8	17.7
Italy	81.1	69.0	73.8	87.2	18.4
Netherland	88.8	62.2	83.3	72.5	30.9
Poland*	87.0	77.8	80.0	96.1	15.6
Portugal	91.5	87.0	88.2	99.0	6.7
Russia	68.0	60.9	60.7	70.9	8.8
Spain*	82.6	70.7	73.9	77.3	17.4
Thailand	92.3	89.9	92.0	77.9	9.5
UK	90.7	72.0	88.4	84.0	23.9
USA	54.3	53.2	40.5	108.4	20.9

*Data are for 2003 since data for 2004 are unavailable.

Source: International Monetary Fund, *Government Finance Statistics Yearbook*, 2005.

and 87.8 percent for Chile, 87.1 percent and 80.8 percent for France, 27.4 percent and 22.2 percent for Germany, 68 percent and 60.9 percent for Russia, 92.3 percent and 89.9 percent for Thailand, 90.7 percent and 72 percent for the United Kingdom, and 54.3 percent and 53.2 percent for the USA. It can be seen that the shares of China's central government revenue and expenditure are lower than that of many other countries.

However, as Oates (1972), Rondinelli (1981), and Bennet (1990) recognized, decentralization is concerned with decision-making power, and cannot simply be measured by the shares of the subnational government revenue and expenditure in the total revenue and total expenditure. It should be measured by the decision-making power of the local governments. For example, under the highly centralized fiscal system in China before 1978, most revenues, both taxes and sequestered profits, were collected at the local level. In 1978, local governments collected 84.5 percent of China's total budgetary revenues, primarily through the enterprises located in their jurisdictions. Expenditures, on the other hand, were more evenly divided. In 1978, the central government accounted for nearly half of all expenditures, 47.4 percent, even though local governments were responsible for providing the bulk of government services such as education and health care. Provinces collected most of the revenue, but the central government decided how these revenues were to be spent, and thus, the system was centralized. The central government controlled the local governments through administrative orders, and local governments did not have much freedom in decision making.

Right now, the central government gets most of the revenue and spends only a small proportion, just the opposite of the situation in 1978. In 2005, the central government revenue share was 52.3 percent, and the central government expenditure share was 26.0 percent. Is the current system more centralized or more decentralized? Compared to the system in 1978, the current system is more decentralized since the local governments have more decision-making powers on its spending. However, the current system is centralized since the central government controls more revenues, allocates a large amount of transfers to provinces, and interferes with the spending decisions of local governments. The local governments are heavily dependent on the central government for revenues. Also, as mentioned earlier, local governments still need to submit their annual budget to the central government for approval. Thus, the Chinese fiscal system is not decentralized. Before 1978, the central government controlled local governments through administrative means, and now the central government controlled the local governments through economic means, i.e., through controlling financial resources.

Table 7.3 also shows the ratio of the central government's expenditures to its revenues and the ratio of grants to the central government revenue for some selected countries. China's central government only spends about 52 percent of its revenue (excluding the revenue from debt issuing). No other country mentioned in Table 7.3 has a smaller ratio of the central government's expenditure to its revenue than the Chinese government. In most countries, the central government revenue and its expenditure are closely related. For example, the ratio of the central government expenditure to its revenue was 87.2 percent in Argentina, 83.4 percent in Chile, 97.9 percent in France, 88.1 percent in Germany, 70.9 in Russia, 77.9 in Thailand, 84 percent in the United Kingdom, and 108.4 percent in the USA. China's central government does not actively involve in the provisions of public goods and services, and it transfers the extra revenues to the local governments.

The last column in Table 7.3 shows the ratio of grants to the central government revenue for selected countries. The ratio of central government grants to local governments to the central government revenue was 69 percent in China, unbelievably high! No other country came even closer to this number. For example, the ratio of central government transfers to the local government to the central government total revenue was 13.4 percent in Argentina, 4 percent in Chile, 9.9 percent in France, 21.9 percent in Germany, 8.8 percent in Russia, 9.5 percent in Thailand, 23.9 percent in the United Kingdom, and 20.9 percent in the US.

The current system causes inefficiency and corruption. The transfer system gives the central government enormous controlling power. The central government has a large amount of extra funds to distribute, and a large portion of the funds are not distributed following strict rules. The central government has a lot of leeway in allocating the funds, and the local governments have no power to check the central government. Every province heavily depends on the transfers from the central government, including the richest provinces such as Shanghai, Guangdong, and Zhejiang, and every province has to beg the central government for money. Every province has to send lobby groups to Beijing to lobby the central government. Some cities and counties also have lobby groups in Beijing. The central government is assumed to be benevolent, super genius, and impartial in allocating the extra funds. But how can the central planner know the amount of funds each province really needs? Such a large amount of funds allocated by the central government may cause misallocation of resources. Also, bribes and other forms of corruption have become widespread. China has changed in many areas, but in the fiscal area, it is still strongly affected by the central planning system.

REVENUES AND EXPENDITURES OF CENTRAL AND LOCAL GOVERNMENTS

This section analyzes the revenue and the expenditure structure of the central and local governments and discusses the missing role of the central government.

Central and Local Government Revenues

The share of taxes in the total tax revenue for the central government is increasing. In 1991, the tax share in the total revenue for the central government was 83 percent, and this ratio increased to about 98 percent in 1994, and it remains at this level.

Noticeably, the central government's burden on subsidizing state enterprises has decreased much more than local governments. In 1991, the central government's subsidies to loss-making enterprises accounted for 25.2 percent of its total revenue. This ratio declined to

2.0 percent in 1994 and to only 0.2 percent in 2004. The central government owns a number of large enterprises which are very profitable. As Lin and Rowe (2006) mentioned, overall the state owned enterprises were making huge amount of profits. The demand for the SOEs to submit a part of profits to the government has recently increased.

Figure 7.2 shows the shares of major taxes in the total tax revenue of the central government from 1996 to 2004 intuitively. The central government depends on VAT, consumption tax, corporate income tax, personal income tax, and tariffs for revenue. The share of consumption tax in the total tax revenue, as well as that of VAT, has declined. In 2004, the share of VAT in the total tax revenue was 46.7 percent. Consumption tax and VAT on imports have increased

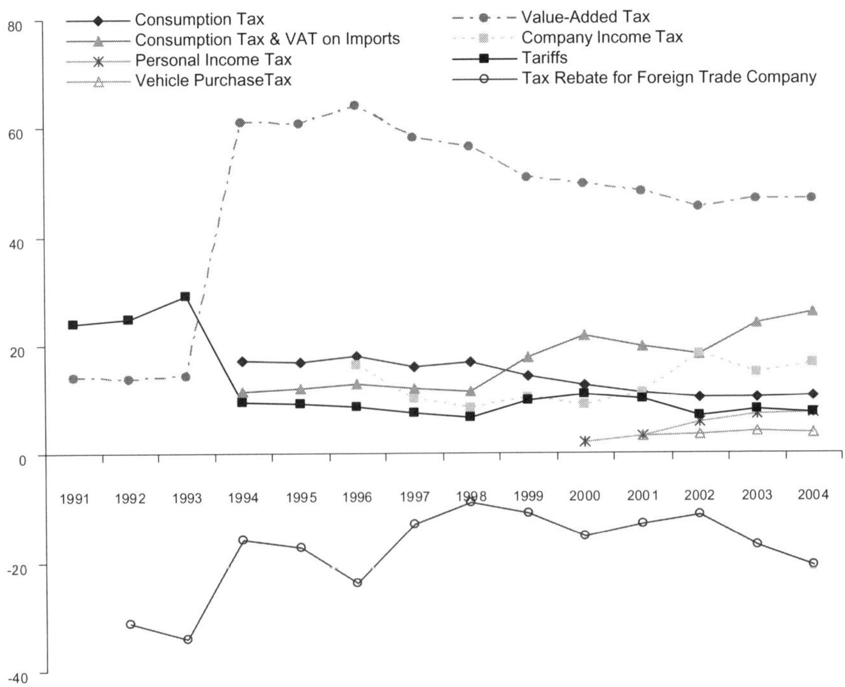

Fig. 7.2: Central government major taxes as percentage of total tax revenue. Data sources: Calculated based on Ministry of Finance, *Finance Yearbook China*, 2000, 2005.

significantly, and the share of consumption tax and VAT on imports was 26.1 percent in 2004. The share of corporate income tax remains at around 16 percent with fluctuation. The share of personal income tax has increased significantly, reaching 7.4 percent of the total tax revenue. The share of tariffs has declined dramatically from 29 percent of the total tax revenue in 1993 to only 7.4 percent in 2004. Also, the share of tax rebates to exporters (negative taxes) accounted for 20.7 percent.[8]

The major component of the local government revenue is tax revenue, but the ratio of taxes in total revenue has declined. In 1991, 99.9 percent of the local government revenue was from taxes; it come down to 95 percent in 1995, to 88.8 percent in 2000, and to only 84.1 percent in 2004. The major non-tax revenue is surtax for education, which accounted for 2.5 percent of total revenue in 2004. The unspecified revenue accounted for 14 percent of total revenue in 2004.[9] This may include the revenues from land sales, which accounted for a large amount of revenue, although detailed statistics is not available. Local governments have to subsidize loss-making state enterprises. The subsidies were considered as negative revenues in China's government accounting system. The subsidies declined from 308.51 in 1994 to 181.98 in 2004, or declined from 13.3 percent of total revenue in 1994 to only 1.5 percent of total revenue in 2004.[10]

Local governments' tax revenues are from local taxes and shared taxes (including individual income and value-added tax). Five major taxes for local governments are VAT, business tax, corporate income tax, personal income tax, and city maintenance and construction tax. In 2004, VAT accounted for 24 percent of the total local tax revenue, business tax 35 percent, corporate income tax 16 percent, personal income tax 7 percent, and city maintenance and construction tax accounted for 6.7 percent.[11] Figure 7.3 shows shares of various

[8] The figures are calculated based on Ministry of Finance (2000, 2005).

[9] The figures are calculated based on Ministry of Finance (2000, 2005).

[10] The figures are calculated based on Ministry of Finance (2000, 2005).

[11] The figures are calculated based on Ministry of Finance (2000, 2005).

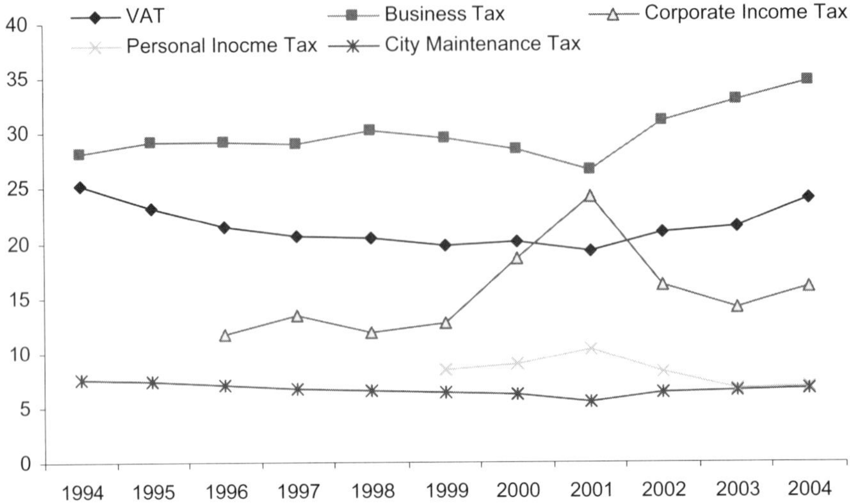

Fig. 7.3: Local government major taxes as percentage of total tax revenue.
Data sources: Calculated based on Ministry of Finance, *Finance Yearbook China*, 2000, 2005.

taxes in the total local government tax revenue from 1991 to 2004. It can be seen that, VAT declined from 25 percent of total revenue in 1994 to 20 percent in 2000 and then came back; the share of corporate income tax increased from 11.7 percent in 1996 to 24.2 percent in 2001, and came down to 16 percent in 2004.

Local governments have become increasingly dependent on taxes from enterprises (VAT, business tax, and corporate income tax). The share of taxes from enterprises was 62.4 percent of total tax revenue in 1996, and increased to 74.7 percent in 2004. The share of city maintenance and construction tax in the total tax revenue declined slightly over the years. Personal income tax deserves some attention. Personal income tax was a local tax based on the tax laws in the early 1990s. However, as the revenue from personal income tax became sizable, the central government decided to share the tax with local governments. The central government has almost unlimited power over the local governments. As a result, the share of personal income tax in the local total revenue declined in recent years.

Central and Local Government Expenditures

Central government expenditures focus on national defense, capital construction, government administration, and interest payment on foreign and domestic debts. In 2004, the central government's total spending was 789.4 billion yuan, of which 217.2 billion yuan was on national defense, 134.4 billion yuan was on capital construction, 58.7 billion yuan was on government administration, 52.1 billion yuan was on culture, education, science, and health care, and 74.1 billion yuan was on interest payment on foreign and domestic debts.[12]

Figure 7.4 shows the share of various central government expenditures in the total central government expenditure over the period of 1991 to 2004. The share of expenditures on capital construction has declined from 33.5 percent of total expenditures to

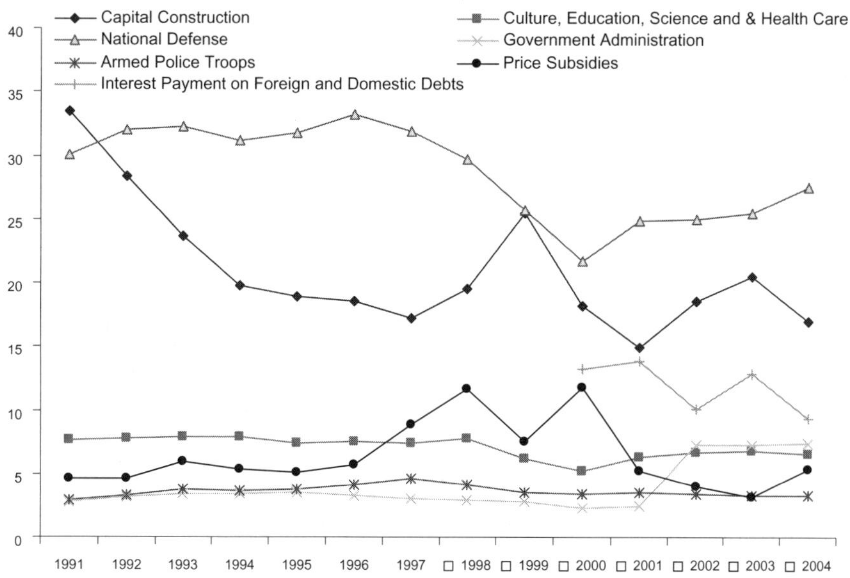

Fig. 7.4: Central government major expenditures as percentage of expenditure. Data sources: Calculated based on Ministry of Finance, *Finance Yearbook China*, 2000, 2005.

[12] The figures are calculated based on Ministry of Finance (2000, 2005).

17 percent of total expenditures. The share of expenditures on national defense was around 30 percent, declined slightly overtime. Meanwhile, the share of the expenditures for government administration increased from 2.8 percent in 1991 to 7.4 percent in 2004! The number of government administrators has increased dramatically in recent decades, and salaries and other expenses for government administrative have also been rising. The share of expenditures on interest on foreign and domestic debts declined from 13.3 percent of total expenditures in 2000 to 9.4 percent in 2004.

Since the Asian financial crisis, China has been very cautious on international borrowing. In addition, the central government revenue has increased much faster than the growth rate of the economy (around 20 percent in recent years). All these explain the decline in the share of the government interest payment on foreign and domestic debts.

Local government expenditures concentrate on education, science and health care, government administration, and capital construction. They are responsible for almost all expenditures on health, education, social services, social security (including unemployment insurance), local infrastructure, and agricultural development. Though education and health care are the largest category of local government expenditures, its share in total expenditures declined steadily. The share of expenditures on education, science, and health care in total government expenditures was 27.2 percent in 1991, 23.6 percent in 2000, and down to only 22.5 percent in 2004. Meanwhile, the share of the expenditures for government administration increased from 13.6 percent in 1991 to 16.9 percent in 2004. The share of expenditures on capital construction increased from 8.5 percent in 1991 to 10.2 percent in 2004. Also, local government expenditures on agriculture was 7.5 percent, on urban maintenance was 5.2 percent, and on social welfare was 2.7 percent. Surprisingly, 26 percent of the total expenditure was unspecified, and thus, more than a quarter of local government expenditures were not transparent.[13] Figure 7.5 shows the share of various government

[13] The figures are calculated based on Ministry of Finance (2000, 2005).

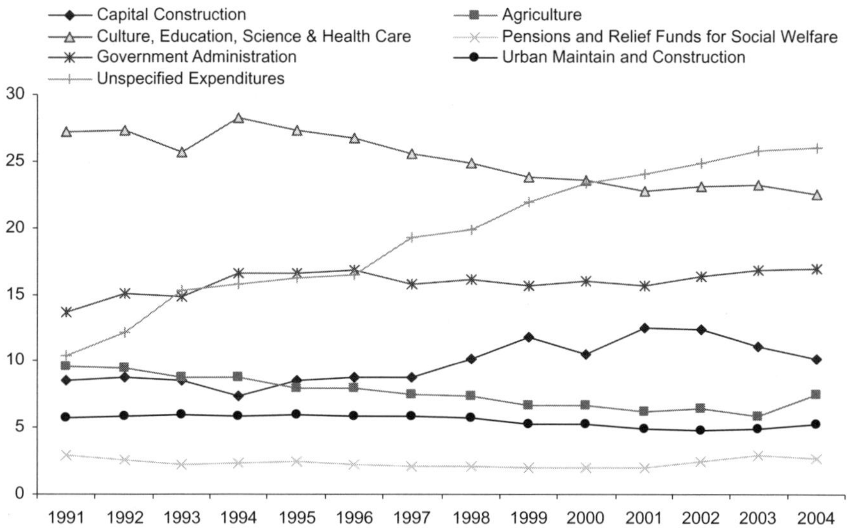

Fig. 7.5: Local government major expenditures as percentage of total expenditure. Data sources: Calculated based on Ministry of Finance, *Finance Yearbook China*, 2000, 2005.

expenditures in the total local government expenditure over the period of 1991–2004.

The Missing Role of China's Central Government

In what area, the role of China's central government is missing? The answer is social security and social welfare. In many countries, the central government administration directly provides goods and services to the general public. In China, the central government designates local governments to provide public goods and services and provide them with financial support. Table 7.4 shows the social contributions in the central government total revenue and social benefits in the central government total expenditure for selected countries in 2004. In all of the countries listed in Table 7.4, except China and Chile, the central government is in charge of social security and other social programs. Australia does not collect social contributions, but finances social benefits by other taxes. The social

Table 7.4: Social contributions in central government total revenue and social benefits in central government total expenditure for selected countries in 2004.

Country	Ratio of social contributions in total central government revenue	Ratio of social benefits in total central government expenditures
Argentina	16.6	33.3
Australia	0.0	41.3
Austria*	40.3	50.5
China	0.0	0.1
Chile	6.6	28.2
Czech Republic	45.4	46.8
France	41.4	47.6
Germany	59.0	71.4
Hungary	33.2	37.5
Italy	34.5	42.8
Netherland	36.9	43.9
Poland*	40.1	45.0
Portugal	30.8	35.6
Russia	27.4	33.6
Spain*	40.5	45.4
Thailand	4.9	16.0
UK	21.7	30.1
USA	42.6	41.6

*Data are for 2003 since data for 2004 are unavailable.
Source: International Monetary Fund, *Government Finance Statistics Yearbook*, 2005.

contributions and social benefits account for a large percentage of the central government total revenue and expenditure. For example, social benefits accounted for 71 percent of the total central government expenditure in Germany, 50.5 percent in Austria, 47.6 percent in France, 46.8 percent in Czech Republic, and 41.6 percent in the US. However, social benefits accounted for only 0.1 percent of the total central government expenditure in China! In China, local governments are responsible for social security programs, which basically cover only urban residents but not rural residents.

Social security program accounts for a large portion of every country's budget. If the social contribution is excluded from the central government budget, many other countries' central government revenue share in total revenue declines dramatically (see Table 7.3). For example, the revenue share of the US federal government was 40.5 percent in 2004, and the revenue share of the German government was 45 percent in 2004.

CONCLUSIONS

This chapter has discussed the fiscal disparity between China's central and local governments, addressed the issue of fiscal decentralization, analyzed the structures of central and local governments' revenues and expenditures, and explained the missing role of the central government.

After the tax reforms in 1994, the central government revenue share in the total government revenue has largely increased, while the central government expenditure share remains unchanged. The central government revenue share in the total government revenue was 52.3 percent in 2005, but its expenditure share was only 26.0 percent in 2005, lower than that in 1993 (28.3 percent). The central government surplus has been increasing, while the local government budget deficit has been increasing. The ratio of local government revenues to local government expenditures was 60.5 percent in 2005, implying that nearly 40 percent of local government expenditures need to be financed by central government intergovernmental transfers.

The central government mainly relies on value-added tax and corporate income tax, and local governments mainly rely on business tax and value-added tax. The central government mainly spent on national defense and investment in fixed assets, while local governments mainly spent on education. Surprisingly, a large proportion of revenues for local governments are unexplained.

Unlike central governments in many countries, China's central government is absent in the area of social security and welfare programs. China's social security and welfare programs are run by local governments currently. As urbanization proceeds and as cross-region labor migration becomes more frequent, centralizing the social security and other social programs will be inevitable. Future fiscal reforms should aim at reducing the central–local fiscal disparity, increasing the local government decision-making power, and increasing central government expenditures on social welfare.

REFERENCES

Bahl, Roy and Christine Wallich (1992), "Intergovernmental Fiscal Relations in China," Working Papers, Country Economics Department, The World Bank, WPS 863.

Bennet, R.J. (1990) *Decentralization: Local Governments and Markets*, London: Clarendon Press.

Brennan, Geoffrey and James M. Buchanan (1980), *The Power to Tax: Analytical Foundations of a Fiscal Constitution*, Cambridge: Cambridge University Press.

China Statistical Bureau (2005), *Statistical Yearbook of China,* Beijing: China Statistical Publishing House.

China Statistical Bureau (2006), *China Statistical Abstract*, Beijing: China Statistical Publishing House.

Hayek, Friedrich A. (1945), "The Use of Knowledge in Society," *American Economic Review* 35, 519–530.

Jin, Hehui, Yingyi Qian and Barry R. Weingast (2007), "Regional Decentralization and Fiscal Incentives: Federalism, Chinese Style," *Journal of Public Economics* 89, 1719–1742.

Knight, John and Shi Li (1999), "Fiscal Decentralization: Incentives, Redistribution and Reform in China," *Oxford Development Studies* 27(1), 5–32.

Lin, Justin, Yifu and Zhiqiang Liu (2000), "Fiscal Decentralization and Economic Growth in China," *Economic Development and Cultural Change* 49(I), 1–21.

Lin, Shuanglin and W. Rowe (2006), "Determinants of the Profitability of China's Regional SOEs," *China Economic Review* 17, 120–141.

Lin, Shuanglin (2005), "Excessive Government Fee Collection in China," *Contemporary Economic Policy* 23, 91–106.

Lin, Shuanglin (2000), "The Decline of China's Budgetary Revenue: Reasons and Consequences," *Contemporary Economic Policy* 18, 477–490.

Lu, Quanlian (2003), "Deepening the Reforms of China's Intergovernmental Transfer System (jinyibu gaige he wanshan woguo caizheng zhuanyi zhifu zhid)," *in China and Oversea Experts on Fiscal Transfers (zhongwai zhuanjia lun caizheng zhuanyi zhifu zhidu)*, Edited by Research Department of Budgetary Committee, The Standing Committee of the National People's Congress, Beijing: China's Finance and Economics Publishing House, pp. 162–170.

Ministry of Finance (2005), *Finance Yearbook of China*, Beijing: China Fiscal Journals Publishing House.

Niu, Meili (2005), PhD thesis, University of Nebraska, Omaha, USA.

Oates, Wallace E. (1972), *Fiscal Federalism*, New York: Harcourt Brace Jovanovich.

Ouyang, Guobin, "Comments and Suggestions on Further Reforms on the Central-Local Government Transfer System (dui jinyibu tiaozheng he wanshan zhongyang dui defang zhuanyi zhifu zhidu de yijianhe jianyi)," in *China and Oversea Experts on Fiscal Transfers (zhongwai zhuanjia lun caizheng zhuanyi zhifu zhidu)*, Edited by Research Department of Budgetary Committee, The Standing Committee of the National People's Congress, Beijing: China's Finance and Economics Publishing House, pp. 254–261.

Rondinelli, D.A. (1981), "Government Decentralization in Comparative Perspective: Theory and Practice in Developing Countries," *International Review of Administrative Science* 47.

Stiglitz, Joseph (1998),"China's Reform Strategies in the Second Stage," A Speech at Peking University, *People's Daily*, November 13.

Tiebout, Charles (1956), "A Pure Theory of Local Expenditures," *Journal of Political Economy* 64, 416–424.

Wong, Christine P.W., Christopher Heady and Wing T. Woo (1995), *Fiscal Management and Economic Reform in the People, Republic of China*, Hong Kong: Oxford University Press.

Zhang, Xiaobo, Shenggen Fan, Linxiu Zhang and Jikun Huang (2004), "Local Governance and Public Goods Provision in Rural China," *Journal of Public Economics* 88, 2857–2871.

Chapter

8

China's Banking Sector Reform: A Critical Survey

*He Liping**

Department of Finance, Beijing Normal University, PRC

Toward the end of 2006, a major American banking corporation, together with several Chinese corporate partners, secured a deal of acquiring a major regional Chinese bank. Immediately after reaching the agreement, the new owners announced that they had appointed an American banker to replace the old, Chinese as the CEO for the acquired bank. The process of acquisition of this significant Chinese bank had been a tortuous one, as the lead bidder underwent long, difficult negotiations and overcame a number of regulatory and cultural obstacles. Both sides tended to regard the deal as a landmark case in China's banking industry, attesting how open the banking sector had been to foreign players and how far the government would let banking reforms go.

* The author would like to thank Dr. Yu Yongding, Dr. Yang Mu, and Professor John Wong for their help in preparing the chapter. My thanks also go to Miss Hu Jiani, a research student assistant at Beijing Normal University, who provided a good deal of timely help.

In the light that China became a World Trade Organization member in 2001 and passed through the "five-year transition" at the end of 2006, this is the time to make an assessment on how banking sector reform has gone during the period. When the country negotiated on the WTO accession, there were remarks on the air that virtually all banks in the country were "technically insolvent" as they presumably encountered an incredibly high amount of non-performing loans. The severe NPL problem would lead to, as believed by quite a number of observers, a major banking and financial crash and crisis when the sector became open to foreign competition. Yet the fact that many international banks showed a great enthusiasm in purchasing equity shares in Chinese banks during the recent years — the above mentioned is just one of numerous similar examples — seems to suggest the contrary: Chinese banks have not been fragile and worthless, but viable and capable to produce returns for investors (Anderson, 2005). This appears puzzling somehow and should be answered with assessment on how successful banking reform in the recent years has been.

This chapter attempts to provide a brief and comprehensive survey on banking reforms in contemporary China. The first section describes the historical background of banking reform in post-Mao China, which is followed by a summary in the second section of main objectives of banking reforms that have been recognized or perceived by the reformers in the country. The third section highlights main policy measures in reforming Chinese banking institutions in the recent years. The fourth section tries to identify significant changes that have happened to these banking institutions, largely based on observable facts. The last section concludes by remarking on future challenges facing Chinese banks.

THREE WAVES OF CHINA'S BANKING REFORM SINCE 1980

Reforming the banking industry in post-Mao China kicked off quite early, but moves have been zigzag and have remained largely incomplete until recently. For the past 25 years or so, we may identify three phases of banking reform movement in the country. The first period is the late 1970s through the mid-1990s, and the second is the last few years in the 1990s, and the third, the latest, is the so-called "WTO transition period" of 2001–2006.

During the first period, the most remarkable reform measure was the establishment of several new banking institutions in the country. Before the end of 1970s, there was virtually one bank only, the People's Bank of China. It conducted all sorts of banking and financial activities, acting as policy decision-maker, regulator, and business operator. Gradually, several business functions of the PBOC were spinned off and absorbed into newly established banking institutions. These included the Agricultural Bank of China, the Bank of China, and the People's Construction Bank of China (later changed Construction Bank of China), together with other semi-banking or non-banking financial institutions. These were often called "specialized banks," in that they were designated to conduct banking business in their own fields. For instance, the Agricultural Bank was mainly serving rural areas and agriculture, Bank of China mainly conducted banking business in foreign exchanges, and the Construction Bank provided long-term credit to state-owned enterprises.

In 1985, the Industrial and Commercial Bank of China was further established by separating the ordinary banking business (deposit taking and credit offering) from the People's Bank of China. Part of the policy motivation was to let the People's Bank of China concentrate on its central banking functions, which it just began to learn about then.

It emerged that many of these "specialized" banks did not really focus on the areas they were earlier "assigned." They tended to enter new areas, not only in the scope of banking and financial service, but also expanding into many various business spheres such as real estate, domestic and foreign trade, etc. During this period, there were a number of other, smaller-scale banking institutions that had been established; many of them were the so-called "share-holding commercial banks" or "urban co-operative banks," with obvious regional or municipal political backgrounds, and in some cases mixed with elements of non-state ownership. In short, many of these banks were competing for market share, and they tended to be risk takers in business conducts.

Here came the second period from the mid-1990s that was marked by consolidation and austerity restructuring in the banking sector. The situation that banks love doing non-banking business and tend not to concern about risk control was deemed undesirable and unsustainable. Several policy measures were undertaken in order to make correction. First, the People's Bank of China was required to become a pure central banking agency, concentrating on its monetary policy and banking regulatory functions. A rationale was that when it no longer has its own business interest, the PBOC would be able or become more able to implement its regulatory function. Second, the central government decided to establish three specialized policy banks, the State Development Bank, the China Import and Export Bank, and the Agricultural Development Bank, separating the policy elements from ordinary banks that earlier had such policy assignments. This way, the old specialized banks should be able to become more like an ordinary commercial bank, free of policy intervention. Third, the government tightened up controls over the new entry in the banking industry and took steps in reorganizing banking institutions of smaller scale, which resulted in a fewer number of banks and their larger, average size.

The banking industry first saw several special laws addressing banking business passed during this period, and this was a welcome sign that regulation in the country was beginning to move toward "rule of law." In practice, however, actual situation was far from what legislative text indicated. Bankers were almost invariably appointed by the government (or the Party-State and its agencies), and many government departments had power to influence credit decision made by banks. Indeed, most banks and bankers believed that it was in their own interest to line up with government influence in conducting ordinary banking business. Economic or commercial principles were thus frequently sacrificed. Business independence that had been reiterated in the banking laws remained largely nominal.

Perhaps, coincidentally, the East Asian financial crisis in 1997–1998 and China's accelerated effort to join the World Trade Organization in the late years of the 1990s helped in bringing both of domestic and international attention to the country's banking system. It surfaced that many began to suspect major problems existed in the banking sector that was dominated by state ownership and heavily influenced by irregular government intervention. Some analysts went to make independent estimate on the possible size of non-performing loans incurred to Chinese banks, based on scarce statistical information and ample anecdote observations. A certainty was that actual situation was more alarming than what the government would like to admit. Some even went to allege that Chinese state-owned banks were virtually "technically insolvent" (Lardy, 1998; Clifford, 2002, among others).

Realizing the potential threat of NPL and low capital adequacy problems in the banking system, the central government began to respond by trying several different methods. First, the central government (through its Ministry of Finance) recapitalized "big four" state-owned banks by injecting a share capital amount of RMB 270 billion yuan in 1998, which was raised by issuing a special government bond to these four banks (the purchase was made possible financially by the central bank's cut in reserve requirement).

Later, this recapitalization was believed insufficient. The central government decided to establish a special debt-relief mechanism and several special agencies in this regard. Four asset management corporations (AMCs) were formed, each dealing with one of "big four" state-owned banks. They carved out NPLs totally amounted to RMB 1.4 trillion yuan for the four banks in a few years from 1999. The policy measure was called "debt-equity swap," i.e., banks that originally held credit claims transferred their claims to designated AMCs who in turn transformed the claims into equity holding to the original borrowers, on the condition that corporate borrowers were a growing concern. The measure, when it was introduced, was also remarked by decision makers as the "last supper" for debt-ridden state-owned banks.

This kind of remark proved to be premature. Bank lending behavior changed too little and too slow, despite repeated calls from the government and regulators. NPLs continued to increase enormously, even if by official estimate. At one occasion, the then governor of the PBOC was quoted to say that the total amount of NPLs incurred to wholly state-owned commercial banks reached RMB 1.8 trillion yuan, or 26.6 percent of their total loans outstanding, at the end of September, 2001 (Dai, 2001). This amount did not involve those that had been earlier transferred to AMCs.

Moreover, it was believed that a bulky part of the huge NPLs has occurred since the mid-1990s when consolidation and organizational restructuring moves began. The new governor of the PBOC once released a result of analysis on the causes of NPLs. According to the study by the PBOC staff, 30 percent of the NPLs were due to government intervention, another 30 percent due to credit policy that supported SOEs, about 10 percent due to deficiencies in the legal system, 10 percent due to the price paid for economic and industrial restructuring and cyclical movements, and the remaining 20 percent were due to banks' poor risk management (Zhou, 2004).

After several years of reform and "bail-out" policy trial measures and extensive policy debate, new consensus has emerged that the country has to open up its banking market, and more radical measures are necessary in order to reshape the banking industry and see to it that it is free of crisis.

Here comes the third and latest wave of banking reform in the country in the recent years, coupled with the country's accession to the World Trade Organization. In fact, whether and how to open the banking market to foreign players was one of focal, contentious issues in the process of negotiation, leading to the final international agreements on China's WTO membership, first with the US and second with the European Union. A new drive for banking reform in the recent years has involved recapitalization, stock market listing, and foreign equity participation.

WHAT ARE OBJECTIVES OF BANKING REFORM?

Many problems in the Chinese banking industry have been identified and recognized by policy decision-makers, pundits, and observers, as well as felt by customers and business partners.

Official documents on banking reform in the past had repeatedly called for restructuring banking industry, improving banking service, and enhancing competitiveness of domestic banking institutions. Official papers had tended to refer to some particular, visible problems, and were often short of addressing the roots of the recognized problems and always vague on long-term objectives of banking reform in the country.

As indicated earlier, there has been consensus emerged on what banking reform should be pursued and how Chinese banks should behave in the ever-changing market environment, especially in the new settings where foreign banks begin to enter as a new competitor. Perhaps, one may believe that many of past reform measures were motivated by crisis prevention or the fear that the Chinese banking system would be heading to crash without major reform measures being undertaken. In the light that the market becomes increasingly open to foreign competitors and external market forces, the issue of making Chinese banking institutions viable in a market environment should inevitably be a long-term one by nature. This in turn should lead us to a question how they would be like in the future or how they are going to be in comparison with their international counterparts.

Bearing this in mind, let us reiterate the following five aspects of the long-term objective of reforming the Chinese bank sector. These are not necessarily equal in importance, but are almost invariably concerned in addressing the objectives of banking reform.

First, restructuring the government–bank relationships. Traditionally, bank managers were all appointed by the government, and banks provided credit supply mainly upon plans and indications they received from the government. In addition, various government agencies and officials tended to intervene irregularly in banks' routine businesses. Reform should cut off the organizational relationship between the government and banks, allowing banks to have an independent mechanism that makes decision on selecting managers based on individuals' performance, capability, and integrity. Also, banks should have legal autonomy in running their own businesses, making decisions on to whom they lend. In general, banks should be able to have their credit policy and criteria, which may not be necessarily in accordance with the so-called "industrial policy" that has been frequently used by the government in directing bank lending. The government should not impose any economic, political, social, ethnical, or cultural obligations on banks, other than what legal standards require banks to do in their ordinary business activities. If the government could not be able to materialize fully this objective, it should at least minimize its influence in these aspects. In practice, bank managers should have rights to reject government officials' intervention, and they would not incur punishment from so doing.

Second, banks should have a multiple structure of ownership, and state ownership should be clarified without ambiguity. Traditionally, large Chinese banks were all state owned, and in some cases there were a few banks of smaller scale that have certain non-state ownership elements. Besides, there was a definitional problem as to who was really representing the state ownership. Many government departments and agencies had actually claimed that they acted on behalf of the state ownership, but in fact their interests and views often conflicted with each other. Reform should clearly address this ownership issue. It should define the ownership issue by equity capital contribution, and clarify the representation issue by allocating voting rights to shareholders only. Non-state and foreign equity participation in traditionally state-owned banks should be permitted as this tends to help define and clarify ownership and representation issues. The multiple structure of ownership mixed with non-state elements would also help banks to become more commercialized in motivation and version. Furthermore, reform should address the issue of corporate governance, especially in the light that many banks still see state dominance in their multiple ownership structure, even after they have conducted a major stock market floatation. Interests, rights, and obligations of different dimensions, such as majority and minority shareholders, the board of directors, the management, and the supervisory body, among others, should all be unequivocally and appropriately defined and respected.

Third, in order to see the market play a greater role in determining which are the fittest and thereby help existing banks to initiate change and move forward, the government should undertake certain steps in liberalizing the banking industry. This should involve allowing non-state institutions to become able to form new banks and related financial service entities when they are judged economically and financially appropriate and feasible, and allowing foreign banks or financial institutions to enter the domestic market when this is judged not incurring any additional, unsound economic and financial risks. In general, the banking industry should have certain institutional flexibility in the sense that various market players are able to initiate organizational restructuring purely based on economic motivation and deliberation through forming new business entities and conducting mergers and acquisitions. Overseeing the process of institutional restructuring, the government may play the role of a watchdog and a law-enforcer in safeguarding the principle of fair transaction and maintaining a competitive market structure.

Fourth, the mode and style of business activity of domestic banks should be transformed. Traditionally, the business of state-owned banks was mainly to take deposits from the public and to provide loans to state-owned enterprises. Problems with this style of banking are many. Personal customers were unable to receive lending and payment services from banks, and non-state enterprises were often treated as a peripheral client in bank lending services. For state-owned enterprises, services they received from banks were also inefficient or insufficient. Modernizing banking business in the country is thus a huge task. For this purpose, banks need to have an impartial attitude toward their customers in general, to respond in a sensible way to what the market demands, and to be innovative in providing banking products to their customers of various kinds. Needless to say, in doing so banks should become more than a profit-maximizing or cost-minimizing agent. They should be concerned with risk prevention, and should have a long-term view on issues such as return, cost, risk, and changes in the market environment.

Fifth, as many Chinese have suffered from huge non-performing loans and low capital adequacy, they need to make great effort in improving their balance sheet results, first with help from the government, and in the longer term primarily by their own resources and initiatives. The balance sheet problems have bearing on the confidence of the public in the Chinese banking system and the ability of the banks to deal with an emergent situation in the case of unexpected happenings. They may also bring severe pressures to domestic banks when the market becomes more open to outside entrants. The task to resolve the balance sheet problems is rather urgent in the sense that the time schedule to open domestic banking market has been fixed by international agreements amid the country's accession to the World Trade Organization.

The above five objectives of reforming China's banking system, namely transforming the government–bank relationships, diversifying the ownership structure and improving the corporate governance, maintaining a competitive market structure, changing the business scope of the banking industry, and revolving balance sheet problems, are all interrelated in one way or another. Yet, we may reasonably believe that when these goals are met, Chinese banks would behave similarly to those in industrial countries and become viable and more competitive, domestic economic growth would be unlikely to suffer from potential banking crisis, and customers of domestic banking industry would benefit enormously.

WHAT HAS BEEN DONE IN BANKING REFORM?

During the past five years or so there have been a number of reform measures undertaken by the Chinese government and the banks themselves. Some of the policy measures were radical, hitting newspaper headlines when they were introduced. Some occurred relatively quietly and were observed at considerable time lags. Let us categorize these reform measures in following aspects.

Recapitalization: A major step was taken by the central government in 2003 that two state-owned banks, the Bank of China and China Construction Bank, received capital injection that amounted to $45 billion in combination. The money came from the central bank's foreign exchange reserves. For the recapitalization purposes, a special agency called the Central Huijin Investment Corporation was formed. The agency used the money to purchase a portion of the two banks' share capital and became their shareholder. This method was once again put into use in 2004 for the Industrial and Commercial Bank of China when the total amount of $25 billion was announced for the bank (the Central Huijin and Ministry of Finance each contributed an equal portion, respectively, in the dollar and RMB denomination). Similarly to the development, the central government and its agencies have efforts in allowing the state-owned banks to materialize their loss reserve accounts and to write off further amounts of non-performing assets. The People's Bank of China is estimated to have purchased NPLs from several large banks (the above three plus the Bank of Communications) that totally amounted to RMB 780 yuan on book value and transferred them to AMCs, between 2004 and 2005 (Ma, 2006). As it happened, the two central government agencies, Huijin (representing the central bank) and the Ministry of Finance, both involved in the process of recapitalization, and this actually helped in clarifying the issue of state ownership in terms of concrete representation.

Allowing foreign equity participation in domestic banks. This occurred as part of the deal with foreign trade negotiators over the process of talks that led to China's accession to the World Trade Organization before 2001. Prior to that year, foreign equity participation in domestic banks was permitted only to some of international financial institutions such as the International Finance Corporation and the Asian Development Bank, on a small scale. Since 2001, there have a good number of foreign private financial institutions, including well-known global banking brands, that have obtained approval to purchase a substantial portion of share capital of Chinese banks. For a single foreign entity, the upper limit of shareholding has set to be 20 percent, and the combined upper limit for all foreign entities in one Chinese bank has set to be 25 percent. At the end of 2006, there were at least 20 Chinese banks that have accepted foreign equity participation. The structure of ownership in many of these Chinese banks is thus diversified and ostensibly internationalized. On the other hand, the government or its various agencies has continued to hold the dominant role in all large banks' capital structure.

Stock market floatation. That Chinese banks venturing into stock markets to raise capital and long-term finance first occurred in the early 1990s, but it happened to a small number of banks and on a small scale. A few more regional, medium-sized banks conducted a major initial public offering in domestic stock markets many years later. Amid this background it became a headline news that the central government decided to allow the country's largest banks to go for stock market floatation. So far, there have been four of them that have successfully conducted IPO: the Bank of Communication in Hong Kong in June 2005 raising HK$14.3 billion, the China Construction Bank in Hong Kong in October 2005 raising HK$71.6 billion RMB 20 billion yuan, the Bank of China successively raising HK$86 billion in Hong Kong in June 2006 and in Shanghai in July 2006 and the Industrial and Commercial Bank of China simultaneously in Shanghai and Hong Kong raising a combined amount of US$19.1 billion in October 2006. A smaller bank, China Merchants Bank, also conducted an IPO in Hong Kong in September 2006, raising HK$20.7 billion. Each of these banks had invited certain foreign financial institutions to take a portion of their share capital as a "strategic investor." Motivations for this action were presumably mixed: to form a new institutional and organizational style that is acceptable to international stock markets; to woo both of international and domestic investors; and to keep the banks at arm's length from the government. As a result, the structure of ownership of these banks has been vastly diversified, with representatives of many different interests now sitting on the same board of directors in a bank.

Emergence of a few new regional banks. In the recent two years, the voice calling for the government to further liberalize the banking market by allowing regional and private agents to form new banks has become increasingly articulated. Several new banks were approved to be established in certain regional contexts. Among these there are two notable examples. The Bohai Bank was formed in Tianjin in February 2006 by a number of regional institutions, national corporations, and foreign financial institutions. In the Anhui province, the Huishang Bank was formed in December 2005 after restructuring and consolidating several local banks and financial institutions led by the provincial government. The Zheshang Bank was formed in Hangzhou, the Zhejiang province, in April 2004, as a result of restructuring an earlier Sino-foreign joint-venture bank. A number of similar, new banks that have strong regional backgrounds are in the pipeline to be approved by regulators. Compared to many of those regional banks that were established in the 1980s and 1990s, these newly established ones appear to have certain elements of "new style," e.g., more non-state equity capital participation, less constrained by regional divisions, etc. Signs of liberalization in the country's banking industry are emerging.

Encouraging the development in personal banking. Largely inspired by successful examples of modern banking in industrial countries, many Chinese banks began to provide various banking services to personal customers in the late years of the 1990s. Financial regulators also helped in pushing the development of consumer finance in the country, which coincided with privatization moves of urban housing property from the late 1990s. Car loans, student loans, housing mortgages, and credit card financing are now offered virtually by every Chinese bank. Meanwhile, banks have made great efforts in improving their payments service to both corporate and personal customers. In appearance, many Chinese banks have become full-ranged banking service entities, which is remarkably different from what it used to be like a short time ago.

Strengthening credit behavior discipline and toughening punishment of frauds and embezzlement. Many banks are reported to have established an internal risk control mechanism in response to the non-performing loan problems. They have also attempted to formulate schemes of "lifetime" personal responsibility system for credit decision makers at various levels of a bank. In order to strengthen risk management many large banks have undertaken an organizationally centralization approach that shifts the power of management to a higher level in the hierarchy. This has presumably helped in minimizing intervention and irregular influences of regional or local government agencies on these banks' ordinary business activities. Internally, many banks have tightened up supervision and discipline enforcement on fraud and embezzlement behavior, which has coincided with the country's drive of anti-corruption. Numerous recent news reports show a great number of cases involving fraud and embezzlement inside domestic banks. Some of them may have happened, perhaps, because culprits had a new fear for their future fate as banks where they have been working are under rapid transformation and create new uncertainty for some of the old staff.

Downsizing the banking business in unprofitable areas. Many banks, especially those large national banks, have made great effort to reorganize their branch network through which they cut off a great number of "redundant" business offices and staff. There have been criticism that Chinese banks are overstaffed, employed too many workers for too little profit. In many years of the 1980s and 1990s, each of the largest four banks attempted to expand its branch to reach virtually every corner of the country. The situation turned to the opposite direction from the late 1990s, in a quiet way. As shown in Table 8.1, the "big four" all sharply reduced the number of their branches and business offices as well as the number of staff

Table 8.1: Reduction in business offices and staff, Big Four banks, 1998–2004.

	Number of branches and business offices		Number of staff workers	
	1998	2004	1998	2004
Agricultural Bank of China	58,466	31,004	524,484	489,425
Bank of China	15,227	11,307	197,547	164,193
China Construction Bank	30,469	14,458	378,523	254,689
Industrial and Commercial Bank of China	39,386	21,223	567,230	375,781

Source: *China Finance Almanac 1999*, p. 533; *China Finance Almanac 2005*, p. 529.

workers between 1998 and 2004. Most notably, more than a half of the number of branches and business offices of the China Construction Bank were reduced in the period, and that one third of the staff of the Industrial and Commercial Bank of China were reduced at the same time. This was supposedly driven by cost-saving motivation, and should help enhance the performance of these banks.

WHAT HAS BEEN ACHIEVED SO FAR?

After so many years of reform and efforts, many Chinese banks have become different from their earlier appearance. Their financial performance has improved remarkably, based on their published statistical information. We may take special notes on the following aspects of financial performance of Chinese banks in recent years.

Increases in cashflows and liquidity. Between 2001 and 2005, the total amount of deposits outstanding of all domestic banks increased from RMB 13,124.5 billion to 28,179.2 billion yuan, equivalent to an annual average growth rate of 21.1 percent. This is almost double the nominal growth rate of gross domestic product during the same period. The high growth rate in deposit-taking by Chinese banks suggests that not only do Chinese people continue to have a high saving propensity through the domestic banking system, but also they maintain their confidence in the banking system and are willing to make heavy use of the system for their surplus fund. Improved banking service may have helped the fast growth in bank deposit-taking. Perhaps, other, rather macroeconomic, factors that would have also helped the growth in cashflows and liquidity in Chinese banking system during the recent years are foreign money inflows as a result of the country's trade surplus, foreign direct investment inflow, and portfolio investment inflow. Any case, domestic banking system has had a degree of comfortability in seeing rapid increases in their cashflows and liquidity, and has been able to use these resources pleasantly to undertake reform and restructuring measures.

Changes in sources of revenue. As pointed out earlier, Chinese banks used to have a simple model of business: taking deposits from the household sector and lending the money under government direction to state-owned enterprises. It is only until recently that they began to create a great variety of banking service products to personal and corporate customers, largely inspired by examples of foreign bank practices. As a result, they are able to generate revenue in addition to traditional net interests. Several large banks have reported that their revenue from conducting "intermediation services," such as debiting and transferring, banking card service, and advising and consulting, among others, has increased rapidly in recent years. The ratio of net revenue out of intermediation service to net interest revenue has reached 5 to 10 percent for large banks in general, with a few of them exceeding 10 percent. Compared to large banks in many industrial countries, the level that Chinese banks have achieved is still relatively low. The change is, however, significant and considerable.

Improvement in fitness indicators. It has been well known that many Chinese banks had suffered from huge amounts of non-performing loans and financial losses. They were cost inefficient and capital inadequate, and therefore susceptible to external shocks or banking runs. The situation has changed remarkably in recent years after great many policy measures and efforts have been taken by both the government and banks in concern, which we have described above. An example is the Bank of China which has had statistical data published for consecutive years on a fairly consistent base (as shown in Table 8.2). Note its NPL ratio reduced from 27.5 percent to 4.6 percent in 2005, with the provision coverage ratio up from 16.8 percent to 80.6 percent in the same period. Similar changes are believed to have also occurred to other Chinese banks of the same kind. As have been seen earlier, it is because of these changes that three largest banks, together with a few other, smaller ones, have successfully conducted their large scale of IPOs in Hong Kong stock markets recently when their shares were oversubscribed by international investors. Many believe that listed Chinese banks now face questions that are different

Table 8.2: Financial ratios of the Bank of China (%).

	2001	2002	2003	2004	2005
Non-performing loans	27.5	22.5	16.3	5.1	4.6
Provision coverage	16.8	21.1	67.3	68.0	80.6
Cost income ratio	37.9	37.9	39.7	40.0	39.3
Capital adequacy ratio	8.3	8.2	N/A	10.0	10.4

Notes: "Non-performing loans" refer to the percent of total loans outstanding of the bank; "provision coverage" refers to the loss reserve account of the bank given as a percent of its known non-performing loans; "cost income ratio" is expenses plus management expenditures, given as a percent of revenue (net interest income plus non-interest income); "capital adequacy ratio" is calculated according to Chinese financial regulators' standards and criteria, and its statistical scope had a major change in 2003.
Data source: *Annual Report of the Bank of China*, various issues in 2002–2006.

from the ones they faced before, e.g., how they are able to sustain the improved performance in the future and transform themselves into a truly modern, competitive banking corporations.

Evolving market structure. Reforms have brought about notable changes in China's banking industry, perhaps in indirect ways. Traditionally the country's banking industry was dominated by four state-owned banks. They had extensive national branch networks, stretching into almost every city and town in the land. They also enjoyed high political clouts, unmatched by any other financial institutions. Their scope of business was much wider than other, smaller-scale domestic banks or financial institutions. It is only in an increasingly liberalized market environment that other domestic banks or financial institutions could possibly grow at a faster pace than that of the Big Four, and reforms have been, in general, favorable to those smaller-scale domestic banks.

Table 8.3 shows the relative importance of four or five categories of banks, in terms of their weight in the banking industry's total assets, from the mid-1990s to the recent years. The most notable is the decline of the Big Four, with their proportion down from 69.1 percent in 1995 to 53.6 percent in 2004. The fastest-growing

Table 8.3: Major players in China's banking industry, percent in total assets.

	1993	1995	1999	2000	2001	2002	2003	2004
Big Four	69.1	69.1	64.3	62.6	60.5	66.3	55.5	53.6
Shareholding banks[1]	5.8	7.6	11.9	10.2	12.3	14.7	13.8	14.9
City banks	—	1.0	3.7	4.2	4.9	5.6	5.8	5.4
Others[2]	25.2	22.3	20.1	23.0	22.3	13.4	24.9	26.1
Foreign banks[3]	—	2.5	2.1	2.1	2.3	1.4	1.2	1.8

Notes: 1. These include China Merchants Bank, China Minsheng Banking Co., Industrial Bank, Bank of Communications, China Everbright Bank, China CITIC Bank, Guangdong Development Bank, Shanghai Pudong Development Bank, Shenzhen Development Bank, and Huaxia Bank.
2. These include policy banks, rural financial institutions (mainly cooperative credit unions or the likes), investment and trust companies (ITCs), finance companies, the Postal Saving Bureau, and foreign banks in China. There were no data available for this group for 1993.
3. A sub-group of the "Others."
Data source: Figures for years prior to 2004 are from Institute of Economic and Resource Management, Beijing Normal University, ed. "*A Report of Development of China's Market Economy*," 2003 and 2005. Figures of 2004 are calculated by the present author based on data published in *China Finance Almanac 2005*.

category is "shareholding" banks, i.e., those domestic banks that were mainly medium-sized, having strong regional backgrounds, and earlier institutionalized by a form of equity capitalization.

It should be noted, however, that foreign banks as a group of players have been small, and their proportion in the total asset of China's banking industry had been actually falling over the period of 1995–2004. There was a moderate increase between 2002 and 2004, part of the five-year transition period till 2006. It is mainly because policy barriers to a foreign bank entry have been effectively considerable, and they are not expected to reduce significantly until the end of 2006. What may be foreseen for the future is that foreign banks would steadily and moderately increase their business activities over a long span of time.

In short, reforms and liberalization have brought about a good deal of visible change to China's banking industry. Public confidence in the banking system has sustained. Banks were able to find new sources of revenue. They have improved their financial performance enormously. The banking sector is now staged with many different types of players who are expected to interface in a dynamic way, though traditionally state-owned banks would continue to be a heavyweight role.

WHAT HAS TO BE ACHIEVED IN THE FUTURE?

Our above brief discussion has showed that in recent years a good number of reform measures have been adopted in pushing change in China's banking industry, and indeed there have been considerable changes occurred to the banking sector. Chinese banking institutions become different from what they were in many ways.

Yet, there are a number of things that have remained largely unchanged or too little change has been made. Let us briefly describe what they are as follows.

First, the government — or more precisely, the Party-State — still maintains its control over state-controlled banks, holding the power to appoint top management for the banks and sometimes executing the power in an unexpected way. After stock market listing, many traditionally state-owned banks become business entities that have a multiple structure of ownership. But the state holds the majority share in most cases. As such, they become "state-controlled banks" instead of "state-owned banks." The difference has not impinged on the appointment of top management, however. Appointment or change of top management in a bank of this kind is determined sometimes without sufficient prior consulting with or the consent of the board of directors.

Second, related to the above issue, the corporate governance of state-controlled banks has yet to be clearly defined as regard to functions of different bodies in the organization. These involve the board of directors representing shareholders, the executive management representing staff, the supervisory body representing regulatory authorities, and the party committee representing the interest of the Party-State. One may easily find that there is possibly a doubling of representation of the Party-State, through its seats in the board of directors and the party committee in the bank. This duplication would undoubtedly complicate the work of the corporate governance in banks.

Third, the legal framework where a modern banking system may function in directing financial resource flows by the principle of efficiency is still far from perfection. This involves laws and regulation of property rights, foreclosure and mortgage, liquidation of state-owned assets, and market for secondary assets. Many people in the country refers this kind of issues to what they call "financial ecological environment." There is still a long way to go for people to see significant changes in the situation. Because of this, banks in the country still need to maintain a "good" relationship with the government at various levels, and compromise their commercialism with politics, thus sacrificing its independence from time to time.

Fourth, internal reorganization that focuses on efficiency and risk management got started just recently and will take time to complete. As it is known, the organization structure that many Chinese banks have adopted is a regional center approach, i.e., individual regional or local offices of a same bank doing business rather independently, quite loosely interconnected by uniform banking products or service standards (this is also accompanied by an effectively weak control by the headquarters over regional or local centers' business activity). Several large banks have begun to try a model of organization that focuses on products, and this is just a start and will need a good deal of time to pursue through.

Fifth, and perhaps the most challenging one, the money market in the country has not become open such that the question of sustainability of China's banking system is still untested. The fact that the currency is not convertible or capital account liberalization has not completed means either domestic or foreign financial institutions may not freely move their funds across the border. Threats to Chinese banking system from sudden changes in international financial markets are thus supposedly small. Therefore, domestic banks are able to enjoy a relatively "quiet" life in one sense. Moreover, as we have seen, foreign banks are a newcomer in the domestic banking market, and they are still constrained by a number of factors that are not conducive to their rapid growth here. Competition between Chinese banks and foreign banks in the same market has yet to be unfolded fully.

Bearing in mind of those above-mentioned "changes" and "unchanges," we may quickly conclude that with regard to the fundamental goals of reforms there is a long way to go for Chinese banks to complete their transformation. What they have achieved in the recent five years of transition period is remarkable, but is still not sufficient. Both the government and the banking industry should make further, greater efforts in pursuing reforms and transformation toward the fundamental goals.

REFERENCES

Anderson, Jonathan (2005), "The Great Chinese Bank Sale," *Far Eastern Economic Review*, September.

Bank of China (2000–2005), *Bank of China Annual Report*.

Bradsher, Keith (2004), "Informal Lenders in China Pose Risks to Banking System," *New York Times*, November 9.

China Construction Bank (2004–2005), *China Construction Bank Annual Report*.

Clifford, Mark (2002), "Are China's Banks Caught in Quicksand?" *BusinessWeek*, November 25.

Dai, Xianglong (2001), Speech at the Beijing 2001 NPL Forum, Beijing, October.

The Economist (2006), "China's Biggest Bank IPO: A Dragon Stirs," *Economist*, October 12.

The Economist (2006), "Chinese Capital Markets: Out of the Shadows," *Economist*, December 13.

Industrial and Commercial Bank of China (2003–2005), *Industrial and Commercial Bank of China Annual Report*.

Lardy, Nicholas (1998), *China's Unfinished Economic Revolution*, Washington, DC: Brookings Institution Press.

Li, Kui-Wai and Jun Ma (2001), *China's WTO Accession and Policy Options for Banking Reform,* September.

Lu, Ding, Thangavelu M. Shandre and Qing Hu (2005), "Biased Lending and Non-performing Loans in China's Banking Sector," *The Journal of Development Studies* 41(6), 1071–1091.

Ma, Guonan (2006), "Who Pays China's Bank Restructuring Bill?," CEPII Working Paper No. 2006-04.

Ma, Guonan and Ben S.C. Fung (2002), "China's Asset Management Corporations," BIS Working Paper No. 115, August.

Nanto, K. Dick and Sinha Radha (2002), "China's Banking Reform," *Post-Communist Economies* 14(4), 469–493.

People's Bank of China (1995–2005), *China Finance Almanac*.

Song, Wonho and Yunjong Wang (eds.) (2004), *Finance and Economic Development in China,* KIEP, March.

Szapary, Gyorgy (2002), "Banking Sector Reform in Hungary: What We Learned and What Are the Prospects?," *Comparative Economic Studies*.

Zhou Xiaochuan (Governor of the People's Bank of China) and Mingkang Liu (President of the China Banking Regulatory Commission) (2004), "Speeches and Q & A," *Xinhua News Agency*, text available at http://www.sina.com.cn, March 11.

Chapter 9

China's Capital Market Reform: Problems and Prospects

Lu Ding

Sophia University, Tokyo, Japan

Li Ning

Department of Business Policy, NUS Business School, Singapore

INTRODUCTION

Through two-and-a-half decades of hyper-economic growth, China has successfully transformed itself from a low-income underdeveloped economy featured by poverty and isolation to a middle-income, newly industrialized, and booming economic giant that has changed world economic geography. Meanwhile China's economic system has moulted from an inward-looking, centrally planned socialist command system into a predominantly market-based one with considerable openness to trade and foreign investment.

In these transitions, the country's financial system has experienced fundamental changes. First of all, the pre-reform socialist mono-banking system has been restructured into a modern central banking system based on fractional reserves of its commercial-bank members. The formerly state-owned specialized banks have been overhauled and incorporated into commercial banks and some of them have successfully listed themselves in stock markets. Apart from the big-four dominant state-owned banks,[1] there have also emerged quite a lot second-tier commercial banks formed on share-holding basis as well as many financial institutions engaged in various forms of merchant and investment banking activities. China's two stock exchanges in Shanghai and Shenzhen, launched about 16 years ago, grew rapidly through the 1990s. The capitalization of the domestic equity market started from virtually zero in 1990 and peaked at 4.6 trillion yuan (US$31 billion), or nominally 53 percent of GDP, at the end of 2000.[2] Corporate bond market has also emerged during the recent years.

These institutional changes have allowed the financial system to play an active role to support the country's two-and-a-half-decade long hyper-economic growth. A major driving factor of the growth has been a high rate of capital formation sustained and backed by a saving rate that is astonishingly high by international comparison. China's gross saving rate has been above 35 percent of GDP in most years since the mid-1980s and climbed to above 40 percent during most part of the 1990s and early 2000s. According to the World Bank (1997), apart from the effects of rising income and changing demographics, the banking sector's systemic efforts to attract deposits and mobilize savings were one of the most important institutional factors that contributed to this phenomenon. The banking-sector asset that

---

[1] The big-four state-owned banks are Bank of China (BOC), the Agricultural Bank of China (ABC), the China Construction Bank (CCB), and the Industrial and Commercial Bank of China (ICBC). These four banks accounted for 54 percent of total bank assets by the end of 2003.

[2] Statistics are cited from China State Statistical Bureau (various years). A factor that may overstate China's financial depth is a very high level of corporate deposits (accounting for one-fourth of total deposits) since firms are obliged to keep them as collaterals. Excluding that, China's financial depth is still relatively high for its per-capita income, reflecting China's financial system unequivocally successful in mobilizing savings (See Farrells *et al.* (2006) for more detailed discussions).

grows at 35 percent per annum has channeled a huge pool of savings to finance the fast capital accumulation that drives the GDP growth.

Despite these achievements, the financial system has exhibited serious flaws that have put the sustainability of China's dynamic growth in question. China has a highly unbalanced financial structure built almost solely upon the banking sector. In 2004, for instance, roughly 93.6 percent (or US$300 billion) of firms' formal finance came from the banking system; only about 1.4 percent (US$4.5 billion) came from the bond market and 5 percent (US$16 billion) came from the sale of shares on domestic exchanges.[3] Few market-based economies have ever had such a high concentration of corporate finance in the banking sector. Unfortunately, the banking sector that finances most of the business capital needs has been notoriously inefficient. This situation implies high financial risks for both the lenders and the borrowers as well as limited business opportunities for entrepreneurs. The equity market, on the other hand, has lost its early momentum of rapid growth in recent years due to systemic weaknesses in corporate governance.

This chapter aims to examine these problems in China's capital market. We will first discuss in the second section why China needs to develop a more balanced structure for capital financing. We will then in the following section probe the causes of the domestic equity market's failure to become a major source of capital finance. In the fourth section, we will review the recent spate of reforms since China launched the split-share-structure reform in April 2005. The last section comments on the prospects of capital market development.

NEEDS TO DEVELOP A MORE BALANCED CAPITAL MARKET STRUCTURE

China's highly unbalanced financial structure has largely been a legacy of the pre-reform economic system. From the early 1950s to the end of the 1970s, China's domestic banking business was operated by

[3] McGregor, R., "China looks to Banks for 99 percent of all Financing," *Financial Times*, May 29, 2005.

the People's Bank of China (PBOC), which was in essence an accounting subsidiary of the Ministry of Finance. There was no division of roles between a central bank and commercial banks in the system. The PBOC simply functioned as a mono-bank to provide financial assistance for the fulfillment of the state physical production plan. It centralized deposits, allotted credits to production units for their partial working capital needs (mainly wage payments), and primarily issued currency to fill the mismatch between deposits and loans.[4] Such a mono-bank system corresponded well to the centrally planned economic system, in which firms' fixed capital formation was financed mainly through the state budget.

Two major reforms were introduced in 1983 and 1984. One was the so-called "*li gai shui* (利改税)" (taxes-for-profits), which sought to dismantle the system where all profits after subtracting a small retained portion for the enterprise were simply returned to the state. The reform aimed to adopt a corporate tax that would allow financial autonomous at the firm level. By 1986, almost all enterprise profits were taxed, instead of being remitted to the government. The other reform was the so-called "*bo gai dai* (拨改贷)" (loans-for-grants), which strove to move away from the provision of investment funds on a grant basis from the state budget toward the allocation of working capital and investment funds through the financial intermediaries.

In a series of reforms from the mid-1980s to the mid-1990s, the PBOC became a central bank and the regular banking businesses were delegated to the state-owned "specialized banks." Relying on a credit ceiling imposed on all banks and depository institutions and its direct control over the interest rates, the PBOC conducted national credit planning till the late 1990s. The promulgation of a central bank law and a commercial bank law in 1995 finally established the framework of a modern central banking system based on fractional reserves of the member commercial banks.

Despite being restructured and incorporated, most of the state-owned banks have been slow to learn to play by commercial banking

---

[4] For a more detailed discussion of the pre-reform monetary system in China's centrally-planned economy, see Peebles (1991).

rules in a market-based economy. After tax-for-profit and loan-for-grant reforms, the state budget no longer finances the capital needs of state-owned enterprises (SOEs). Instead, the state-owned banks had to take over the role to meet the SOEs' financial needs through lending credits. This inherited obligation to support the many financially nonviable SOEs has been a major cause of poor performance by the state-owned commercial banks since the mid-1990s. Operational efficiency of the state-owned banks have further suffered from their bureaucratic management structure and lack of commercial banking expertise and experience.

The weakness of the state-owned-bank dominated banking sector is evident in several phenomena. Just a few years ago, the major state-owned banks were technically insolvent in the swamp of non-performing loans. At the peak of this crisis, the NPL ratio officially amounted to over one-fourth of bank assets. Thanks to combined measures of bad-loan write-off, "*zhai-zhuan-gu* (债转股)" (debt-for-equity) swaps, and huge public fund injection, most of these banks have substantially improved their balance sheets by achieving the so-called "double declines" of both NPL balance and NPL ratios for over four subsequent years since 2002. With improved bank balance sheets, major Chinese state-owned banks have either enticed foreign banks or financial institutions to partner with them as "strategic investors" or successfully launched IPOs on overseas stock markets since 2005. However, the real improvement in their operational efficiency is still doubtful. As estimated by Farrell *et al.* (2006), of the substantial reduction of non-performing loans of the big-four state-owned banks between 2001 and 2005, about 59 percent was due to transfer of bad loans to asset management companies. The remaining reduction came from NPL resolution and dilution due to growth in new loans.

The state-owned banks' inherited linkage to the state-owned enterprises has resulted in a highly biased corporate-loan lending portfolio that favors the state-owned sector. A study by CASS (1998) shows that, although the SOEs contributed to only one-third of GDP, they received two-third of the total domestic loans in the mid-1990s. A recent count by Farrell *et al.* (2006) reveals that the wholly and partially state-owned companies continue to absorb most of the funding from the financial system. In 2003, wholly state-owned companies received 35 percent of bank credit and accounted for all equity and bond issues, despite the fact that they only contributed to 23 percent of GDP. The many shareholding enterprises that are partially state-owned and the collective enterprises took up another 38 percent of credit, though they produced only 25 percent of output. Private and foreign enterprises, being the engine of China's growth and producing 52 percent of GDP, received only 27 percent of bank loans. Meanwhile, the small and medium-sized enterprises (SMEs),[5] which provide 75 percent of jobs and create 55 percent of GDP, receive merely 16 percent of total bank loans in the recent years.

Banks have also been more risk-taking (or less cautious in dealing risks) when giving loans to SOE borrowers. Lu *et al.* (2005) used a sample of 268 public listing companies in China for the period 1994–1999 to test the relation between firms' bank borrowing and their loan default risks. The study shows that, at all default risk levels, firms with higher state-owned share ownership ratios tend to get more loan credits than those with lower ones. In particular, the SOEs with higher risks also tend to get more money from the banks after controlling other factors that affect borrowing/lending decisions. Podpiera (2006) examined data from 1997 through 2004 and found that the large state-owned commercial banks (SCBs) have slowed down credit expansion, but that the pricing of credit risk remains undifferentiated and banks do not appear to take enterprise profitability into account when making lending decisions. Farrell *et al.* (2006) identifies several operational weaknesses prevailing in many Chinese banks, including lack of good internal credit-assessment, lack of external information on the credit histories and the financial condition of potential borrowers, and ineffective performance-management systems.

The inability of the bank-dominated formal financial system to meet the financial needs of the SMEs and private businesses has forced the latter to turn to informal/underground finance. The rising

[5] SMEs are defined in China as enterprises with 8–2000 employees, less than US$50 million assets, and less than US$37 million sales (which varies depending on sector). About 80 percent of SMEs were estimated to be private by Citibank in 2001.

importance of such finance in filling up the gap left by the formal system has drawn research interests in recent years (Tsai, 2001; Guo and Liu, 2002; Mao, 2005; Gonzalez, 2006). These studies show that the booming private businesses in China have for years relied primarily on informal finance (the so-called "curb market") for their start-up and working capital needs. The informal financing mechanisms range from loans between friends and relatives to sophisticated financing arrangements that circumvent national banking laws in creative ways. Underground lending organizations operate actively in the coastal regions, functioning like deposit institutions and granting loans to local entrepreneurs at interest rates as high as 15–20 percent. It is estimated by some researchers that lending from these institutions amounts to 800 billion yuan (3 percent of total bank deposits), providing 6 percent of corporate loans. On top of that, lending based on personal arrangements (among family members and friends) could be as high as one-fourth of the bank deposits (Farrell *et al.*, 2006). The prevalence of the high-cost informal finance highlights the potential to improve the efficiency of China's financial system.

In China, the banking sector intermediates nearly 75 percent of the capital in the economy. This ratio is remarkably higher than those in other Asian countries (43 percent in India, 35 percent in Japan, and 33 percent in South Korea) and the US (19 percent). Excluding the value of non-tradable equity shares, China's equity market capitalization was only 17 percent of GDP by 2004, much lower than that in many developed and developing countries (29 percent in Poland, 56 percent in India, 63 percent in South Korea, 79 percent in Japan, 139 percent in the US). China's net corporate debt was only about 1 percent of GDP, one of the lowest in the world (Farrell *et al.*, 2006). Such a high concentration of capital finance in a shaky banking sector implies huge potential risks and inefficiency for the economy.

Fueled by another wave of bank lending binge, China has experienced a new capital formation boom in recent years. The immediate outcome of this round of bank-lending and investment boom is the macroeconomic overheating since 2004, which has signaled more problematic loans ahead. As pointed out by Hale (2005), "China's lending boom of 2003 and 2004 could lead to another wave of defaults this year and next. In 2004, the investment share of GDP rose to 45% — one of the highest levels in recorded financial history — as banks financed a huge expansion of property development and manufacturing capacity. Now, the largest banks are claiming significant increases in non-performing property loans, while the glut of new industrial capacity implies that some firms may not have adequate profits to service their debts."

The trend of macroeconomic efficiency has been alarming. For economies experiencing fast industrialization, infrastructure building and fast capital accumulation are normally reflected in a high incremental capital to output ratio (ICOR). It is, however, rather worrying that China's ICOR has gone up substantially in recent years and is clearly higher than those of Japan, South Korea, and Taiwan during the latter's high-growth periods (Table 9.1). As shown in Fig. 9.1, China's ICOR has exhibited a steep rising trend since the early 1990s.[6]

Table 9.1: Incremental capital to output ratio (ICOR): China compared to Japan, South Korea, and Taiwan in their high-growth periods.

	Period	Investment share of GDP		GDP growth rate		ICOR	
China[a]	1991–1995	33.2	*32.6*	12.0	*12.2*	2.8	*2.7*
	1996–2000	35.1	*32.6*	8.3	*8.6*	4.3	*3.8*
	2001–2005	45.1	*40.4*	8.7	*9.5*	5.1	*4.3*
Japan[b]	1961–1970	32.6		10.2		3.2	
S. Korea [b]	1981–1990	29.6		9.2		3.2	
Taiwan[b]	1981–1990	21.9		8.0		2.7	
India[c]	1995–2004	21.2		5.6		4.1	

Note: Numbers in italics are based on adjusted GDP statistics in NBSC (2006a).
Source: [a]Compiled from NBSC (various issues) and NBSC (2006a); [b]Kwan (2004); [c]Farrell *et al.* (2006).

[6] China carried out a nationwide census on its secondary and tertiary industries in 2004. Based on the survey results, the National Bureau of Statistics of China adjusted up the country's GDP in 2004 by 16.8 percent and recalculated GDP statistics for years back to 1993 (NBSC, 2006a).

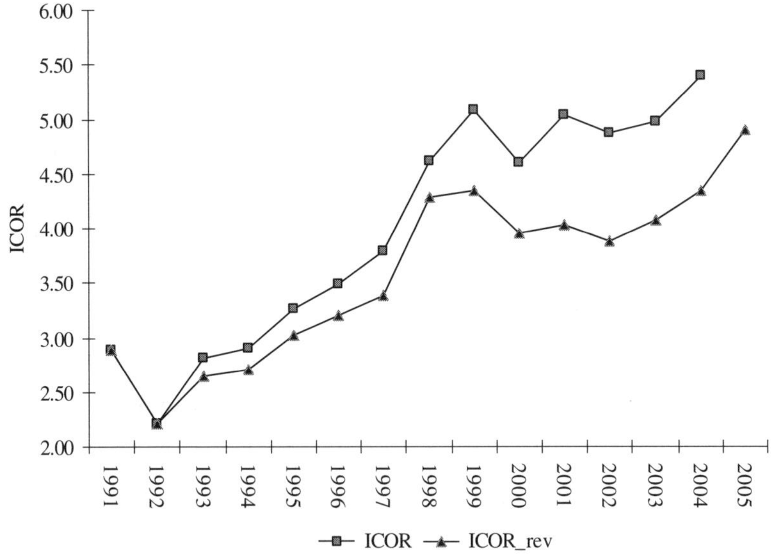

Fig. 9.1: Incremental capital–output ratio (1991–2005).
Note: ICOR is the ratio between fixed capital investment to GDP ratio and real GDP growth rate. ICOR_rev is based on the adjusted values in NBSC (2006a).
Source: National Bureau of Statistics of China (NBSC).

Thanks to the suppressed interest rates, capital account control, and underdeveloped corporate capital-bond market, the banking sector has been able to absorb almost the entire pool of household savings and provide them as low-cost capital to support the nation's investment-driven growth in the past two decades. High concentration of corporate finance in an inefficient banking sector not only increases overall financial risks for both the lender and the borrower but also constrains business opportunities for entrepreneurs. This model of capital misallocation and high-cost growth will face increasing challenges in future as the Chinese economy becomes more mature and open. The worrying trend of rising ICOR indicates an increasingly unsustainable growth path. Further financial reforms are essential for China's future growth efficiency. Farrell *et al.* (2006) estimates that reforms to improve banking efficiency, to modernize the payments system, and to diversify the mix of financing vehicles available to companies could save US$62 billion per year, which nearly equals the amount of foreign direct investment that China receives each year, or 3.2 percent of GDP. On top of that, reforms that enabled a larger share of funding to go to the more productive private enterprises would, over time, increase investment efficiency and raise GDP by up to 13 percent.

Why, 16 years after the launch of stock exchanges, China's equity market is yet to become a major source of capital finance? This is the issue to be discussed next.

INSTITUTIONAL FLAWS OF THE EQUITY MARKET

China's market-oriented reform was accelerated after the Communist Party leadership reached a consensus at the Party's National Congress in October 1992 to establish the "socialist market economic system" as the goal of the reform. In November, the following year, the Party's Central Committee passed a 50-article "Decision" on the strategies of further reforms, which led to a series of centrally initiated reforms to build the bedrock of a modern market economy in the 1990s.

The Party's 1992 Decision immediately accelerated reforms in all fronts, including the banking and financial sector. China's two stock exchanges in Shanghai and Shenzhen, launched on an experimental basis around 1990, started to grow by leaps and bounds after the establishment of the State Council Securities Committee (SCSC) and the Chinese Securities Regulatory Commission (CSRC) in October 1992.

From October 1992 to mid-1998, the SCSC was the immediate supervisory body over the CSRC, which was set up as a specialized independent regulatory body in charge of day-to-day monitoring of the securities market and market participants. When the SCSC was dissolved in 1998, the CSRC was upgraded to the equivalent rank of a ministry with extensive authorities, including the supervisory role over brokerage houses and stock exchanges in Shanghai and Shenzhen. China's first *Securities Law*, which took effect in July 1999, further strengthened the CSRC's supervisory power.

The "split share structure"

In many aspects of its legal framework, China's stock market was patterned after the U.S. stock market since the Chinese policy makers regarded the latter as a model of efficient corporate governance.[7] However, ever since its birth, China's stock market has been burdened by political–economic interests of state-owned enterprises. The development of stock market started as a part of the government's program to reform the state-owned enterprises. It was hoped that stock market would become a fresh source of funding to help the state-owned enterprises to ride through the difficult times of market-oriented transition. Meanwhile, it was also expected that the discipline of stock market would provide extra incentives for the SOE managers to improve the performance of their firms. It is therefore no wonder that the most remarkable feature of China's capital market is that almost all of the listed companies are SOEs or dominated by state-owned shares.

By Marxist ideology, public (state) ownership is one of the main features of socialism. The principle of public ownership being the "mainstay" of the economy has been sanctioned by China's constitution. In order to ensure the state's dominant share and control of the SOEs after they get listed in the stock market, the policy makers created a unique system of "tradable shares" and "non-tradable shares." Under this so-called "split share structure," the listed companies' shares are classified by the ownership type of shareholding into four categories, namely state-owned shares, legal persons' shares, staff shares, and public shares. When a state-owned enterprise was incorporated into a shareholding company, the state assets were converted to state-owned shares, the assets belonging to other (mostly state-owned) enterprises were converted to legal persons' shares, and the shares issued to employees were converted to staff shares. State-owned shares are not tradable in the stock market. The legal persons' shares, representing the assets owned by other state-owned enterprises, are also not allowed to be traded. Employee-owned staff shares can be traded only after being approved by the majority employees in the company. Only the public shares, which were issued to the public on

[7] Tam (1999).

or after IPO, can be traded in the domestic stock exchanges. Most of the tradable shares are called "A-shares," which are quoted and priced in Chinese yuan. The rest are "B-shares," which are quoted and priced in foreign currencies (mainly US dollar and HK dollar). Besides, there are "H-shares," which are shares issued and traded in Hong Kong stock exchanges by companies registered in China.

Table 9.2 gives a general picture of share structure in China's stock market from years 1992 to 2005. It shows that on average the

Table 9.2: Share structure of all listed firms (1992–2005); unit: percentage of all shares.

Year	Non-tradable shares				Tradable shares			
	State-owned shares	Legal persons' shares	Others	Total	A-shares	B-shares	H-shares	Total
1992	42.10	26.60	1.20	70.00	15.90	14.90	0.00	30.80
1993	49.10	20.70	2.50	72.20	15.80	6.40	5.60	27.80
1994	43.30	22.50	1.10	67.00	21.00	6.10	6.00	33.00
1995	38.70	24.60	1.10	64.50	21.20	6.70	7.70	35.50
1996	35.40	27.20	2.20	64.80	21.90	6.40	6.90	35.20
1997	31.50	30.60	3.20	65.30	22.80	6.00	5.70	34.60
1998	34.30	28.30	3.30	65.90	24.10	5.30	4.70	34.10
1999	36.10	26.60	2.30	65.00	26.30	4.60	4.00	35.00
2000	38.90	23.80	1.60	64.30	28.40	4.00	3.30	35.70
2001	46.20	18.30	0.80	65.30	25.30	3.10	6.40	34.70
2002	47.20	17.30	0.80	65.30	25.70	2.90	6.10	34.70
2003	47.39	16.63	0.71	64.72	26.67	2.73	5.87	35.28
2004	46.78	16.40	0.77	63.95	27.87	2.76	5.42	36.05
2005	45.00	10.20	6.99	62.20	29.90	2.86	5.45	38.20
Average	41.57	22.12	2.04	65.75	23.77	5.34	5.22	34.33

Notes:
(1) The figures are the number of shares as a percentage of outstanding shares, which are computed through data from *China Securities and Futures Statistical Yearbook* (2006).
(2) H-shares are shares of companies registered in China but listed in Hong Kong stock exchanges.

state-owned share accounts for 41.57 percent of the total shares, while the legal persons' share accounts for 22.12 percent, and the public A-share accounts for 23.77 percent. During 1992–2004, before the reform of split-share structure was launched in 2005, the proportion of legal persons' shares decreased from 26.60 percent to 16.40 percent while the proportion of state-owned shares increased from 42.10 percent to 46.78 percent. Despite the fact that the proportion of public A-shares rose from 15.90 percent to 27.87 percent, the number of total non-tradable shares remained almost a double of that of the total tradable shares by the end of 2004: the non-tradable shares accounted for 66.02 percent of the total shares, leaving only 34.03 percent for the tradable ones. The ownership structure is further described by Table 9.3. On average, in about 49 percent of the companies, the state-owned shares accounted for the largest proportion while in about 32 percent of the firms, the legal persons'

Table 9.3: Ownership structure of listed companies (1993–2001).

Year	Number of firms	Dominated by state-owned shares (percent)	Dominated by legal persons' shares (percent)	Dominated by A-shares (percent)	Dominated by non-tradable shares (percent)
1993	173	52.02	34.68	12.72	89.02
1994	285	47.37	31.93	20.70	84.56
1995	321	45.17	30.22	24.30	83.49
1996	523	46.08	35.37	17.97	88.34
1997	726	50.83	31.68	17.08	90.22
1998	838	51.79	31.74	15.99	90.10
1999	918	49.78	31.81	17.97	88.78
2000	1037	48.79	29.12	21.89	83.99
2001	1082	48.15	27.63	24.12	81.79
Average		48.89	31.58	19.19	86.70

Notes: In this table, the firms are divided into different groups according to their ownership structure. The percentage figures are the proportion of firms dominated by different types of ownership, which are computed through data from the website www.cninfo.com.cn.

shares made the largest proportion. Only about 19 percent of the firms were dominated by public A-shares. Therefore, in about 86.7 percent of the firms, non-tradable shares dominated the ownership structure.

From Tables 9. 2 and 9.3, we can observe that: (a) over two-thirds of the shares were not tradable in stock exchanges and over 86 percent of the listed firms had their ownership dominated by non-tradable shares; (b) the state ownership had the absolute control rights in about 48.89 percent of the total firms; (c) the public shareholders hold about only 23.30 percent of the total shares while the A-share ownership dominated in less than one-fifth of the total firms; and (d) the status of legal persons' shares was in between the state-owned shares and the public tradable shares.

The weighty state ownership in the listed companies makes the principal-agent problem between shareholder and management more complicated than in a conventional private-ownership-based corporate system. With state dominance of shareholding, the government authorized various levels of state assets management authorities to manage the state assets on behalf of the state treasury. These state assets management authorities in turn appointed state-owned or state-controlled holding companies, investment companies, industrial groups, or other legal-person agencies to function as representatives of state ownership. The directors assigned by these agencies directly manage the state-owned companies or supervise the managers they have nominated to undertake the routine management.

Therefore, in those companies, there are multiple layers of principal-agent relationships, i.e., the relationship between the state treasury and the state asset management authorities, the relationship between these authorities and their agencies, the relationship between the state-appointed agencies and the company directors, the relationship between the directors and the managers, and finally, the relationship between the managers and the public shareholders. In each of these layers, the agents may not act in the interests of the principals.

Such a maze of principal–agent relationships has exposed the equity market to fights for political interests and controls. As observed by Walter and Howie (2001), there had been a continuous power struggle among the People's Bank of China (PBOC), Ministry of Finance (MOF), and other bureaucracies over the control of the securities industry. Such a struggle often leads to fragmentation in the regulatory framework. What makes things worse is the conflicting policy missions assigned to the CSRC. As noted by Heilmann (2002), the agency's (implicit) policy mission to provide preferential capital access for state-owned enterprises and to increase the value of state assets constantly conflicts its role of being an impartial supervisory and regulatory authority.

Weak corporate governance

China's capital market is weak in corporate governance in two senses. On the one hand, the rights of public shareholders are under-represented and poorly protected. On the other hand, no one is the real owner of state-owned shares who acts in the interests of "the state." Since both the directors and the managers of the listed state-owned companies are government-appointed or approved, there exists more shared than conflicting interests between them. Being insiders who have access to advantageous information and are in direct charge of corporate control, both of them may be tempted to collude in pursuing their common interests at the expense of the public shareholders and the state treasury. Among all layers of the principal–agent relationships, the interest conflict between these insiders and the public shareholders is the most acute.

The institutional features of the split-share structure have made insiders' collusion possible and easy since under this system the retail investors are particularly vulnerable to expropriations. For instance, the reference value (or negotiable price) of each non-tradable share is net asset per share. Therefore, every time the company reissues stocks or issues right-shares at a price above net asset per share, the non-tradable shareholders will benefit from the rise of their non-tradable share values as long as they themselves do not purchase or purchase very few reissued or right-issued shares. Thus the stock market becomes a cheap cash cow from which those controlling (non-tradable) shareholders could raise funds without seriously rewarding the shareholders. Despite such expropriations, the conventional mechanisms to protect the interests of public shareholders have not worked effectively.

First of all, the voting right on important corporate matters, such as the elections of the board of directors and mergers and acquisitions, are undoubtedly the most important legal right that could be used by the shareholders to exercise their influence (Manne, 1965; Easterbrook and Fischel, 1983). Although China's stock market regulation follows the "one-share-one-vote" rule practiced in the UK and US, it is very unlike that the votes of the public shareholders, especially the retail investors, could make much difference, given the fact that all that the public shareholders held was only one-third of the total shares in a typical company. Given this situation, the rational public individual shareholders would not bother to vote in the shareholders' meeting.

Secondly, minority shareholders may not rely on the listed company's supervisory board to protect their interests. China's listed companies have a similar supervisory board as in Germany, which is comprised of employees and representatives of shareholders. It is supposed to supervise the management to prevent the illegal behavior or misconduct that may impair the interests of the company. Following the German model, the main function is to balance the interests among the stakeholders of the company, namely, the executives, the shareholders, and the employees. The supervisory boards of China's listed companies generally do not have representatives of retail shareholders and almost all the board members are insiders of the company, mainly the representatives of non-tradable share owners and the employees. The few "independent" board members are often appointed or recommended by either the state representative agencies or the management. Although many employees also own the company shares, when confronted with conflicting interests, they would often place the insiders' interests above those of retail shareholders, especially in the case of mergers and acquisitions.[8]

Thirdly, protection for the interests of individual shareholders may come from the institutional investors, who are observed in the US and UK to have played active role in corporate governance. For an average retail investor, it is usually not worth monitoring closely the operations of the company of which she/he owns the shares because the cost of collecting and analyzing the necessary information far exceeds the benefit of doing so. In such a case, it is more cost-effective for an institutional investor to undertake the monitoring function. Aware of this, China's policy makers have been trying to foster a regulatory environment conducive for institutional investors, including the Qualified Foreign Institutional Investors (QFII). However, the influence of institutional investors on the corporate governance have to be exerted either through internal mechanism such as voting in the shareholders' meeting or through the equity investment in the open market. Here again the two-third majority of the non-tradable state- and legal-person shares has severely limited the possible functions of institutional investors. Compared to the bank-centered capital markets like those in Germany and Japan, the Chinese banks have been unable to excise active influence on listed companies' management since they were prohibited from investing in the stock market till recently. The banks, as creditors to the firms, are generally not allowed to take over the companies dominated by state- and legal-person shares even if the latter default the interest and principal payments.

Next, since two-thirds of the shares issued on China's domestic exchanges were owned directly or indirectly by the state and legally non-tradable, it was extremely difficult to launch hostile takeover or corporate raiding, which is the major instrument of market discipline in the market-based Anglo-Saxon capital markets. The corporate

[8] For instance, in September 2004, after the China International Trust and Investment Securities Limited Company (Zhongxin) announced its takeover bid at the Guangfa Securities Limited Company (Guangfa), the employees of Guangfa immediately set up an investment agency called Shenzhen Jifu to block the takeover bid by buying back Guangfa's shares. After a few weeks, Shenzhen Jifu made deals with three of Guangfa's largest shareholders to collect enough shares to foil the takeover.

takeover was theoretically possible only in about 19 percent (see Table 9.3) of the companies where the number of tradable A-shares exceeded the number of the state- and legal-person shares. Even when mergers and acquisitions did happen, they were usually the deals made among the bureaucracies and the legal persons who controlled or owned the non-tradable shares.[9] In such deals, the change of the non-tradable share ownership was conducted outside the stock exchanges at prices and conditions not transparent to the public. Such deals have been restricted among the state-owned enterprises or government organizations and subject to approval by the state assets management authorities. These beyond-the-market deals among bureaucracies and SOE managers have greatly reduced operational transparency of the listed companies and created the leeway for insider trading and manipulation, which have often been in favor of the vested interests of non-tradable share owners or controllers.

Finally, the minority public-share holders' last resort is to exert their influence indirectly on the management by dumping the shares. Such influence can be effective only if the selling-caused fall of the share prices can make the managers feel the pain. This may happen when the managers' rewards are associated with the market performance of the company under incentive contracts, or when the managers' jobs or reputation would be marred if the undervalued company becomes a target of takeover. Share-price linked incentive contract is still rather new in China and has yet to be widely practiced. It is also not certain whether the enforcement of incentive contract alone is enough to discipline the managerial behavior through a slumping share price. Since successful hostile takeovers have been rare in China's capital market, the managers may not feel the pain even if the share price falls.

Crisis of equity market

From the above discussions, we can conclude that the structure of China's stock ownership is highly unfavorable to the minority holders

[9] The number of M&A cases in China was 176 in 2003, 160 in 2004, and 127 in 2005 (Jinrong Shibao, August 3, 2006).

of public tradable shares. Under the system, many listed companies care more about raising money from the shareholders by all means than about improving the returns to shareholders' investment. If they are compelled to pay dividends, they would pay stocks rather than cash, or would pay very little cash. The minority shareholders can do little to change that because they can hardly excise any influence over such decisions. Gradually, since the practice of not paying cash dividends become so popular, even the well-performing companies would choose not to pay or pay very little cash. Disappointed by the dismal prospects of real returns on the invested equity, more and more shareholders would choose to behave like speculators, who place the hope of earning solely on capital gains and no longer care about the companies' fundamentals. Without active monitoring by the shareholders, the listed companies would become more lax in performance and greedier in raising capitals from the shareholders. In such a vicious cycle of poor corporate governance, poor performance, and poor returns to shareholders, it is no wonder that China's stock market has done a poor job to effectively discipline the listed state-owned companies to perform well.

The overall performance of the listed companies has exhibited a deteriorating trend over years. As indicated in Table 9.4, the average return on equity decreases from 14.28 percent in 1992 to as low as 5.35 percent in 2001. The average earnings per share decreased from 0.35 yuan in 1992 to 0.13 yuan in 2001. From 1994 to 2005, the number of loss-making listed companies displayed a rising trend and the proportion of such firms in the total increased from 5.5 percent in 1995 to 18.3 percent in 2005 (Fig. 9.2).

The impact of poor corporate governance is also reflected in the financial behavior of the listed companies. As discussed earlier, under the split-share structure, the controlling shareholders are tempted to increase the reference value (or negotiable price) of their holdings of non-tradable shares through seasoned equity issues to the public at prices above net asset per share. This behavior is evident in Table 9.5, which shows the changes of capital structure from 1992 to 2002 classified by the share ownership. During this period, the number of listed companies' shares rose 85 times from 6.88 billion

Table 9.4: Overall performance of listed companies (1992–2005).

Year	Debt ratio (percent)	Net asset per share (yuan)	ROE (percent)	EPS (yuan)
1992	65.01	2.44	14.28	0.35
1993	48.76	2.43	14.68	0.36
1994	50.8	2.39	13.15	0.31
1995	54.41	2.31	10.78	0.24
1996	53.72	2.41	9.59	0.23
1997	50.06	2.47	9.69	0.24
1998	49.49	2.48	7.45	0.19
1999	52.57	2.48	8.23	0.20
2000	53.49	2.69	7.63	0.20
2001	55.65	2.49	5.35	0.13
2002	64.75	2.49	5.65	0.14
2003	67.99	2.39	7.37	0.19
2004	69.65	2.71	9.12	0.25
2005	71.86	2.74	8.19	0.22

Note: ROE = Return on equity; EPS = earning per share.
Source: *China Securities and Futures Statistical Yearbook*, edited by CSRC (2006).

to 587.5 billion. About 70.1 percent of this rapid expansion came from IPOs, 22.6 percent from stock dividends, and 7.3 percent from seasoned equity issues. Although state- and legal-person shareholders had nearly 65 percent of the increased shares, they only purchased less than 29 percent of right-issued shares and less than 10 percent of re-issued shares. In contrast, holders of tradable shares (A, B, and H) account only for 35 percent of increased shares but they purchased 61 percent of right-issued shares and 86 percent of re-issued shares!

Despite that the seasoned equity issues account for only a small percentage of total of share number increase (7.3 percent for 1992–2002), they accounted for 38 percent of total capital raised from the equity market (during 1993–2004), as shown in Fig. 9.3. The mismatch between their small proportion of increased shares and their large proportion of the capital raised reflects the extent of expropriation of the public investors by the controlling (non-tradable) shareholders.

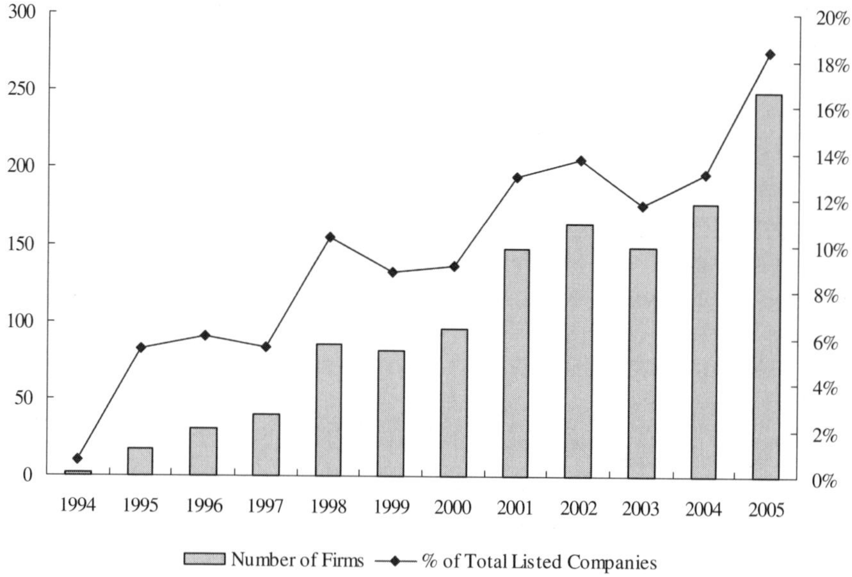

Fig. 9.2: Loss-making companies listed in stock market (1995–2005).
Sources: Compiled from CSMAR (Chinese Stock Market and Accounting Research) financial database, produced by GTA information Technology Co. Ltd. and China Accounting and Finance Research Center of the Hong Kong Polytechnic University.

Although the listed companies were enthusiastic in raising funds, they were parsimonious in paying dividends to the shareholders. As displayed in Table 9.6, on average, there were 60 percent of companies that paid dividends to the shareholders during 1994–2005, among which 45 percent of firms paid stock dividends instead of cash dividends. The proportion of firms paying stock dividends remained above 45 percent of all dividend-paying firms until the end of 1999. Furthermore, the cash payment was often trivial compared to its market price as the average dividend yield was about 0.86 percent, which was only a fraction of the three-month fixed deposit rate (about 1.7 percent).[10]

With poor corporate governance and transparency, China's stock market has exhibited very high volatility over years. Since

[10] *Shanghai Securities News*, August 14, 2004.

Table 9.5: Changes of share structure of listed companies (1992–2002); unit: 100 million shares.

Type of shares	Total changes	IPO	Stock dividend	Seasoned equity issue		Other changes
				Rights issue	Re-issue	
State-owned shares	2745.78	2228.32	396.98	47.71	9.72	63.55
Sponsors' legal persons' shares	677.4	509.33	253.55	24.10	2.38	−111.49
Foreign legal persons' shares	50.46	30.84	21.85	1.90	0.36	−4.49
Private placement of legal persons' shares	275.64	127.03	114.79	13.37	−0.16	20.61
Staff shares	13.88	82.91	26.92	7.17	0.44	−103.56
Others	27.33	76.25	11.89	23.46	5.33	−89.59
A shares	1509.49	605.8	445.01	179.27	64.47	204.01
B shares	156.28	63.05	43.89	5.72	32.98	11.32
H shares	349.83	347.87	0	0	10.5	1.71
All shares	5806.58	4071.4	1314.86	302.71	126.01	−7.94
In each category of share changes						
state- and legal-person shareholders' percentage	64.57	71.12	59.87	28.77	9.76	
tradable (A, B, H) shareholders' percentage	34.71	24.97	37.18	61.11	85.67	

Source: Compiled from *China Securities and Futures Statistical Yearbook* (2003).

shareholders could not get fair returns through cash dividends, their hope of investment returns lay heavily on capital gains from buying and selling the stocks. Capital gains also enjoy great tax advantageous over cash dividends, which is subject to 20 percent taxation. In a market where stock prices are relatively stable, the chance would be slim for shareholders to capture capital gains. Retail investors' appetite for capital gains in a volatile market also motivated the

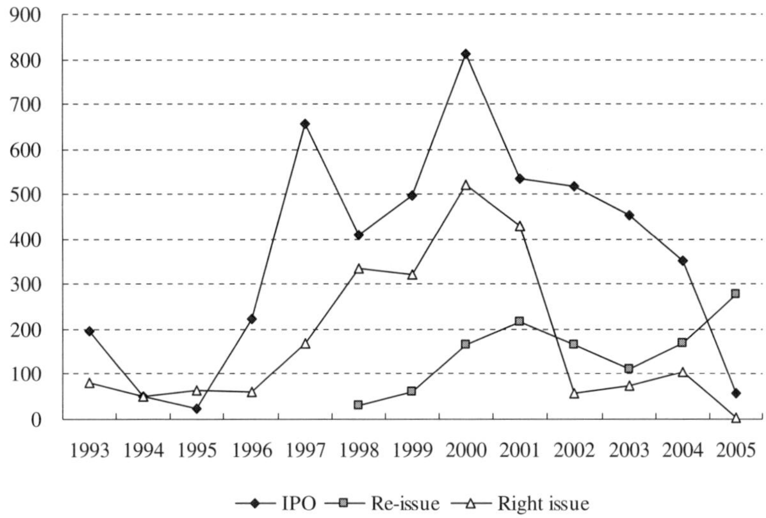

Fig. 9.3: Fund raised from equity market (1993–2005). Unit: 100 million yuan. Source: *China Securities and Futures Statistical Yearbook* (2005) and CSRC website.

institutional investors and dominant shareholders to manipulate the market prices, resulting in greater fluctuation of stock prices. Price manipulation is made easy by the fact that only one-third of the total shares were tradable and more than 99 percent of investors have been retail ones. Lack of transparency in the deals among non-tradable share owners has allowed rumors and fabricated news to cause great impact on prices.

As shown in Table 9.7, from 1992 to 2005, the turnover velocity in Shanghai Securities Exchange (SHSE) and Shenzhen Securities Exchange (SZSE) was, on average, above 400. The figure was even as high as 950 in Shenzhen in 1996. In contrast, the average turnover ratios were only 72, 74, and 47 in New York, London, and Tokyo, respectively.

In the first decade after its launch, China's stock market won the reputation as a vehicle for the government to unload the financial burdens of keeping many mammoth SOEs afloat to the retail investors. The poor accounting standards, weak corporate governance, lack of transparency, and scandals of insider trading further marred the public

Table 9.6: Summary of A-share firms paying dividend (1994–2005).

Year	Total number of firms	Firms paying dividend		Firms paying cash dividend		Firms paying stock dividend	
		Number	As percent of total firms	Number	As percent of total firms	Number	As percent of total firms
1994	287	225	78.40	155	54.01	174	60.63
1995	311	272	87.46	224	72.03	153	49.20
1996	514	332	64.59	198	38.52	216	42.02
1997	720	470	65.28	175	24.31	353	49.03
1998	825	448	54.30	232	28.12	275	33.33
1999	923	447	48.43	270	29.25	239	25.89
2000	1060	428	40.38	313	29.53	178	16.79
2001	1136	781	68.75	733	64.52	197	17.34
2002	1200	746	62.17	700	58.33	164	13.67
2003	1263	622	49.25	586	46.40	110	8.71
2004	1353	687	50.78	623	46.05	234	17.29
2005	1358	769	56.63	738	54.34	169	12.44
Average			60.53		45.45		28.86

Source: Compiled from www.cninfo.com.cn and CSMAR (Chinese Stock Market and Accounting Research) financial database, produced by GTA Information Technology Co. Ltd., and China Accounting and Finance Research Center of the Hong Kong Polytechnic University.

confidence in this emerging market. At the turn of the century, the market capitalization value experienced a slump, sharply contrasting the bank credit expansion amidst the economic boom after China joined the World Trade Organization (Fig. 9.4). Thanks to the slump, China's market capitalization ratio, once peaked at 53 percent of GDP in 2000, declined to under 20 percent of GDP in 2005 (Fig. 9.5).

Consequently, the amount of capital raised from stock issuance in China's equity markets at the Shanghai and Shenzhen stock exchanges has slumped from its peak of 154 billion yuan at year 2000 down to 78–86 billion yuan annually during 2002–2004. In recent years, Hong Kong stock market has risen to replace the Shanghai and

Table 9.7: Turnover velocity: China vs. major world markets (1992–2005).

Year	Turnover velocity				
	SZSE	SHSE	New York	London	Tokyo
1992	265.5		47.0	43.0	20.0
1993	324.4		53.0	81.0	26.0
1994	691.8		53.0	77.0	25.0
1995	309.6	519.4	59.0	77.7	26.8
1996	949.7	760.1	59.1	58.3	27.1
1997	662.3	535.0	65.7	44.0	32.9
1998	411.1	355.3	69.9	47.0	34.1
1999	371.6	421.6	74.6	56.7	49.4
2000	396.5	504.1	87.7	69.3	58.8
2001	190.0	216.7	86.9	83.8	60.0
2002	200.7	208.7	94.8	97.3	82.6
2003	217.0	268.6	89.5	106.6	67.9
2004	311.8	308.3	89.8	116.6	97.1
2005	350.6	290.7	99.1	110.1	115.3
Average	407.8	409.8	71.5	73.7	46.7

Notes: The turnover velocity is defined as the ratio of the number of transactions to the number of tradable shares.
Source: Compiled from *China Securities and Futures Statistical Yearbook* (2006); World Federation of Exchanges, website: www.world-exchanges.org/WFE/home.asp.

Shenzhen markets to become the main source of equity-financed capital for China's companies (Fig. 9.6). The marginalization of the mainland stock markets highlights the urgency of carrying out fundamental reforms to improve corporate governance and recover investors' confidence.

IMPROVEMENTS IN CORPORATE GOVERNANCE

Year 2006 is the fifth year after China gained accession to the WTO and is also the last year that China must fulfill its pre-accession commitments to open up the domestic banking-financial sector for foreign entrants. The country's highly unbalanced financial structure, however, has resulted in a very high concentration of corporate

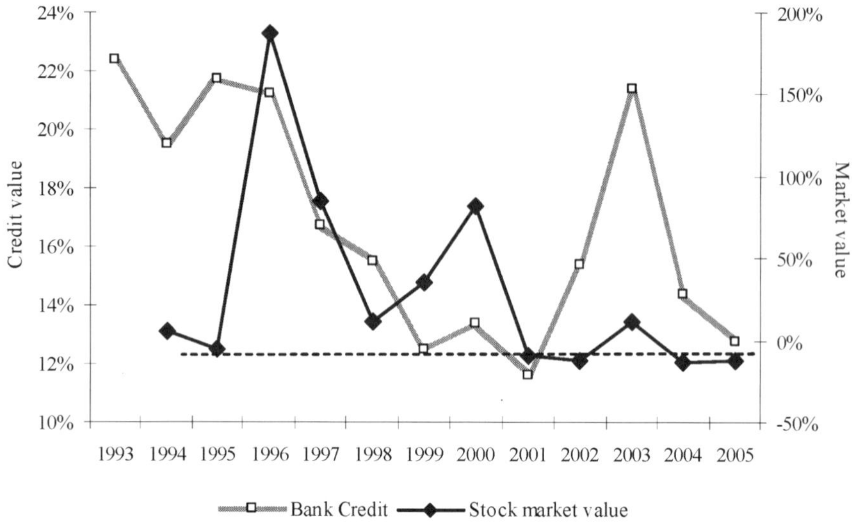

Fig. 9.4: Annual growth rates of bank credit and stock market capitalization value (1993–2005).
Source: *China Statistical Yearbook* (various years).

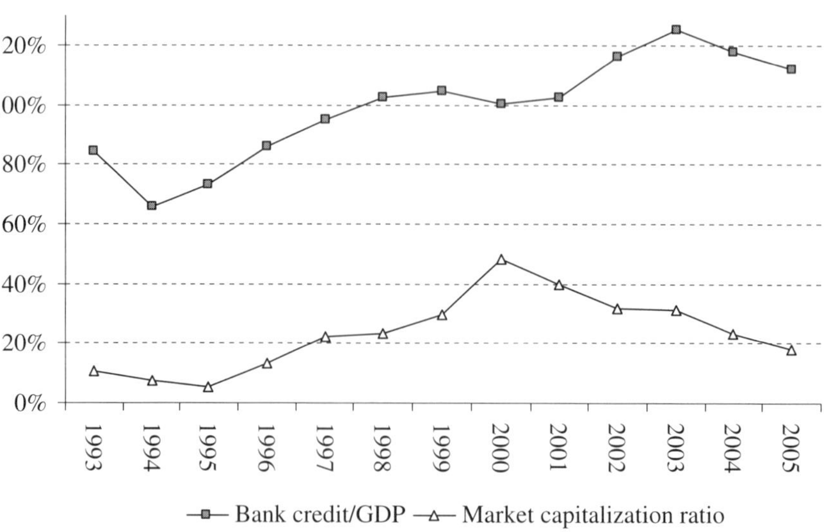

Fig. 9.5: Market capitalization ratio and bank-credit-to-GDP ratio (1993–2005).
Source: *China Statistical Yearbook* (various years).

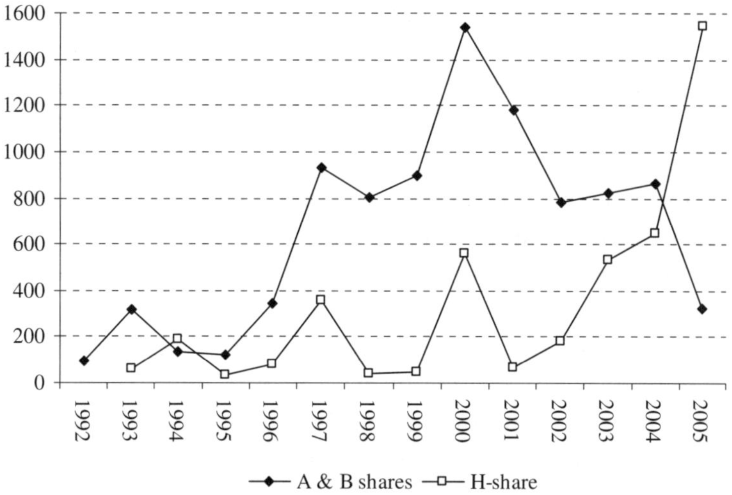

Fig. 9.6: Capital raised from share issuance (1992–2005). Note: From June 2005 to May 2006, new stock issuance was suspended in the A- and B-share markets for reform of split-share structure (see details in the section, "Open the equity market for entry of institutional investors").
Source: *China Securities and Futures Statistical Yearbook* (2005), CSRC website: www.csrc.gov.cn.

finance in a largely inefficient banking sector. In a fast-growing economy, this corporate finance structure could easily cause the companies to be over-leveraged and the banks to be swamped by the piling up of another round of non-performing loans. Facing such a potential disaster, the Chinese policy makers are eager to promote the role of equity market in capital finance. That is why, the sudden loss of the equity market's growth momentum after the turn of the century caused great concerns to the government, which has made serious efforts in recent years to improve the protection of shareholders' rights and corporate governance.

Improve the legal framework for corporate governance

Patterned after the U.S. model of stock market regulation, the Securities Law of People's Republic of China (1998) required listed companies to correctly and regularly publish and report their financial statements and operational conditions to the China Securities Regulatory Commission (CSRC). In case there are important events which may have significant influences on the trading prices of the shares but so far unknown to the investors, such as conclusions of significant contracts, heavy debts, or major lawsuits, the company is obliged to publish and submit a special report without delay. In practice, however, it is not unusual for listed companies to conceal or delay the disclosure of crucial information that may have adverse effects on their share prices. The regularly published financial statements may also be unreliable. The profits may be manipulated through different accounting methods. The so-called "earnings management" that manipulates accounting rules is not a rare phenomenon among the listed companies and even some auditing institutions have been involved in such manipulations (Lu, 2002).

Apart from government supervisions and regulations that require companies to disclose such information honestly without delay, the ultimate check on the management comes from shareholders themselves. However, as shown in the previous section, the practice of paying very little cash dividend has severed the link between individual shareholders' returns and the company's performance. With dismal prospects of real returns to their investment, most minority shareholders would "rationally ignore" their rights to monitor the management and increasingly behave like speculators. That in turn would lead to greater volatility of stock prices and weaker linkage between price movements and the listed companies' fundamentals. A stock market as such certainly cannot exert effective governance on the corporate management.

Both theoretical and empirical studies in the literature suggest a link between high dividend payouts and good corporate governance (Lintner, 1956; Gordon, 1959). For investors, the present value of the all-equity firm is the sum of all the current and expected cash flows discounted at the market rate. A firm's ability to distribute dividends is based on its earnings. Companies with good performance have better cash flows and therefore can afford to pay higher dividends than relatively poorly performing firms. In return, the shareholders would reward the companies with higher dividend payouts by bidding up their stock prices. Meanwhile, if shareholders receive cash dividends regularly, they will be better motivated to actively monitor the firm's performance.

To improve China's corporate governance, an important reform in recent years is the policy to enforce cash dividend payout. In March 2000, the CSRC released a "Supplementary Circular on the Rights Issues of Listed Companies," which stipulated that the details of cash dividend distributions in each year since being listed were required to report in the Rights Issue Prospectus. Since then, a series of regulations have been introduced to enforce cash dividend payout. The "Directives on the Management of New Share Issues of Listed Companies" promulgated by CSRC in February 2001 requested the underwriters to pay more attention to the firms that had not paid cash dividends in past three years without reasonable explanations. At the end of 2004, the CSRC released the "Regulations on the Reinforcement of the Social Public Shareholders' Rights Protection," which stipulated that listed firms having not paid cash dividends subsequently for three years would not be allowed to issue new shares.

With the impact of the reform, there appeared some changes in the pattern of equity issuing and dividend paying in recent years. As shown in Table 9.6, more than half of the companies did not pay cash dividends in 1999–2000. In 2001, however, the percentage of firms paying cash dividends leaped to 69 percent, which was nearly three-thirds higher than it was in 2000. Compared to the late 1990s, both the number and percentage of firms issuing stock dividends decreased sharply in the period 2001–2005. Li and Lu (forthcoming) empirically investigate China's listed companies' dividend policy over 1994–2003 and find that the cash-dividend-enforcement policy did have impact on the managerial behavior to a certain extent.

After the cash-dividend-enforcement reform, the CSRC released the "Directives on Establishing the Institution of Independent Members of Board of Directors" in August 2001. The Directives specify the requirement and qualifications of the independent members of the board of directors. The CSRC also issued the "Code of

Corporate Governance for Listed Companies in China" in January 2002, which spells out the criteria of corporate governance. In October 2005, China's *Company Law* and the *Securities Law* were both revised for the fourth time since 1997 to further consolidate institutions for corporate governance. These laws took effective on January 1, 2006. Furthermore, the "Regulations on Shareholders' Meeting of Listed Companies" and the revised "Guidelines on the Statute of Listed Companies" were promulgated in March 2006 with immediate effect. Meanwhile, the "Guidelines on the Statute of Listed Companies" has been revised for the first time since 1997 to be made compatible to the new editions of the *Company Law* and the *Securities Law*. The main amendments were reflected in the sections of Shares, Shareholders and Shareholders' Meeting, and the Board of Directors. Table 9.A1 in the Appendix summarizes the major protections for shareholders' rights in these regulations.

Open the equity market for entry of institutional investors

In 2002, China announced the Qualified Foreign Institutional Investors (QFII) scheme to allow foreign funds and securities companies to enter China's equity market. Since then, the government has allowed domestic insurance funds, social security funds, and corporate pension funds, to invest in the stock market. In early 2005, the PBOC, CBRC, and CSRC jointly promulgated a pilot scheme to allow a limited number of commercial banks to enter into the fund management business on a trial ("*shidian*" in Chinese) basis.[11] The rationale of this scheme is two-fold. One is to diversify banks' sources of revenue beyond interest income, which accounts for more than 90 percent of revenue for most banks. The other is to facilitate the growth of capital market and financial deepening process. By diversifying commercial banks' businesses, the move was not only meant to reduce banks' operation risks but also to give a boost to the development of equity

[11] "Officials of PBOC, CBRC, and CSRC answered media questions about the pilot scheme on commercial banks' operation of fund management business," www.cbrc.gov.cn, February 20, 2005.

financing market. In consistence to this move, the new version of *Securities Law* that took effect in January 2006 removed its previous version's ban on banks' funds to enter the equity market.

By March 2006, the number of fund management companies rose to 54, three commercial banks had conducted fund management business on an experimental basis, and fund managed shares reached a total number of 476.8 billion, accounting for 14.4 percent of the market value of domestic tradable shares. A total of 35 foreign institutions had been approved for QFII status.[12] In April 2006, the People's Bank of China announced the formal launch of the Qualified Domestic Institutional Investor (QDII) scheme. Under the QDII scheme, domestic financial institutions, including banks, insurance companies, and fund management firms will be allowed to raise funds (in foreign currencies or RMB), to apply for quotas from the State Administration of Foreign Exchange (SAFE) to convert RMB into foreign currencies, and to invest in overseas securities including bonds, money market products, and equities. In September 2006, CSRC, PBOC, and SAFE jointly promulgated the "Regulations on QFII Investment in Domestic Securities," which lowers the qualification requirements for QFIIs. By the end of September 2006, a total of 48 foreign institutions had been approved for QFII status with foreign exchange quota of U.S.$7.845 billion.[13] The QFII and QDII schemes are making China's financial system and capital market more open for both domestic and foreign institutional investors.

The impact of the entry of these institutional investors on China's equity market development is expected to increase over time. For instance, by the end of 2005, the fund under the management of China's National Social Security Fund (NSSF) was 212 billion yuan.[14] Just this money alone is equivalent to 24 percent of all money raised from the domestic stock market from 1991–2004. By

---

[12] China security news net, April 29, 2006.

[13] CSRC spokesman on Regulations on QFII investment in domestic securities, CSRC website www.csrc.gov.cn, September 27, 2006.

[14] Deutsche Bank Report, "China's QDIIs and Outlook for Overseas Investments," April 17, 2006.

October 2006, shares held by institutional investors had risen to 30 percent of the total traded shares.[15]

Reform of the "split share structure"

Compared to all the reforms described above, breaking up the "split share structure" of tradable and non-tradable shares is the most formidable task. With two-thirds of the shares being owned directly or indirectly by the state and kept out of market trading, it is virtually impossible to keep various governmental authorities from mingling with business interests, ensure fairness and transparency in corporate governance, and protect minority shareholders' rights. However, if all the non-tradable shares became tradable and flooded the market, the sudden rise in the supply of shares would cause the stock prices to slump, hurting all shareholders, especially those who have invested in the tradable shares.

Aware that the split share structure had become a major obstacle to stock market development, the State Council tried to initiate reforms to release the non-tradable shares for market trading in June 2001 by issuing the "Temporary Management Measures of Reducing State-owned Shares and Raising Social Security Fund." The attempt, however, immediately caused panic selling in the stock market and triggered a sharp fall of stock prices (Figs. 9.4 and 9.5). The reform also caused uproar of opposition mainly from the retail investors who held tradable shares.

To avoid a crash of the market, the government had to shelve the reform for three years. In February 2004, State Council tested the public sentiment by releasing the "Guidelines on Promoting Reform, Opening-up and Steady Development of China's Capital Market." Apart from explaining the necessity and importance of the reform, the Guidelines specified the principle of this reform: "To solve this problem, we must respect the law of market, make the reform conducive for market stability and development, and ensure protection for the legal rights of investors, especially the investors of the public."

---

[15] *Xinhuanet News*, October 6, 2006.

Under these guidelines, the reform of the split-share structure was re-launched in April 2005, when the CSRC issued a "Notice on Some Issues Regarding the Split Share Structure Reform Experimented on Selected Listed Companies" (CSRC, 2005, Circular No. 32). The notice detailed the operation procedures of the reform based on several important principles, namely, "market stability and development, fair and consistent rules, choice of measures through consultation, decisions to be approved by the holders of tradable shares, and orderly and sequential implementation." From May to July 2005, the reform was experimented with over two dozens of listed companies. In August 2005, five major government authorities, namely, the CSRC, State Asset Management Commission, Ministry of Finance, People's Bank, and Ministry of Commerce, jointly promulgated the "Guiding Propositions for the Split Share Structure Reform of Listed Companies" (CSRC, 2005, Circular No. 80) to kick off the overall reform for all listed companies. In September 2005, the CSRC issued the "Management Measures of Share Structure Reform for Listed Companies" (CSRC, 2005, Circular No. 42) to give more detailed instructions on the operation procedures.

To many observers' surprise, the reform turned out to be quite successful. By the end of the first half of 2006, of the totally 1300 plus listed companies, 1092 companies had already completed the reform or had been going through the reform procedures. These reformed companies' market value amounts to 3445.7 billion yuan, or 81.25 percent of all listed companies' market value.[16] By September 2006, the number of reformed companies rose to 1169, accounting for 93 percent of total market value.[17] Meanwhile, as shown in Figs. 9.7 and 9.8, the stock market price started to recover from its bottom in June 2005 and lifted up the market values since then, reflecting investors' regained confidence in the stock market. As more shares become tradable and started to enter the trading, the tradability ratio of stocks has been sharply rising since the reform was launched.

[16] *Xinhuanet News*, July 3, 2006.

[17] *Shanghai Zhengquan Bao* (Shanghai Securities News), September 28, 2006.

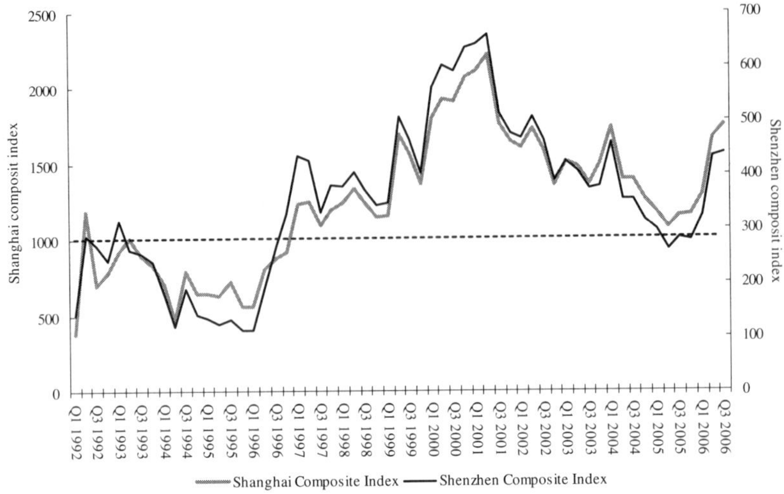

Fig. 9.7: Stock market price index (Q1. 1992–Q3. 2006).
Source: CSRC website: www.csrc.gov.cn.

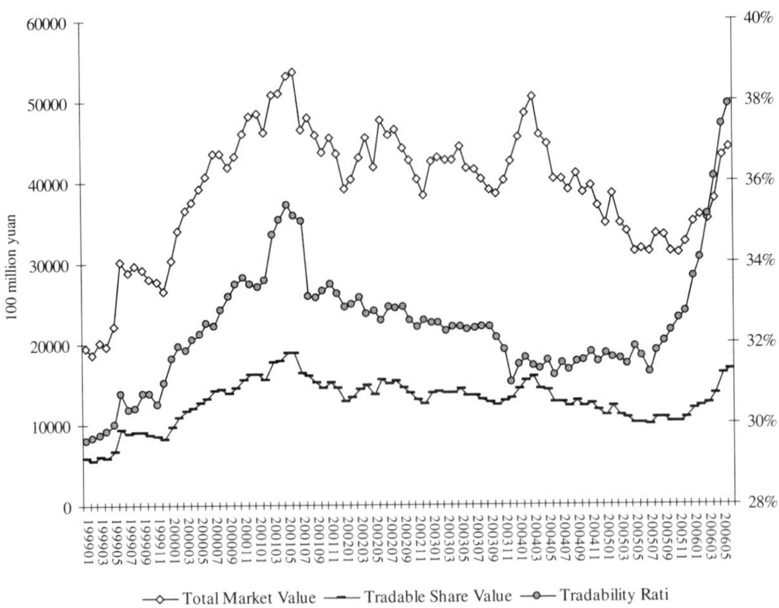

Fig. 9.8: All share market values and tradable share market values (Jan 1999–June 2006). Note: Tradability ratio = tradable share value divided by total market value.
Source: CSRC website: www.csrc.gov.cn.

How did the reformers achieve this remarkable success? Several important policy choices have made this possible.

First, several measures are taken to ensure that the tradable shareholders' interests will not be hurt. These mainly include:

- The reform package, proposed on the principle of consensus by the non-tradable shareholders, should win two-thirds of all the tradable shareholders' (by one-share-one-vote rule) support before it can be implemented.[18]
- In principle, for every 10 shares held by the tradable shareholders, they are to receive about 3 (converted) shares from the non-tradable shareholders as a "compensation" for their risks and potential losses that may arise from the conversion of non-tradable shares to tradable ones. The exact compensation ratio is subject to the decision of shareholders' meeting in each company.
- The Ministry of Finance waived stamp duties, corporate, and individual income taxes for all the share transfers related to the reform.
- There are also rules to specify monitoring institutions and procedures as well as standards for information disclosure regarding the companies undergoing the reform.

Second, there are also a number of measures to stabilize the share price of the companies undergoing the reform. These include:

- Before the reform package is announced at the tradable shareholders' meeting, the company's stock trading at the exchanges should be suspended. The stock trading will be resumed only after the package wins the approval of the tradable shareholders' meeting.
- Listed companies are allowed to buy back their own shares to boost the demand for the stocks.
- The controlling shareholders are allowed to increase their shareholdings by purchasing shares from the market.

[18] By April 2006, in a total of 11 listed companies, the reform package proposed by the non-tradable shareholders had failed to win the two-third approval votes by the tradable shareholders (*China Securities News*, May 1, 2006).

- The non-tradable shares' sale prices may be pre-determined and the associated purchasing right options may be traded in the market.
- Within 12 months after the reform package is implemented, the non-tradable shares are not allowed to be transferred or traded in or outside the stock exchanges.
- Those major non-tradable shareholders (each of whom owns more than 5 percent of the total shares of the company), they are not allowed to sell more than 5 percent of the total shares in the first 12 months after the 12-month no-sale period expires. Nor can they sell more than 10 percent of total sales in the first 24 months after the no-sale period expires.
- Any listed company has to wait for six months after the completion of the reform (i.e., resumption of stock trading) before it can raise new funds from the stock markets (by re-issuance or right issuance).

Finally, there are measures to stabilize the overall stock market. For instance, from June 2005 to May 2006, the CSRC suspended all IPOs, re-issues, right issues, and convertible bond issues in Shanghai and Shenzhen markets for one year. To boost demand for shares, the government allowed the investment funds to hold and invest in the non-tradable purchasing right options during the reform. A series of reforms to open up the equity market to institutional investors and banks were also announced and implemented from early 2005 to 2006 to breathe some life into market confidence.

A brief review of the reform process since April 2005 illustrates the effectiveness of some of these measures. When the first few companies were selected for experimental reforms of the split-share structure in May 2005, the stock market responded negatively like it did in the year 2001 to the previous reform attempt. After the second group of about 20 listed companies started the reform, the market plunged and Shanghai composite index fell below the psychological threshold of 1000 points for the first time since 1996 (Fig. 9.7) on June 6, 2005.

Within the following two weeks, however, the government released a series of news to boost retail investors' confidence. These include: the listed companies would be allowed to buy back their shares; the control shareholders would be allowed to increase shareholding by purchasing shares from the market; stamp duties and income taxes would be waived for stock transfers due to the reform; and option rights of pre-determined converted share prices would be allowed to be traded. The series of news immediately lifted the market index from the trough. The recovery of the stock got another dose of stimulus in August when the "Guiding Propositions for the Split Share Structure Reform of Listed Companies" was issued by five major government authorities. An important policy announced in this circular was that A-share companies that also issue B-shares and H-shares should let their A-share holders discuss and decide the split-share-structure reform programs. The promulgation of the CSRC's "Management Measures of Share Structure Reform for Listed Companies" in September 2005 further institutionalized the policies that secure the minority shareholders' rights and market stability. China's two stock exchanges finally shook off the bearish mood and hopped into a new round of bull-market race.

PROSPECTS OF CAPITAL MARKET DEVELOPMENT

Reform of the split-share structure has removed a major obstacle to further development of China's equity market. As the reform has come to an end, a few more regulatory-policy changes have been introduced.

First, to prepare for the resumption of IPO after one year of suspension, the CSRC declared a new set of regulatory rules for IPO procedures in April 2006. On the one hand, the new rules have removed some previous restrictions on IPO companies to make the procedure more in line with the practices in matured equity markets. The most important changes include canceling the one-year "guiding" (waiting) period for companies qualified for IPOs and removing the constraint that the maximum amount of capital raised though IPO should be no more than twice the company's net asset value. These changes should greatly enhance the attractiveness of China's equity market (especially the A-share market) to good-quality companies and thus reverse the recent-year marginalization trend of the domestic exchanges. On the other hand, the new regulations define greater responsibility to the IPO intermediary institutions for the accuracy and completeness of the IPO-company's publicized information. Meanwhile, the new regulations give clearer, stricter, and more detailed requirements for the IPO-company's corporate governance and financial conditions.[19]

The CSRC also revised the rules for re-issuing shares. The successful reform of the split-share structure has substantially reduced the chances for controlling shareholders to expropriate the minority shareholders by right issues. Since there are no more non-tradable shares, the control shareholders would not benefit by not exercising the rights if the right issue price is attractively low. If the right issue price is too high, the minority shareholders can avoid the risk of losing money by forgoing the rights. The new CSRC rules provide an additional safeguard for shareholders' rights: if no more than 70 percent of the right issue shares are purchased by the shareholders, the right issue should automatically become void and all the money raised should be reimbursed to the shareholders with interests. As for re-issues, the new regulation stipulates that all re-issued shares must be offered at the prevailing market price.[20] With these new rules in place, only the companies with good business prospects can benefit from using seasoned equity issues to raise capital.

Success of the split-share structure reform also facilitates the corporate control market for mergers and acquisitions (M&A). By mid-2006, proportion of A-shares held by controlling shareholders dropped to below 40 percent from over 67 percent before the reform, thanks to the use of share transfer as compensation to the tradable shareholders in the reform. These developments have made M&A more likely to happen. To ensure a level-playing field and protect the minority shareholders' rights, the CSRC timely promulgated the "Regulations on Acquisition of Listed Companies" to take effect on September 1, 2006. According to the new regulations,

---

[19] CSRC, "Regulations on initial public offering (draft)", April 28, 2006.

[20] *People's Daily* (overseas edition), June 7, 2006, www.xinhuanet.com.

once an investor's holding of a company's shares reaches 30 percent threshold of total shares, the investor is obliged to propose a tender offer to all shareholders to purchase either all shares or no less than 5 percent of the total shares. This clause is more flexible than the previous regulation that only allowed the tender offer to purchase all shares. Meanwhile, the new regulations also allow the acquirer to use (other companies') stocks for payment of takeover purchase. The CSRC also simplified its approval procedure for takeover applications. On the other hand, the new regulations provide better protection for the shareholders. These include the rule that tender offer should be non-discriminative and fair to all shareholders and more stringent qualifications for the acquirer, especially regarding the latter's financial track record, current financial status, and ability to make the payment. Besides, under the new rules, if the original controlling shareholders or actual controllers have made any damage to shareholders' interests, they must have cleared up the damage, compensated or arranged for compensation to the public shareholders before the acquisition can be completed.

Since the launch of split-share structure reform in April 2005, the scale, intensity, and comprehensiveness of reforms in China's equity market has been unprecedented in its 16 years' development. It should not be exaggerating to call these reforms a "big-bang" package. With all these reforms, the prospect of China's capital market development looks brighter than any time since its first launch for the following reasons.

First, these reforms have created conditions to further improve corporate governance and protection of shareholders' right. In particular, they have addressed the major weaknesses of China's corporate governance system as discussed in the section, "Weak corporate governance."

Second, although it is still early to evaluate the full effects of these reforms, the reaction by China's investors so far has been very positive. As shown in Fig. 9.7, both Shanghai and Shenzhen exchange indices indicate a rapid recovery of China's equity market after the split-share structure reform showed the first sign of success. The number of new accounts also started to pick up. Although the

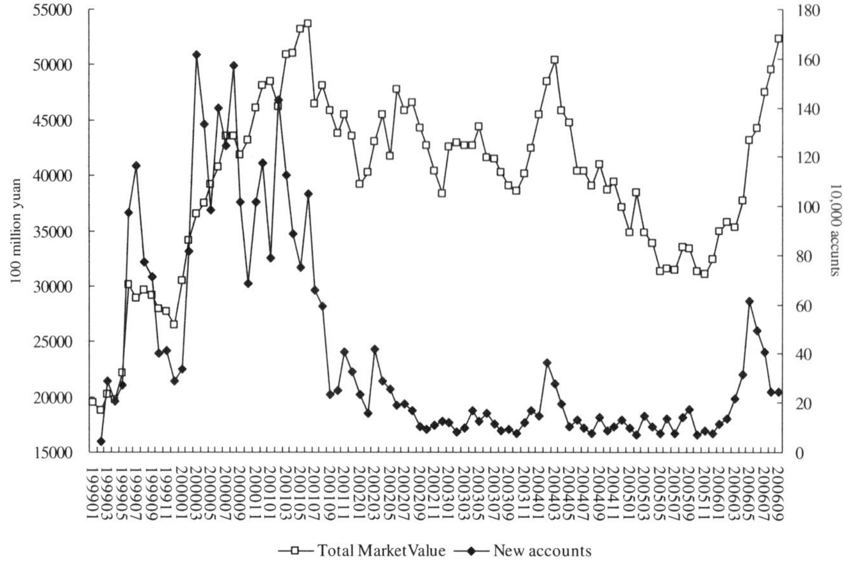

Fig. 9.9: Total market value and newly-opened investor accounts (January 1999–September 2006).
Source: CSRC website: www.csrc.gov.cn.

increase is still much lower than those in the previous boom in the late 1990s (Fig. 9.9), the trend parallels well with the upward swing of the market value.

Finally, the experience of the much limited reforms in the past may serve as a reference. For instance, as discussed in the section, "Improvements in corporate governance," China's regulatory authorities started to enforce cash dividend payout in 2000–2001, along with some other reforms to improve the legal framework of corporate governance in the following years. It is interesting to note that the overall performance of China's listed companies started to show signs of improvements in 2001–2005 in terms of debt ratio, net asset per share, return on equity, and earnings per share (Table 9.4). These signs of improvements bode well for the much more comprehensive reforms since April 2005 and for the future of China's capital market development.

APPENDIX

Table 9.A.1: Highlights of protections for shareholders' rights in China's corporate legal framework.

Rules	Description	Source
Information disclosure and transparency	*Articles 64, 65, 66, and 67* specify requirements for the announcement of IPO **prospectus** and the relevant **financial statements**; the submission of a **mid-term report**; the submission of an **annual report**; and the announcement of **a major event**. *Article 68*: The directors and senior managers of a listed company shall subscribe their **opinions for recognition** in the periodic report of their company **in written form**. The board of supervisors of a listed company shall carry out an examination on the periodic report of its company as formulated by the board of directors and produce the **relevant examination opinions in writing**.	*Securities Law of the People's Republic of China* (2006), Chapter 3 — Transaction of securities, Section 3 — On-going disclosure of information Articles 64–68.
Tender offer	*Article 86*: Where an investor, through securities trading at a stock exchange, comes to hold or holds with any other person **5% of the shares** as issued by a listed company by means of agreement or any other arrangement, the investor shall, **within three days** as of the date when such shareholding becomes a fact, **submit a written report** to the securities regulatory authority under the State Council and the	*Securities Law of the People's Republic of China* (2006), Chapter 4 — Acquisition of listed companies, Articles 86 and 88.

(*Continued*)

Table 9.A.1: (*Continued*)

Rules	Description	Source
	stock exchange, notify the relevant listed company and announce the fact to the general public. Within the aforesaid prescribed period, the investor may not purchase or sell any more shares of the listed company. In case an investor holds or holds with any other person 5% of the shares as issued by a listed company by means of agreement or any other arrangement, he shall, pursuant to the provisions of the preceding paragraph herein, **make report and announcement of each 5% increase or decrease** in the proportion of the issued shares of the said company he holds through securities trading at a stock exchange. Within the reporting period as well as two days after the relevant report and announcement are made, the investor may not purchase or sell any more shares of the listed company. *Article 88*: Where an investor holds or holds with any other person **30% of the stocks** as issued by a listed company by means of agreement or any other arrangement through securities trading at a stock exchange and **if the purchase is continued**, he shall **issue a tender offer** to all the shareholders of the said listed company to purchase all of or part of the shares of the listed company.	

(*Continued*)

Table 9.A.1: (*Continued*)

Rules	Description	Source
Special shareholders' meeting	*Article 101*: Under any of the following circumstances, a special shareholders' meeting shall be held within 2 months: (1) The number of directors is less than two-thirds of the number of directors as required by this law or the number of directors as prescribed in the articles of association; (3) At the request of the shareholders separately or aggregately holding 10% or more of the company's shares; (4) The board of directors deems it necessary; (5) At the request of the board of supervisors.	*The Company Law of the People's Republic of China* (2006), Chapter 4 — Establishment and organizational structure of a joint stock limited company, Section 2 — Shareholders' meeting, Articles 101, 103.
Proposal of a shareholders' meeting	*Article 103*: The shareholders separately or aggregately holding 3% or more of the shares of the company may put forward a written temporary proposal to the board of directors 10 days before a shareholders' meeting is held. The board of directors may notify other shareholders within 2 days and submit the temporary proposal to the meeting of the shareholders' meeting for deliberation.	
Shares blocked before meeting	*Article 103*: If the holders of unregistered stocks attend the shareholders' meeting, they shall have their stocks preserved in the company during the period from 5 days before the meeting is held to the day when the shareholders' meeting is closed.	

(*Continued*)

Table 9.A.1: (*Continued*)

Rules	Description	Source
Voting at the shareholders' meeting	*Article 104*: When a shareholder attends the shareholders' meeting, he shall have one voting right for each share he holds. However, the company has no voting right for its own shares it holds. *Article 75*: When general resolution is to be made by the shareholders' meeting, it shall be adopted by shareholders representing more than half of the voting rights of the shareholders in presence. However, the special resolution shall be adopted by shareholders representing 2/3 or more of the voting rights of the shareholders in presence.	*The Company Law of the People's Republic of China* (2006), Chapter 4 — Establishment and organizational structure of a joint stock limited company, Section 2 — Shareholders' meeting, Article 104. *The Guidelines on the Statute of Listed Companies* (2006), Chapter 4 — Shareholders and shareholders' meeting, Section 6 — Voting and resolution of shareholders' meeting, Article 75.
Cumulative voting system	*Article 106*: When the shareholders' meeting elects directors or supervisors, it may, according to the articles of association or resolution of the shareholders' meeting, adopt a cumulative voting system. The term "cumulative voting system" as mentioned in this Law refers to a system of voting by shareholders for the election of directors or supervisors at a session of the shareholders' meeting in which the shareholder can multiply his voting rights by the number of candidates and vote them all for one candidate for director or supervisor.	*The Company Law of the People's Republic of China* (2006), Chapter 4 — Establishment and organizational structure of a joint stock limited company, Section 2 — Shareholders' meeting, Article 106.

(*Continued*)

Table 9.A.1: *(Continued)*

Rules	Description	Source
Proxy voting	*Article 107*: A shareholder may entrust an agent to attend a shareholders' meeting. The agent shall present a power of attorney issued by the shareholder to the company, and shall exercise his voting rights within the authorization scope. *Article 55*: The notice of shareholders' meeting shall include the following: ... (3) Indicate in clear writing that: All shareholders are entitled to attend the shareholders' meeting, and are able to entrust an agent to attend a shareholders' meeting and vote for the resolution. The agent may not necessarily be a shareholder of the company.	*The Company Law of the People's Republic of China* (2006), Chapter 4 — Establishment and organizational structure of a joint stock limited company, Section 2 — Shareholders' meeting, Article 107. *The Guidelines on the Statute of Listed Companies* (2006), Chapter 4 — Shareholders and shareholders' meeting, Section 4 — Proposal and notice of shareholders' meeting, Article 55(3).
Special meeting of the board of directors	*Article 111*: The shareholders representing 1/10 or more of the voting rights, or 1/3 of the directors, or the board of supervisors may bring forward a proposal on holding a temporary meeting of the board of directors. The chairman of the board of directors shall, within 10 days after he receives such a proposal, convene and preside over a meeting of the board of directors.	*The Company Law of the People's Republic of China* (2006), Chapter 4 — Establishment and organizational structure of a joint stock limited company, Section 3 — Board of directors, managers, Article 111.

(Continued)

Table 9.A.1: (*Continued*)

Rules	Description	Source
Voting at the meeting of the board of directors	*Article 112*: No meeting of the board of directors may be held, unless more than half of the directors are present. When the board of directors makes a resolution, it shall be adopted by more than half of all the directors. As for the voting on a resolution of the board of directors, a director shall have one vote only.	*The Company Law of the People's Republic of China* (2006), Chapter 4 — Establishment and organizational structure of a joint stock limited company, Section 3 — Board of directors, managers, Article 112.
Independent directors	*Article 123*: A listed company shall have independent directors. And the concrete measures shall be formulated by the State Council. Details refer to "The Directives on the Establishing the institution of Independent Members of Board of Directors" (2001), and "Code of Corporate Governance for Listed Companies in China" (2002) Chapter 4 Section 5	*The Company Law of the People's Republic of China* (2006), Chapter 4 — Establishment and organizational structure of a joint stock limited company, Section 5 — Special provisions on the organizational structure of a listed company, Article 123.
Voting of a connection enterprise is prohibited	*Article 125*: Where any of the directors has any relationship with the enterprise involved in the matter to be discussed at the meeting of the board of directors, he shall not vote on this resolution, nor may he vote on behalf of any other person. The meeting of the board of directors shall not be held unless more than half of the unrelated directors are present at the meeting. A resolution of the board of directors shall be adopted by more than half of the unrelated directors. If the	*The Company Law of the People's Republic of China* (2006), Chapter 4 — Establishment and organizational structure of a joint stock limited company, Section 5 — Special provisions on the organizational structure of a listed company, Article 125.

(*Continued*)

Table 9.A.1: *(Continued)*

Rules	Description	Source
	number of unrelated directors in presence is less than 3 persons, the matter shall be submitted to the shareholders' meeting of the listed company for deliberation. *Article 79*: Where any of the directors has any relationship with the enterprise involved in the matter to be discussed at the meeting of the board of directors, he shall not vote on this resolution. The number of stocks with voting rights represented by the director shall not be included in the effective votes. The resolution of shareholders' meeting should fully disclose the voting situation of non-relationship shareholders.	*The Guidelines on the Statute of Listed Companies* (2006), Chapter 4 — Shareholders and shareholders' meeting, Section 6 — Voting and resolution of shareholders' meeting, Article 79.
Lawsuit filed by shareholders	*Article 34*: Should the content of the resolution of the shareholders' meeting or directorates' meeting violate the law and regulations, shareholders are entitled to request the court to deliver a verdict of "nullity" within 60 days since the resolution was made. *Article 35*: Should the directors, senior executives, or Board of Supervision violate the law and regulations, shareholder, who owns 1 percent of shares alone or collectively with other shareholders in consecutive 180 days, is entitled to file a lawsuit to the court.	*The Guidelines on the Statute of Listed Companies* (2006), Chapter 4 — Shareholders and Shareholders' Meeting, Section 1 — Shareholders, Articles 34 and 35.

(Continued)

Table 9.A.1: (*Continued*)

Rules	Description	Source
Dissolution	*Article 183*: Where a company meets any serious difficulty during its operation or management so that the interests of the shareholders will be subject to heavy loss if it continues to exist and it cannot be solved by any other means, the shareholders who hold 10 percent or more of the voting rights of all the shareholders of the company may plead the court to dissolve the company. *Article 178 (5)*: Same content as above.	*The Company Law of the People's Republic of China* (2006), Chapter 10 — Dissolution and liquidation of a company, Article 183. *The Guidelines on the Statute of Listed Companies* (2006), Chapter 10, Section 2 — Dissolution and liquidation, Article 178(5).
Liquidation	*Article 187*: The residual assets that result from paying off the liquidation expenses, wages of employees, social insurance premiums and legal compensation premiums, the outstanding taxes and the debts of the company with the assets of the company may, in the case of a limited liability company, be distributed according to the proportions of capital contributions of the shareholders, and in the case of a joint stock limited company, according to the proportions of stocks held by the shareholders.	*The Company Law of the People's Republic of China* (2006), Chapter 10 — Dissolution and liquidation of a company, Article 187.

(*Continued*)

Table 9.A.1: (*Continued*)

Rules	Description	Source
Increase of stocks	The stocks of a company can be increased through (3) Paying stock dividend to the existing shareholders; (4) Transferring funds from capital reserve account.	*The Guidelines on the Statute of Listed Companies* (2006), Chapter 3 — Stocks, Section 2 — Increase and deduction of stocks and repurchase, Article 21(3) and (4).
Incentive contracts	A listed company is allowed to implement incentive stock plan by giving restricted stocks and stock option or use other approved ways to its directors, senior executives, and other staffs.	*The Directives on the Incentive Stocks of Listed Companies* (2006).

REFERENCES

Chinese Academy of Social Sciences (CASS) (1998), "Macro situations, financial risk and external shock," *Economics Research Journal (Jin Ji Yan Jiu)* 3, 3–14.

Easterbrook, Frank H. and Daniel R. Fischel (1983), "Voting in corporate law," *Journal of Law and Economics* 26, 395–427.

Farrell, Diana, Susan Lund, Jaeson Rosenfeld, Fabrice Morin, Niyati Gupta and Ezra Greenberg (2006), *Putting China's Capital to Work: The Value of Financial System Reform*, San Francisco: McKinsey Global Institute.

Gonzalez, Michael (2006), "Informal finance: encouraging the entrepreneurial spirit in post-Mao China," *2006 Index of Economic Freedom*, Washington, DC: Heritage Foundation, Chapter 4.

Gordon, M. (1959), "Dividends, earnings and stock prices," *Review of Economics and Statistics* 44, 91–105.

Guo Bin and Liu Manlu (2002), "Private finance and development of small-&-medium-sized enterprises: an empirical study on Wenzhou city," *Jingji Yanjiu Journal of Economic Research*, No. 10.

Hale, David (2005), "China's Banking Revolution, www.project-syndicate.org.

Heilmann, Sebanstian (2002), "The Chinese Stock Market: Pitfalls of a Policy-drive Market," Working Paper, Center for East Asian and Pacific Studies, Trier University, Germany.

Li, Ning and Ding Lu (forthcoming), "The information content of cash dividends and its policy implication in China's stock market," *Zhongguo Jinrong Yanjiu (China Financial Economics Review)*.

Lintner, J. (1956), "Distribution of incomes of corporations among dividends, retained earnings, and taxes," *American Economic Review* 46, 97–113.

Lu, Ding, Shandre M. Thangavelu and Qing Hu (2005), "Biased lending and non-performing loans in China's banking sector," *Journal of Development Studies* 41(6), 1071–1091.

Lu, Yujian (2002), "The empirical studies on the earnings management behavior for the rights issue qualification of listed companies," *Nanjing She Hui Ke Xue (Nanjing Social Science)* 3, 26–32.

Manne, Henry G. (1965), "Mergers and the market for corporate control," *Journal of Political Economy* 73(2), 110–120.

Mao, Jinmin (2005), "On private financial market: a survey and analysis on the cases of private finance in Shanxi Province," *Jinrong Yanjiu*, No. 1, 2005.

Peebles, Gavin (1991), *Money in the People's Republic of China: A Comparative Perspective*, Sydney: Allen & Unwin.

Podpiera, Richard (2006), "Progress in China's banking sector reform: has bank behavior changed?" *IMF Working Paper*, WP/06/71.

Tam, On Kit (1999), *The Development of Corporate Governance in China*, Northampton, MA: Edward Elgar Publishing.

Tsai, Kellee (2001), Beyond banks: the local logic of informal finance and private sector development in China," KSG/HBS/MIT, Cambridge, MA, 11–13, September.

Walter, Carl E. and J.T. Howie Fraser (2001), *To Get Rich Is Glorious: China's Stock Markets in the 80s and 90s*, London: Palgrave Press.

World Bank (1997), *China 2020*, Washington, DC: World Bank.

Chapter

10

Chinese Government Spending on Primary Education: Inequality and Trend

Zhao Litao and Tan Soon Heng

East Asian Institute, Singapore

China's spectacular economic growth has fueled human capital investment. From 1990 to 2004, educational expenditures from all sources have increased from 65.9 billion yuan to 724.3 billion yuan, an annual growth of 18.7 percent, higher than the GDP growth in this period.[1] This rapid increase in educational expenditure can help correct a long-standing policy bias that favors physical capital investment over human capital investment, but it is less clear to what extent it corrects other policy biases that favor urban human capital investment over rural human capital investment, and favor coastal regions over inland provinces.[2]

It is widely known that localized financing of education, coupled with growing regional disparities in economic development,

---

[1] For the 1990 figure, see *China Education Yearbook* 1991, p. 123; for the 2004 figure, see *China Educational Finance Statistical Yearbook* 2005, p. 2.

[2] For a discussion on policy biases in human capital investment, see James J. Heckman, "China's Human Capital Investment." *China Economic Review* 16 (2005): 50–70.

exacerbates unequal distribution of human capital investment nationwide. Concerns have been raised regarding unequal access to education among school-age children.[3] The tax-for-fee reform aiming at reducing peasant burdens — a major financial source of rural education — can only make the problem worse. Clearly aware of this problem, the central government has set up special programs to promote compulsory education in poor regions, with increased funds from central appropriation. In 2001–2002 alone, a multiple-year program that sought to upgrade dilapidated school buildings mobilized 12 billion yuan, with 3 billion yuan from the central government.[4] Since 2001, the central government has also increased financial transfer to the central and western provinces, to make up local losses from the tax-for-fee reform. Despite larger financial support from the central government for poor regions, it remains unclear whether such support is large enough to narrow the regional disparity in educational expenditure.

We aim to fill in the gap in this chapter. Our focus is on the nine-year compulsory education, the basic education that the Chinese government has sought to expand till it is universalized nationwide. The right to free compulsory education has been written into the education law, and the enrollment rate for primary school-age children is above 97 percent nationwide throughout the 1990s. The national-level statistics nonetheless conceal considerable local variations. Dropout rates are high in some localities,[5] and insufficient educational funds are among the most important factors

[3] Jennifer Adams and Emily Hannum, "Children's Social Welfare in China, 1989–1997: Access to Health Insurance and Education," *The China Quarterly* 181 (2005): 100–121; Mun Tsang, "Costs of Education in China: Issues of Resource Mobilization, Equality, Equity, and Efficiency," *Education Economics*, 2 (1994): 287–312; Loraine West and Christine Wong, "Fiscal Decentralization and Growing Regional Disparities in Rural China: Some Evidence in the Provision of Social Services," *Oxford Review of Economic Policy* 11 (1995): 70–85.

[4] *China Education Yearbook* 2003, p. 337.

[5] Rachel Murphy has found in a county in Jiangxi Province that only 68 percent of students in the primary school intake graduated in 1999. See Rachel Murphy, "Turning Peasants into Modern Chinese Citizens: 'Population Quality' Discourse, Demographic Transition and Primary Education," *The China Quarterly* 177 (2004): 1–20.

causing regional gaps in educational attainment. In this chapter we focus on (1) how the government spending on primary school education varies across provinces, and (2) how this provincial-level inequality changes over time. Our primary data sources are official statistics that report budgetary spending on primary school per student by province from 1992 to 2003. In the first section, we briefly describe educational reforms in the past two decades within the larger context of financial reforms that affect the pattern of government spending on education. Based on official statistics, the second section shows how educational expenditures change over time, in both absolute and relative terms. The third section focuses on provincial-level inequality in per pupil budgetary expenditure on primary education, how this inequality changes over time from 1992 to 2003, and what accounts for the temporal change. The fourth section concludes with a discussion on the role of the central government in narrowing the regional gap in educational expenditure.

FINANCING CHINA'S COMPULSORY EDUCATION

Ever since China began the transition from a state socialist economy to a market-oriented one in the late 1970s, education was emphasized as a strategic area for producing a skilled labor force and for promoting social and economic development.[6] As part of the larger economic reform, major educational reforms were initiated in the mid-1980s. Two developments are particularly noteworthy. First, the Compulsory Education Law was passed in 1986 to formally institute a nine-year compulsory education system. Aware of large regional gaps, the Law set requirements and deadlines tailored to local conditions. The government aimed to make lower secondary education universal in urban areas by 1990 and nationwide by 2000.

[6] As Jennifer Adams and Emily Hannum noted, Chinese education laws continue to show this orientation. See Jennifer Adams and Emily Hannum, "Children's Social Welfare in China, 1989–1997: Access to Health Insurance and Education," *The China Quarterly* 181 (2005): 100–121. For discrepancies between national enrolment figures and local ones in the 1980s, see Suzanne Pepper, *China's Education Reform in the 1980s: Policies, Issues, and Historical Perspectives*, Institute of East Asian Studies, University of California at Berkeley.

Second, school administration and financial responsibility were decentralized to local authorities in 1985. Fiscal decentralization granted more control to county and township governments over how funds were used, but also required them to share in the responsibility for financing education. A hierarchical system for financing education was thus instituted, with little change over the next decade. The central government ran and financed certain institutions of higher education; down the hierarchy, provincial, county, township, and village governments, respectively, were financially responsible for schools at the tertiary, upper secondary, lower secondary, and primary education.[7] In rural areas, throughout the 1990s, township governments were responsible for financing lower secondary education and wages of "state-run" teachers (*gongban jiaoshi*) in primary and lower secondary schools, while villages were responsible for building and maintaining school facilities, and financing wages of "people-run" teachers (*minban jiaoshi*).

Against the backdrop of growing regional disparities, localized financing mechanism has a profound impact on the regional gap in educational expenditures. The central government required local governments to meet the target of universalizing the nine-year compulsory education without providing needed funds. This created problems for many poor rural areas. With little revenue from industry or commerce, local governments could barely finance *gongban* teachers' wages. Other costs such as classroom supplies, facility maintenance, and wages for *minban* teachers must be borne locally, through charges and levies collected from households, collective contributions, school-generated revenues, or fees charged to students.[8] A survey of poor counties in the central region finds that

---

[7] Keith Lewin, Angela Little, Xu Hui and Zheng Jiwei, *Educational Innovation in China: Tracing the Impact of the* 1985 *Reforms* (Harlow: Longman, 1994).

[8] Jennifer Adams and Emily Hannum, "Children's Social Welfare in China, 1989–1997: Access to Health Insurance and Education," *The China Quarterly* 181 (2005): 100–121. Rachel Murphy, "Turning Peasants into Modern Chinese Citizens: 'Population Quality' Discourse, Demographic Transition and Primary Education," *The China Quarterly* 177 (2004): 1–20. World Bank, "China: National Development and Sub-National Finance: A Review of Provincial Expenditures," 2002.

in 2000, non-governmental inputs accounted for as high as 70 percent of total educational expenditures in many schools.[9]

The 1994 tax reform exacerbated the situation by altering the revenue structure in favor of the central government without changing the expenditure structure. A survey shows that in 1999, township-level governments accounted for 78 percent of government spending on compulsory education, with another 9 percent from county-level governments, 11 percent from provincial and prefectual-level governments, while only 2 percent from the central government.[10] With little revenue from industry and commerce and limited subsidies from upper levels of government, local governments in poor areas were forced to levy surcharges on peasants, meanwhile delaying wage payments to teachers and investing little in upgrading dilapidated school buildings. Educational surcharge became the chief contributor to the growing peasant burden, especially in the central region which had a much less developed economy than the eastern region, and much less financial transfer from the central government than the western region.[11]

Increasing peasant burdens led to a sustained rise in social protests in the 1990s, forcing the central government to begin a new round of reform in 1999 that aimed at reducing the peasant burden.[12] By consolidating legitimate fees into a single tax, the tax-for-fee reform effectively reduced arbitrary and unwarranted levies

---

[9] Li Xiangyun, "Zhongguo gonggong caizheng kuangjia xia gonggong yiwu jiaoyu caizheng zhidu goujian" [Establishing a Financial System for Public Compulsory Education within the Framework of China's Public Finance], Paper presented at the International Symposium on Public Finance Reforms and China's Economic Development, Beijing, China, 2006.

[10] Zhang Zhiyong, "Guanyu difang caizheng guanli tizhi zhidu anpai wenti de huibao" [A Report on Problems of the Local Fiscal Management System], 2005, cited from Wang Shaoguang, "Xiangzhen caizheng de guoqu, xianzhuang ji weilai" [The Past, Present and Future of Township Finance], *Hong Fan Pinglun* [*Journal of Legal and Economic Studies*] 3 (2006): 81–96.

[11] Shi Qinghua, "Nonghu jiating shuifei fudan jiqi chengdu yanbian qushi" [Peasant Burdens and Temporal Changes], *Kaifa yanjiu* [*Exploration Research*], 4 (2004).

[12] Thomas P. Bernstein and Xiaobo Lu, *Taxation without Representation in Contemporary China* (New York: Cambridge University Press, 2003).

collected from peasant households. The "miscellaneous fees" charged directly to students were also substantially reduced in poor areas. In 2003, the central government made an unprecedented move to abolish the agricultural tax altogether nationwide in three to five years. As can be predicted, the tax-for-fee reform had an immediate, exacerbating effect on rural compulsory education, even to the point of hindering school functioning. The problem of wage arrears became more acute in areas previously plagued by insufficient funds; many teachers left for other occupations; and there seemed no solution to the dilapidating school buildings.[13]

To make up local losses from the tax-for-fee reform, the central government began to increase financial transfers to local governments in 2001, starting with Anhui and several other provinces, and expanding to more provinces that undertook the reform. In 2001, the central government transferred 8 billion yuan to cover the cost incurred by the tax-for-fee reform; in 2002, the transfer increased to 24.3 billion yuan.[14] Plans were made to substantially increase the transfer in the upcoming years.

Apart from these developments, the central government also established special programs to help fund compulsory education in poor areas. Realizing that some local governments were unable to make the compulsory education universal by 2000, the central government began to intervene by establishing multiple-year programs for promoting compulsory education in poor areas. A five-year project of Compulsory Education for State-Designated Poor Areas was launched in 1995. By the end of 2000, a total of 12.5 billion yuan was spent on compulsory education in state-designated poor counties, with 3.9 billion yuan from the central government.[15] Despite the effort, 522 county-level governments still fell short of making compulsory education universal within their jurisdiction. The second project of Compulsory Education for State-Designated Poor Areas

---

[13] Thomas P. Bernstein, "Luoshi xin zhengce: yi 'nongmin jianfu' wei li" [Implementing New Policies: "Peasant Burden Reduction" as a Case], *Hong Fan Pinglun* [*Journal of Legal and Economic Studies*] 3 (2006): 31–57.

[14] *People Daily*, October 11, 2003.

[15] *China Education Yearbook* 2001, p. 272.

was thus launched in 2001. The central government earmarked 5 billion yuan for this project.[16] To upgrade dilapidated school buildings, the central government launched another project, also in 2001. By the end of 2002, this project had spent 12 billion yuan on upgrading dilapidated school buildings, with 3 billion yuan from the central government and another 1.1 billion yuan from the second project of Compulsory Education for State-Designated Poor Areas.[17] From 2003 to 2005, the central government planned to spend 2 billion yuan each year on the project.[18]

Given that the tax-for-fee reform created problems for township governments, the central government decided that from 2001 on, county governments should take over the responsibility and finance wages of primary and secondary school teachers. The central government would provide subsidies to poor counties in the central and western regions to make up shortfalls, if any.[19]

Evidence shows that the Chinese government's commitment to universalizing the compulsory education has produced higher levels of school enrolment nationwide, even in poor areas.[20] At the same time the localized financing mechanism has led to a rising dependence on the ability of the community and household to pay for social services such as education and health care, raising concerns about the regional disparity in human capital investment and educational attainment. Some studies have suggested that such disparity is on the rise in the reform period.[21]

Aware of the conflict between the regional disparity and the goal of making compulsory education nationwide by 2000, the central government has increased the financial transfer since 1995, and

---

[16] *China Education Yearbook* 2002, p. 327.

[17] *China Education Yearbook* 2003, p. 337.

[18] *China Education Yearbook* 2004, p. 332.

[19] *China Education Yearbook* 2002, p. 62.

[20] Jennifer Adams and Emily Hannum, "Children's Social Welfare in China, 1989–1997: Access to Health Insurance and Education," *The China Quarterly* 181 (2005): 100–121.

[21] Xiaobo Zhang and Ravi Kanbur, "Spatial Inequality in Education and Health Care in China," *China Economic Review* 16 (2005): 189–204.

intensified such effort in the new millennium. It is self-evident that if the transfer from the central government is large enough, poor regions can catch up with rich ones in educational expenditures. Tibet is such an example.[22] But the question is: When the transfer from the central government has to be shared by more than half of the provinces, many of which require much more financial resources than Tibet, the central transfer may be too small to have any visible impact on the regional gap in educational expenditures. This gap is likely to widen if the central transfer fails to make up local losses from the tax-for-fee reform and the abolition of the agricultural tax. The net effect of these reforms on the regional inequality in educational expenditure thus far remains unclear.

EDUCATIONAL EXPENDITURES: CHANGING ROLES OF GOVERNMENT APPROPRIATION

We begin with a descriptive analysis of temporal changes in educational expenditures, followed by an analysis of expenditures on compulsory education. We then focus on the share of government appropriation in education expenditures, especially government appropriation for the compulsory education. The purpose is to show a general pattern of educational expenditures, and compare expenditures on the compulsory education to this general pattern.

Table 10.1 reports total expenditures on education and as percentage of GDP. It shows that in absolute terms, educational expenditures have been increasing throughout the 1990s. There is no sign of slowing down into the new millennium. Of course, we are more interested in how this increase compares with the growth of GDP. Some have argued that China's policy favors physical capital investment over human capital investment, resulting in underinvestment in education by international standards.[23] Table 10.1 shows that this

[22] Yan Wang, "Inequality in Education in China and in the World," Paper presented at the International Symposium on Public Finance Reforms and China's Economic Development, Beijing, China, 2006.

[23] James J. Heckman, "China's Human Capital Investment," *China Economic Review* 16 (2005): 50–70.

Table 10.1: Total expenditures on education as a percentage of GDP.

Year	Total expenditures on education (billion yuan, 1990 price)	Educational expenditure as percentage of GDP
1990	65.9	3.55
1991	70.8	3.38
1992	78.8	3.25
1993	84.0	3.07
1994	95.1	3.19
1995	102.4	3.27
1996	113.9	3.38
1997	124.0	3.46
1998	145.6	3.83
1999	167.7	4.16
2000	192.0	4.36
2001	229.7	4.84
2002	273.7	5.27
2003	306.4	5.32

Source: Authors' calculation based on *China Statistical Yearbook*, 2004.

is particularly true for the early 1990s. Despite substantial increase in absolute terms, educational expenditure as percentage of GDP was declining from 1990 to 1993. However, this trend was a short-term one. The next decade witnessed a steady increase in educational expenditures as percentage of GDP, a net gain of more than two percentage points (5.32 percent in 2003 versus 3.07 percent in 1993). It is clear that China has been making progress in correcting its unbalanced investment strategy, which favors physical capital over human capital.

Table 10.2 singles out the expenditure data of the nine-year compulsory education and breaks down into primary and lower secondary education. It should be noted that such data are available for a much shorter period, beginning with 1997. It is clear that both primary and lower secondary educational expenditures follow the general trend revealed in Table 10.1. For most years, they both increase in absolute terms and as percentage of GDP, indicating that investment in the basic education is able to catch up with the growing

Table 10.2: Total expenditures on primary education and lower secondary education.

Year	Primary education			Lower secondary education		
	Total expenditure (billion yuan, 1990 price)	As percentage of GDP	As percentage of total expenditures on education	Total expenditure (billion yuan, 1990 price)	As percentage of GDP	As percentage of total expenditures on education
1997	40.9	1.14	33.0	27.1	0.76	21.8
1998	45.4	1.19	31.2	25.2	0.66	17.3
1999	49.8	1.23	29.7	27.6	0.68	16.5
2000	54.0	1.23	28.1	30.6	0.70	15.9
2001	63.1	1.33	27.5	36.5	0.77	15.9
2002	72.3	1.39	26.4	42.9	0.83	15.7
2003	77.7	1.35	25.4	47.6	0.83	15.5

Source: Authors' calculation based on *Educational Statistics Yearbook of China*, 2004.

economy. However, it is worth noting that the share of primary and lower secondary education in total educational expenditures is declining from 1997 onwards. Therefore, the educational expansion (in terms of expenditures) is attributed primarily to non-compulsory education rather than compulsory education. This is understandable given that school enrollment has reached a much higher level for compulsory education than for non-compulsory education, and that the government has allowed the non-compulsory education to charge for higher tuition fees.

We move on to examine the role of government appropriation in financing education, especially the compulsory education. In general, China's education is funded by a number of sources. The government appropriation has been a major one. Its main component is the budgetary expenditure on education (*yusuan nei jiaoyu jingfei*) that finances teachers' wages, construction costs, research funds, and other related costs. It also includes non-budgetary expenditures on education, such as the investment of enterprises in enterprise-run schools, educational surcharges in urban and rural areas, and school-generated revenues. Other than government appropriation for education, social organizations and individuals are a major source for non-state schools run by these organizations and individuals. Additional financial sources for education include social donations and fund-raising, and tuition and miscellaneous fees. The nine-year compulsory education is tuition-free by law, but students have to pay "miscellaneous fees," which are often arbitrarily levied and become a source of grievance in many poor areas. For non-compulsory education, the state allows schools to charge tuitions. The central government initiated educational reforms in the mid-1990s to promote private spending on vocational education and tertiary education. Tuition fees have been increasing rapidly since then, and are perceived by the general public as excessively high in recent years.

Table 10.3 shows government appropriation for education, as percentage of GDP and as percentage of total expenditures on education. In absolute terms and as percentage of GDP, government appropriation for education follows the general trend of

Table 10.3: Government appropriation for education as a percentage of GDP.

Year	Government appropriation for education (billion yuan, 1990 price)	Government appropriation as percentage of GDP	Government appropriation as percentage of total expenditures on education
1990	56.4	3.03	85.5
1991	59.8	2.85	84.5
1992	66.2	2.73	84.0
1993	68.8	2.51	81.9
1994	75.0	2.52	78.9
1995	77.0	2.46	75.2
1996	84.2	2.50	73.9
1997	91.2	2.55	73.6
1998	100.4	2.64	68.9
1999	114.5	2.84	68.3
2000	127.8	2.90	66.6
2001	151.4	3.19	65.9
2002	174.3	3.35	63.7
2003	190.0	3.30	62.0

Source: Authors' calculation based on *China Statistical Yearbook*, 2004.

educational expenditures. Considering that government appropriation is by far the largest source of educational expenditures throughout the 1990s, it can also be said that the general pattern of educational expenditures is largely shaped by the temporal pattern of government appropriation. As percentage of GDP, government appropriation declined in the early 1990s, followed by an upward trend until 2003. It seems that the government took its commitment to education more seriously since the mid-1990s as the deadline was approaching for making compulsory education universal nationwide by 2000.

We have shown in Table 10.2 that compulsory education has been declining in terms of share in total educational expenditures. The same pattern also holds for government appropriation.

It accounted for 85.5 percent of educational expenditures in 1990; but its share has been declining all the way to 62 percent in 2003. Comparing Tables 10.1 and 10.3, we can see that the rapid growth of educational expenditures is primarily due to the surging private spending on education. While government appropriation for education is able to keep apace with the GDP growth since the mid-1990s, private spending on education increases much faster in the same period.

Our next analysis focuses on government appropriation for compulsory education in the period of 1997–2003. For primary education and lower secondary education, we report total appropriation, appropriation as percentage of GDP, and appropriation as percentage of total expenditures on each level of education. In absolute terms, government appropriation for either primary education or lower secondary education has been increasing for most years. This is in line with the temporal pattern we observed for total educational expenditures, for educational expenditures on primary and lower secondary education, and for government appropriation for education. In relative terms, government appropriation as percentage of GDP has been on the rise for most years, suggesting that government appropriation for compulsory education is more than able to keep apace with the growing economy. This is also in line with the general trend shown in previous tables.

There are also some significant divergences, however. We have shown that government appropriation as percentage of total educational expenditures has been on the decline for the entire observation period, from 85.5 percent in 1990 to 62.0 percent in 2003. In contrast, Table 10.4 shows a different pattern regarding the role of government in financing compulsory education. As percentage of total expenditures on primary education, government appropriation actually increased from 76.4 percent in 1997 to 80.5 percent in 2003. For lower secondary education, government appropriation has been very stable around 75 percent. It is clear that the government has been adjusting its investment priority in the past decade. While allowing the market force and private spending to play an

Table 10.4: Government appropriation for primary education and lower secondary education.

Year	Primary education			Lower secondary education		
	Total appropriation (billion yuan, 1990 price)	As percentage of GDP	As percentage of total expenditures on primary education	Total appropriation (billion yuan, 1990 price)	As percentage of GDP	As percentage of total expenditures on junior secondary education
1997	31.3	0.87	76.4	20.4	0.57	75.4
1998	34.6	0.91	76.2	18.6	0.49	73.8
1999	38.6	0.95	77.5	20.7	0.51	74.8
2000	42.4	0.96	78.4	22.9	0.52	74.8
2001	50.7	1.07	80.3	27.6	0.58	75.5
2002	58.1	1.12	80.4	32.1	0.62	74.8
2003	62.6	1.09	80.5	35.3	0.61	74.3

Source: Authors' calculation based on *Educational Statistics Yearbook of China*, 2004.

increasingly larger role in financing non-compulsory education, the government has consolidated its role in financing compulsory education.

In sum, using national-level statistical data, we find that (1) in absolute terms, educational expenditures have been increasing. This is true for both compulsory and non-compulsory education, although expenditures on non-compulsory education increase faster than compulsory education. Government appropriation for education in general and for compulsory education in particular is also on the rise. (2) In relative terms, educational expenditures as percentage of GDP declined in the early 1990s, and began to increase from the mid-1990s onward. The same pattern also largely applies to expenditures on compulsory education, government appropriation for education, and government appropriation for compulsory education. Since the mid-1990s, educational expenditures have been more than able to keep apace with the growing economy. (3) In terms of share of total educational expenditures, compulsory education has been declining relative to non-compulsory education. As school enrollments reach a high level for compulsory education, educational expansion (in terms of educational expenditures) mainly occurs at the non-compulsory level. (4) Government appropriation remains a major source of educational expenditures, but its importance is declining in relative terms, as percentage of total educational expenditures. However, for compulsory education, government appropriation is not only by far the largest source of expenditures, its share has also increased for primary education and is stable for lower secondary education in the period of 1997–2003.

PROVINCIAL INEQUALITY IN EXPENDITURES ON COMPULSORY EDUCATION: 1992–2003

At the national level, we find that government appropriation is by far the largest financial source for primary education. In this section, we focus on provincial-level variations. In Table 10.5, we list five provinces where government appropriation accounts for the largest share of total educational expenditures and five provinces where

Table 10.5: Provinces with the highest or lowest levels of government appropriation for education: 1997–2003.

Year	Top five provinces with the highest percentages of educational expenditure from government appropriation	Bottom five provinces with the lowest percentage of educational expenditure from government appropriation
1997	Tibet (99.0%) Qinghai (88.1%) Xinjiang (88.0%) Gansu (85.6%) Yunnan (85.5%)	Hubei (58.2%) Guangdong (62.0%) Hunan (63.2%) Zhejiang (65.9%) Henan (68.1%)
1998	Tibet (95.3%) Qinghai (88.7%) Xinjiang (86.2%) Yunnan (83.3%) Ningxia (82.3%)	Hubei (56.0%) Hunan (58.2%) Guangdong (58.4%) Zhejiang (60.2%) Henan (66%)
1999	Tibet (96.3%) Qinghai (87.0%) Xinjiang (84.8%) Yunnan (83.8%) Gansu (80.1%)	Hubei (56.8%) Hunan (57.3%) Guangdong (59.4%) Zhejiang (60.8%) Chongqing (64.4%)
2000	Tibet (94.6%) Qinghai (86.0%) Yunnan (84.8%) Xinjiang (81.4%) Gansu (79.4%)	Hunan (56.3%) Hubei (56.8%) Zhejiang (58.2%) Guangdong (59.8%) Jiangsu (62.7%)
2001	Tibet (93.1%) Qinghai (85.0%) Yunnan (84.3%) Xinjiang (82.1%) Ningxia (78.2%)	Hunan (56.3%) Hubei (57.3%) Jiangsu (59.0%) Zhejiang (60.1%) Guangdong (60.9%)
2002	Tibet (95.0%) Qinghai (85.0%) Yunnan (82.7%) Ningxia (77.2%) Guizhou (76.2%)	Hunan (54.7%) Hubei (56.1%) Jiangsu (57.8%) Zhejiang (58.1%) Jiangxi (58.5%)

(Continued)

Table 10.5: *(Continued)*

Year	Top five provinces with the highest percentages of educational expenditure from government appropriation	Bottom five provinces with the lowest percentage of educational expenditure from government appropriation
2003	Tibet (94.4%) Qinghai (84.1%) Yunnan (79.8%) Inner Mongolia (75.6%) Ningxia (74.5%)	Hunan (51.8%) Hubei (53.7%) Jiangxi (54.3%) Shaanxi (55.2%) Jiangsu (56.0%)

Source: Author's calculation based on *Educational Statistical Yearbook of China*, 2004.

government appropriation makes up the smallest share. A quick look suggests that wide variations exist at the provincial level regarding the role of government in financing education. At one extreme is Tibet which relies heavily on government appropriation, as high as 99 percent in 1997 and 94.4 percent in 2003. At the other extreme is Hunan Province where government appropriation only accounted for 51.8 percent in 2003, with nearly half of its educational expenditures from other sources.

Table 10.5 shows that provinces in the western region rely more on government appropriation. Tibet and Qinghai are constantly the top two provinces in the period of 1997–2003. Other provinces that appear regularly in the top five list include Yunnan, Ningxia, Xinjiang, and Gansu, all located in the western region and with large proportions of minority population. By comparison, the central region relies more on non-government sources. For most years, Hunan and Hubei are the two provinces where government appropriation makes up the smallest share of total educational expenditures. Three provinces in the eastern region — Guangdong, Zhejiang, and Jiangsu — also appear regularly on the bottom five list. It seems that the central region neither benefits as much from the economic growth as the eastern region, nor benefits as much from the central government's transfer as the western region.

Gini Coefficient: Provincial Inequality in Budgetary Allocation

Of particular interests to us is the provincial-level inequality in government appropriation for compulsory education. Our focus is on primary education, which the central government takes much effort to universalize and provide substantial appropriation. We analyze both the data of per student budgetary allocation for primary education (*xiaoxue shengjun yusuan shiye fei*) and a portion of it that is the budget for school functioning or "public expenditures" (*xiaoxue shengjun gongyong jingfei*).[24] *China Education Yearbook* reports figures by province for the two indicators, but no information is available prior to 1992. Our analysis is therefore confined to the period of 1992–2003.

In measuring provincial inequalities in per student budgetary allocation for primary education and per student budgetary allocation for "public expenditures," we use the number of primary school students as the weight to calculate the Gini coefficient, which is a typical measure of inequality. It ranges from 0, which represents perfect equality, to 1, which represents perfect inequality. Without the luxury of sub-provincial data, inequalities within the province are ignored, and not reflected in the Gini coefficients reported below.

Table 10.6 presents Gini coefficients for both indicators year by year from 1992 to 2003. In terms of per student budgetary allocation for primary education, inequalities at the provincial level are quite stable. There is almost no net increase or decrease in this period.

[24] Budgetary allocation for education includes allocation for individual expenditures (*geren zhichu bufen*) and allocation for public expenditures (*gongyong zhichu bufen*). The first component — allocation for individual expenditures — mainly includes payments to individuals in the form of wages, allowances, bonuses, welfare benefits, and social security provisions. The second component — allocation for public expenditures — includes items such as administrative and office expenses, purchasing of equipment and facilities, and maintenance expenses.

Table 10.6: Gini coefficient of per student budgetary allocation for primary education (小学生均预算事业费) and per student budgetary allocation for public expenditures (小学生均公用经费): 1992–2003.

Year	Per student budgetary allocation for primary education	Per student budgetary allocation for primary school public expenditures
1992	0.191	0.412
1993	0.221	0.465
1994	0.223	0.469
1995	0.234	0.459
1997	0.241	0.417
1998	0.243	0.441
1999	0.234	0.480
2000	0.227	0.498
2001	0.216	0.469
2002	0.202	0.433
2003	0.214	0.422

Source: Authors' calculation based on weighted provincial data from various years of *China Educational Yearbook*.

The Gini coefficient starts with a low 0.191 in 1992 and arrives at a low 0.202 a decade later. But within the 10-year span, there have been notable increases from 1992 to 1998, a net gain of about five percentage points. Subsequently, the Gini coefficient has been declining from 1998 to 2002, amounting to a net loss of about four percentage points, suggesting that there may be some policy adjustment around 1998.

However, when we single out the Gini coefficient for the second indicator — budget allocation for "public expenditures," some interesting contrasts emerge. First, the Gini coefficient is considerably higher for the second indicator than for the first one. As explained earlier, the first indicator includes budgetary allocation for both "individual expenditures" in the form of wages, bonuses and welfare benefits paid to teachers and staff, and "public expenditures" that are associated with classroom supplies, facility maintenance and office expenses. Excluding "individual expenditures" from the budgetary allocation, the second indicator captures the budgetary allocation for "public expenditures." To the extent that the latter directly affects the students more than the wages paid to teachers and staff, our analysis suggests that government appropriation for primary education is quite unequal across provinces.

Second, for the first indicator, the provincial-level inequality began to decline after 1998, while for the second indicator, the process began after 2000. It is also noteworthy that while the level of inequality is much higher for the second indicator than for the first one, it also declines much faster for the second indicator than the first one. In the period of 2000–2003, the Gini coefficient was lowered by 7.6 percentage points for the budgetary allocation for public expenditures, compared to 1.3 percentage points in the same period for the budgetary allocation for primary education in general.

Regional Inequality: Varying Growth Rates of Budgetary Allocation

We further explore the causal factors behind the temporal changes of the two Gini coefficients. It is widely known that the government policy has a regional bias, which is the root cause of unequal distribution of social services. It is therefore very likely that when the government spending on some provinces increases more rapidly relative to other provinces, the regional disparity will change accordingly. In the subsequent analysis, we group 31 provinces (including four centrally administered municipalities and five minority autonomous regions) into five mutually exclusive categories, based on a combination of factors to minimize the differences within the category and maximize the differences between the categories. We first single out the four centrally administered municipalities into a separate category, because the government investment policy has an entrenched urban bias, especially for the large cities.[25] We then single out the five minority autonomous regions, given the fact that the central government has favorable educational policies

[25] Prior to 1997, there were three centrally administered municipalities as Chongqing was still part of Sichuan Province.

Table 10.7: Average per student budgetary allocation for primary education (yuan) by region: 1992–2003.

Year	Centrally administer municipality	The eastern region	The central region	The western region	The minority autonomous region
1992	359.4	147.0	111.4	135.0	172.3
1993	485.8	183.7	124.9	154.3	204.8
1994	692.4	265.2	182.3	219.6	257.7
1995	886.8	295.8	207.8	235.1	295.5
1997	820.1	377.1	258.9	282.0	356.0
1998	857.7	426.6	277.0	317.4	427.2
1999	975.1	481.4	313.5	352.3	463.7
2000	1103.9	573.1	379.1	414.4	549.1
2001	1384.5	737.0	507.0	555.9	764.3
2002	1596.0	944.9	663.5	676.7	913.0
2003	1842.8	1118.7	746.2	748.1	1015.8
Annual growth rate:					
1992–1998	15.6%	19.4%	16.4%	15.3%	16.3%
1998–2003	16.5%	21.3%	21.9%	18.7%	18.9%
1992–2003	16.0%	20.3%	18.8%	16.8%	17.5%

Note: The centrally administered municipality includes Beijing, Tianjin, Shanghai, and Chongqing; the eastern region includes Fujian, Guangdong, Hainan, Heilongjiang, Jiangsu, Jilin, Liaoning, Shandong, and Zhejiang; the central region includes Anhui, Henan, Hubei, Hunan, Jiangxi, and Shanxi; the western region includes Gansu, Guizhou, Qinghai, Shaanxi, Sichuan, and Yunnan; and the minority autonomous region includes Guangxi, Inner Mongolia, Ningxia, Tibet, and Xinjiang.
Source: Various years of *China Educational Yearbook*.

toward them. For the remaining 22 provinces, we divide them into the "eastern region," the "central region," and the "western region," in accordance with the official definition.

Table 10.7 presents per student budgetary allocation for primary education by region for 1992–2003. It is clear that there are wide variations across the five regions. Not surprisingly, the centrally administered municipalities have large advantages over other regions throughout the period. Thanks to the financial support from the central government, the minority autonomous region is largely comparable to the eastern region. By comparison, the central region and the western region lag behind the other regions throughout the period of 1992–2003.

Our interest is in why the Gini coefficient was on the rise between 1992 and 1998 and began to decline afterwards. Table 10.7 provides some clue. At the bottom of the table, we report the annual growth rate by region for the period 1992–1998, 1998–2003, and the two periods combined. For the period 1992–1998, the western region, with a lower level of per student budgetary allocation than the centrally administered municipality, the eastern region, and the minority autonomous region in 1992 also had a lower annual growth rate than these three regions, suggesting that the gap actually widened in this period. The central region, which had the lowest level of per student budgetary allocation, showed no signs of catching up either. In fact, the gap between the central region and the eastern region widened considerably. In 1992, the eastern region was 32 percent higher than the central region in terms of per student budgetary allocation; in 1998, the eastern region was 54 percent higher. The slower growth rate of the western region and the widened gap between the central and the eastern region thus led to the increasing regional inequality.

It is a different story for the period of 1998–2003. The central region, which started with the lowest level of per student budgetary allocation in 1998, registered the highest growth rate between 1998 and 2003. About 15 percent lower than the western region in terms of per student budgetary allocation in 1998, the central region caught up with the western region in 2003. Meanwhile, the four centrally administered municipalities, which had the highest level of per student budgetary allocation in 1998, had a lower growth rate than the other four regions. Taken together, the regional gap narrowed, and the Gini coefficient declined.

If we focus on the entire period of 1992–2003, we have a better view of how the regional inequality evolves. It is clear that different regions play a different role in shaping the overall trend of regional disparity, some tending to increase it, while others tending to reduce it. Surprisingly, the centrally administered municipality plays an equalizing role in the overall trend of regional inequality. Despite having the highest level of per student budgetary allocation, it was overtaken by the other four regions in terms of the annual growth rate. By contrast, the eastern region plays a disequalizing role. It has the highest growth rate in the period of 1992–2003. As a result, the gap has increased between the eastern region and the other three regions (the central region, the western region, and the minority autonomous region). By and large, the western region also plays a disequalizing role. Starting at a comparatively low level of per student budgetary allocation, the western region grew at a slower rate than other regions except the centrally administered municipality. As Table 10.6 shows, the equalizing effect of the centrally administered municipality and the disequalizing effect of the eastern and the western regions seem to have canceled each other out, leading to little change in the regional inequality between 1992 and 2003.

Table 10.8 breaks down the budget for "public expenditures" by region from 1992 to 2003. Comparing Tables 10.7 and 10.8, one striking observation is that there is relatively little amount of money going into "public expenditures" as compared to the total appropriation, indicating that most of the budgetary allocation goes into paying the wages of teachers and staff. Similarly, one can observe that the centrally administered municipalities receive the lion's share of the budget, while the central and western provinces receive the least. Comparing the two tables, it is clear that the regional gap is larger for the budgetary allocation for "public expenditures" than the budgetary allocation in general for primary education.

The drop in the Gini coefficient of the budgetary allocation for public expenditures after 2000 observed in Table 10.6 can be explained by comparing the growth rate of each region. Into the new millennium, the budget going into "public expenditures" has substantially increased nationwide except the minority autonomous region. Most remarkable is the central region, which had the lowest level of budgetary allocation and the lowest growth rate from 1992 to 2000, uncharacteristically registered the highest annual growth

Table 10.8: Average per student budgetary allocation for primary school public expenditures (yuan) by region: 1992–2003.

Year	Centrally administer municipality	The eastern region	The central region	The western region	The minority autonomous region
1992	88.7	16.0	9.8	14.7	20.3
1993	105.5	20.6	8.8	15.9	20.7
1994	122.3	20.6	9.5	14.2	20.2
1995	168.2	24.8	13.5	18.9	23.4
1997	167.7	34.4	23.4	25.3	31.8
1998	147.2	34.8	20.2	28.4	52.1
1999	161.6	37.1	17.2	30.3	63.3
2000	166.6	41.9	16.1	30.9	62.7
2001	219.5	58.0	22.9	30.0	45.0
2002	263.0	74.8	34.6	43.6	60.3
2003	345.2	108.5	55.2	55.9	66.5
Annual growth rate					
1992–2000	8.20%	12.7%	6.4%	9.7%	15.1%
2000–2003	27.5%	37.3%	50.8%	21.8%	2.0%
1992–2003	13.1%	19.0%	17.0%	12.9%	11.4%

Source: Various years of *China Educational Yearbook*.

rate of 50.8 percent from 2000 to 2003. This may reflect the policy adjustment associated with the tax-for-fee reform. In the central region, the overwhelming bulk of budgetary allocation often goes into teachers' wages, implying that non-budgetary surcharges have to become the primary source for schools' public expenditures. By eliminating a large part of such surcharges, the tax-for-fee reform forced the central government to increase its financial transfer and shift the financing mechanism from educational surcharges to budgetary allocation, leading to a surge in budgetary allocation for the central region from 2000 to 2003. The central region thus becomes a major factor that contributes to the drop in the Gini coefficient. But it is noteworthy that the centrally administered municipality and the eastern region had impressive growth rates as well, considerably higher than the western region and the minority autonomous region. If the trend continues, the declining regional inequality is likely to be reversed in the years to come.[26]

DISCUSSION AND CONCLUSION

China has taken its commitment to the nine-year compulsory education seriously, especially since the mid-1990s when the deadline was approaching for making the compulsory education universal nationwide by 2000. Our analysis shows that educational expenditures on compulsory education and government appropriation for compulsory education not only increase rapidly in absolute terms, but also increase faster than the rapidly growing economy in recent years in terms of the annual growth rate. Moreover, in contrast to the non-compulsory education where government appropriation is declining as a source of educational funds, the government's role in financing compulsory education remains stable and strong. In fact, its importance has increased for financing primary education. Against this backdrop, it can be expected that the Chinese government will continue to play a pivotal role in universalizing and developing its compulsory education.

There is a problem, however. While the central government has been accustomed to establish development goals, it has to rely on the decentralized fiscal structure to accomplish them. Fiscal decentralization has led to a rising dependence on the ability of the household and community to pay for social services. This is less a problem for economically more developed regions, whose booming economy can generate funds for development targets set by the central government. But for poor regions, compulsory education has been a burden for local governments, communities, and households. There is great concern that without interference from the central government, the widening regional gap in economic development

[26] We projected the Gini coefficient from 2003 to 2010, assuming that each region has the same annual growth rate as in the period 2000–2003. Our calculation suggests that the provincial-level inequality will continue to decline until 2004, and will rise again afterwards. The Gini coefficient for 2010 will be 0.475.

will translate into the growing regional disparity in human capital investment.

The problem loomed large in the mid-1990s as it was increasingly clear that poor regions could not meet the target of universalizing the compulsory education by 2000. The central government responded by increasing the financial transfer on the one hand, and pressuring local governments to invest more on the other. In the wake of the tax-for-fee reform, the central government increased its transfer to make up local losses from the reform. To the extent that such transfers largely go into poor regions, it is expected that the regional inequality in human capital investment can be alleviated.

Our analysis does not assess whether transfers from the central government are adequate to compensate for local losses from the tax-for-fee reform. Our focus is instead on the temporal changes in government appropriation for primary education. We find that the regional gap in government spending on primary education has been diminishing since the late 1990s, suggesting that poor regions have been catching up with economically more developed regions, though at a very slow pace. In terms of per student budgetary allocation for primary education, the provincial-level inequality measured by the Gini coefficient was on the decline from 1998 to 2002, a reversal of the upward trend observed for years prior to 1998. There is also a declining trend for the provincial-level inequality in the portion of budget that goes into "public expenditures."

Our analysis suggests that the provincial-level inequality declines mainly because per student educational budget has been growing slower for centrally administered municipalities than for most other regions, and the central region has overtaken the eastern region and centrally administered municipalities in the annual growth rate of educational budgets. These are the positive sign that China has partially corrected the entrenched policy bias that favors urban human capital investment over rural human capital investment, and coastal regions over inland provinces.

Our findings, however, cast doubt on the optimistic prediction that the declining trend will continue into the future. Despite the central government's effort to help poor regions, financial transfers from the central government have been inadequate for the western region and the minority autonomous region to catch up with the eastern region. Over the last decade, the eastern region has increased the gap with the western region and the minority autonomous region in terms of per student educational budget. If the trend continues, the provincial-level inequality is like to rise again, driven by the widening gap between the east and the west. The central government therefore has to play a larger role in balancing regional investment in the compulsory education. Poor counties in the central and western regions should receive more financial transfer from the upper levels of government.

Chapter 11

China's Demographic Dividend and Economic Growth

Wang Dashu

Department of Finance, School of Economics, Peking University, Beijing, PRC

INTRODUCTION

Two key priorities for developing countries are economic development and population control. China's answers to these were the reform and the open-door policy, and the one-child policy.[1] In these areas, China has produced two miracles.

During the last two decades, China has undergone economic as well as demographic changes. Economically, China has completed its transition from a centrally planned economy to a market-based economy. In the last two decades, China has become one of the most dynamic and fast-growing economies in the world. This is the first miracle. Demographically, the one-child policy put China's explosive population under control and fertility rates have declined to below-replacement levels. This is the second miracle.

[1] One-child policy in China means that an urban couple can have only one child, but a rural couple can have a second child if the first is a girl.

In a matter of a few decades, China's population will start to shrink.[2]

In fact, the decline in fertility rates, the slow-down in population growth, and changes in age structure have contributed to China's economic success. The purpose of this chapter is to use the concept of the "demographic dividend" to examine the relationship between China's demographic transition and economic development. In the light of the recent and future changes in China's age structure, it also examines and speculates on the role of population age structure changes in affecting China's prospects for economic development in the coming decades. The chapter explains the current and future challenges China faces and proposes policies to deal with them to support economic growth in the world's most populous country.

THE DEMOGRAPHIC DIVIDEND

The relationship between population growth and economic development remains a subject of endless debate among economists and demographers. "Population pessimists," who trace their lineage to Thomas Malthus, have insisted that high fertility rates and rapid population growth have a negative impact on development (Ehrlich, 1968). Their main concern is that excessive population growth is a threat to food supplies and natural resources. This view contributed to the rationale for widespread funding of family-planning policies and program in the 1960s. Conversely, "population optimists" have argued the opposite position — that rapid population growth and large population sizes can promote economic prosperity by furnishing abundant human and intellectual capital and increasing the market size. For example, Kuznets (1960) argues that large societies, with the capacity to take advantage of economies of scale, are better positioned to develop, exploit, and disseminate the increased flow of knowledge they receive. Proponents of both views can point to the evidence from research to support their cases, but on the whole, the evidence has been inconclusive and the link

[2] Some experts have forecasted that this will occur in 2030.

between demographic transition and economic growth seems to be rather ambiguous.

There is a third view: "population neutralism" argues that population growth, in isolation from other factors, has little impact on economic performance. This position is supported by a sizable body of economic research and stimulates a complete reconsideration of the population factor.

Focusing on population size and growth, the debate mentioned above tends to largely ignore a critical demographic dimension: the age structure of the population (the way in which the population is distributed across different age groups). Now economists have decided to stop focusing entirely on the overall population indicators such as population size and growth rate, but to turn their attention to the age structure of the population. It is found that the production potential and consumption patterns tend to closely follow the life cycle of individuals as important variations are observed across age groups from childhood to adulthood and old age. Since each age group in a population behaves differently, changes in age structure can significantly affect economic performance. Adulthood is characterized by a very high production/consumption ratio, and the number of adults available for the workforce relative to the rest of the population represents a crucial factor of economic potential. Not surprisingly, nations with a high proportion of young or old dependents tend to devote a relatively high proportion of resources to these groups, often limiting economic growth. By contrast, nations in which a relatively large portion of the population has reached the prime ages for working and saving may enjoy a boost to income growth stemming from the higher share of the working-age population, the accelerated accumulation of capital and the reduced spending on dependents. This phenomenon is known as the "demographic dividend" (Bloom and Williamson, 1998; Mason, 2001; Bloom *et al.*, 2002). Simply stated, the demographic dividend arises because the demographic transition when birth rates are low and the elderly population is not yet burgeoning induces changes in the age structure that increase the share of the population concentrated at the productive ages. The demographic dividend is also called the "demographic gift" by Williamson (2001), the "demographic bonus" or the "window of opportunity" by Birsall and Sinding (2001), the "demographic opportunity" by Fargues (2001), and the "demographic golden age" by Vallin (2002).

The relationship between population change and economic growth has taken on added salience in the past few decades because of demographic trends in the developing world. At varying rates, developing countries are undergoing a demographic transition to lower rates of mortality and fertility, producing a boom generation that is gradually working its way through the nation's age structures. When the baby-boomers reach working age, a country will experience a demographically induced economic boost, provided this demographic cohort is productively employed. Thus, many developing countries face opportunities to translate their ongoing demographic transitions into economic gains.

In China, the child dependency ratio[3] declined from 72.6 percent in 1965 to 41.5 percent in 1990, and will decline further to 25.3 percent in 2030; the old dependency ratio[4] was fluctuating around 8 percent during 1965–1990, then went up in 1990 and will reach 24.4 percent in 2030. The dramatic decline in fertility rates since the late 1960s has created a demographic window of opportunity. As a matter of fact, the total dependency ratio declined to levels below 50 percent in 1990 (Table 11.1). This "golden age structure" characterized by the total dependency ratio being below 50 percent, will last approximately 40 years (from 1990 to 2030). After 2030, the total dependency ratio will rise above 50 percent due to the fact that the population ageing drives up the old dependency ratio.

CONTRIBUTION FROM THE DEMOGRAPHIC DIVIDEND

The demographic dividend occurs when a decline in fertility rates changes the age distribution, so that fewer investments are needed to

---

[3] The child dependency ratio is defined as the ratio of the population aged 0–14 to the working-age population, which is defined as the population aged 15–64.

[4] The elderly population is defined as the population aged 65 and plus. The old dependency ratio is defined as the ratio of elderly population to the working-age population.

Table 11.1: Dependency ratios in China.

Year	Ratio of 0–14	Ratio of 65+	Total dependency ratio
1965	72.6	7.9	80.5
1970	70.9	7.7	78.6
1975	70.4	7.8	78.3
1980	59.4	7.9	67.2
1985	47.0	8.1	55.0
1990	41.5	8.4	49.9
1995	39.3	9.1	48.4
2000	36.3	9.9	46.2
2005	30.1	10.7	40.8
2010	27.0	11.5	38.5
2015	25.7	13.4	39.1
2020	26.4	17.1	43.5
2025	26.2	20.0	46.2
2030	25.3	24.4	49.7
2035	24.7	30.8	55.5
2040	25.1	35.9	61.0

Source: United Nations (2004 and 2003).

meet the needs of the young age groups and resources are released for investment in economic development and family welfare. As a matter of fact, a falling fertility rate makes for a smaller population at young dependent ages and for relatively more people in the working-age groups who comprise the productive labor force. This makes for faster economic growth and fewer burdens on families.

Obviously, the demographic dividend as a favorable factor contributes to economic growth. There is some research that substantiates this. For instance, Bloom and Williamson (1998), Bloom *et al.* (2000), and Mason (2001) have investigated the role of the demographic dividend in the successful East Asian "Tiger" economies, and Bloom and Williamson (1998) have concluded that as much as one-third of growth in the "East Asia Miracles" can be accounted for by the demographic dividend. Bloom and Canning (2003) have analyzed Ireland's more recent transformation into Europe's "Celtic Tiger." Bloom *et al.* (2003) have provided a negative example: the absence of demographic change accounts for a large portion of Africa's economic debacle.

As far as China is concerned, it is suggested that the rapid growth in China partially benefits from the demographic dividend (Chen and Song, 2006). More specifically, Wang and Mason (2005) believe that the demographic dividend accounted for 15 percent of China's economic growth between 1982 and 2000. A recent synthesis attributed over one-quarter of China's economic growth to changes in its age composition (Vermeer, 2006).

Chinese demographers use dependency ratios to quantify the demographic dividend. According to Cai's (2005) calculation, a reduction of one basic point in dependent ratios leads to an increase of 0.115 percentage points in the rate of economic growth. From 1982 to 2000, the dependency ratios fell by 20.1 percent, leading to economic growth of 2.3 percent. During the same time the GDP per capita increased by 8.6 percent annually and the contribution from the demographic dividend was 26.8 percent.

THREE CONTRIBUTING MECHANISMS TO GROWTH

How does the demographic dividend help economic growth? According to Bloom *et al.* (2003), the dividend is delivered through three mechanisms: labor supply, savings, and human capital. This section will analyze the contributing mechanisms in the case of China.

The Quantity of Labor Force

Labor is an important factor of production. Due to family planning, women now have fewer children than before and are able to take jobs outside of the home. As suggested by Birsall and Sinding (2001), the rising female participation in the labor force strengthens the demographic bonus. More importantly, baby-boomers from the last round finally leave the dependent years and as a result the availability of manpower is increased. These two factors jointly provide an abundant labor supply.

Lewis' (1954) classical two-sector model[5] claims that labor supply is assumed to be infinitively elastic at the initial phase of development. This was just what happened to China in the last quarter of the 20th century. During this period, the labor supply in China seemed to be unlimited mainly on account of the migration of farmer workers.[6] It is estimated by Research Office of the State Council (2006) that there are 120 million migrant farmer workers and 80 million local farmer workers in China.

Because farmer workers receive lower levels of education and training than the general labor force, they are the group most directly obliged to rely upon physical effort to earn a living. Not surprisingly, their employment opportunities are principally in low-paying, physically demanding jobs.

It can be found from Table 11.2 that the majority of farmer workers earn less than 800 yuan (approximately US$100) per

Table 11.2: Farmer worker wages (RMB yuan).

Monthly wages	Percent of farmer workers who earn this wage
Below 300	3.58
300–500	29.26
500–800	39.26
Above 800	27.90

Source: Research Office of the State Council (2006).

[5] In fact, there are two turning points in the Lewis model that explains rural migration in a dual economy (Lewis, 1954): the first one is at the stage of transition of rural labor forces from unlimited supply to limited surplus; the second one is at the point that rural wage equals urban wage when rural surplus labor forces are totally absorbed by the expansion of urban non-agricultural sectors. Before the first turning point, the supply of rural labor is unlimited, and labor demand from the expansion of the urban industry sectors does not face the shortage of rural workers. When it passes the first turning point, the supply of rural labor forces becomes limited with certain elasticity. If enterprises do not adjust wage rates at this time, they will have certain difficulties in hiring rural workers.

[6] In this chapter, farmer workers are defined as workers who are from rural areas. They are also called rural workers or migrant workers.

Table 11.3: International comparison of annual average manufacturing wages.

Country	Year				
	1995	1996	2000	2001	2002
China	619	679	1057	1181	1329
Japan	35569	31296	32638	29376	28366
USA	25667	26520	29786	30701	31803
United Kingdom	25997	26902	31345	31530	34412
South Korea	17486	18813	16993	15824	17812
Singapore	18264	19740	21132	20876	21137
Malaysia	4801	5318	4383	4835	

Notes: (1) Figures in this table are exchanged into U.S. dollars according to the exchange rate of each individual country;
(2) Because of differences in wage statistics, hour wages in USA and United Kingdom are multiplied by 40 h per week and then by 52 weeks to get the annual wages; monthly wages in others are multiplied by 12 months to get the annual wages.
Source: International Labor Organization (2005).

month. The unlimited labor forces (mainly farm workers with very low pay) enable manufacturing industries to maintain low wages in China.

Table 11.3 shows that by international standards the average wage in Chinese manufacturing industries is very low. Low wages constitute low prices which make goods produced in China competitive and Chinese exports are flooding in the world market. Obviously, exports are one of the driving forces for economic growth.

Since 2003, there has been a shortage of farmer workers in China. Despite government figures that indicate there are 150 million farmer workers waiting to transfer from rural to urban areas, signs have emerged to show that the country's labor resource is on the decline. Fewer and fewer farmer workers are willing to take unskilled low wage jobs.

Although the booming Guangdong Province has sucked up more than 19 million farmer workers, its annual labor shortfall remained at two million. Factories found it hard to employ migrant workers with low wages any more. Another enterprise survey conducted by the Guangdong Bureau of Statistics in 2005 showed that one-third of enterprises in the Guangdong Province offered higher wages to solve hiring difficulties, but there was still a recruitment gap of one million. Of the 503 enterprises surveyed, 57.1 percent had plans to hire new workers, meaning more than half reported that they still had unfilled job vacancies. Compared with the initial plan, the recruitment of ordinary workers came to 73.2 percent, while the recruitment of skilled workers was only 58.6 percent, 14.6 percentage points less than the former. The shortage of rural workers intensified in 2005 and spread to the Yangtze River Delta area and north coastal regions. Even in Hunan, Jiangxi, and Henan provinces, enterprises run into similar difficulties when hiring farmer workers.

The shortage of workers in China is expected to push up wages. As this trend continues, products manufactured in China will not be of such a bargain around the world. A survey by the Ministry of Labor and Social Security shows that in 2006, construction engineering and machine building enterprises in prosperous coastal areas are willing to pay workers at least 1000 yuan (about US$125) per month, almost equal to the local salary of college graduates. Three years ago these enterprises were paying only 600 yuan to workers every month.

The shortage of farmer workers symbolizes a turning point in China's rural surplus labor forces from the previous unlimited supply to limited surplus. This phenomenon is the outcome of the interaction between high-speed export growth after China's accession to the WTO and a new-round economic growth. From the viewpoint of resources allocation, this new trend has important implications to the development of China's labor market.

The Quality of Labor Force

Human capital[7] is regarded as a primary source of long-term economic growth along with physical capital (Azariadis and Draxen,

[7] In this chapter, the human capital stock is represented by the average years of schooling per capita for the population in the age group of 15–64.

1990; Mankiw *et al.* 1992). Empirical research suggests that human capital may play a stronger role in the growth process once it reaches a certain threshold. Upper secondary and tertiary achievement is important for economic growth to translate into steady growth (WEIP, 2002). As far as China is concerned, it is estimated by Wang and Yao (2003) that augmented human capital has contributed 46.3 percent to China's growth during the pre-reform period and 11 percent during the reform period from 1978 to 1999.

In fact, the demographic dividend not only contributes to the size but also the productivity of the working-age population. Because of light child dependency, more family income can be placed upon better food for children, and the next generation may become healthier. Furthermore, income can go toward education for children to improve their prospects. Therefore, families can afford to focus on better child health and educational attainment.

In this area, the central and local governments also play an important role. The spending on public education is increased and universities and colleges are allowed to recruit more students as a result of education reforms. Public and private investment in education raises new cohorts of workers with enhanced human capital, which as expected, benefits the economy and society. Indeed, China has taken advantage of the light child dependency burden and has increased basic education. The average years of schooling of the working-age population increased from 3.2 years in 1964 to 8.3 years in 2004. The improvement is more obvious in urban areas. For example, average years of schooling of the working-age population in rural areas was 7.3 years, but this figure in urban areas was 10.2 years.

The public and private investment in education and effective education reform has raised the level of educational attainment, boosting the accumulation of human capital. The young school-age cohorts are the beneficiaries of additional education. As a result, the quality of labor forces is enhanced and this contributes to human capital formation. Now China has a fast growing educated labor force.

There is a new phenomenon in China: students graduate from universities and colleges but cannot find jobs. In 2006, for example, the number of university graduates increased to 4.13 million but demand for them was only 1.66 million. The accumulating number of unemployed tertiary graduates presents a challenge to governments.

Personal and National Savings

During the period of the demographic window, "increased personal saving and investment become possible" (Merrick, 2002). Indeed, the demographic transition interacts with the fundamental feature of any economy — its life cycle variation in consumption and production. Humans have an extended period of economic dependency at the beginning of their lives and at the end. The young require intensive investment in health and education and the aged require health care and retirement incomes. During these ages of dependency, individuals consume more than they produce. Conversely, during the prime working ages, individuals produce more than they consume. In fact, age structure matters significantly to income growth prospects.

For a long time, Chinese people have traditionally saved money for the future. Now personal savings are encouraged by the government. As a result, personal savings deposits have dramatically increased.

Personal savings serve as a partial resource for industrial investments that fuel economic growth. The demographic dividend can have long-lasting effects if savings are invested in the form of physical or human capital, and/or institutional development.

It should be noted that national savings is not only of personal business, but governments should also play a role in this area. However, if attention is given to government savings, we will hear a different story as governments suffer from long-lasting deficits. Since the late 1970s, government spending has been greater than revenue, accumulating a huge amount of fiscal deficits in China.

Another problem being faced now is the lack of a nationwide pension system. In the 1950s, China set up an urban pension system, and it seemed to work for some decades seeing as state-owned enterprises and government offices were primarily new and staffed with young adults. By the 1980s, however, the system became less and less able to pay out its unfunded liabilities because staff and workers started retiring (see World Bank, 1997 for a background of China's pension system). In fact, China does not have much of a functioning social security or pension provision for rural residents, and its urban system is burdened with unsustainable commitments. Eberstad (2006) surmises that these prospective pensioners will not be supported through China's current state pension arrangement.

CONCLUDING REMARKS

China has already reaped the benefits from the one-off demographic window of opportunity deriving from a decline in fertility rates. Obviously, changes in age distribution create a supply-side effect and a potential for economic growth. Whether or not this potential is captured depends on the policy environment in which the population change is occurring.

It should be noted that there is nothing automatic about the link from the demographic dividend to economic growth. During the next 10 to 20 years demographic conditions could be favorable for growth, but their effect is by no means inevitable. To reap the dividend, it is necessary to support it with appropriate economic, social, and political institutions and policies. Otherwise it will only lead to higher levels of unemployment. In fact, it is the combined effect of this "dividend" and effective policies that stimulates growth. If the Chinese government takes suitable actions, then the dividend may become real rather than potential. On the contrary, if it fails to do so, China may struggle with the social unrest of millions of unemployed working-age adults. While demographic pressures are eased whenever fertility falls, some countries take better advantage of it than others. Some countries will act to capitalize upon the released resources and use them effectively, while others will not. Then eventually, when the window of opportunity is closed, those who do not take advantage of the demographic dividend will face renewed pressures while finding themselves in a position that is weaker than ever.

The demographic dividend does not last forever. There is a limited window of opportunity. With time, the age distribution changes again, as the large adult population moves into the older, less-productive age brackets and is followed by the smaller group of people born during the decline in fertility rates. When this occurs, the dependency ratio rises again, this time involving the need to care for the elderly, rather than the need to take care of the young. For some countries, the demographic bonus can become a demographic onus as described by Ogawa *et al.* (2005) for Japan. In China (and elsewhere), the dividend is a persistent but ultimately transitory phenomenon. As the demographic transition proceeds, growth in the working population will eventually become slower than that of the total population. The effect will be to depress growth in per-capita output and consumption. Clearly the challenges are massive and must be dealt with soon before population aging accelerates rapidly, because favorable policies take time to establish and take effect. Therefore, those developing countries whose transition is advanced need to look to the future, adopting policies to cope with an aging population and optimize the remaining years of low dependency ratios.

The demographic factor was a favorable factor in China's growth during the last quarter century. China's demographic dividend is created by rapidly falling fertility rates, and materialized at the same time that China underwent its most radical economic transitions and faced the strongest unemployment pressures.

Being an early achiever brings with it some costs. As a consequence of such a forced demographic transition, China will soon enter a long period of decline in labor supply, and will face a rapid increase in the older population that cannot be reversed easily or quickly. Now the shortage of farmer workers with low wages indicates that the demographic dividend has been reaped at low levels. If the authorities intend to increase the labor supply, the one-child policy needs to be reconsidered. China could choose to relax the one-child policy and other restrictions on childbearing, so that future birth cohorts will not be as small as they are today. This could produce more working adults in two decades, just as the workforce is becoming older and the elderly population is growing most rapidly. They could then help to financially support the large aged dependent population. If China maintains its coercive population control programs, there is another way to address this problem. As argued by Kosai *et al.* (1998), it is possible that labor shortages will provide a stimulus to technological development and to higher productivity resulting from an increase in capital per worker. Therefore, China should change its growth pattern. Since university graduates seem to be over-supplied now, the development in technology-intensive and capital-intensive industries should absorb more of this human capital. In fact, a larger, better-educated workforce will yield benefits only if the additional workers find suitable jobs.

A nationwide pension system is needed to provide an essential protection for all young and old citizens. In this area it is desirable for China to collect social security tax as a reliable source for the nationwide pension system so that not only urban residents but also rural residents are covered. It should be noted that to establish any kind of viable pension system, the authorities will be forced to raise the ages at which people can retire and/or expect a pension. China established a very young legal retirement age in the 1950s when life expectancies were shorter than they are today. Men were entitled to retire at 60, while women could retire at 55 if they have white-collar jobs and 50 for blue-collar jobs. Today in China, men at 60 can expect to live 15 more years, and women at 55 have a further life expectancy of 24 years. In the future, as they are still needed in China's economy, workers should be encouraged or required to spend more years in the workforce.

REFERENCES

Azariadis, C. and A. Draxen (1990), "Threshold externalities in economic development," *The Quarterly Journal of Economics* 105(2), 501–526.

Birsall, N. and S. Sinding (2001), "How and why population matters: new findings, new issues," in Population Matters, eds. N. Birsall, A. Kelley and S. Sinding, Oxford University Press.

Bloom, D., D. Canning and P. Malaney (2000), "Demographic change and economic growth in Asia." *Population and Development Review* 26 (Suppl.), 257–290.

Bloom, D., D. Canning and J. Sevilla (2003), "The demographic dividend: a new perspective on the economic consequences of population change," *Population Matters Series*, Santa Monica, California: Rand.

Bloom, D. and D. Canning (2003), "Contraception and the celtic tiger," *The Economic and Social Review* 105(3), 229–247.

Bloom, D. and J. Williamson (1998), "Demographic transitions and economic miracles in emerging Asia," *World Bank Economic Review* 12: 419–456.

Cai, Fang (2005), "China's demographic dividend," *Financial Economics*, October.

Chen, Wei and Jian Song (2006), "Age and gender structure of the population in China," *Population Research* 30(2), 84–88.

Eberstad, N. (2006), "Growing old the hard way: China, Russia, India," *Policy Review*, No. 136.

Ehrlich, P.R. (1968), *The Population Bomb*, New York: Ballentine.

Frazier, Mark (2005), "What's in a law?: China's pension reform and its discontents," in *Engaging the Law in China: State, Society and Possibilities for Justice*, eds. Neil Diamant *et al.*, Stanford University Press, pp. 108–130.

International Labor Organization (2005), *Yearbook of Labour Statistics 2005*, http://laborsta.ilo.org/.

Kosai, Y., J. Saito and N. Yashiro (1998), "Declining population and sustained economic growth: can they coexist?" *American Economic Review* 82(2), 412–416.

Kuznetz, Simon (1960), "Population change and aggregate output," in *Demographic and Economic Change in Developed Countries*, Princeton, NJ: Princeton University Press.

Lewis, A. (1954), "Economic development with unlimited supplies of labour," *The Manchester School* 22, 139–191.

Mankiw, N.G., D. Romer and D. Weil (1992), "A contribution to the empirics of economic growth," *The Quarterly Journal of Economics* 107(2), 407–437.

Mason, Andrew (ed.) (2001), *Population Change and Economic Development in East Asia: Challenges Met, Opportunities Seized*, California: Stanford University Press.

Merrick, T. (2002), "Population and poverty: new views on an old controversy," *International Family Planning Pespectives* 28, 41–46.

Ogawa, N., M. Kondo and R. Matsukura (2005), "Japan's transition from the demographic bonus to the demographic onus," *Asian Population Studies* 1(2), 207–226.

Research Office of the State Council (2006), A Report on Farmer Workers in China, http://gov.ce.cn/data/button/200604/26.

Research Team of the Ministry of Agriculture (2005), "Migration and employment of rural labor forces: current situation, problems and countermeasures," *Journal of Rural Economic Surveys*, No. 5.

United Nations (2004), World Population Prospects: The 2004 Revision, http://esa.un.org.unpp.

United Nations (2003), World Urbanization Prospects: The 2003 Revision.

United Nations (2002), World Population Prospects: The 2002 Revision, Volume II: Sex and Age.

Vermeer, E.B. (2006), "Demographic dimensions of China's development," in The Political Economy of Global Population Change, 1950–2050, eds. P. Demeny and G. McNicoll, Population Council, pp. 114–144.

Vallin, J. (2002), "The end of the demographic transition: relief of concern?" *PDR* 28(1), 105–109.

Wang, F. and A. Mason (2005), "Demographic Dividend and Prospects for Economic Development in China," Paper presented to UN Expert Group Meeting on Social and Economic Implications of Changing Population Age Structures, Mexico City, August 31–September 1.

Wang, Y. and Y. Yao (2003), "Sources of China's economic growth 1952–1999: incorporating human capital accumulation," *China Economic Review* 14, 32–52.

World Education Indicators Programme (WEIP) (2002), *Financing Education-Investment and Returns: Analysis of the World Education Indicators*, UNESCO Institute for Statistics and OECD.

Williamson, J. (2001), "Demographic changes, economic growth, and inequality," in *Population Matters*, eds. N. Birsall, A. Kelley and S. Sinding, Oxford University Press.

World Bank (1997), *Old Age Security: Pension Reform in China*.

Chapter

12

Problems and Prospects of China's Health Reforms

Åke Blomqvist

Department of Economics, National University of Singapore, Singapore

INTRODUCTION

Between 1980 and 2005, real per capita GDP in China is estimated to have risen by some 8.5 percent per year on average, increasing its level by a factor of almost 8. China has had a surging economy, indeed. Over roughly the same period, per capita spending on health care rose at an even faster rate. While health care cost was estimated to have accounted for only some 3 percent of GDP at the beginning of the period, in the early 2000s, its share had risen to almost 5.5 percent.

The rapid growth rate of the economy has, of course, corresponded to a dramatic increase in average living standards in the population. It is often said that since 1980, China's economy has grown fast enough to lift several hundred million persons out of poverty.[1] However, the rapid growth in health care spending is usually not thought of as having benefited the majority of people in China in this way. On the contrary, the large increase in aggregate spending on health care is often thought of as something that, in individual cases, may have *reduced* human welfare, as the cost associated with serious illness has sent many individuals and families into poverty.

The dramatic changes that took place as China moved away from the earlier system of a centrally planned economy to one where resources were allocated through the global market mechanism to a much greater extent are usually thought of as constituting a program of economic reform. Large changes also took place in the health care sector, as the government reduced its role in funding and managing it, and in a recent report issued as a series of papers in a special issue of *China Development Review*, these changes are referred to as "reforms" of the health care sector as well (Development Research Center of the State Council (2005); henceforth referred to as "DRC Report").[2] The main thesis in the report is that in this sector, the reduced role of the government has not had the same kinds of beneficial effects as elsewhere in the economy. Moreover, the authors are also critical of the initiatives that have been undertaken in the last 10 years or so to remedy some of the deficiencies of the current system. (These include the introduction of the Basic Urban Insurance plan that is intended to provide

[1] A recent paper (Ravallion and Chen, in press) provides new estimates which imply that in the 1980s, some 500 million people in China lived in poverty; by 2001, this number had fallen to a little over 100 million.

[2] The report's description of the way the health care system was organized and funded during the "planned economy period" (roughly 1950–1980), and the changes that took place after that time, essentially reinforce descriptions elsewhere in the literature. A good background discussion of the situation in the 1990s is in Economist Intelligence Unit (1998). Recent discussions on changes in Chinese health policy in the last several years include Asian Development Bank (2002), Bloom (2003, 2004), Gu (2004, 2005), and Liu (2002). A broad-brush review is also available in an unsigned essay originally published in China Development Brief, available on the website www.chinadevelopmentbrief.com. A similar and even more recent summary is Blumenthal and Hsiao (2005).

employment-related health insurance for urban workers and retirees, and the attempts to revive the Cooperative Medical System in rural areas.) Based on the shortcomings they identify in the way the system now functions, and the limited impact that they expect current policy initiatives to have, they outline a somewhat radical new approach involving a return to a considerably larger role for the state in the funding and management of China's health care system, in both urban and rural areas. Later in the discussion, I will refer to this proposal as the "DRC model"; it is most clearly articulated in the concluding paper in the report, written by Ge (2005). In concrete terms, what the report proposes is an initiative under which the government would take responsibility for providing basic medical care and drugs for all Chinese citizens through a publicly funded and managed network of government clinics.

In this chapter, I first summarize the way China's health care system was organized and funded during the planned economy period, and the way it was affected by the process of dismantling the system of central economic management after 1980. I relate the discussion of the problems that have arisen since that time to the Western literature on the potential sources of market failure in the health care sector.[3] I then review the main elements of the current government initiatives for health sector reform in urban and rural areas, and assess the more radical approach advocated in the DRC model. In the final section, I consider the possibility of a synthesis approach under which the proposals in the DRC model would be integrated with the approaches currently being pursued to strengthen the Basic Urban Insurance system and the Cooperative Medical System in rural areas.

THE HEALTH CARE SYSTEM IN THE PLANNED ECONOMY PERIOD

Not surprisingly, the current problems in China's health care system have invited comparisons with the way it was organized during

---

[3] The discussion of these topics draws heavily on the more detailed treatment in Blomqvist (2006).

what is now often referred to as the "planned economy period," roughly spanning the decades 1950–1980. To many observers, the way the system functioned at that time seems a great deal more efficient and equitable than the way it operates today.

Then as now, health care funding and services provision was organized very differently in cities and in the countryside. In the cities, there were two parallel funding systems, one covering those who were classified as regular government employees (including retirees and family members), the other covering employees of State-Owned Enterprises (again including retirees and, at least partially, dependents). The latter, variously referred to in English as the Labour Insurance System (LIS) or the Labour Insurance Medical System, was based on the principle that responsibility for the health care of current and retired workers and their dependents rested with the enterprise (work unit) to which they belonged. In most cases, basic (primary) health care was supplied in a clinic or hospital owned and operated by the enterprise, or an independent one with which the enterprise had an agreement.[4] Higher-level care (in hospitals) would only be supplied based on a referral from the primary-care unit. Hospitals charged fees for the services they rendered; these were paid by the enterprise, though with some co-payments by patients.[5] However, the fees charged by hospitals were regulated by the state at relatively low levels (as were the prices of pharmaceuticals), and hospitals only covered part of their operating costs from the fees they charged; most of their costs were paid directly by the state, which in most cases was the owner of the hospital.[6]

The plan that covered government employees (current and retired) and their dependents (variously referred to as the Government Insurance System (GIS) or the Public Medical System) functioned in essentially the same way as the LIS, although there

---

[4] Gong (2005, p. 111) uses the term "franchised hospital" to describe the relation between the SOEs and the hospitals with which they had contracts to treat their staff.

[5] When dependents incurred costs in external hospitals, the plan essentially paid 50 percent of the cost (with some exceptions).

[6] Some large government agencies and SOEs actually owned their own hospitals, however.

were some small differences in the benefit package to which covered individuals were entitled. Also, under the LIS, each work unit was individually responsible for the costs of its employees' health care, whereas under the GIS, the costs for all state employees in a county were pooled rather than allocated to individual departments (work units). As contemporary observers have noted, however, the difference in the funding methods between the two plans was not very important from a substantive point of view. Since SOEs were, by definition, owned by the state and hospitals were as well, all health care costs except the out-of-pocket costs to the patients ultimately became a charge on the state budget. Deficits were often tolerated in individual SOEs, and the strength of the incentives on decision-makers to make efficient use of their resources depended on the extent to which they faced sanctions from the state if they overspent their budgets or spent their funds wastefully.

With respect to rural areas, the health care system that China built up over the 1950–1980 period has been regarded by many as one of the PRC's most successful achievements, and it continues to be held up as a model for developing countries today. It was organized as part of the system of collectives into which the farming population was divided during that period, and was based on a three-tiered model of health services provision. At the top were the state-owned county hospitals (typically with several hundred beds and medical staff which included physicians in a number of the major specialties). The next level was the township (commune) hospital or health center with a small number of beds and no more than one or a few physicians. Formally, the township health centers were either owned by the state or by the commune, and their operating costs were shared between the two. Their responsibilities included provision of public health services (that is, sanitation, control of epidemics, etc.), prevention, and maternal and child health services, as well as provision of basic curative services. At the lowest level were village health stations with only some basic equipment and a supply of common pharmaceuticals, and staffed by personnel (such as the famous "barefoot doctors") with only basic medical training; the staff typically practiced on a part-time basis only.

The village level of health care was supervised by the township health centers, and at least partially paid for by the villages, with at most very low charges collected from patients. Treatment in second or third tier hospitals was only allowed on the basis of a referral from lower-level providers, and was partially financed on the basis of fees charged to the users. However, the fees (and the charges for medication that patients received) were controlled by the state at relatively low levels, and as in the cities, the fees charged by hospitals only were enough to cover a portion of their total cost of operation, with the difference paid for by the state. Moreover, the burden of hospital fees and payments for pharmaceuticals was largely borne by the Cooperative Medical System (CMS) to which most of the rural population belonged, and which was organized and funded by villages and communes.

Although neither the urban nor the rural health care funding systems were universal in the sense of covering all residents, coverage extended to the vast majority of the population. It has been estimated that in the early 1980s, 90 percent of rural residents were covered by a CMS (Wang, 2005, p. 155), and that perhaps 70 percent of the urban population was covered through membership in either the LIS or the GIS (Gong, 2005, p. 111). Moreover, since hospitals' service charges were lower than they would have had to be if they had been the hospitals' only source of revenue, there was at least an implicit state subsidy for hospitalization and medication costs for every Chinese resident.

It is clear that by contemporary standards, the health care that was supplied during this period could not have been very advanced, since China at that time still was a very poor country with a low per capita GDP, and since the resources devoted to health care corresponded to no more than about 3 percent of GDP. Nevertheless, the system did produce a remarkable improvement in basic health indicators such as average life expectancy and infant mortality.[7]

[7] Lei *et al.* (2005, p. 91) cite estimates of an increase in average life expectancy from 35 years before liberation to almost 68 years in 1981, and a decrease in infant mortality from 20 percent to about 3.8 percent over the same period.

THE CHANGES SINCE THE 1980

Since the end of the planned economy period, China's health care system has undergone a dramatic transformation. Essentially, the changes have mirrored those that have taken place in the management of the economy generally.

The dismantling of the earlier system of nationwide central planning of the economy involved decentralization not only from the state to enterprises, but also a large transfer of both funds and authority from the state (central government) to lower levels of government (provincial and below). In the countryside, a dramatic change took place as the collective work brigades and communes were dissolved and replaced by the "household contract responsibility system" under which individual farm families, rather than the collective, became the decision-making units in agricultural production. The decentralization of authority to enterprises and rural farm families was accompanied by increased financial responsibility, so that these units were given more or less complete responsibility for balancing their own budgets. That is, the earlier "soft budget constraints" under which the commune or the state effectively guaranteed to cover any deficits were replaced by a system of harder budget constraints. By the same token, production units were also allowed to keep any surpluses they were able to generate, and no longer required to turn them over to the state or commune. These changes extended to hospitals as well, giving them an increased incentive to control costs and to increase the amount of revenue collected from patients. Although the state formally continued to own most hospitals, the staff often became the *de facto* residual claimants on surpluses from their operations, as periodic salary bonuses tied to the hospital's net revenue became common.

As a strategy for general economic policy, decentralization of authority and responsibility to farm households, enterprises, and local governments clearly was a major success, as it was the foundation for the remarkable economic transformation that China has gone through over the last several decades. However, it also resulted in dramatic changes in the health care sector, some of which had unintended and undesirable side effects.

In the countryside, the abolition of the system of collective farming and the communes meant the end of the collective funding of village-based primary health care by barefoot doctors and others, as village health posts were closed or privatized and the rural doctors became private practitioners. Many township hospitals began experiencing financial stringency as responsibility for funding them was delegated downward, from the province to county and township governments. This process typically led to a reduction in government funding, and to an expectation that the hospitals would finance their operations to a greater extent via charges paid by patients. As county hospitals were subject to the same kind of pressures, the referral system broke down. With both county and township hospitals wanting to increase service volumes to collect more fees, they effectively started competing for patients, and county hospitals were more than happy to treat, and collect fees from, patients who equally well could have been treated in a township facility. When rural patients had a choice, they often chose to go directly to the better-equipped county hospital rather than to the township hospital. This pattern was reinforced as some of the more skilled doctors found that they were able to treat more patients (and thus raise their incomes) in county hospitals than in township facilities. As a result, township hospitals in many places became underutilized. At the same time, township government were under some pressure to protect rural employment, so the number of staff often did not fall in proportion to the declining patient load (China Development Brief, 2003; Bloom, 2003).

Another consequence of the changes was the breakdown of the CMS network under which rural residents could get reimbursement for all or most of their bills if they needed hospital treatment. With the collapse of the village-based collectives and with no well-developed system of local taxation by townships, these schemes could no longer be sustained.

In urban areas, the consequences of the decentralization reforms manifested themselves somewhat differently. As enterprises became subject to harder budget constraints, some of them ran into financial difficulties and started cutting back on funding the hospitals and clinics that they ran for their employees, retirees, and dependents, and as well as on paying for the cost of the medical services that were supplied by higher-level hospitals for those with serious illness. Moreover, an increasing share of the labor force obtained employment in private firms or on short-term contracts. Since these workers were not covered by the GIS/LIS system, they added to the ranks of urban residents without insurance coverage who had to pay out of pocket for their medical services. In a 2003 survey, it was estimated that only 43 percent of urban residents had "some sorts of social medical security," as opposed to the 70 percent before the reform period cited earlier (Gong, 2005, p. 121). At the same time, government-owned hospitals tried to earn more revenue by increasing their service volumes, as they also became subject to harder budget constraints and reduced funding from the state and provincial governments.

With reduced government subsidies to health care, and with more people in both urban and rural areas becoming uninsured, one might have expected that aggregate health care spending would have decreased. In fact the opposite happened: aggregate (public plus private) spending on health care has increased very rapidly. As noted earlier, in the beginning of the 1980s, health care spending as a percentage of GDP was estimated at a little above 3 percent; 25 years later, the figure had risen to some 5.5 percent. While this might not seem like a very striking increase (especially in comparison with the figures that apply in the US and other advanced countries), it must be borne in mind that this increase has occurred at the same time as China's GDP per capita has been growing at an average rate of some 8.5 percent. To increase its share in GDP as much as it has, health care spending must have been rising at some 11 percent per year in real terms, a remarkably high rate. What this suggests is that the increased incentives on individuals to reduce their health care spending when they had to pay a larger share of the cost out of pocket were more than counterbalanced by the increased incentive on health services providers to produce a larger volume of services and/or raise their fees.[8]

A particularly unfortunate consequence of the decentralization process was a trend toward a distorted pattern of medical services provision, under which a large proportion of hospital resources were devoted to highly sophisticated and expensive methods of diagnosis and treatment, even in cases where their medical value was questionable, whereas not enough resources were devoted to simple and less expensive interventions of proven medical effectiveness. A similar pattern applied with respect to pharmaceuticals, in the form of a trend toward overuse of new and sometimes very expensive drugs even when older and cheaper ones would have been equally effective. These patterns resulted partly because the government continued to enforce controls on the fees for established types of diagnostic and treatment services and commonly used drugs, but gave hospitals considerably more freedom to set their own charges for newer "state of the art" diagnostic and treatment services, often those involving the use of expensive machinery and equipment. Similarly, the margins that the hospitals could charge on newer (and hence often expensive) types of drugs were less strictly regulated.

Aggregative statistics on population health status, while incomplete, are also consistent with the impression that the health care system has functioned with much less efficiency in the last 25 years than it did before 1980. While indicators such as life expectancy and infant mortality have shown some improvement, the gains have been much smaller since 1980 than they were during 1950–1980.[9] In the case of

---

[8] This pattern is consistent with much of the Western health economics literature in which it is concluded that in health care, incentives on providers ("supply-side incentives") are more important determinants of resources use than incentives on patients ("demand-side incentives"). See, for example, Glied (2000).

[9] Lei *et al.* (2005, p. 101) provide a table that shows average life expectancy and infant mortality increasing by two years and decreasing by 1.1 percentage points, respectively, between 1980 and 1998. Both are much smaller than the corresponding figures cited for typical low-income and middle-income countries (three years, 2.9 percentage points, and five years, 2.3 percentage points, respectively).

contagious disease, there has even been some degree of reversal of the earlier declines in the incidence of conditions such as hepatitis, tuberculosis, and schistosomiasis. In part, these unfavorable trends are likely to be due to the increased inequality of access to preventative and curative health care, between cities and rural areas, the insured and the uninsured, and, more generally, the rich and the poor.

WHY HAVEN'T MARKETS WORKED IN HEALTH CARE?

In general, the justification for moving away from a system of allocating economic resources through central planning was the expectation that greater efficiency could be attained if producers were allowed to make their decisions more in response to consumers' demand, as reflected by market prices, and less in response to central directives, and to finance their activities from the revenues they could earn rather than from budgetary allocations of state funds. In most cases, this expectation clearly appears to have been correct, as the result was the remarkably successful economic performance that China has enjoyed since 1980. The decision to reduce subsidies to hospitals and other health service providers was part of this move toward greater reliance on private incentives and the market mechanism. But as discussed above, the contemporary view in the literature on the Chinese health care system is that in the health care sector, this strategy has had disappointing results. The question therefore arises: why has the move toward greater reliance on the market mechanism worked so much less well in the health care sector than elsewhere in the economy? The answer can be sought partly by looking at the way that the state and local governments in China managed the process of health system reform, but partly also in certain characteristics of the markets that make up the health care sector. These characteristics have been extensively analyzed in the international literature on health economics, and I will briefly review them here.

Health Services with Externalities

Conventional economic analysis suggests that for most goods and services, there is no significant difference between their value to society, on the one hand, and to the individual who enjoys them, on the other. For such goods, it is efficient to let the quantity produced depend on the amounts that people want to spend on them out of their own funds. However, there are some goods and services for which the benefits to society clearly are different from the benefits to the individuals who use them. Technically, production and consumption of such goods and services are said to have "external effects" or "spill-over effects," meaning that they impinge, at least to some extent, on the welfare of other people than those for whom they are produced.

The majority of curative health services do *not* have significant external effects. For example, treatment to soothe the pain of someone who has been in an accident certainly is valuable to the person who is treated, but it does not directly benefit anyone else. However, for diseases that are contagious, prevention and treatment typically *do* have external effects, in that not only they benefit the treated individual directly, but also benefit others since they reduce the probability that other people will contract the disease. Indeed, for certain kinds of public health services (such as control of mosquitoes, or the snails that carry schistosomiasis), the external effects are their main benefits since they do not involve treatment of individual patients.

For the cases of public health services and prevention and treatment of contagious disease, the market mechanism will not work well, since individual purchase decisions will not fully reflect their value to society. As a result, there is a strong case for government intervention to subsidize or directly produce these services, and a reform that gives an expanded role for the market mechanism in the health care sector that needs to make special provision for safeguarding their production. In the case of China, the need for a well-functioning system to deal with contagious disease was of course brought into sharp focus during the SARS epidemic, and the threat of an avian flu epidemic contributes to continued preoccupation with the issue.[10]

[10] Another growing problem in China's urban areas is the spread of tuberculosis among migrant workers; the problem was recently described in the *Asian Wall Street Journal* (November 2, 2006, p. 9).

Information Asymmetry Between Patients and Health Service Providers

Allowing production and resource allocation to be governed by market demand may be problematic when buyers have less information than sellers regarding the characteristics of the good or service they buy. As has been emphasized in the health economics literature, this problem certainly applies to health services, where consumers who are ill typically do not know much about the prognosis of the diseases they have, or the likely outcomes of different methods of treatment or use of different drugs, whereas the sellers (providers) have much more information. It is also often difficult to assess the value of health services even after they have been received, since even in cases when the consumer gets better, this might have happened even without treatment, and also since not all patients get better even if they are treated in the best possible way. To a large extent, therefore, users of health services have to rely on the information and advice of providers when they are sick. Moreover, because decisions about treatment may have to be done quickly and often involve face-to-face contact with the provider, it is difficult for consumers to compare suggested treatment methods and fees of different providers. In markets where health services and pharmaceuticals are sold directly to consumers, therefore, competition among providers will not be very effective in preventing them from charging high fees, or from treating patients with more expensive methods and drugs than their diseases would warrant.[11]

Because of these problems, governments in many countries have tried to control the prices of most medical services and drugs. However, designing an effective system of price controls is not easy, and the pattern of health services production may become biased if the regulated prices make some types of treatment methods more

[11] The problem of "overtreatment" of particular conditions when providers recommend more, or more expensive, services than patients would use if they were better informed is referred to in the health economics literature as "supplier-induced demand" or SID. One of the leading American textbooks in health economics devotes almost an entire chapter to this issue; see Folland *et al.* (2001, Chapter 10).

profitable than others, or if the prices of some types of services and drugs are left unregulated. This of course is what has been happening in China since the 1980s, as noted above.

Markets for Health Insurance

Most kinds of illness typically strike in a highly random and unpredictable fashion. In any given year, most people will essentially be well, and not need very large amounts of health services. However, a minority will contract various kinds of serious illness, with some needing treatment or drugs that can be very costly in relation to their income or the resources they have. Because it is not known in advance who will be stricken by illness, everyone who is at risk fears that it may be him or her. In these circumstances, the community can be made better off by putting in place a system of risk-pooling to which everyone contributes, but whose resources are used to help pay for the cost of the health care only when needed by one of the few people who is seriously ill in a given year.

A system where the state produces and pays for the health services that the population needs, therefore, plays a dual role. In addition to providing health services, it also implicitly supplies a system or risk-pooling (it collects tax revenues from everyone, and pays for the health services of those who fall ill). But this also means that if the state withdraws from supplying health services and expects their production to be financed by revenues earned by providers, private markets must fill both these roles. That is, there must be functioning markets both for health services *and* for health insurance.

But markets for private health insurance also tend to be affected by problems associated with imperfect and asymmetric information. In particular, as has been extensively discussed in the health economics literature, their functioning is likely to be impaired by *moral hazard* and *adverse selection*.[12]

[12] Extensive discussion of the moral hazard and adverse selection problems can be found in Cutler and Zeckhauser (2000, Chapter 11), in the current standard reference work on health economics.

The moral hazard problem arises because under conventional private insurance plans, the decisions with respect to what services the patient will be using are made jointly by the patient and the provider, who have more information about the patient's condition than the insurance plans do. When most of the cost of the care is paid for by the insurer, doctors and patients typically have an incentive to choose the best possible treatment, even if it involves a large volume of expensive services. This is especially so if the doctors' income depends on the amount or revenue earned from the treatment. Even if insurers believe that this effect sometimes leads to more expensive treatment patterns than necessary, they typically cannot show that this is so without the doctor's cooperation. As a result, aggregate costs of care are likely to be high when many patients are covered by conventional insurance of this type, that is, of a type that implicitly subsidizes the patient's utilization of health services and rewards doctors for supplying a large volume of services.

Adverse selection arises when different individuals face different risks of illness. In order to avoid losing money on insurance for high-risk people, insurers will then try to charge higher premiums for those in that category. But sometimes it is difficult and costly to identify which individuals are in high-risk groups, since individuals may have information about their own risks of illness that they will not tell the insurer about. For this reason, insurers often follow conservative rules with respect to whom they will enroll, and spend considerable resources on medical examinations of people who apply for coverage. This contributes to raising the administrative costs of insurance, which may be high to begin with.[13] The end result is that private insurance will be costly and not available everywhere, at least not to individual buyers (although employment-based group insurance may be less expensive and more widely available).

When the CMS system in the countryside collapsed after 1980, and with the decline in the proportion of urban residents who were

[13] The administrative costs of private insurance include the amounts that insurers spend on marketing, which can be substantial.

covered by the GIS/LIS systems, the proportion of China's population that was not covered by collective or state-organized insurance became very large, and this happened at a time when the cost of a typical treatment episode rose dramatically as hospitals tried to generate more revenue. The need for a well-functioning system of health insurance therefore increased substantially. However, the extent of privately supplied insurance in China has not expanded enough to come close to filling this gap. In view of the problems with private insurance markets that have just been discussed, this is hardly surprising.

RECENT GOVERNMENT INITIATIVES AND THE DEVELOPMENT RESEARCH CENTER PROPOSALS

Although the trend toward decentralized economic management and greater reliance on the market mechanism has produced remarkable success for the Chinese economy as a whole, there is now widespread agreement that the performance of the health care sector has not been nearly as good as that of the economy generally, and strategies to improve it are intensely debated. While the debate has become more active in the last several years, some of the special problems in the management of the health sector have been recognized for a long time, particularly since the mid-1990s. A particularly noteworthy event was the State Council promulgation of the reform of the urban social health insurance system at the end of 1998. This reform, in turn, had its roots in the experiences with cost control and experiments with different social insurance mechanisms that had taken place in various parts of China throughout the 1990s.

Briefly,[14] the new system (often referred to as the Basic Urban Insurance, or BUI) is intended to cover workers (current and retired) in all private and public-sector enterprises (but not dependents). It is managed independently by Social Insurance Bureaus in major cities. Funding is through payroll deduction (at a minimum rate of 6 percent from the employer and 2 percent from the

[14] For more detail, see, for example, Gong (2005), or Liu (2002).

employee), and the amount contributed is divided into an individual account that can be used to pay for outpatient medical care, and a social pooling account that can be used to pay for hospital expenses. Coverage of hospital costs is subject to a deductible equivalent to 10 percent of the worker's annual wage, and a co-insurance rate that varies from city to city. It is also subject to an upper limit equal to four times the average annual wage prevailing in the city. An important feature is that health costs are only be eligible for reimbursement if they are incurred for services from providers that are on the Social Insurance Bureau's list, and the SIB can negotiate with listed providers regarding rates and other conditions that govern payments. Although the scheme is scheduled to ultimately cover all urban workers, enrollment is not yet compulsory, and statistics for 2003 indicate that only about half those in the eligible groups had enrolled at that time (Gong, 2005, p. 121).

With respect to strengthening the rural health care system, policy initiatives have focused to a large extent on efforts to reconstruct the Cooperative Medical System (CMS). There have been a series of state resolutions encouraging this approach since 1990, the latest one coming in 2003 and containing explicit promises of fixed per capita subsidies for renewed CMS plans in various parts of China. At the same time, local governments, often working together with international organizations, have organized pilot projects aimed at testing out different models for reviving the CMS system. However, there are several factors that have led critics to question whether current efforts are likely to be successful.[15]

First, under current rules in China regarding the rights of local governments to impose taxes, contributions to CMS plans cannot be made compulsory. Even with subsidies from the state and local governments, it has been proved difficult to induce large proportions of residents in rural communities to pay the voluntary contributions required for membership. Moreover, when membership is voluntary, the plans are subject to the problem of adverse selection (that is,

[15] For a detailed description of the problems with reviving CMSs, see Wang (2005, especially pp. 162–166).

that those who sign up tend to be the ones most likely to need expensive health services). Second, many current CMS plans only offer coverage for inpatient treatment in hospital, not the cost of outpatient care. In one sense, this is understandable, since the cases when large health care costs have sent rural families into poverty have typically involved hospital care. But surveys in the 1990s showed that only about 3 percent of rural residents had episodes of inpatient care in any given year. When membership is voluntary, it is likely to be difficult to retain subscribers over time when plan benefits only are experienced so infrequently.

The DRC Report

As noted above, in the 2005 collection of papers on health system reform by the Development Research Centre of the State Council (the DRC report), the authors tend to be pessimistic regarding the prospects for success of the current approaches to reform, with respect to both the urban and rural systems. In particular, they imply that the policy of making health services providers more dependent on the revenues they collect from patients, and their freedom to set the prices of many kinds of services and medication, have had detrimental effects in many cases. Moreover, they are not optimistic regarding the effectiveness of the efforts to protect the population against the risk of ruinous health care expenditure by strengthening the urban BUI plan and reviving the CMS model in the countryside. As an alternative, the concluding essay in the collection (Ge, 2005) advances a radically different alternative, under which responsibility for public health and preventative services, as well as basic curative services, would be transferred to a network of government-owned and operated clinics which would provide such services (and pharmaceuticals) at low regulated prices, and receive their funding from the state budget.

It is of course difficult to tell whether these critical views of developments in the health care system are shared by many among those responsible for health policy in China, and whether a change of course as drastic as that proposed in the concluding essay could be regarded as consistent with the principle of "feeling the stones while crossing the river." Nevertheless, the proposals deserve to be subject to serious debate, and in the next section, I will briefly consider to what extent they would constitute a good way of dealing with the kinds of problems that China's health care system has been experiencing since 1980. Or, to put the question differently: In the previous section, I referred to several sources of potential market failure that motivate a substantial role for the government in the health care sector. To what extent would the model proposed by the DRC be effective in overcoming these potential problems?

Health Services with External Effects

The need for an effective system to deal with public health services and control of epidemics and contagious diseases is one of the main arguments in favor of a model such as that proposed by the DRC. The fact that these services have deteriorated under current approaches, in part because existing agencies have been under pressure to raise more revenue, has been well documented. At the same time, it is clear that there often are significant synergies between the provision of public health services and provision of basic medical care, especially in rural areas with a dispersed population. Even if some version of the CMS model continues to be the main approach to reform, arrangements under which these public health services and basic curative services are provided together, by the same or closely related agencies, certainly make sense, and even in urban areas it is efficient for there to be close coordination between the two.

The Risk-Pooling Function

A model under which basic medical care is provided at little or no cost to users through a network of government-funded clinics implicitly accomplishes the objective of risk-pooling for the cost of such services. It therefore would, at least in part, address the market failures associated with a system that relies exclusively on private insurance. In this sense, the DRC model can also be seen as an alternative to the BUI system in urban areas and to the CMS model in the countryside, since the main purpose of these schemes is to provide at least some degree of risk pooling.

However, a key issue in this regard is how the concept of "basic medical care" is defined. In the DRC report no precise definition is given beyond saying that care would be given in government clinics to those suffering from "common diseases and frequently-occurring diseases" (Gong, 2005, p. 249), while "non-basic" medical care would have to be paid for by individuals either out of pocket, or through commercial insurance (ibid., p. 251), perhaps arranged by enterprises, or in rural areas by collective organizations (villages?). In comparing the DRC model to the BUI and CMS models, the report seems to imply that the idea of these schemes is to insure against "expenses on serious diseases" while they require individuals themselves to pay for "common disease and frequently occurring diseases" (either out of pocket, or out of their individual accounts, for individuals covered by BUI); see Gong (2005, pp. 245–246). The wording here seems to suggest that the definition of "basic medical care" that the report has in mind principally refers to services that currently are provided on an outpatient basis, since the existing BUI and CMS schemes would cover most types of inpatient services. If that is so, the DRC model would not really provide much protection against the financial risk associated with serious illnesses requiring hospital treatment; many would regard the lack of such protection for many people as one of the most important problems of the Chinese health care system today.

Dealing with patient–provider information asymmetry

From the literature, it is clear that the inability of the current health care system to deal with the problem of patient–provider information asymmetry is a major reason for the rapidly rising cost of health care in China today, and also for the distorted pattern of care under which certain advanced treatment methods and new and expensive drugs are used more frequently than can be medically justified. Under the DRC model, personnel in the government clinics would have no financial incentive to provide expensive services or drugs, and the charges that patients would pay for basic medical services and drugs would be strictly controlled. Thus the problems of rising costs and a distorted pattern of care could be significantly reduced if the DRC proposal were implemented. With no financial incentive on providers to produce a high volume of services, patients may even be worried that their diseases would not be treated intensively enough, or with enough care, but the professional ethics of health care workers can of course be expected to reduce the risk that this would happen.

The fact that the DRC model would remove the incentive on providers of basic medical care to overuse intensive high-cost treatment and to prescribe expensive drugs is one of the major arguments in its favor. Once again, however, the extent to which this would resolve the problem of patients being subject to large financial risk in cases of serious illness would depend on the frequency with which patients would have to turn to hospitals for treatment going beyond basic care, and the costs and treatment patterns in hospitals.

Complementary Measures to the DRC Model

The DRC report constitutes a very illuminating and comprehensive analysis of China's health care system over the past several decades, and the case it makes for a network of government-funded providers of basic medical care for everyone, at low cost, is very carefully motivated. Given the apparent readiness of the policy-makers to have the state take a more active role in the management of the system than it has been doing in recent years, a reorientation of current approaches to health system reform along these lines may perhaps be in the cards.

As implied by the discussion in the previous section, a major question about the proposal is what range of services would be provided in the basic-care clinics. If the range is defined too broadly so as to include many of the services currently being provided in hospitals, the system could become very costly to the state budget, and management of a system that would encompass not only primary outpatient care but most of the hospital sector as well would present a formidable challenge.[16] A network of clinics that essentially would provide public health services and a more narrowly defined range of outpatient services would be a more realistic option. Such a model could borrow features from the UK approach of providing primary care through independent General Practitioners, often practicing in groups (in the so-called Primary Care Trusts), or the Japanese system in which most primary care services are supplied through independent general practitioners who sometimes operate small clinics that can provide certain basic inpatient services as well.[17]

An important issue that would have to be addressed in a system of the type proposed in the DRC report would be whether patients would have a choice between different providers. One model would be to simply assign individuals to specific clinics based on where they live. However, this would leave patients with no choice, and would remove any incentive for clinics to maintain a high quality of service in order to compete for patients. An alternative model (similar to what is practiced in the UK) would be to require patients to choose a specific clinic with which to register in order to be entitled to care from it, and letting the clinic's aggregate budget depend on the number of patients registered with it. Such a payment system

[16] The essay in which the DRC proposal is outlined provides a very insightful discussion of why it is necessary to set a relatively low ambition level regarding the degree of coverage that should be provided in a plan that would be universally available (Ge, 2005, pp. 245–247). Its arguments in this regard are similar to those underlying the simulation exercise offered in Blomqvist (2000).

[17] Blomqvist (2002) provides a summary of the organization of the primary-care based health care system in the UK. A good description of some important features of the Japanese health care system is Imai (2002).

(referred to as capitation) gives the clinic an incentive to provide care to a large number of patients, but not to produce a high volume of expensive services for each one.[18]

If a version of the DRC model of primary care reform is chosen as the basis for health system reform, however, a strong case would remain for government intervention to protect individuals against the financial risk associated with serious illness that would require advanced hospital treatment, since private insurance is unlikely to be an effective option for most people. One approach would be to continue to expand the BUI and CMS plans currently under development, so that they would cover larger shares of the population. That is, these plans would complement the DRC model, providing financial protection against the potentially high cost of non-basic medical care needed in cases of serious illness that could not be treated in the government-funded clinics.

As discussed above, many observers believe that part of the reason for the high cost of hospital care, and the tendency for hospitals to overuse advanced diagnostic and treatment technology and expensive drugs, is the fact that hospitals can increase their total revenue by billing each patient for a large volume of services, and charge high prices for certain of them. Indeed, it is to remove this type of incentive that the DRC model advocates a system of funding of basic medical care that is independent of the amount of revenue the clinics (primary-care providers) collect from patients. But this logic can be extended to non-basic medical services provided in hospitals as well. Under the BUI plan, the Social Insurance Bureau that is responsible for managing each city's plan can negotiate with providers regarding the way they will be paid for their services, and they can refuse to pay for services rendered by hospitals who have

[18] The list of registered patients entitled to seek care with each primary-care provider is often referred to as a patient "roster," and the system itself is sometimes called "rostering" in the literature. As in the UK, patients would register with a clinic for a fixed period of time, at the end of which they would be allowed to change to another one if they wanted. For a comprehensive review of the literature on the performance of different systems of primary-care provision involving different payment methods, see Scott (2000).

not concluded agreements with the plan about payment methods. One way to remove the incentives for hospitals to overuse expensive procedures and drugs would be for the Bureaus to negotiate agreements under which each insured person would be registered with a specific hospital which then would receive a fixed sum per patient enrolled in return for providing all necessary services to the patient, subject only to limited out-of-pocket fees. (That is, the capitation principle could be applied to hospitals as well as to the government clinics providing primary care.[19]) The choice of hospital to register with could be made by the patient or, more reasonably, by the primary-care clinic where the patient was registered.

A variant of this approach would be for the BUI or the CMS plan to use the government primary care clinics as "gatekeepers" for hospital care. Under this model, patients would only be allowed to seek hospital care on the basis of a referral from the government clinic. The clinic could then be given an incentive to control the patients' use of hospital care by requiring that it pay a part of the cost of their hospital care. In return, the BUI or the CMS plan would pay an additional capitation fee to the clinic where the patient was registered. This would be similar to the model that was used under the so-called fundholding system in the UK, a system that is in the process of being strengthened under the reforms that provide for reorganization of general practitioners' practices into Primary Care Trusts.

Should Opting Out of the Government Plan be Allowed?

The major advantage of the plan proposed by the DRC is that it would give every citizen guaranteed access to basic medical care in a government-funded and government-managed clinic. However, the plan would not necessarily require that these clinics would be the *only* ones providing basic care. The advantage of universal guaranteed access could be preserved even if enterprises and rural collectives were allowed to provide care in independent clinics that

[19] For a discussion of an experiment with this kind of payment mechanism for hospital services in China, see Yip and Eggleston (2004).

they themselves were managing, or that were privately managed under contracts with the enterprises or rural collectives. If this were allowed, those having access to such clinics would lose the right to receive care in the government clinics, and all or part of the funding that would have gone to the government clinics to pay for the care of these persons would be channeled instead to the independent clinics. Indirectly, therefore, allowing this form of "opting out" from the government system could induce a certain degree of competition for patients between government clinics and independent ones, something that could be beneficial for ensuring that all clinics had an incentive to provide care of high quality.

CONCLUSION: MARKETS AND COMPETITION IN THE DELIVERY OF UNIVERSAL HEALTH CARE

The kind of health care system discussed in the last few paragraphs would be an equitable one, in that every citizen would be guaranteed access to basic medical care at reasonable cost. To the extent that enrollment in BUI or CMS plans could be expanded to cover larger proportions of the urban and rural populations, it would be even more equitable in this sense. By guaranteeing everyone access to basic care, some of the most serious consequences of market failure, namely those associated with private health insurance markets, would be neutralized to a significant extent. At the same time, the amount of waste and inefficiency arising from factors such as moral hazard and patient–provider information asymmetry, can be reduced by choosing payment methods that reward efficient use of health care resources and diminish providers' incentive to drive up health care costs. Finally, the system could also be designed with a renewed emphasis on prevention and public health, hallmarks of the best elements of the system that existed in China before the 1980s.

While all this could be accomplished through an increased degree of government intervention and regulation, a system reformed along the lines discussed in the last section would also retain significant elements of choice for individual patients, employers, and rural collectives. This in turn would induce a degree of competition among providers for patients, something that could be beneficial in that it would give providers an incentive to offer care of high quality. By offering some degree of choice and competition, the system would differ in an important way from the pre-1980s centrally planned one, and might thus be able to avoid some of the problems that the centralized economic management at that time gave rise to. But it would also be designed in such a way as to counteract the most important sources of market failure observed in systems that are managed and regulated with insufficient attention to the special factors affecting health care markets. Importantly, it would also be more compatible than a purely market-based system with the idea that guaranteed access to basic health care is one of the most important elements of the social policy in a society that aspires to be an equitable one.

REFERENCES

Asian Development Bank (2002), *People's Republic of China: Toward Establishing a Rural Health Protection System* (Report 090902, by Yuanli Liu, Keqin Rao, and Shanlian Hu), Manila: Asian Development Bank.

Blomqvist, Åke (2000), "Financing Health Care in Developing Economies: Simulations for China," (with Susheng Wang and Lijing Zhu) in *Social Security Reform: Options for China*, eds. Jason Z. Yin and Shuanglin Lin, Singapore: World Scientific, pp. 315-333.

Blomqvist, Åke (2002), *Canadian Health Care in a Global Context: Diagnoses and Prescriptions* (Benefactors Lecture), Toronto: C.D. Howe Institute.

Blomqvist, Åke (2006), "Governments, Markets, and the Health Care Sector," in *China into the Hu-Wen Era*, eds. John Wong and Lai Hongyi, Singapore: World Scientific, pp. 437–466.

Bloom, Gerald (2003), "China's Rural Health System in a Changing Institutional Context," Institute of Development Studies, University of Sussex, Working Paper 194.

Bloom, Gerald (2004), "China's Health System in Transition: The Next Stage," paper presented at an International Conference on 'Comparative Health Policy and Reforms in East Asia' organized by National University of Singapore.

Blumenthal, David and William Hsiao (2005), "Privatization and Its Discontents — The Evolving Chinese Health Care System," *New England Journal of Medicine* 353, 1165–1170.

China Development Brief (2003), "The Physician Will Not Heal Himself," available on www.chinadevelopmentbrief.com/node/262.

Cutler, David M. and Richard J. Zeckhauser (2000), "The Anatomy of Health Insurance," in *Handbook of Health Economics, Volume 1A*, eds. Anthony J. Culyer and Joseph P. Newhouse, Amsterdam: Elsevier, pp. 563–644, Chapter 11.

Development Research Center of the State Council, Beijing (2005), *China Development Review* (Special Issue on Health Policy and Reform) 7(1), 1–259.

Economist Intelligence Unit (1998), *Healthcare in China into the 21st Century*, London: The Economist Intelligence Unit.

Folland, S., A. Goodman and M. Stano (2001), *The Economics of Health and Health Care*, Upper Saddle River, NJ: Prentice-Hall.

Ge, Yanfeng (2005), "Report Eight: A Conceptual Framework for the Reform of the Health System in China," pp. 237–259 in DRC (2005).

Glied, Sherry (2000), "Managed Care," in *Handbook of Health Economics, Volume 1A*, eds. Anthony J. Culyer and Joseph P. Newhouse, Amsterdam: Elsevier, pp. 707–753, Chapter 13.

Gu, Xin (2004), "Health Care Regime Change in Urban China: Unmanaged Marketization and Reluctant Privatization," paper presented at an International Conference on 'Comparative Health Policy and Reforms in East Asia' organized by National University of Singapore.

Gu, Xin (2005), *Health Care Marketization in Urban China*, EAI Background Brief No. 228, Singapore: East Asia Institute, National University of Singapore.

Gong, Sen (2005), "Report Four: Review and Prospects of Medical Security System for Urban Staff and Workers," pp. 109–136 in DRC (2005).

Imai, Yutaka (2002), "*Health Care Reform in Japan*," Economics Department Working Paper 321, Paris: OECD.

Lei, Haichao *et al.*, "Report Three: A Review and Recommendations on Building and Remodeling China's Public Health System," pp. 81–108 in DRC (2005).

Liu, Yuanli (2002), "Reforming China's Urban Health Insurance System," *Health Policy* 60, 133–150.

Ravallion, Martin and Shaohua Chen (in press), "China's (Uneven) Progress Against Poverty," *Journal of Development Economics*.

Roberts, Marc J., William Hsiao, Peter Berman and Michael R. Reich (2004), *Getting Health Reform Right: A Guide to Improving Performance and Equity*, Oxford: Oxford University Press.

Scott, Anthony (2000), "Economics of General Practice," in *Handbook of Health Economics, Volume 1B*, eds. Anthony J. Culyer and Joseph P. Newhouse, Amsterdam: Elsevier, pp. 1175–1200, Chapter 22.

Wang, Liejun (2005), "Report Five: Review and Recommendations on the Construction of Rural Medical Security System in China," pp. 137–177 in DRC (2005).

Yip, W. and Karen Eggleston (2004), "Addressing Government and Market Failures with Payment Incentives: The Case of Hospital Reimbursement in Hainan, China," *Social Science and Medicine* 58, 267–277.

Index